Japanese Environmental Philosophy

Japanese Environmental Philosophy

Edited by J. BAIRD CALLICOTT
AND JAMES MCRAE

Oxford University Press is a department of the University of Oxford. It furthers
the University's objective of excellence in research, scholarship, and education
by publishing worldwide. Oxford is a registered trade mark of Oxford University
Press in the UK and certain other countries.

Published in the United States of America by Oxford University Press
198 Madison Avenue, New York, NY 10016, United States of America.

Library of Congress Cataloging-in-Publication Data
Names: Callicott, J. Baird, editor. | McRae, James, 1976– editor.
Title: Japanese environmental philosophy / edited by J. Baird Callicott and James McRae.
Description: New York : Oxford University Press, 2017. |
Includes bibliographical references and index.
Identifiers: LCCN 2016035607 (print) | LCCN 2016053677 (ebook) |
ISBN 9780190456320 (cloth : alk. paper) | ISBN 9780190456337 (pbk. : alk. paper) |
ISBN 9780190456344 (pdf) | ISBN 9780190683269 (ebook) |
ISBN 9780190456351 (online course)
Subjects: LCSH: Environmental ethics—Japan. | Human ecology—Japan—Philosophy. |
Environmental policy—Moral and ethical aspects—Japan.
Classification: LCC GF80 .J36 2017 (print) | LCC GF80 (ebook) | DDC 179/.10952—dc23
LC record available at https://lccn.loc.gov/2016035607

We dedicate this book to our friend and colleague,
YAMAUCHI Tomosaburō, without whom this project
would not be possible.

CONTENTS

FOREWORD | BACK TO THE FUTURE?

CARL B. BECKER

The great culture gaps between Japan or China and America today are not so much differences between Tokyo or Shanghai and New York, as internal differences between the rich and poor, urban and rural, young and old. In each of these countries, centuries-old lifestyles and death rituals are rapidly giving place to lives devoid of ritual meaning and styled only after media images—simulacra, in a word. Years ago, American media had taught me to believe subconsciously that typing rapidly was superior to handwriting slowly, that a "Big Gulp" (liter of liquid) was more satisfying than a sip of tea, and that half-naked teenage Miss Universes strolling the beach were more beautiful than octogenarians.

My first few weeks living in a temple in Japan transformed that worldview. I witnessed an eighty-eight-year-old calligrapher brush a scroll that combined art and wisdom in a way no typing could. I sat on my heels for hours in a tearoom to receive a sip of tea more deeply memorable and satisfying than any liter of cola. I watched the slender hands and ageless face of an octogenarian classical dancer perform with more grace and beauty than any Miss Universe.

As the media's blinders fell from my eyes, I gained hope for humanity. If speed, size, and youth were all that mattered, then all adult humanity would have to forever remain wretchedly longing to be swifter or bigger or younger than it could ever be—and people who are slower or smaller or older would be forever doomed to inferiority. But it is precisely these animalistic values that Japan had transcended in the classical arts and lifestyle that it had cultivated.

With locally made paper and brush or kimono, the Japanese calligrapher and dancer achieved self-cultivation and communicated elegance that all could admire and seek to cultivate in themselves. As long as our basic needs for hydration (and food and shelter) are achieved, it is more sustainable—indeed more human—to appreciate the tea-making of a single cup, than to consume far more calories than our bodies need. To be sure, the late-teen age is the most biologically desirable time for human bodies to reproduce, but this is no reason for our entire value system to be debased to biological reproduction. Rather, for a species that lives more years after than before reproduction, to cultivate grace and elegance in movement can remain a more fulfilling goal for the remainder of our days.

Rapid modernization of any society intensifies the cultural gaps between traditional and modern worldviews and lifestyles. When I moved to Japan in the early 1970s, most homes were inhabited by five to ten family members belonging to several generations. Japan retained many of its classical values and attitudes toward life, death, and aging. Although urban-rural, younger-elder, and north-south variations could be found, they were largely outweighed by the common worldview and value systems shared by the majority of Japanese. Japan prided itself on the fact that most of its citizens were "middle class," that farmers, laborers, and housewives were respected for their roles, that the gap in salary between a production-line worker and a CEO was among the world's lowest, and that its crime rate was the lowest in the developed world.

Living in three-generational families, honoring their ancestors at family altars, Japanese ostensibly epitomized a culture conscious of its continuity with the past and its indebtedness to its forefathers. Ceremonies of tea, flowers, meditation, calligraphy, aikido, and many similar arts were precisely the kind of "paths" (michi 道) in which the cultured sensibilities of maturity could find expression; people became potentially more, rather than less, valuable through age. Moreover, ideas of reciprocal obligation and interdependence dictated that elders be cared for, not because they might again contribute to society, but because they had already contributed to those now in a position to repay that obligation.

After leaving the temple complex for university, I lived with an educated family in a typical country home built in earlier centuries. We shared rooms of traditional tatami grass matting, on which we unfolded low tables for eating and working that we exchanged at night for the futons on which we slept. Local vendors peddled fresh tofu and vegetables to our doorsteps daily. Homes had neither ovens nor freezers, air conditioners, dishwashers, nor clothes dryers; our well had recently been fitted with a motorized pump. We washed ourselves at public bathhouses, and many toilets were little more than outhouses. Bare fluorescent lamps provided light, while hibachi charcoal braziers provided minimal heat through the cold winters. Adults commuted by bicycles and trains, while children played with insects and bamboo in the backyard.

This lack of modern Western amenities was somewhat offset by a strong sense of family cooperation. We huddled together around the hibachi in the winter to keep warm, and washed each other's backs in the public bath. The entire family pitched in to replaster walls or repair the paper shoji screens and scrub the floors. Doors were not locked, and neighbors regularly exchanged gifts from their gardens; any neighbor could tell our parents where the younger children were playing.

In the past thirty-odd years, radical economic and demographic changes have disturbed those traditional lifestyles. The 1980s witnessed an unprecedented boom in the Japanese economy, leading to a spate of debates about its sustainability, and followed by similar booms in Taiwan and Hong Kong, Southeast Asia, and China. The boom led to an economic bubble, in which such two-, three-, and four-generation families built separate residences and moved from their traditional country estates into anonymous suburban apartment complexes. Today, most Japanese live with only three people to a domicile. They eat hamburgers while sitting on Western-style chairs, sleep on beds, and drive cars. Now city people have their own bedrooms, enjoying heating and air conditioning, electrically heated baths and toilet seats, high-definition widescreen digital televisions, and air- as well as water-filtering systems—no more communal cleaning, huddling, or bathing. Many parents insist that their children carry cell phones as the only way to keep track of them.

Superficially obvious changes hide greater changes in the ways people think and relate to each other. The Japanese language contains dozens of terms of respect for seniors, and dozens of terms for deprecating oneself out of politeness. These are no longer used by the younger generation; teenagers and octogenarians speak completely different dialects of the same Japanese language. When Japanese gymnasts swept the Tokyo Olympics in 1964, they publicly attributed their glory to their coaches and seniors, or apologized for bringing their coaches only silver medals instead of gold. When Japanese athletes win at sports meets today, they personally gloat over their successes but no longer apologize to their seniors for their failures.

Max Weber devastatingly critiqued the devaluation of the Protestant work ethic from an ethic that valued good work itself to an ethic that reduced to the byproduct of work (viz., capital). Now it may be time for us to critique the devaluation of the sports ethic from an ethic that valued sportsmanship and self-cultivation itself to an ethic that reduced it to the byproduct of sports (viz., winning, self-aggrandizement, and ultimately capital). If all human values become reducible to competition for capital and ego, then the environment and the majority of the human species are in grave danger.

Today, I live on a hillside in rural Japan, surrounded by terraced rice paddies and ridges of forest. My good neighbor plows and harvests the surrounding paddies with an agile vigor that defies his seventy-odd years. He spends not only time, but major expense, to pay for his small gasoline tractor and combine, for dung and fertilizer, as well as for the pesticides required by Japan's agricultural association to allow him to market his rice. In the last few years, as aging hunters in the vicinity have hung up their rifles, my neighbor has also had to invest heavily in fences and traps to avoid the depredations of the mushrooming populations of boar and deer. Although he receives some subsidy for growing rice from the Japanese government, more often than not, his expenses outweigh his profits, leaving him with a loss at the end of the year.

When I first moved to his valley, I asked him about the profitability of his farming. He responded with evident pride tinged with indignation: "My ancestors owned this entire valley for centuries. Hideyoshi granted it to my forefathers for their military services [in the 1580s]. For four hundred years, my ancestors have maintained these forests and terraces, planting and harvesting this land with their hands and sweat. They had years of plenty, and years of famine, but none of them said, 'Times are hard, so I'll give up farming to labor in a city.' Only their commitment to this land made it possible for us to live here. Only my commitment to this land can make it possible for my descendants to live here, and for Japan to continue to eat the rice from these fields. We do not 'own' the land; the land is here before us and will be here after us. It is our responsibility to care for the land during the short time we live on it, so that others may live on it in the future. Farming is not for the sake of making money; it is for the sake of preserving the land for future generations."

I was deeply impressed and humbled by his explanation. At the same time, the fact that he could respond in this way shows that his family was not yet totally destitute or desperate. The countryside of Japan is littered with the remnants of abandoned farms and terraces. In fact, the hills directly behind our own were once totally covered with tiny terraces on which rice was hand grown, before tractors reformed farming and made plots that are too small for tractors uneconomical. In a mere generation or two since their abandonment, the terraces have crumbled, allowing good soil slowly to wash away, and the remaining soil has become overgrown with thickets of bamboo, with a root system too shallow to preserve the hillside from landslides, but too toughly intertwined to allow newcomers to readily farm again.

Today, as TPP[1] threatens national governments with lawsuits from corporations whose profits are in jeopardy, it also threatens the topsoil of Japan's mountainous islands. The case of India is tragically illustrative. Every year during its monsoon season, Asia—from India to Japan—receives meters of rainfall within just a few weeks. Our terraced paddies serve as miniature dams, trapping the rainwater that falls during this short period, allowing it to slowly seep into the soil and water table over the following months, while nourishing the wet-paddy rice and discouraging weeds and pests that cannot survive in the water. Before the British Raj dominated India, much of India's land was devoted to terraced rice farming. Backed by a new market economy, British entrepreneurs urged India to farm cotton, indigo, tea, and spices in large fields rather than water-gathering terraces. Indian farmers abandoned their terraces for broad-field agriculture suited to countries where rain is far less plentiful and more evenly timed. In the absence of terracing, the monsoon torrents gradually washed the best topsoil down to the rivers and downstream to the sea. Within a century, the soil had lost much of its lighter and richer organic matter, retaining only heavier silt and clay resistant to the monsoon floods, facing much of India with desertification despite its concentrated rainfall.

Japan has argued against TPP demands on the grounds that rice is a sacred part of its history and culture. It might be more persuasive to point out that, if TPP forces Japan to buy foreign rice, much of Japan's terraced paddy land will be abandoned to the incursions of bamboo, while its best topsoil washes away to the sea every year. This is not a reversible process. Foreign foods will become increasingly expensive as the cost of fossil fuel transportation rises. In the future, when the costs of long-distance transportation, food-mileage taxes, or carbon taxes make local Japanese rice once again economically competitive with foreign rice, Japan's good topsoil will already have washed to the sea, and its paddies overgrown with bamboo. Not only Japan, but the entire world, needs the wisdom of my neighbor, who values maintaining the arability of his land even over personal convenience or expense.

Such insights are not unique to Japanese farmers, but can be found in traditional agriculture around the world. The problem is how modern agriculturists can vocalize these insights against the onslaughts of transnational corporations that value the world only in terms of short-term profits, regardless of the long-term disasters they create in loss of topsoil or eradication of pollinating insects.

At the same time, traditions of respect for elders and elder care, of home doctors and community cooperation have declined. While the yen replaces more traditional values as a common denominator of self-worth, retirees face psychological crises of self-worth, housewives prefer remunerative part-time jobs to caring for their elders, and economically motivated crimes have soared. Growing gaps between rich and poor parallel growing diversity in values, especially between urban and rural, young and old, north and south. While it used to be somewhat possible to speak of Japan in one breath, it is increasingly difficult to make generalizations about Japan as a single entity. If America's diversity can be called a melting pot or salad bowl, Japan's diversity may be analogized to the fragmentation of a melting polar ice floe, or the cracking of a clear glass marble thrown into ice water. And it may be argued that from its beginnings, Japan had a less unified or articulated worldview than America, which self-consciously grounded itself on biblical and philosophical texts.

So there are great lessons to be learned from Japan, both about traditional and sustainable values, and about their rapid erosion in the face of media imagery and so-called globalization. Some of these may be gleaned from the writings of Japanese thinkers like ISHIDA Baigan[2] and NINOMIYA Sontoku; others may better be deduced from lifestyles and practices like those alluded to above. I hope that this book will prove not only a provocative introduction to historical thought but also a challenge to all readers to discover and adopt more sustainable values and lifestyles for a world that increasingly needs them.

Notes

1. TPP stands for "Trans-Pacific Partnership," a trade agreement among Brunei, Chile, New Zealand, and Singapore. Australia, Canada, Japan, Malaysia, Mexico, Peru, the United States, and Vietnam are in the process of negotiating to join this partnership, and Taiwan and South Korea have expressed an interest in joining. The TPP would allow

corporations to sue governments for billions of dollars if they were "harmed" by laws or policies designed to protect public health or the environment.

2. Most of the time, Japanese names are presented in this volume in traditional order: the surname comes first with all letters capitalized, followed by the given name (e.g., WATSUJI Tetsurō or NISHIDA Kitarō). Whenever an author is referred to by surname only, the name is capitalized in the usual way (e.g., Watsuji or Nishida). Japanese scholars who regularly publish in English typically have their names presented in Western order, with only the first letter of the surname capitalized (e.g., D. T. Suzuki or Yuriko Saitō).

ACKNOWLEDGMENTS

J. Baird Callicott: I thank YAMAUCHI Tomosaburō for what has proved to be a fairly long and sustained relationship going back to his kind and generous efforts securing the translation into Japanese of my book *Earth's Insights: A Multicultural Survey of Ecological Ethics from the Mediterranean Basin to the Australian Outback*, in 2009. He also arranged for me to make a two-week lecture tour of Japan in 2010. I thank my coeditor, Jim McRae, who, it must be confessed, did all of the yeoman work (including the cat-herding) and at least half of the intellectual work on this book. When I say that this book would not have existed except for Jim's efforts, that's the gospel truth. If I attempted to draw up a list of all the scholars, friends, and intimate associates who have, either directly or indirectly, contributed to the confluence of thoughts and events that have resulted in this book, there would not be any room left for the book itself—and even then I am sure that I would have left some unnamed. I consider myself to be but a medium through whom ripples in the cognitive ether are amplified, for which I can take no credit (or blame) except the words that embody them. So the authors of the ideas themselves that my words express are numberless and largely unknown to me.

James McRae: Many thanks to YAMAUCHI Tomosaburō (aka "Yama-Sensei") for envisioning this project and inviting me to be one of its editors. Thanks also to my coeditor, Baird Callicott, for his friendship and mentorship as we worked on our second book together. I am indebted to my wife, Heather Thornton McRae, who has always helped me to be my best. I offer sincere thanks to my parents, John and Derrill McRae, and my wife's parents, John and Catherine Thornton, for their love and support. Many thanks to my research assistants, Katie McMurtrey, Tyler Haulotte, Yuzhou Wang, and Shrijan Amatya, for their hard work on this project. I give genuine thanks to Ron and Dianne Winney and Travis Traylor for their generous support of my research. Finally, I offer my gratitude to the staff at Oxford University Press, with whom it has been a great pleasure to work. *Dōmo arigatō!*

CONTRIBUTORS

Carl B. Becker holds a Ph.D. in comparative philosophy from the University of Hawai'i at Mānoa with a specialization in Japanese Buddhism. Subsequently he taught Asian philosophy at Southern Illinois University and the University of Hawai'i, and comparative thought at Japan's National Osaka, Tsukuba, and Kyoto Universities. He serves on the editorial boards of *Mortality* and the *Journal for the Study of Spirituality*. His books on environment include *Japan's Wisdom: How it Can Save the Future; Danger in Daily Life* (both Tokyo: Eihosha, 2011 and 2000); and *Asian and Jungian Views of Ethics* (Westport, CT: Greenwood Press, 1999).

Steve Bein is Assistant Professor of Philosophy at the University of Dayton. He earned his Ph.D. from the University of Hawai'i at Mānoa, specializing in Japanese philosophy and ethics. His publications include *Purifying Zen: Watsuji Tetsuro's Shamon Dogen* (University of Hawai'i Press, 2011) and *Compassion and Moral Guidance* (University of Hawai'i Press, 2011). He is also a science fiction and fantasy novelist, and publishes essays on philosophy and science fiction in Blackwell's Pop Culture and Philosophy series.

Augustin Berque holds a Ph.D. in geography from the University of Paris and served as a Director of Studies at the EHESS (School of Advanced Studies in the Social Sciences). He has also served as Director of the Maison Franco-Japonaise in Tokyo, an invited researcher at the Nichibunken (Centre for International Research on Japanese Culture, Kyoto), and a Professor at Miyagi University, Sendai. His numerous publications include the books *Le Sauvage et l'Artifice: Les Japonais Devant la Nature* (Paris: Gallimard, 1986), *Être Humains Sur la Terre: Principes* *d'Éthique de l'Écoumène* (Paris: Gallimard, 1996), and *Milieu et Identité Humaine: Notes Pour un Dépassement de la Modernité* (Paris: Editions Donner Lieu, 2010). A member of the Academia Europaea, he was in 2009 the first westerner to receive the Fukuoka Grand Prize for Asian cultures.

J. Baird Callicott holds a Ph.D. in philosophy from Syracuse University and recently retired as University Distinguished Research Professor and Regents Professor of Philosophy at the University of North Texas. He is one of the founders of environmental ethics and philosophy, teaching the world's first course on the subject in 1971. He has served the International Society for Environmental Ethics as President and Yale University as Bioethicist-in-Residence. He is the author or editor of a score of books, including *Thinking Like a Planet* (New York: Oxford University Press, 2013), *Environmental Philosophy in Asian Traditions of Thought* (with James McRae, Albany: SUNY Press, 2014), *Earth's Insights* (Berkeley: University of California Press, 1994), *In Defense of the Land Ethic* (Albany: SUNY Press, 1989), and *Beyond the Land Ethic* (Albany: SUNY Press, 1999). The anthology *Nature in Asian Traditions of Thought* (Albany: SUNY Press, 1989), which he coedited with Roger T. Ames, was the world's first book on the subject of comparative environmental philosophy.

GODA Hiroko holds a doctorate in social anthropology from Tokyo Metropolitan University. After retiring as a professor at Hyogo Prefectural University in 2011, she founded the Institute of Environmental Anthropology, where she has continued to study the correlation of society and environment, especially focusing upon the environmental ethics reflected in folk customs and rituals in Japan. Some of her recent publications on these topics are *The Environmental Anthropology of Miyaza and Touya* (Tokyo: Fuukyo-sha, 2010) and "Amphibious Gods Linking Mountain, River and Sea and Irrigation Technology," in KUWAKO Toshio's *Topology of Japanese Culture* (Tokyo: Toushin-do, 2008).

INUTSUKA Yū is a doctoral student at the University of Tokyo, currently preparing a Ph.D. thesis on the thought of WATSUJI Tetsurō in the context of environmental philosophy and ethics. She is a visiting researcher of the Research Center for International Japanese Studies at Hosei University (since December 2015). Her publications include the article "From Environmental Ethics to the Ethics of the Ecumene: The Landscape of the Genetically Modified Crops" in the Center for Applied Ethics and Philosophy's *Applied Ethics: Ethics in an Era of Emerging*

Technologies (Sapporo: Center for Applied Ethics and Philosophy, Hokkaido University, 2014).

ISHIDA Masato holds a Ph.D. in philosophy from the Pennsylvania State University and currently teaches in the philosophy department of the University of Hawai'i at Mānoa. He specializes in classical American philosophy, history and philosophy of logic, and traditional Japanese philosophy. His recent works include "The Geography of Perception: Japanese Philosophy in the External World," in Arindam Chakrabarti and Ralph Weber's *Comparative Philosophy without Borders* (New York: Bloomsbury, 2015) and "The Sense of Symmetry: Comparative Reflections on Whitehead, Nishida, and Dōgen" in *Process Studies* 43, no. 1 (2014): 4–34.

Midori Kagawa-Fox was born and raised in Japan. She holds a Ph.D. in Asian studies from the University of Adelaide, Australia, and specializes in ethics and Japanese environmental policy. She is currently teaching the Asian studies course at the University of Adelaide. Her publications include *The Ethics of Japan's Global Environmental Policy: The Conflict between Principles and Practice* (New York: Routledge, 2012) and "Environmental Ethics from the Japanese Perspective," *Ethics, Place and Environment* 13, no. 1 (2010): 57–73.

Leah Kalmanson received her Ph.D. in philosophy from the University of Hawai'i at Mānoa in 2010. She is currently Assistant Professor in the Department of Philosophy and Religion at Drake University (Des Moines, Iowa) with research interests in comparative philosophy and postcolonial studies. Her publications include articles in journals such as *Comparative and Continental Philosophy, Continental Philosophy Review, Frontiers of Philosophy in China, Hypatia, Philosophy East and West,* and *Shofar*, and edited volumes including *Levinas and Asian Thought* (with Frank Garrett and Sarah Mattice, Pittsburgh: Duquesne University Press, 2013) and *Buddhist Responses to Globalization* (with James Mark Shields, Lanham, MD: Lexington Books, 2014).

KUWAKO Toshio holds a doctor of arts and letters from the University of Tokyo with a specialization in philosophy. He currently serves as Professor of Philosophy at the Graduate School of Decision Science and Technology, Tokyo Institute of Technology. His publications include the books *Philosophy of Environment* (Tokyo: Kodansha, 1999), *Philosophy in Landscape* (Tokyo: University Tokyo Press, 2008), and *Philosophy of Life and Landscape* (Tokyo: Iwanami Shoten, 2013).

James McRae holds a Ph.D. in comparative philosophy from the University of Hawai'i at Mānoa with specializations in Japanese philosophy and ethics. He currently serves as Vice-Chair of the Faculty and Associate Professor of Asian Philosophy and Religion at Westminster College in Fulton, Missouri. His publications include the books *Environmental Philosophy in Asian Traditions of Thought* (with J. Baird Callicott, Albany: SUNY Press, 2014) and *The Philosophy of Ang Lee* (with Robert Arp and Adam Barkman, Lexington: University Press of Kentucky, 2013).

Steve Odin has taught in the philosophy department at the University of Hawai'i at Mānoa since 1982. He has also served as Visiting Professor at Boston University, Tohoku University, and the University of Tokyo. He has received several fellowships for one-year periods of research and teaching in Japan, including those from the National Endowment of the Humanities and Japan Foundation, and two Fulbright awards. Among his publications are *Process Metaphysics and Hua-Yen Buddhism* (Albany: SUNY Press, 1982), *The Social Self in Zen and American Pragmatism* (Albany: SUNY Press, 1996), and *Artistic Detachment in Japan and the West: Psychic Distance in Comparative Aesthetics* (Honolulu: University of Hawai'i Press, 2001). His most recent book is *Tragic Beauty in Whitehead and Japanese Aesthetics* (forthcoming).

Graham Parkes earned his Ph.D. in philosophy from the University of California, Berkeley. After three decades at the University of Hawai'i at Mānoa, he moved to University College Cork where he served as a Professor of Philosophy, Head of the Department of Philosophy, Head of the School of Sociology and Philosophy, and Director of the Irish Institute of Japanese Studies. His numerous publications include the books *Heidegger and Asian Thought* (Honolulu: University of Hawai'i Press, 1987), *Nietzsche and Asian Thought* (Chicago: University of Chicago Press, 1991), *Composing the Soul: Reaches of Nietzsche's Psychology* (Chicago: University of Chicago Press, 1994), and a translation of Nietzsche's *Thus Spoke Zarathustra* (Oxford: Oxford University Press, 2005).

Yuriko Saitō, born and raised in Japan, received her Ph.D. in philosophy from the University of Wisconsin at Madison and is Professor of Philosophy at the Rhode Island School of Design. Her writings on everyday aesthetics, Japanese aesthetics, and environmental aesthetics have appeared in a number of journals and book chapters, some of which have been translated into Finnish, French, Polish, and Portuguese. Her *Everyday Aesthetics* was published by Oxford University Press in 2008. She is Associate Editor of *Contemporary Aesthetics*, an online, free-access, and peer-reviewed journal.

TAKAHASHI Takao graduated from the University of Tokyo and holds a Ph.D. in philosophy from Kyushu University. He is now Emeritus Professor and Visiting Professor at Kumamoto University, Japan. His publications include *Logic of "Co-existence with Disasters"* (Fukuoka: Kyushu University Press, 2013) and *Life, Environment, and Care* (Fukuoka: Kyushu University Press, 2008), and he is the editor of *Taking Life and Death Seriously: Bioethics from Japan* (Amsterdam: Elsevier, 2005).

TOYODA Mitsuyo is Associate Professor at Niigata University's Center for Toki and Ecological Restoration. She holds master's degrees from both the University of North Texas and University of Hawai'i, and Ph.D. from Tokyo Institute of Technology. Her primary research interest is to combine environmental ethics, which she studied with Baird Callicott at the University of North Texas, with the dialogue-based educational method "philosophy for children" that she learned at the University of Hawai'i. She examines philosophical issues that arise through collaboration with the public and governmental sectors for sustainable development, and attempts to construct democratic processes of environmental conservation. Her article "Revitalizing Local Commons," appeared in *Environmental Ethics* 35, no. 3 (2013): 279–293.

YAMAUCHI Tomosaburō is an emeritus professor at Osaka University of Education and has served as a visiting scholar at many academic institutions, including Kyoto University, Kobe University, and Monash University. His numerous publications on the subject of ethics include *A History of Western Ethics* (Tsukuba: Gakujutsu Tosho, 1983), *Putting Oneself in Another's Shoes: The Moral Philosophy of R.M. Hare* (Bunkyō-Ku: Keiso-Shobo, 1991), and *Reading Singer* (Tokyo: Showado, 2008). He has translated a number of books into Japanese, including J. Baird Callicott's *Earth's Insights* under the Japanese title *Chikyū no Dōsatsu* 地球の洞察 (Tokyo: Misuzu-Shobo, 2009).

Japanese Environmental Philosophy

Introduction |

I.1. How This Book Came About

The dedication of this collection of papers on Japanese environmental philosophy to YAMAUCHI Tomosaburo is intended both to honor a dedicated senior Japanese philosopher and to acknowledge that creating a volume devoted to Japanese environmental philosophy was his idea.

Professor Yamauchi believes that the traditional Japanese sociopolitical order embedded in a distinctly Japanese worldview had once, not so long ago, preserved "the integrity, stability, and beauty" (in Aldo Leopold's oft-quoted words) of the Japanese islands. *The Green Archipelago* by Conrad Totman indicates that Professor Yamauchi is not just nostalgically romanticizing the environmental condition of Japan before the modernization (that is, westernization) of Japan over the course of the previous century and a half. Totman's ecological history of Japan confirms that the Japanese archipelago actually was in a condition of environmental integrity, stability, and beauty in the relatively recent past. Professor Yamauchi, as any philosopher would, thinks that that is due in large part to the traditional Japanese worldview, to the pervasive cognitive atmosphere once breathed in by the Japanese people.

As KUWAKO Toshio points out in his contribution to this volume, the environmental crisis faced by Japan is more acute than in many other regions of the world. Climate change will bring more intense storms and flooding to the island nation, as it will for lots of other maritime countries. But, in addition, the northeastern quadrant of the ring of fire girdling the Pacific Ocean is entering a more active phase of plate tectonics, according to Kuwako, likely resulting in an increased frequency of large earthquakes, such as the one that struck offshore on March 11, 2011. That earthquake caused the huge tsunami that inundated the Fukushima Daiichi nuclear plant, which subsequently melted down, and released high-level radioactive materials into the environment. The time is certainly ripe for the development of a distinctly Japanese environmental philosophy and an associated environmental ethic.

I.2. How We Came to Edit This Book

The editors have complementary backgrounds in relation to the focus of this collection of essays. J. Baird Callicott is a member of the first generation of environmental philosophers, which coalesced as a distinct field of philosophy during the 1970s. James McRae is a specialist in Japanese philosophy, which he studied, during the first half decade of the present century, in the philosophy department of the University of Hawai'i, a department that uniquely specializes in Asian and comparative philosophy.

In the mid-1980s, Callicott was awarded a fellowship in the Institute of Comparative Philosophy, a six-week summer program for midcareer college teachers of philosophy sponsored by the National Endowment for the Humanities. It was held in Honolulu, and several members of the UH philosophy department served as faculty, supplemented by several visiting scholars. The idea was to provide college philosophy teachers with an intensive introduction to Hindu, Buddhist, Daoist, Confucian, and Shinto traditions of thought, hoping that they would develop courses in these areas for their students or insert segments devoted to these areas into the syllabi of courses already in the curriculum. Callicott, however, came with his own agenda: to persuade the area specialists and comparativists that they had something of great value to contribute to environmental philosophy.

Roger T. Ames, a specialist in Chinese philosophy, had a receptive ear. During their noonday runs up the beautiful Mānoa Valley above the UH campus, Callicott and Ames hatched a plan. The annual meetings for the Society for Asian and Comparative Philosophy were themed and Ames was the program chair. So the theme for the upcoming meetings of the SACP at congresses of the American Academy of Religion and the Eastern Division of the American Philosophical Association was set: "Conceptual Resources in Asian Traditions of Thought for Environmental Ethics." Participation in these panels by known environmental philosophers was also solicited.

In 1987, the best of these papers would be published in special issues of *Environmental Ethics* and *Philosophy East and West*—those by the comparativists appearing in the former; those by the environmental ethicists appearing in the latter. And so the field of comparative environmental philosophy and ethics was born. Callicott and Ames went on to coedit a collection of papers titled *Nature in Asian Traditions of Thought*, which was published in 1989. The year before that, Callicott had returned to the University of Hawai'i as a visiting professor. As a deliverable to the East-West Center, a US State Department entity that partly supported his second stint in Honolulu, Callicott wrote a monograph titled *Earth's Insights: A Multicultural Survey of Ecological Ethics from the Mediterranean Basin to the Australian Outback*, published in 1994, which adds discussions of North and South American Indian, Polynesian, African, and Australian environmental thought to that indigenous to South and East Asia.

The guiding principle of *Earth's Insights* is the construction of environmental ethics embedded in a wide variety of cultural worldviews, with an emphasis on difference and diversity. The idea is not to steal the discourse of the Other, but to sketch a diverse network of different environmental ethics embedded in regional thought worlds—regional cognitive atmospheres, as it were. How they might be interconnected and harmonized was a challenge, but to get into that issue in this introduction would be digressive. One purpose of that book was also to provoke area specialists into critiquing Callicott's outsider's take and stimulate them to do a better job of teasing environmental ethics out of regional worldviews than he had done. As a result, comparative environmental philosophy might grow both in expanse and in depth.

As Midori Kagawa-Fox notes in her contribution to this volume, it was the opinion of some members of the first generation of academic philosophers in Japan that there was "no philosophy in Japan" at the turn of the twentieth century. (Many Anglo-American analytic philosophers would heartily agree.) Thus that generation began to study Western philosophy as if it were the only philosophy—other traditions of thought being just that—traditions of thought, not philosophy. Callicott will have more to say about this in the afterword, but here, to make a longer story shorter, the result, principally by the famous Kyoto school, was a wonderful fusion of European philosophy and theology with such Buddhist metaphysical concepts as no-self and emptiness. Schooled at the University of Hawai'i, not Kyoto, Callicott shared no such narrow conception of philosophy, and the Japanese conceptual resources on which he drew for *Earth's Insights* were the classical texts, not those of the sophisticated Kyoto school.

Now back to Professor Yamauchi and this book. Upon reading *Earth's Insights*, Yamauchi realized that if Japanese philosophers thought there was no philosophy in Japan before they latterly created it, Callicott and the area specialists and comparativists upon whose work he depended thought that there was. Further, he was delighted to also realize that Callicott had sketched a Japanese ecological ethic drawing on premodern Japanese philosophy, also confirming his conviction that the integrity, stability, and beauty of premodern Japan were fostered by the traditional Japanese worldview. Yamauchi secured the publication of *Earth's Insights* by a leading Japanese press, Misuzu-shobo, in 2009. And, at Yamauchi's urging, the Uehiro Foundation sponsored Callicott's two-week lecture tour of Japan, following the publication of the book in Japanese translation.

Meanwhile, Callicott was invited to give a talk for the annual Symposium on Democracy at Westminster College in Fulton, Missouri, in 2007. Chatting with McRae after the talk, Callicott learned that McRae used *Nature in Asian Traditions of Thought* as a textbook in one his courses and that McRae had been a student of Roger Ames, Callicott's old friend and coeditor. Callicott was delighted to learn that the inaugural text of comparative environmental philosophy was still useful, but noted that it was dated and rashly suggested that getting together a sequel might be even more useful. And so a new plan was hatched, which eventually took the form of *Environmental Philosophy in Asian Traditions of Thought*, which was published by SUNY Press in 2014. Having productively worked together on that project, we accepted Yamauchi's request to edit a whole volume devoted to Japanese environmental philosophy by a diverse group of scholars. And now at last, you, dear reader, hold that book in your hand (or perhaps, as one sensitive to environmental issues, you hold your e-reader in your hand with that book downloaded onto it).

I.3. How This Book Is Structured

Japanese Environmental Philosophy is a collection of papers, which respond to the environmental problems of the twenty-first century. Many of the authors draw on Japanese philosophical traditions to illuminate our relationships with other humans, nonhuman animals, and the natural environment. It contains articles from fifteen scholars from Japan, the United States, Europe, and Australia. The essays cover a broad range of Japanese thought, including Zen Buddhism, Shintoism, the Kyoto school, Japanese art and aesthetics, and traditional Japanese culture. Most of the material has been written specifically for this volume; only two articles have been previously published in scholarly journals. This anthology is divided into five major parts, each of which deals with a particular aspect of Japanese environmental philosophy.

The first part addresses conceptions of nature in Japanese thought and the implications these conceptions have for environmental ethics. In chapter 1, "Thinking the Ambient: On the Possibility of *Shizengaku* (Naturing Science)," Augustin Berque considers the philosophical implications of *shizen* (nature). IMANISHI Kinji (1902–1992) attained international acclaim as the initiator of a paradigm shift in primatology by recognizing the animal's subjecthood, sociality, and capacity for cultural learning. Imanishi was also an entomologist, ecologist, and anthropologist and a great mountaineer, but he was fundamentally a philosopher of nature, life, and biological evolution. He summarized his epistemological stance not in terms of *shizen kagaku* 自然科学, the natural sciences, but rather as *shizengaku* 自然学, a "naturing science" in which the scientist participates in the general subjecthood of nature, and thus is able to know it hermeneutically—that is, from the inside—making science itself a particular aspect of nature's general dynamics. This way of thinking is opposed to the modern distinction between subject and object, and its relevance is grounded in both the Japanese language and attitudes toward nature, which in fact imply an *ambient* rather than a *subject*.

Chapter 2 features Leah Kalmanson's "Pure Land Ecology: Taking the Supernatural Seriously in Environmental Philosophy." Kalmanson investigates the concept of nature from the perspective of Pure Land Buddhism, which uses the term *jinen* rather than *shizen* to refer to the supernatural power of Amida's compassion that facilitates rebirth in the Pure Land. Though it has been traditionally overlooked as a type of superstition, the supernatural can be a relevant medium for philosophical discourse, particularly in the area of environmental philosophy. Pure Land Buddhism provides a set of guidelines that can minimize human beings' interference with the natural world by emphasizing selfless action and universal compassion.

In chapter 3, "From *Kyōsei* to *Kyōei*: Symbiotic Flourishing in Japanese Environmental Ethics," James McRae discusses *kyōsei* (symbiosis), a Japanese philosophical paradigm that is the cornerstone for the Caux Round Table Principles of business ethics. Though this notion comes from the idea of mutualistic symbiotic relationships in the biological sciences, it has only recently been applied to the discipline of environmental ethics. *Kyōsei* is a normative ethical principle, and the adoption of *kyōsei* (symbiosis) by individuals, corporations, and governments can promote *kyōei* (mutual flourishing). The concept of noninterference (*jū*) promotes ethical conduct by encouraging respect for others and minimizes waste through the promotion of maximal efficiency. By using *kyōsei* as the guiding principle for international business and politics, we can create policies and laws that allow us to live sustainably and to flourish, both economically and ecologically.

The second part deals with the Japanese understanding of the person as a being fundamentally grounded in a social and environmental context. In chapter 4, "Kūkai and Dōgen as Exemplars of Ecological Engagement," Graham Parkes argues that the current environmental crisis is largely due to a particular conception of the human relationship to nature. Common in anthropocentric traditions of Western thought, this view depicts human beings as separate from, and superior to, all other beings in the natural world. Traditional East Asian understandings of this relationship are quite different and remarkably unanthropocentric, especially as exemplified in the ideas of Chinese Daoism and Japanese Buddhism. This essay examines the human-nature relationship in the philosophies of Kūkai (aka Kōbō Daishi, 774–835) and Dōgen (1200–1253), who offer a notion of somatic practice designed to bring about a transformation of experience. Both thinkers advocate philosophy as a way of life that can help us to engage the world in an ecologically responsible manner. This article was originally published in the *Journal of Japanese Philosophy* 1 (2013): 85–110.

Chapter 5 features INUTSUKA Yū's "Sensation, Betweenness, Rhythms: Watsuji's Environmental Philosophy and Ethics in Conversation with Heidegger." She uses the philosophy of Japanese ethicist WATSUJI Tetsurō to challenge the traditional understanding of "environment" as something nonhuman. Criticizing Heidegger, especially for his analyses of equipment and of mood, Watsuji first emphasizes participation of the environment in our self-understanding through sensation. He further proposes that repetitive phenomena of *fūdo* or climate form a certain human way of life, where human existence is understood as in betweenness, the existence with individual-social duality. Finally, Watsuji comes up with an understanding that it is human existence that has a rhythmic nature. The rhythms of human life integrate the environment which in turn founds our ethical life. Beyond an opposition between the individual and the environment, Watsuji's philosophy provides a base for a new anthropocentric ethics in which the environment is a part of human existence.

Chapter 6 contains Steve Bein's "Climate Change as Existentialist Threat: Watsuji, Greimas, and the Nature of Opposites." Bein uses Watsuji's models of *ningen sonzai* (人間存在), *fūdo* (風土), and *seken* (世間) to make sense of why climate change is an existential threat in the now ordinary-language sense (it threatens our very existence) and also an existentialist threat (as it threatens our mode of being-in-the-world). Applying the semiotic squares developed by Algirdas Julien Greimas, the distinction emerges between two types of opposites: antithesis (where X and anti-X annihilate each other) and countermeasure (where X and counter-X push and pull against each other in the act of self-becoming). The human drives toward individualism (*nin*) and collectivism (*gen*) are each other's countermeasure, just as humanity's existence in and expansion through the lived world (*fūdo* 風土) plays the role of countermeasure to the lived world itself. Climate change is an existential threat because even by the most conservative estimates, it threatens to topple all of those carefully counterbalanced relationships.

Part III deals with environmental aesthetics, a subdiscipline of both environmental philosophy and philosophical aesthetics that deals with the beauty of the natural world. In chapter 7, "Whitehead's Perspectivism as a Basis for Environmental Ethics and Aesthetics: A Process View on the Japanese Concept of Nature," Steve Odin investigates parallels between the Buddhist concept of Indra's Net and the notion of moral perspective-taking. According to Alfred North Whitehead's process metaphysics, the aesthetic continuum of nature is an organization of *perspectives*, whereby each occasion is akin to a Leibnizian monad, or metaphysical point, each functioning as a living mirror that reflects the entire universe from its own unique standpoint as a microcosm of the macrocosm. Odin first analyzes the metaphysical perspectivism underlying Whitehead's ecological concept of nature along with a brief consideration of how Whitehead's perspectivism illuminates the Japanese aesthetic concept of nature as visualized by the poetic metaphor of Indra's Net, wherein an event is likened to a brilliant jewel reflecting the whole cosmos from its own viewpoint. He then shows how Whitehead's Leibnizian perspectivism as reformulated by George Herbert Mead, and later by Lawrence Kohlberg and Jürgen Habermas, can be integrated into an ethical procedure for moral perspective-taking, whereby free moral agents learn to put themselves into the perspectives of others in the community. Odin ultimately argues that this procedure for moral perspective-taking can be used as the basis for a new environmental ethic and aesthetic.

Chapter 8 features Yuriko Saitō's "Japanese Gardens: The Art of Improving Nature," which argues that gardens represent an idealized form of nature in which human beings reshape the natural world according to specific aesthetic paradigms. Unlike Western formal gardens, which are characterized by symmetry and rigid order, Japanese gardens present a more "natural" appearance by articulating the native characteristics of the materials, such as rocks and plants. This chapter draws from the philosophy of Zen Buddhism, as well as the time-honored garden design principle of "following the request," to show how Japanese garden designers are inspired by—and possibly improve upon—nature in their art and how a respectful attitude toward nature is expressed aesthetically in Japanese gardens. This article first appeared in *Chanoyu Quarterly* 83 (1996): 40–61.

Part III concludes with chapter 9, YAMAUCHI Tomosaburō's "KUKI Shūzō and Platonism: Nature, Love, and Morality." The aesthetic system of Japanese philosopher KUKI Shūzō exposes the value systems at the heart of our current environmental crisis. Kuki's anthropology and aesthetics stand in sharp contrast to the Platonic metaphysics that form the historical basis of Western value schemes. By focusing on becoming and nothingness rather than the permanence of the forms, Kuki develops a philosophy in which the love of nature is the fundamental ground of value. This forms the basis of an environmental aesthetic and ethic in which human flourishing is ultimately tied to the good of the environment.

Part IV investigates the critical role that nature plays in Japanese culture, which in turn informs Japanese environmental ethics and aesthetics. In chapter 10, "Recollecting Local Narratives on the Land Ethic," TOYODA Mitsuyo explores some of the indigenous Japanese narratives about the land and its relation with human societies that have been handed down from generation to generation as guides to appropriate human conduct. Though Japan has a rich heritage of narratives about nature, their value has not been properly appreciated because of the development of modern epistemology, which is primarily based on scientific reasoning. Japanese mythological accounts of the world provide a treasure trove of ideas for constructing a land ethic rooted in local traditions. Aldo Leopold's land ethic offers the notion of biotic community based on his actual observation of nature from an ecological perspective, treating humans as plain members and citizens of the biotic community. Japanese nature narratives provide guidance for living safely and sustainably in harmony with the natural world around us. The collection of these narratives, therefore, is an important source for a Japanese land ethic built upon the unique cultural heritage of Japan.

Chapter 11 features Midori Kagawa-Fox's "The Crucial Role of Culture in Japanese Environmental Philosophy." She argues that Japanese culture has been as important in shaping Japanese environmental ethics as have philosophical values. Japan has an extensive cultural heritage that has been built on mythology and folklore, and on religious beliefs and practices, and these ingredients have influenced the Japanese ethical consciousness. The indigenous Shinto religion, which evolved from animism, teaches that the ever-present *kami* (spirits) bind the Japanese to their environment. Their presence imparts a strong moral consciousness. Thus an understanding of the relationship of the *kami* to the Japanese people is essential for appreciating Japanese environmental ethics. Most Japanese have an intuitive belief in the *kami* that has been significant in forming their caring attitude toward the natural world.

The fourth part concludes with GODA Hiroko's "*Kagura*: Embodying Environmental Philosophy in the Japanese Performing Arts." Goda, a cultural anthropologist, argues that by studying the *kagura* dance performances of the Kyushu regions of Takachiho and Gokase, the environmental anthropology of Japanese mythology can be revealed. The traditional Shinto religious and philosophical ideologies embodied in these ritual dance performances illustrate how the invisible power of divinity can become manifest in the environment. While nature in the Japanese tradition is morally neutral, the human response to the divinity present in nature is not; humans have an obligation to pursue a harmonious relationship with the natural world via the divinity present in it.

The final part of the book deals with the ways that humans can respond to, prepare for, and prevent natural disasters such as the tsunami that caused the meltdown of the Fukushima Daiichi reactor in 2011. Chapter 13 contains TAKAHASHI Takao's "Disaster Prevention as an Issue in Environmental Ethics." He argues that while the Great East Japan Earthquake in 2011 gave Japan the opportunity to reconsider the basic relationships between humans and nature, the scale of this disaster was not limited to Japan. It may be said that all of us live in "the age of co-disaster" in which we must realize that disasters are unavoidable. The earthquake brought forth a new agenda for environmental ethics, that is, disaster prevention. However, little research has been done in this area by environmental ethicists, many of whom have focused on the conservation of nature. Disaster prevention may be introduced into environmental ethics by examining Japanese mythology, which can help us develop new ways of forming, maintaining, and restoring good relationships between humans and nature.

In chapter 14, "Nondualism after Fukushima? Tracing Dōgen's Teaching vis-à-vis Nuclear Disaster," ISHIDA Masato argues that humans and environment form a single continuum, part of a larger cosmic life. This, however, seems to imply that we are continuous even with the radioactive waste produced by the nuclear meltdown in Fukushima. There is nothing surprising about this, Ishida suggests, since in Buddhism no substance is considered to have intrinsic self-nature such as "clean" or "dirty." On the other hand, Ishida points out that there remains a clear distinction between purifying and nonpurifying *acts*, if Dōgen's view of human agency in relation to the environment is correctly applied in our present-day context. Taking Fukushima as an example, and scrutinizing Dōgen's many passages on Buddha-nature, washing, and wrongdoing, Ishida underscores our responsibility to participate in nature's self-purifying process rather than making questionable appeals to "nondualism."

The final chapter of this part, "Planetary Philosophy and Social Consensus Building," KUWAKO Toshio discusses his work in applied environmental ethics. The Ohashi River, which runs through Matsue City in the Izumo region and feeds the Hii River, has recently undergone extensive modification for flood control. This controversial project has been politically polarizing because of the tensions between human welfare, traditional cultural beliefs, sustainability, and environmental aesthetics. Kuwako develops the idea that changing the spatial structure of a community is both a cultural and historical project that must take into account traditional beliefs about the relationship between human beings and the environment. The decision-making process for the development of social infrastructure should be grounded in meaningful citizen participation and should reflect the environmental values of the people.

Comparative environmental philosophy is valuable because it forces us to challenge many of the foundational assumptions that have led to the shortsighted thinking responsible for much of the environmental degradation that we see today. The editors and authors of this anthology hope that the Japanese philosophical, religious, and cultural traditions can provide meaningful insight to address the current environmental crisis.

PART I | Nature in the Japanese
Tradition of Thought

CHAPTER 1 | Thinking the Ambient
On the Possibility of Shizengaku
(Naturing Science)

AUGUSTIN BERQUE

1.1. Subject, Nature, and Japanese Language

It is generally assumed that one of the main ingredients of the modern Western paradigm was science as instituted by the scientific revolution of the seventeenth century; that is, as founded on the will to objectify phenomena, measure these objects, and ascertain their laws through experimentation. This supposed an ontological stance, called *dualism*, in which the object is essentially distinguished from the subject who observes it. The institution of the modern subject was thus correlative to the institution of the modern object. A telling image of this essential distinction was given by the discovery and implementation of the laws of linear perspective, which placed the observer's eye outside and behind the picture, converting the scene represented by the latter into a strictly measurable object.[1] This setting of the observer's position out of the picture symbolized the abstraction of the modern subject's being out of an objectified world. The same ontological withdrawal of the subject's essence out of objective reality was to be later clearly formulated by Descartes's distinction between res extensa (the extended thing, i.e. the object) and res cogitans (the thinking thing, i.e., the subject), e.g., in the following passage of the *Discourse on Method:* "I knew thereby that I was a substance whose whole essence or nature is only thinking, and who, in order to be, needs not any place, nor depends on any material thing."[2] This virtual abstraction of the modern subject's essence from any particular place or object was perfectly in tune with the universality of the scientific observer's eye, with its supposed gaze from nowhere onto pure objects. This is what made the modern natural sciences ontologically possible, since nature thus became an object.

Native speakers of European tongues like English or French are generally unaware of the homology between this universal abstraction of the modern subject's subjecthood from an objectified nature, on the one hand, and on the other hand that which they symbolize in everyday speech with the use of their, by far, most frequent word: the personal pronoun "I" (*je, ich, io, ja,* etc.). I am "I" always and everywhere, independently from any place or object, and even from my own body: be it male or female, black or white, old or young, I am always "I." True, since antiquity, grammarians had been conscious of this duality between a person's concrete singularity and the universality of personal pronouns; this is why they rendered the grammatical idea of person with the word "mask" (*prosopon, persona*). Indeed, a mask remains the same even when the actor or the scene is not the same. Yet Europeans did not really question this strange duality between concrete beings and personal pronouns until the nineteenth century, e.g. when Rimbaud wrote, "I is an other" (*Je est un autre*).[3]

Perhaps it took a poet to denaturalize the coincidence of "I" and "my selfhood (substance, essence or nature)" in our languages; but the fact is that such a coincidence is not natural at all in some other languages. This is the case in Japanese, where the notions of "subject" (*shugo* 主語) and "personal pronoun" (*ninshō daimeishi* 人称代名詞) were artificially introduced, under Meiji, by grammarians who strove to make the "national tongue" (*kokugo* 国語) fit into the categories of European grammars, deemed to be universal paradigms of modernity.[4] In fact, the basic structure and functioning of the Japanese language is profoundly alien to those of the main European tongues, which are commonly represented with the triad S-V-C (subject-verb-complement), as in "I (S) see (V) Mary (C)." This is not all. The same model also governs (since Aristotle) the basic structure of logic, that is, the dyad S-P (subject-predicate), as in "Mary (S) is sad (P)." Now, this also does not directly apply to Japanese; so much so that, in the last century, NISHIDA Kitarō (1870–1945) turned Aristotle's "logic of the subject" into a "logic of the predicate" (*jutsugo no ronri* 述語の論理), also called a "logic of place" (*basho no ronri* 場所の論理).[5]

In both cases (grammar and logic), the problem centers on that which, since Aristotle, we call the subject (*hupokeimenon, subjectum*). I intend to show here the incidence of this double question on the way nature can be grasped, not only in general or traditional terms, but even in the field of science, especially in the case of the evolution of species.

1.2. The Sound of a Windbell

My stance here follows what I shall call *a historicized Sapir-Whorf hypothesis*. This amounts to acknowledging, at the same time, both the reality and the contingency of the link between language and worldview. There *is* a link, but it works differently according to the circumstances. This is to say that it does not belong to *causality* (the binary relation "A causes B"), but to *motivation* (the ternary relation "A becomes B for C"). For instance, the Western view of reality as an objective substance (*ousia*, which at the same time is a logical subject) owes much to the basic structure of European languages. Indeed, in our tradition of thought, "substance & accidents in metaphysics correspond to subject & predicate in logic."[6] Now, this basic structure is the same as that of Sanskrit—also an Indo-European tongue—in which was expressed, as in Buddhism, an entirely different conception of reality (including the conception of language itself: Panini's grammar did not center, as Aristotle's, on the notion of the subject). Is this to say that there is no link between language and worldview? No, it is to say that, owing to the concrete circumstances of history, the link is contingent, not abstractly, timelessly mechanical. This is what I intend to show in greater detail with the Japanese case.

Let us take the following haiku, which is, in the original Japanese, grammatically a perfectly regular, complete, and ordinary sentence:

風鈴の	*Fūrin no*	The windbell's
ちひさき音の	*chiisaki oto no*	tiny chime:
下にゐる	*shita ni iru*	I am under

In YAMAMOTO Kenkichi's *New Seasonal of Haiku*,[7] this poem by Ōshi is classed with the "season words" (*kigo* 季語) of summer. Haikus compulsorily include a season word, which here is the windbell, *fūrin*. A windbell is hung in summer from a branch in the garden. Its tongue is fit with a small sail (a piece of paper) that makes it chime at the slightest puff of wind. As is the case here, this sound makes people, inside in the mugginess of the house, synesthetically feel the breeze as if they were outside, "under the tiny chime of the windbell." This synesthesia in itself is a telling trait of the Japanese sense of reality. Windbells were not invented in the West because westerners tend to put the identity of subjects (substances) over their relation. Accordingly, sounds (A) are not supposed to be coolers (non-A).[8] On the contrary, Buddhism taught the Japanese that there is no such thing as substance; all is relation, and thereby hangs the reality of synesthesias. But this is not only a matter of Buddhism; it is also perfectly in tune with the basic traits of the Japanese language. In the haiku above, the verb *iru* (to be somewhere) has no subject (a noun or a pronoun like "I," "she," etc.); and its form, also, is impersonal. So we literally cannot know *who* is there, under the windbell. What is said is a *scene*: the windbell's tiny chime, and a certain presence thereunder. True, we could manage to render something like that if we translated *shita ni iru* with, for example, "being thereunder"; but that would not be natural at all. English does not work that way; it needs a subject, whereas Japanese does not.

What the Japanese language needs to have, on the other hand, is a predicate, and to organize and codify that predicate in all sorts of ways. In the above example, if put in the normal syntax of the English language, the translation should be: "I" (or "you," "grandpa," or whoever equals the subject S) "am (are, is) under the tiny chime of the wind bell" (which equals the predicate P). First S, then P. Now, the original haiku has only P, without an S. The English translation is *obliged* to invent that S in order to fill the blank (which in Japanese is not a blank at all); exactly in the same way as our grammar has invented an impersonal and fictional "it" in order to say *"it" rains ("il" pleut, "es" regnet*, etc.[9]), while the fact is only rain, i.e., P; whereas indeed, according to the circumstances, Japanese can simply say *futteiru* ("raining")—and, for that matter, Chinese also only says *xiayu* 下雨 ("downrain"), etc. Of course, Japanese *can* also express the subject (as in *ame ga futte iru*, "rain is falling"); but the important fact is that, in ordinary speech, it does not *need* to.

How is this possible? Because the concreteness of a real *scene* (*bamen* 場面), if expressed verbally, in fact necessarily implies the existence of a speaker. The accent is put on this *implication*; and therefore, in inverse ratio, *explicating* that existence is not necessary. Japanese does not need to, and in fact generally does not, say explicitly "I" (or "you," "Mary," etc.); what it needs, on the other hand, is to be precise about what is going on, and in which circumstances. Yet it can say with perfect precision that subject "I" (etc.), if necessary *according to the circumstances*, that is, according to the *bamen*.

1.3. An *Ambient* Instead of a Subject

Bamen, indeed, is the clue. The word itself structurally means "facing (*men* 面) the place (*ba* 場)." *Who* then is "facing the place" of the action, i.e., the scene? It is that which we call the subject, e.g., expressed by the pronoun "I"; but, in a concrete scene, the essential fact is *facing that scene*, that is, the *aspect* of the scene; in other words, the phenomenon as such (*phainein*: to appear). This is why, in Japanese, aspective forms are so frequent. An aspective form is a form that implies the existence of the interpreter of a scene. Whereas in European languages *and* logic we rely on the binary structure S-P (S is P), Japanese relies on the ternary structure S-I-P (S is P for I), where I is the interpreter of the scene. For example, whereas we can say in English "Mary (S) is sad (P)," unless Mary herself is speaking (saying "Mari" instead of "I," as can be done by young women), Japanese cannot say the equivalent, "Mari wa (S) kanashii (P)"; it must say, "Mari wa (S) kanashisō da (P)," i.e., "Mary looks sad"; that is, "S is P for I" (the speaker, who is not Mary and therefore cannot express Mary's intimate feelings in her place, but only can tell her aspect). Yet that speaker does not verbalize his or her own existence with a pronoun (e.g., "for *me*, Mary is sad"). There is no need to do so, because this existence is implied by the aspective form *kanashisō da*.

Interestingly enough, *men* also means a mask; e.g., in *nōmen* 能面, a Noh mask. Yet, contrary to the Greek *prosōpon* or the Latin *persona*, this "mask" did not evolve into meaning a substantial and individual "person"; it clung to the acceptation of "face" or "aspect," which implies both the own figure of a thing and the existence of those for whom things figure something; that is, a certain relation.

A *bamen*, then, is a certain set of such relations in which one's existence is implied by the things themselves. The person implied in such a relationship could certainly not say, as Descartes did, "I knew thereby . . . (etc.)"; that is, express the transcendence of the modern Western subject, an "I" able to say *sum qui sum*, literally "I am who I am," as our Vulgate makes Yahweh say on Mount Horeb (Ex. 3:14). This is what I shall call "the principle of Mount Horeb," according to which the human subject, absolutizing his or her own subjecthood, is her or his own predicate "I."[10] Indeed, as Benveniste stressed in several articles after the Second World War,[11] "is I who says 'I'" (*est je qui dit 'je'*"). This entails that other beings (unless one's own human fellows), virtually deprived of any subjecthood at all, become objective machines; and this principle is indeed the essence of mechanicism. On the other hand, the person implied in a Japanese *bamen* would rather pronounce a purely immanent *sum id, ubi sum*: "I am that, where I am." And in fact, this is precisely the case in the above haiku, where the person in question is not expressed as such, but only as a certain ambience. Subjecthood here is not concentrated into an "I," it is diffused into the whole *bamen*. Indeed, "being under the tiny chime of the windbell" is nothing else than being that particular set of circumstances: an ambience. That being, then, is not that which we call a subject, and especially not our modern subject as opposed to the object; it is *an ambient*, being there in the things around and the atmosphere thereby. A thorough *Dasein*, as Heidegger might have put it.

The Japanese did not only figure reality according to this *ambienthood*; they consciously elaborated it along history, and created the necessary concepts for it. In the oldest anthology of poetry, the *Man'yōshū* (eighth c.), one of the categories of poems is called "letting things express one's feelings" (*mono ni yosete omoi wo nobu* 寄物陳思). About the tenth century appeared the concept of *mono no aware* 物の哀れ, "the pathos of things," which was later to be analyzed in detail by the great philologist MOTOORI Norinaga (1730–1801). Yet the most telling historical fact is the development and codification of the haiku itself, at about the time when the modern paradigm was established in Europe, i.e., the seventeenth century. True, as a poetical genre, the haiku progressively emerged from a long tradition, but what concerns us here is its codification by authors like IHARA Saikaku (1642–1693), MATSUO Bashō (1644–1694), and MASAOKA Shiki (1867–1902). The most conspicuous trait of the haiku is its briefness (three verses of 5-7-5 syllables). This is made possible because the haiku immediately evokes a whole set of codified relations with the Japanese milieu (I shall define this word in the following section, 1.4), symbolized by what is called a *season word* (*kigo* 季語). Season words represent something or custom associated with one of the five seasons (spring, summer, autumn, winter, new year). In the haiku above, it is the windbell, a *kigo* of summer. These season words are itemized and classified in *seasonals* (*saijiki* 歳時記), which nowadays can count up to seven thousand *kigo*. The first Japanese seasonal,[12] the *Nihon Saijiki* by KAIBARA Ekiken, a botanist, was published in 1688, but the first one especially dedicated to haiku, the *Haikai Saijiki*, was published by TAKIZAWA Bakin in 1803.

The necessity of including a *kigo* in a haiku amounts to a syntax of the unwritten context of the poem, that is, the Japanese milieu. This syntax, in inverse ratio, diminishes the necessity to express verbally what the matter is about. A few words will suffice for arousing an impression. Curiously enough, in the same period when the genre of haiku was established, the Japanese language underwent a peculiar evolution, that is, an extraordinary multiplication of onomatopoeias expressing not only sounds, but also any kind of other impressions (the former are called *giseigo* 擬声語, the latter *gitaigo* 擬態語). It is said that contemporary Japanese numbers more than two thousand of these *impressives*, out of which four hundred to seven hundred are in current use.[13] They immediately evoke an ambience, out of the linear order of speech. For example, the chime of a windbell will be evoked by *chirin, chirorin, chinchin, chiririn* ... According to the context, *chira chira* will evoke the way snowflakes or flower petals fall down, or stars twinkle faintly in a summer night, or something or somebody fleetingly appears and disappears, or a rumor is heard here and there ... *Uja uja* is the way insects or cars are milling about, etc. Now, the peculiarity of these impressives is that they need no grammatical construction. They can stand alone, and their meaning is immediately felt, out of any syntax. I surmise that, on the other hand, their historical diffusion has something to do with the *syntactization of the Japanese milieu* as a whole. That is to say, systematically ordering (cosmizing) the milieu as a whole, as in seasonals, made possible, in direct ratio, the diffusion of these *desyntactized* words, their sense stronger as they are linked to real impressions rather than, grammatically, to other words.

But then, what is a milieu?

1.4. From Environment to Milieu

According to *The Concise Oxford Dictionary*, the word *milieu* means "environment, state of life, social surroundings." This can correspond to the way Auguste Comte understood it in his *Cours de Philosophie Positive* (1830–1842), that is, as an objective ambient system interacting with an organism.[14] This led one of Comte's disciples, the physician Charles Robin (1821–1885), one of the founders of the Société de Biologie, to propose at its inaugural session, on June 7, 1848, the constitution of a study of milieus, which he dubbed *mésologie*.[15]

The field of this mesology was more encompassing than that of ecology, later introduced by Haeckel; it might be defined as an addition of ecology and sociology. That was too much for a single positive discipline, and it is probably the reason why mesology, in the twentieth century, eventually faded out of the scientific realm. Yet it was to be reborn on a new ground in the works of Jakob von Uexküll (1864–1944), who introduced a radically different point of view, that is, to consider the animal not as a machine, determined by an objective environment, but as a machinist interpreting the environment in its own subjective way.[16] Accordingly, von Uexküll made a revolutionary distinction between what he called *Umwelt* on the one hand, and *Umgebung* on the other hand. The Umwelt is an animal's ambient world (*Welt*), whereas the Umgebung is constituted with the objective data (*Gebung*) of the environment, as they can be grasped by a modern science like ecology.

Through classical scientific protocols, von Uexküll has proven that what concretely exists for an animal is its proper Umwelt, not the general Umgebung. I use here "milieu" as an equivalent for the former, and "environment" for the latter. In that sense, *a* milieu is what really exists for a certain living being, while *the* environment is what is abstractly considered from the nowhere point of view of modern science. A milieu is singular, the environment is universal. Accordingly, mesology (the study of milieus: *Umweltlehre*) must not be confused with ecology (the study of environments: *Ökologie*). In the realm of ecology, binary statements like "S is P" (e.g., "Water is H_2O") can be made altogether; in that of mesology, what must be made are ternary statements like "S is P for I," where I is the interpreter of a certain milieu (i.e., von Uexküll's "machinist"), e.g., "Rain (S) is good (P) for plants (I)." Yet human reason is also able to acknowledge this objectively, and conclude that "rain (S) is good for plants (P)"; and this is indeed what makes mesology scientifically possible. Nevertheless, we should not forget that it is first for plants that rain is good (S-I-P), because if it were not the case, we would not be there to state that S-P.

At about the same time when von Uexküll introduced *Umweltlehre* in the natural sciences, a similar stance was defined, in the humanities, by the Japanese philosopher WATSUJI Tetsurō (1889–1960) in his essay *Fūdo* (*Milieus*, 1935),[17] which also distinguished milieu (*fūdo* 風土) from the natural environment (*shizen kankyō* 自然環境). Correlatively, Watsuji introduced the concept of *fūdosei* 風土性, which he defined as "the structural moment of human existence" (*ningen sonzai no kōzō keiki* 人間存在の構造契機). This concept expresses the dynamic coupling (moment) of a human being with her or his milieu. Basing on Watsuji's definition, I have translated it with "mediance" (*médiance*).[18] It renders the fact that in a concrete, eco-techno-symbolic human milieu (not in an abstract, purely physical environment), reality is never a pure S (the logician's subject = the physicist's object), but, ternarily, an interpretation of S as P by a certain being (I), either individual (e.g., a certain person, or organism) or collective (e.g., a society, or a species), since the existence of that milieu is a function of that being's existence, and vice versa.

1.5. From Species to Speciety

The fact that mediance was conceived of in Japanese by a Japanese is probably not a coincidence. This concept is just another name for the structural moment that, eleven centuries earlier, had made ŌTOMO no Yakamochi think of the category of "letting things express one's feelings," and later made MOTOORI Norinaga put forward the "pathos of things" as properly Japanese. Mediance is certainly a universal trait of human existence—of existence tout court, in fact—but it took Japanese culture to grasp it as such. Though he created plenty of neologisms to constitute his mesology, von Uexküll did not think of that ontological, overarching concept. True, the word *fūdo* existed already in Japanese, with the acceptation of natural features of a certain region; yet Watsuji gave it a special turn, which we might interpret as "the way (*fū* 風 = P) a certain land (*do* 土 = S) is interpreted [by its inhabitants = I]"; that is, the triadic structure S-I-P. This is homologous with the basic structure of the Japanese language. The dyadic structure S-P, for sure, does not so easily allow us to think of mediance; it is much more in tune with the abstraction of the modern subject out of an objectified environment—no wonder since, structurally, S-P does not suppose I.

A double-blind trial of the Japanese mediance can be found in the works of the great naturalist IMANISHI Kinji (1902–1992). Indeed, though he did not use Watsuji's terminology, nor even that of von Uexküll, Imanishi based his interpretation of nature on two postulates, which amount not only to acknowledging mediance, but to making it a clue for reinterpreting the natural sciences themselves. The first one was to consider that a living being does not face an external and objective environment as such, but in the course of a mutual process that he called "subjectivation of the environment, environmentalization of the subject" (*kankyō no shutaika, shutai no kankyōka* 環境の主体化、主体の環境化). This principle was laid out as early as his first book, entitled *The World of the Living* (*Seibutsu no sekai*, written in 1941), and tenaciously reaffirmed in numerous works thereafter. The second one was to consider that any living being, including the human, is a member of a global society, which Imanishi called *seibutsu zentai shakai* 生物全体社会, "the whole society of the living," on which grounds a scientist is entitled to feel something in common with the animal he or she observes, and penetrate, so to speak hermeneutically, into this animal's proper world.

Imanishi began his research as an entomologist in the twenties. It is by studying mayflies in their nymphal state in a nearby stream that he came to define a concept that was to become the pillar of his later theories: *sumiwake* 棲み分け, which associates the two ideas of inhabiting (*sumi*) and dividing (*wake*). Imanishi himself later translated this concept with *habitat segregation*.[19] One of his disciples, SANO Toshiyuki, preferred to render it with *lifestyle partitioning*, adding the following quotation from the *Iwanami seibutsugaku jiten* (*Iwanami Dictionary of*

Biology): "Biologically, the phenomenon of sumiwake can be defined as follows: two or more species, with the same potential to live in a given 'place,' divide the place into exclusive habitats."[20] Yet this cannot do justice to the richness of the concept, which implies not only the spatial fact of segregation, but also the temporal fact of speciation. Indeed, *wake* means here both the division of habitat and that into (sub)species. This is why I prefer to render *sumiwake* with the neologism "ecospecy."

Ecospecy also implies one of Imanishi's most fundamental ideas, which he represented with the concept of *shushakai* 種社会. This literally means "species (*shu*) society (*shakai*)." This expresses the socialness of species both intrinsically (the members of a species form a society) and extrinsically (the relations between different species form a society). The latter aspect leads to the concept of whole society of the living, as just noted. This idea of *shushakai* differs profoundly with that of population, which dominates the neo-Darwinian theory of evolution. A population is a purely statistical sum of individual organisms. On the other hand, a society implies some kind of integrative principle or, better said, some kind of self-consciousness. A population is a mechanical combination of objects, whereas a society is a sensible integration of subjects.

Indeed, Imanishi professed correlatively that living beings are subjects (*shutai* 主体), not machines. They are endowed with subjecthood or selfhood (*shutaisei* 主体性) at all levels, ranging from the cell to the whole society of the living. One of Imanishi's last books is titled, precisely, *Shutaisei no shinkaron* (*Subjecthood in Evolution*, 1980). Needless to say, this view is totally discrepant with that of Darwin, which classically belongs to the modern Western paradigm of mechanicism. In other words, whereas neo-Darwinism, in compliance with the Mount Horeb principle, only acknowledges in evolution an objectified binary combination of chance (mutation) and necessity (the statistical laws of selection), Imanishi's theory of evolution implies a ternary combination in which any fact (S) is concretely interpreted in a certain way (P) by a certain selfhood (I); that is, once again, it relies on the triad S-I-P.

I shall add that Imanishi's theory of evolution implies a thorough realism, as opposed to the nominalism of twentieth-century neo-Darwinian theory—e.g., Dawkins's thesis of the selfish gene. Indeed, whereas the latter—as Mrs. Thatcher said of society: that "there is no such thing"—amounts to saying that there is no such thing as species but only populations, Imanishi professed that evolution implied some kind of choice by the species itself; that is, as a *shushakai*.

For that reason, I think that translating *shushakai* deserves in its turn a neologism, that of "speciety." This implies the proper selfhood of a species. It is the aspective way that a species appears to itself through its own members (which in its turn implies the selfhood of these members, and so on from the cell to the whole society of the living and the other way round). One should remember that *species* originally meant view, aspect (hence spectacle, etc.). If you are a modern Western *Homo sapiens sapiens*, for instance, speciety is that which generally makes you ashamed to appear in the nude in front of another person, but not in front of a cat (*Felis silvestris catus*).

It should now be clear that Imanishi's position in front of natural phenomena can be opposed to the classical modern Western worldview as characterized on the whole (there are of course exceptions, like Nietzsche, Leopold ...), especially so in the Anglosphere, by a bent to dualism, mechanicism, nominalism, utilitarianism, and methodological individualism. Is this to say that Imanishi's stance is not scientific?

1.6. From the Theory of Evolution to Naturing Science

Imanishi's scientific status is not a simple question. On the one hand, he has been internationally recognized as the initiator of a paradigm shift in primatology, the essence of which consists in acknowledging the animal's subjecthood, sociality, and culturalness. Yet he was much more than a primatologist. Also an entomologist, ecologist, anthropologist, and great mountaineer, he was fundamentally a thinker of nature, life, and evolution. In his later years, he summarized his epistemological stance in the concept of *shizengaku* 自然学, as opposed to *shizen kagaku* 自然科学, the natural sciences. Though robot translators recognize no difference between the two terms, what is at stake here is in fact an alternative between two radically different conceptions of reality, one (*shizen kagaku*) in which, in accordance with the classical modern Western scientific paradigm, nature is considered as an object, and another one (*shizengaku*) in which the scientist participates in the general subjecthood of nature, and thus is able to know it hermeneutically, i.e., from the inside, making science itself a particular aspect of nature's general bent. This is why I propose to translate *shizengaku* with "naturing science."

Needless to say, from the first point of view, this is a totally heretic, unscientific stance. This discrepancy was best illustrated with respect to the theory of evolution. All his life long, Imanishi was highly concerned with evolution, and published abundantly about it, tenaciously contesting the neo-Darwinian dogma. His late book *Subjecthood in Evolution* is a good example of what his naturing science can consist of in such matters. No surprise, his theses were discarded by the academic world (though he was himself titular of a prestigious chair at the University of Kyoto); e.g., a recent book, titled *Why Is Evolution a Philosophical Question?*,[21] in which a team of nine Japanese philosophers of science, in nearly three hundred pages, accomplish the feat of not mentioning his name even once. This is more or less like a book on ontology that would ignore the name "Heidegger." My stance here is different. I do consider that naturing science, for better or worse, is a highly philosophical question, which deserves much more attention than that kind of *mura hachibu* 村八分 (village ostracism). We should remember that, during a whole generation, if not totally ignored, Imanishi's primatology was laughed at in the West as childishly anthropomorphic, before it became so naturally paradigmatic as to make young Western primatologists unaware of its origin.[22] Yet it was and remains consistent with his *shizengaku*. The question fundamentally relies on the modern distinction between subject and object and its relevance, on the one hand, to Japanese realities (language, attitudes toward nature, etc., which, as we have seen, in fact imply an ambient rather than a subject), and on the other hand to reality in general, beyond the classical modern Western scientific paradigm. Is science to remain within the gauge of *shizen kagaku*, or can we conceive of scientifically "naturing" science itself?

In such matters, the essence of modernity has been embodied by physics. Physics is that science to which any other natural science has to refer, directly or not, if it is to be deemed scientific. True, some scientists have contested the validity of this reference. A great quantifier of biological data, Haldane, for one, in his *Philosophy of a Biologist* (1935), professed that for biology, it is physics that is not an exact science.[23] Yet Imanishi's naturing science, as a contestation of reigning dogmas in the natural sciences, went much farther. He was able, for example, to write the following: "[In the same way as] 'if the baby stood up, it is because he had to stand up (*tatsu beku shite tatta*),' . . . evolution evolved because it had to (*kawaru beku shite kawatta*). Saying that it changes because it must change is to see evolution no longer from a mechanistic point of view, but as a course (*kōsu*)."[24]

This is undoubtedly a teleological, unscientific stance, which, mutatis mutandis, one can compare with the idea of "intelligent design" in cosmology. Yet we are facing here a series of problems that neo-Darwinism cannot rationally address. The most fundamental one is the infinitesimal probability of life as we know it, given the number of possible combinations of natural protein chains. Chance alone *can mathematically not* have produced it;[25] hence the unscientific idea of intelligent design. If one is to remain scientific, then, one has to make another hypothesis; that is, to suppose that life itself has determined its own course as it went along, taking into account the path already followed for *choosing*, in some way or other, the path to follow next.

Such a hypothesis is of course not consistent with mechanicism, because it amounts to recognizing nature as having some kind of subjecthood; and this is precisely what, starting with his primatology, Imanishi's naturing science amounts to. But then, why should science be equated with mechanicism? Why should nature be reduced to a mere object? This is an ontological bias that in itself owes nothing to science, but much to religion. It ensues from the Mount Horeb principle more than from physics itself. Did not one of the great physicists of the last century, Werner Heisenberg, write, "If one is allowed to speak of the image of nature according to the exact sciences of our time, one has to understand thereby, rather than the image of nature, the image of our relation to nature. . . . Science, ceasing to be the spectator of nature, recognizes itself as part of the reciprocal actions between nature and man. . . . [C]onsequently, the method can no longer be separated from its object"?[26]

Though expressed in a different language, this attitude amounts to acknowledging the mesological ternary structure S-I-P, which we have seen at work in the Japanese case, ranging from haikus to Imanishi's naturing science. True, in his rejection of the modern Western paradigm as exemplified by neo-Darwinism, Imanishi went too far. The "course" he speaks of has a scent of teleology, rather than of the contingency entailed by the ternary structure S-I-P that, nowadays, one should reasonably substitute for the mechanical alternative of chance and necessity in biological processes. Just as dinosaurs did not "have to" become birds, our ancestors did not "have to" stand up. They *came to* stand up, as certain small dinosaurs came to exapt their feathers to flying.

Why did some dinosaurs exapt to flying? This is a question that mechanicism cannot reasonably answer. Mechanicism considers S-P (functions), not S-I-P (reasons). Machines have no reasons, but only functions. For instance, as Gould wrote, feathers (S) formerly worked as thermoregulators (P); and they (S) were exapted to flying (P').[27] Here the only interpreter (I) of this exaptation is Gould himself, because he is the only subject. Yet neither chance nor necessity can explain that exaptation. The only reasonable hypothesis is that, at some time of their own history, in their proper milieu, these dinosaurs came to have enough subjecthood for interpreting (I) their feathers (S) as something for flying (P'). How can we know? Certainly not if we cling to the Mount Horeb principle, which will forever deny nature any subjecthood at all; so, as physics already has done in its own way, perhaps in biology also, following the path opened up in ethology by von Uexküll's *Umweltlehre* and Imanishi's primatology, should we "nature" science a little more decidedly . . . ? That is, should we clear the way to *biohermeneutics*? Evolution then, involving subjecthood, would have to be reconceived also in terms of milieu, rather than only of environment.[28] Reality (S-I-P) is not ours only, is it?

Notes

1. Erwin Panofsky, *La perspective comme forme symbolique* (*Perspective as a Symbolic Form*) (Paris: Minuit, 1975).

2. "Je connus de là que j'étais une substance dont toute l'essence ou la nature n'est que de penser, et qui, pour être, n'a besoin d'aucun lieu, ni ne dépend d'aucune chose matérielle." René Descartes, *Discours de la méthode* (Paris: Garnier-Flammarion, 2008), 38–39.

3. In a famous letter addressed to Paul Demeny, dated May 15, 1871. See Arthur Rimbaud, *Œuvres complètes* (*Complete Works*) (Paris: Gallimard, 2009).

4. See KANAYA Takehiro, *Nihongo ni shugo wa iranai* (*There Is No Need of a Subject in Japanese*) (Tokyo: Kōdansha, 2002) and YANABU Akira, *Kindai nihongo no shisō* (*The Thought of the Modern Japanese Language*) (Tokyo: Hōsei Daigaku Shuppankai, 2004).

5. NISHIDA Kitarō, *Basho* (*Place*), in *Nishida Kitarō zenshū*, vol. 4 (Tokyo: Iwanami, 1966). See also NISHIDA Kitarō, *Bashoteki ronri to shūkyōteki sekaikan* (*Logic of Place and Religious Worldview*), in *Nishida Kitarō zenshū*, vol. 11 (Tokyo: Iwanami, 1966).

6. See the entry for "substance" in *The Concise Oxford Dictionary of Current English*, ed. H. W. Fowler et al. (Oxford: Oxford University Press, 1964).

7. YAMAMOTO Kenkichi, *Saishin haiku saijiki* (*New Seasonal of Haiku*), vol. 2 (Tokyo: Bungei Shunjū, 1977), 149.

8. It is said that, in a certain experiment, letting people hear the chime of a windbell made the temperature of the skin of Japanese participants actually drop, while that of other participants (unaware of windbells) did not change (sankei.jp.msn.com/life/news/120723/art12072307430002-n1.htm).

9. Whereas in Spanish (*está lloviendo*), etc., it is the form of the verb that indicates that fictional "third person."

10. The essential distinction between subject and predicate makes it difficult for us to figure *subjectpredicates*, but this category explicitly exists in Chinese grammar, where it is called *zhuweiweiyu* 主謂謂語; e.g., in *neige ren zui dadade* 那個人嘴大大的 (literally "That man mouth big big of", i.e., "That man has a big mouth"), where *zui* (mouth)

is both the predicate of *ren* (man) and the subject of *da* (be big). The structure here is S-(P:S)-P, whereas the English translation comes down to S-P: "That man (S) has a big mouth (P)." Though Chinese and Japanese belong to two different families, that same structure S-(P:S)-P also exists in Japanese, where the translation would be *ano hito wa kuchi ga ōkī*.

11. For instance in the following: "It is in and by the language that man constitutes himself as a subject; because only language founds in reality, in *its reality* which is that of Being, the concept of 'ego.' The 'subjectivity' which we are here dealing with is the capacity of the speaker to pose himself as a 'subject.' It is defined, not by the feeling everyone experiences to be oneself (this feeling, inasmuch as one can report it [*dans la mesure où l'on peut en faire état*], is only a reflection), but as the psychic unity that transcends the whole of the lived experiences it gathers, and which ensures the permanence of consciousness. Now, we assume that this 'subjectivity,' be it posed in phenomenology or in psychology, is only the emergence of a fundamental propriety of language. Is 'ego' who *says* 'ego.' We find here the foundation of 'subjectivity,' which is determined by the linguistic status of the 'person.'" See Émile Benveniste, *Problèmes de linguistique générale* (*Problems in General Linguistics*), vol. 2 (Paris: Gallimard, 1966), 259–260 (originally published in *Journal de Psychologie*, July–September 1958).

12. The genre itself, pronounced *suishiji* in Chinese, began in China in the sixth c. AD.

13. TSUJI Sanae, *Les impressifs japonais* (*Japanese Impressives*) (Lyons: Presses Universitaires de Lyon, 2003).

14. E.g., when he wrote the following: "According to the universal law of the necessary equivalence between reaction and action, the ambient system could not modify the organism unless the latter, in its turn, exercised a corresponding influence." Original French in *Cours de philosophie positive; Œuvres*, 3 :235. Quoted by François Jacob in *La logique du vivant: Une histoire de l'hérédité* (*The Logic of the Living: A History of Heredity*) (Paris: Gallimard 1970), 172.

15. Georges Canguilhem, *Études d'histoire et de philosophie des sciences concernant les vivants et la vie* (*Studies in the History and Philosophy of Sciences Concerning the Living and Life*) (Paris: Vrin, 1968), 72.

16. "Whoever wants to cling to the conviction that living beings are only machines, abandons the hope to ever have a glimpse of their milieus (*ihre Umwelten*). . . . Animals are thus pinned as pure objects [*reinen Objekten*]. One forgets then that one has, from the start, suppressed the essential; that is, *the subject* [*das Subjekt*], the one who uses the means, perceives with them and acts with them. . . . Now, who considers that our sensorial organs serve our perception, and our motor organs our action, will see in beasts not only mechanical devices, but will discover the machinist [*den* Maschinisten], who is embodied in the organs just as we are in our body. Then one will no more address animals as mere objects, but as subjects [*als Subjekte*], whose essential activity consists in perceiving and acting." This is my own English translation of Jakob von Uexküll, *Streifzüge durch die Umwelten von Tieren und Menschen* (*Incursions in the Milieus of Animals and Humans*) (Hamburg: Rowohlt, 1965), 21–22.

17. Watsuji, who stayed in Germany in 1927–1928, may have heard of von Uexküll's works through Heidegger, who at the time was profoundly influenced by these discoveries. He dealt with the question in detail in his 1929–1930 seminar, published after his death as *Die Grundbegriffe der Metaphysik: Welt-Endlichkeit-Einsamkeit* (*The*

Fundamental Concepts of Metaphysics: World-Finitude-Loneliness) (Frankfurt am Main: Klostermann, 1983), particularly in the second part. See also WATSUJI Tetsurō, *Fūdo: Ningengakuteki kōsatsu* (Tokyo: Iwanami, 1935).

18. *Mediance* derives from the Latin *medietas*, which means "half." One of these "halves" is the concerned being; the other one is that being's milieu. Only joining the two "halves" makes a concrete being. *Mediance*, like *milieu*, stems from the Latin root *med-*, which is equivalent to the Greek *meso-*; hence "mesology."

19. E.g., p. 90 in IMANISHI Kinji, *Seibutsu shakai no ronri* (*The Logic of the Societies of Living Beings*) (Tokyo: Heibonsha, 1994).

20. SANO Toshiyuki, "The Effect of Culture on the Development of Scientific Theory: Imanishi and Darwin," *Nara Women's University, Faculty of Human Life and Environment, Annual Report of the Graduate Division of Human Culture*, vol. 19, 241.

21. MATSUMOTO Shunkichi, *Shinkaron wa naze tetsugaku no mondai ni naru no ka* (*Why Is Evolution a Philosophical Question?*) (Tokyo: Keisō shobō, 2010).

22. Frans De Waal, "Silent Invasion: Imanishi's Primatology and Cultural Bias in Science," *Animal Cognition* 4, no. 6 (2003): 293–299.

23. Quoted by Georges Canguilhem, *La connaissance de la vie* (*The Knowledge of Life*) (Paris: Vrin, 2009), 195.

24. IMANISHI Kinji, *Shutaisei no shinkaron* (*Subjecthood in Evolution*) (Tokyo: Chūōkōron, 1980), 204.

25. Hervé Zwirn, for one, did the following calculation in *La Recherche* 365 (June 2003): 104: "The molecules responsible for nearly all biological functions, enzymes, are proteins, i.e. chains of at least one hundred amino acids placed end to end. Natural proteins utilize about a score of amino acids. There are at least 10^{130} possibilities of different proteins. Let us suppose that each atom of the observable Universe (numbering about 10^{80}) is a computer, each one enumerating one thousand billions combinations per second.... It would need 1021 times the age of the Universe to terminate the task of enumeration."

26. Werner Heisenberg, *La nature dans la physique contemporaine* (*Nature in Contemporary Physics*), trans. Ugné Karvelis and A. E. Leroy (Paris: Gallimard 1962), 33–34.

27. See p. 1721 in the French translation of Stephen Gould's *La structure de la théorie de l'évolution* (*The Structure of Evolutionary Theory*), trans. Marcel Blanc (Paris: Gallimard, 2006). The original was published in English by the Belknap Press of Harvard University Press in 2002.

28. I develop this argument in *Poétique de la Terre: Histoire naturelle et histoire humaine, essai de mésologie* (*Poetics of the Earth: Natural History and Human History, an Essay in Mesology*) (Paris: Belin, 2014) and *La mésologie, pourquoi et pour quoi faire?* (*Mesology, Why and What For?*) (Nanterre: Presses de l'Université de Paris Ouest, 2014).

CHAPTER 2 | Pure Land Ecology

Taking the Supernatural Seriously in Environmental Philosophy

LEAH KALMANSON

Such nature is the brilliant light that has passed through darkness. The
awareness of this darkness is not found in Saigyo, or Ippen, or Basho. Nor
is it seen in Dogen. Shinran alone delved down through the darkness within
the self and encountered the light of nature or Buddha.

—OMINE AKIRA[1]

SCHOLARS IN JAPANESE environmental philosophy have pointed out that
the use of the Japanese term *shizen* (自然) to translate the English word
"nature" is problematic, because the traditional Japanese understanding
of the natural environment does not make a sharp distinction between the
human world and a supposedly pristine (i.e., human-free) wilderness.[2] Yet,
for precisely this reason, *shizen* has also been praised as a resource for
helping contemporary environmentalism think beyond the human/nature
divide. Here I am interested in another artificial distinction imposed upon
shizen through its association with the English "nature"—namely, a distinction between the natural and the supernatural.

Environmental philosophy tends to deal with the question of the supernatural in one of two ways: On the one hand, it often restricts the universe
of discourse to exclude the supernatural altogether. As one introductory textbook to environmental philosophy states, "nature" should not
be defined broadly as "everything that falls outside of the realm of the
supernatural (if any such realm exists)," but narrowly as "the nonhuman
part of the biosphere."[3] The author explains: "It is true that environmental

philosophers do not focus their attention on supernatural entities such as angels and demons, yet in this respect they are no different from the practitioners of most other academic disciplines."[4] Many might accept this basic assumption that the supernatural does not fall under the purview of environmental philosophy or, most likely, philosophy at all. On the other hand, fields such as deep ecology or new animism, which tend to be critical of positivism and materialism, are perhaps more willing to take seriously claims regarding panpsychism, pantheism, or other notions of holistic spirituality.

However, neither approach seems adequate to account for the specificity of supernatural entities—an exclusion that, as I argue here, renders certain progressive perspectives in environmentalism invisible to philosophical inquiry. Consider, as a starting point, an example from the Hawaiian tradition. In Hawaiian cosmology the taro (Haw. *kalo*) plant is named as an ancestor, the elder brother Hāloa. In the context of a 2002 dispute between the University of Hawai'i and indigenous Hawaiians over the status of patented taro seeds, one local farmer rejected the University's right to ownership over the taro, because "from a Hawaiian perspective, any *kalo* is our ancestor."[5] Here, the taro does not symbolize a Hawaiian ancestor, nor is it a metaphor for Hawaiian heritage—rather, *any* taro plant is the ancestor Hāloa.

What is the appropriate attitude of supportive environmental philosophers toward environmental activism that presupposes and prioritizes the involvement of supernatural forces? If we restrict the universe of discourse to exclude the supernatural altogether, then we simply fail to take the Hawaiian perspective seriously, at least with regard to this issue. However, if we incorporate Hāloa into some sort of general panpsychism, or render him one manifestation of a general "world spirit" or "world consciousness," then we lose the specificity of Hawaiian cosmology and cosmogony. We lose the sense in which Hāloa is an elder brother within a particular family. I suggest that, to avoid either condescending toward the Hawaiians or subsuming Hawaiian cosmology within a general spiritual holism, we must make the supernatural visible as a subject of philosophical discussion.

Precisely on this issue, recent work in Japanese philosophy has important contributions to make. In a forthcoming book on Shin Buddhism and Marxism in Japan, Melissa Anne-Marie Curley explains that the Western dichotomy between transcendence and immanence is inadequate to account for the function of the Pure Land paradise in Japanese Buddhist thought. The Pure Land is not located in some transcendent beyond, nor is it simply already present or pervasive in the world here and now—rather, Curley claims, we should understand the Pure Land as a supernatural force with the power to intervene in present conditions.[6] The transcendent/immanent paradigm fails to register this dramatic potency, that is, the power to effect change in the "real" world. The potency of the Pure Land also drives the environmental activism of several prominent Jōdo and Jōdo Shin priests in Japan today, who have advocated successfully for environmental protection in the name of instantiating the Pure Land on earth. As with Hāloa in Hawai'i, this is not a metaphorical or symbolic "Pure Land"—it is an actual earthly environment permeated with, and hence transformed by, the infinite compassion of Amida.[7] In both cases, the palpable forces of Hāloa and Amida within environmentalism are diminished if we insist on slotting them into one of the two dominant categories, transcendent or immanent. Following Curley's lead, I suggest that appreciating Pure Land thought as a resource in the academic context of Japanese environmental philosophy will require taking the supernatural seriously.

To begin the project of making visible a category such as "supernatural" in this context, I rely on the different uses of both *shizen* (自然) and its variant *jinen* (自然) to recover the supernatural connotations once intimately associated with the natural world in Pure Land thought. I first give a brief overview of the religious dimensions of the exclusion of the supernatural from philosophical discourse. In the historical development of the concept of "religion" in the West, we see the attempt to distinguish "legitimate" religious entities from supernatural beings and, accordingly, legitimate religious practices from superstitious ones. By tracing the importation of these distinctions into Meiji-era Japan, we find the origins of the natural/supernatural divide that over time shaped the definition of *shizen*. Next, I look at earlier uses of these same *kanji* in the term *jinen* as this is used to describe the power of Amida's compassion to facilitate birth in the Pure Land. And, finally, I return to the work of Curley and other recent scholars who have advocated Pure Land thought as an overlooked resource for progressive political philosophy as well as political activism. As these scholars show, this school of Buddhism is potent precisely because of, not in spite of, the supernatural power of the Pure Land to intervene in earthly conditions. Building on their work, we see that Pure Land Buddhism has a similarly progressive perspective to contribute within the field of Japanese environmental philosophy.

2.1. The Role of the Supernatural in Distinguishing Superstition from Religion

Mapping the distinction between the natural and the supernatural in the history of European thought embroils us in the (at times) tensely negotiated distinctions between "legitimate" religion and "paganism," between science and superstition, and, accordingly, between the rational and the irrational. We might say that, even as early as Aristotle, we see a basic association between rationality and the contemplation of the divine. But we certainly see assumptions about rationality and religiosity at play throughout European history in the attempt to differentiate Christian practices from the supposedly irrational rituals of so-called pagans. As Tomoko MASUZAWA shows, the earliest uses of the word "religion" were associated with Catholicism only. Both Judaism and Islam were occasionally counted as religions (because they seemed to recognize a universal, rational God), but they were often counted instead as pagan or tribal (because they also seemed to worship a specific deity with apparently arbitrary power over a particular group of people).[8] Robert Ford Campany points out that "well into the nineteenth century, there 'were' only four religions: Christianity, Judaism, Islam, and a fourth variously named Paganism, Idolatry, or Heathenism."[9] This fourth term is, perhaps more precisely, a nonreligion, or that against which legitimate religion defined itself. Over time, this four-part schema became strained, as Europeans discovered—slowly and piecemeal—traditions such as Buddhism and Confucianism. Eventually, more and more traditions were shifted from the category "pagan" to the category "religion," bringing us up to the ten or so "world religions" recognized today in common parlance (or the 9,900 recognized, as Campany says somewhat playfully, among scholars in religious studies).[10]

As Jason Ānanda Josephson discusses, the Japanese began encountering the evolving term "religion" as early as the 1600s, although *shūkyō* (宗教) was not devised as a suitable translation until the late 1800s, following the forceful opening of the country's borders to trade. The colonial context here is important—a term for "religion" only became necessary because European powers imposed on Japan multiple trade treaties, which included clauses demanding that the government recognize "religious freedom."[11] Prior to this, the Japanese tended to classify what they knew of Christianity as a deviant Buddhist school,[12] showing that Buddhism functions here as a *category* that might include Christianity and not as a *type* of tradition that might be included, alongside Christianity, in some larger category "religion." As Josephson points out, the word selected to translate religion (i.e., *shūkyō*) was itself of Buddhist origin, referring to doctrinal differences between Buddhist sects. So, even after translation, Buddhism continues to function in part as the category "religion," not a member of that category: "Put differently, 'religion' was Buddhism (or a subset of Buddhism). Buddhism, on the other hand, was not a religion."[13]

In its function as a category, Buddhism in the Japanese context was associated closely with monasticism on the one hand, and on the other, popular rituals for laypeople to generate karmic merit. Confucianism, or what I prefer to call Ruism,[14] was another major category in Japan, associated with a range of scholarly, professional, and ritual activities, encompassing what we might call today the social sciences, the natural sciences, literary studies, statecraft, training in the arts and gymnastics, and the ritual veneration of ancestors. The eventual importation of Western categories such as philosophy and religion redefined these traditions and remapped their relation to each other.

One particular episode from Meiji history is a useful lens through which to understand this remapping process, namely the antisuperstition campaign of Japan's affectionately titled "Dr. Monster," INOUE Enryō. Inoue was a tireless cataloger of regional Japanese beliefs about ghosts, monsters, and other supernatural entities. His larger project, however, was the eradication of so-called superstitious practices from Buddhism, so as to whittle the tradition down to what he perceived as its fundamental core—the apprehension of an absolute reality, which is not irrational, but which does transcend human reason. On the one hand, Inoue associates the absolute (*zettai* 絶対) with the existing idea of Buddhist thusness; on the other hand, his understanding of *zettai* reflects, in part, his engagement with freshly minted vocabulary terms, including not only *shūkyō*, but also *tetsugaku* 哲学 (philosophy) and *meishin* 迷信 (superstition), all of which were translated from European languages into Japanese around the same time. As Josephson comments, "A key aspect of the way that Inoue represents religion in *Meishin to shūkyō* [*Superstition and Religion*] is the foundational assumption that the core of religion is a series of beliefs rather than practices. While this might seem straightforward, as contemporary scholars SHIMAZONO Susumu and ISOMAE Jun'ichi have both observed, in the pre-Meiji period Buddhism was largely understood as something one did, not something one believed. It was only under the influence of the Western concept of religion that Buddhism became a commitment to a series of propositions rather than rituals."[15]

I am particularly interested in how Inoue tackles the dilemma of differentiating the legitimate religious beliefs of Buddhism from the superstitious ones. When he defines superstitious beliefs as *irrational* and legitimate religious beliefs as *transrational*, he engages a very Western-inflected sense of the term "religion"—a sense rooted in long-standing theological connections between the rational and the divine but also extending to eighteenth-century discourses on so-called natural religion (i.e., religious truths that all humans can access via reason alone, needing no revelation). As Josephson says, Inoue does not consider people's beliefs in Buddhas, bodhisattvas, or *kami* as superstitious: "[These] are not founded upon irrational belief in false entities; instead they are provisional names awarded to the true absolute reality that is beyond reason. This distinction between 'irrational' and 'beyond reason' allows Inoue to divide the supernatural world with buddhas and the gods on one side and other darker manifestations of the supernatural on the other."[16] Inoue's "true absolute" may exceed human comprehension, but it is not contrary to either rationality or scientific inquiry since it is, after all, what is ultimately real. From this perspective, Inoue proposes that Buddhism is better than Christianity at successfully merging the projects of religion, rational philosophy, and science.[17]

On the one hand, Inoue gives the impression that Buddhism succeeds where enlightenment Europe fails; on the other, certain Eurocentric values do have (at least part of) the last word, under Inoue's influence. Namely, we see the lines between the natural and the supernatural altered to accommodate a very Western understanding of religion. The already problematic use of *shizen* to translate "nature" is further complicated by this exclusion of many phenomena, once associated with *shizen*, but now relegated to the irrational side of the supernatural. Although we cannot turn back the colonial clock, we can nonetheless familiarize ourselves with these earlier uses of *shizen* and the related term *jinen*. As I hope to show, this broadened sense of *shizen/jinen* expands our understanding of the scope of ecology to include not only natural but also supernatural environments (such as the Pure Land).

2.2. Pure Land, Nature, and Naturalness

Resources from the Shinto tradition, especially the vital living energies of the environment called *kami*, point toward one way that the Japanese sense of nature can expand our ecological thinking, as Kagawa-Fox demonstrates in her contribution to this volume. We can also look to those elements of Buddhism that tend to be underexplored in Western contexts. For example, Josephson describes Inoue's project as "pared-down Buddhism" and comments: "It should be apparent that Inoue has radically re-conceptualized Buddhism."[18] Yet this would not necessarily be apparent to many Americans, including many American Buddhist practitioners, who have inherited precisely the "pared-down Buddhism" that Inoue helped to promote.

As T. Griffith Foulk says, "Westerners interested in Zen ... are often attracted to the 'practices' of seated meditation (zazen), manual labor, and doctrinal study but uncomfortable with the 'rituals' of offerings, prayers, and prostrations made before images on altars."[19] The relative popularity of Zen in the West, as compared to Pure Land Buddhism, is no doubt attributable to the same unease with prayers, offerings, and prostrations that Foulk mentions here. Such activities, common across Zen and Pure Land, speak to Buddhism's rich and robust engagement with unseen forces, including Buddhas and bodhisattvas living in heavenly realms; the spirits of ancestors reborn in nonearthly places; and the powerful force of merit (*kudoku* 功徳), which can be generated by rituals and bestowed on intended recipients, driving a bustling economy of merit exchange. Speaking to the general absence of engagement with such unseen forces in American Buddhism, Foulk observes:

> The underlying assumption is that "merit" is a magical, superstitious, or at best symbolic kind of thing that no rational, scientifically-minded person could take seriously as actually existing. In the East Asian Buddhist tradition of which Japanese Zen is a part, however, people do believe in merit. It is as real to them as, say, money—that other symbolic, magical thing that has no substantial existence but nevertheless serves to organize human societies and get things done.[20]

Just as we take seriously the power of money, I suggest that we take seriously the power of unseen forces in Buddhist thought, such as the Pure Land environment itself, that freely cross what we "rational, scientifically-minded people" believe to be the line between the natural and the supernatural. In particular, I am interested in the power of the Pure Land's paradisiacal ecology to impact conditions in the present world.

To explore this idea, I turn to the role of the natural environment in the teachings of the Jōdo Shin founder Shinran (1173–1263). In line with basic Pure Land beliefs, Shinran teaches that the efforts of the individual practitioner to achieve enlightenment are ineffective because all such efforts are marred by the practitioner's own self-interest in attaining freedom from suffering. Rather than rely on his or her own "self-power" (*jiriki* 自力) the practitioner instead moves toward enlightenment thanks to the "other-power" (*tariki* 他力) of Amida's infinite compassion. The Pure Land is a "buddha field" established by Amida where practitioners can be reborn to continue their journey toward becoming bodhisattvas. Ultimately, these enlightened beings can return to the human world to fulfill the bodhisattva's vow of freeing all beings from suffering.

The notion of nature appears in at least two aspects of Shinran's teachings. On the one hand, he explicitly equates all of reality with Buddhanature: "Buddha-nature is none other than buddha, and this buddha pervades the very stuff of the universe itself. In other words, it is the heart of the entire ocean of life. Plants, trees, the very land itself, all become buddhas."[21] OMINE Akira comments: "Particularly in the last years of his long life, Shinran attained a realm in which Buddha was in actuality none other than nature."[22] On the other hand, Shinran makes use of the term *jinen* to describe the power by which Amida facilitates our rebirth in the Pure Land. Omine is quick to point out that Shinran's use of *jinen* (自然) predates the more contemporary use of these same *kanji* as the *shizen* (自然) that translates the English "nature." Omine comments: "For human beings to be saved by the Buddha—to be reborn in the Pure Land—is a matter of jinen. Jinen is the same word that is now used to mean 'nature' (*shizen*). . . . Today the word 'shizen' (nature) is used as a noun referring to the natural phenomena that exist objectively apart from us. Shinran's jinen, however, is adverb and verb. . . . It is more direct, prior to any objectification."[23]

However, this is not to imply that *shizen* is an entirely misguided translation for "nature," or that there is no conceptual link between the earlier *jinen* and the later *shizen*. To the contrary, the use of *jinen* in Chinese philosophies (Ch. *ziran*) does encompass verbal and adverbial as well as nominal applications. Christoph Harbsmeier provides a detailed linguistic history of *ziran* functioning as an "abstract subject nominalisation" that he defines as "what is so of itself > Nature."[24] Several of the examples that he discusses include Chinese Buddhist discourses on the Pure Land, which establish a precedent for Shinran's use of other-power as both a natural and a supernatural force. Or it is perhaps more precise to say that Shinran did not make an explicit distinction between the natural and the supernatural—other-power is a force of nature, and nature is the body of the Buddha.

Regarding Shinran's verbal and adverbial uses of *jinen*, we see that these are central to his conception of the active functioning of other-power. As he writes: " 'Natural' (*jinen*) means being enabled from the beginning. The pledge of Amida Buddha is, from the very beginning, designed to enable the practitioners to put their trust in the *nenbutsu—namu-Amida-Butsu—* without any judgment, and yet to enable practitioners to judge that they will be received into the Pure Land. As such, the practitioner is not concerned about how good or bad he may be. This is the meaning of 'natural' as I have been taught."[25] As Shinran stresses, the prayer to Amida is effective regardless of the practitioner's intentions. He elaborates: "Because of the pledge of the Tathāgata, *hōni* [dharma itself] implies nothing intended by the practitioner. . . . Everything starts anew when there is no judgment or design by the person. This is the basis of how you should understand the phrase in reference to Amida Buddha's vows, 'making meaning of what has no meaning.' "[26]

The term translated above as "meaning" (*gi* 義) also carries connotations of "right behavior" or "acting rightly." Hence another translation renders the same phrase to say that "no working is true working."[27] This translation emphasizes the idea that our best efforts are, in fact, effortless. On the one hand, we perhaps see the influence of Daoism here—especially on the original phrase (無義為義), which is attributed to Hōnen, and whose 無/為 construction recalls Daoist writings on the *wu*-forms and the efficacy of nonaction. On the other hand, the compassion of Amida functions as a potent facilitator of this nonaction specific to Pure Land thought. As Shinran teaches, the "working" or "meaning" that is negated (無義) is the practitioner's "calculating and designing," while the true working or true meaning (為義) is the other-power of Amida.[28] For the practitioner, his or her *own* enlightenment and compassion are impossible—such is the dilemma of relying on self-power to overcome the self.

In other words, as Omine reminds us, our intentions are self-defeating, especially when we intend to practice, or to be compassionate, or to realize no-self: "Shinran states that human beings are incapable of genuine, thoroughgoing good. Good done for display may be possible, but if there is the least consciousness of having done good, it is defiled by self-satisfaction."[29] Hence Shinran teaches us that, when our own intentions are the problem, we must trust in an other-power, namely, the compassion of Amida—this is precisely the aspect of Pure Land thought that I am suggesting is relevant to contemporary environmental philosophy as well as environmental activism.

2.3. Pure Land and Progressive Politics

I do not mean the compassion of Amida metaphorically or symbolically—rather, I draw on the connotation of *jinen* most familiar to Shinran, that is, the supernatural power of Amida's compassion that facilitates birth in the Pure Land. As we saw earlier, the category "supernatural" in Western contexts is often used in a negative sense. Being associated with the superstitious and the irrational, the supernatural is neither properly religious[30] nor properly scientific nor properly philosophical. However, at least two recent scholars have turned to Pure Land Buddhist philosophy as a tool for progressive politics—and precisely because of, not in spite of, the supernatural status of the Pure Land. As mentioned above, Melissa Anne-Marie Curley uses the notion of "supernatural" to intervene in the Western dichotomy of transcendence and immanence: "In practice, Pure Land tends to generate a vision of space as heterogeneous: within this world, there are multiple sites in which Amida's Western Paradise is established, sometimes entirely and sometimes partially, sometime predictably and sometimes unpredictably. These instantiated Pure Lands are neither strictly transcendent nor strictly immanent. I will suggest that they are best understood as 'supernatural.'"[31]

As Curley goes on to discuss, it is precisely the supernatural force of the Pure Land that heightens its potential to subvert accepted orders of power, whether this is the karmic order that governs death and rebirth or the social order that governs the human world: "As an image of transcendent utopia, Amida's Pure Land offers the possibility of escape from both the law of karma that governs one's own life and the degeneration of the dharma that governs the world. As a supernatural site, Amida's Pure Land opens up as a space in which that escape can be represented. But because the representation and the real are not sharply distinguished, even the representation can trouble the real social order."[32] In other words, it is precisely its supernatural position vis-à-vis the everyday world that enables the Pure Land, as Curley says, to "trouble the real social order." This is why, she concludes, several early Japanese leftists found inspiration in the Pure Land not only as an image for socialist utopia but as a program for enacting that utopia in the present world.

James Mark Shields makes a similar observation about the Japanese Marxist and Shin priest TAKAGI Kenmyō: "Takagi envisioned social change arising from a process of individual transformation, based on a reformulation of the traditional Shin Buddhist concept of *shinjin*—usually translated as 'faith' but with the nuance of 'opening oneself up' to the saving grace of Other-power."[33] Similar to Curley, Shields notes that Takagi takes the existence of the Pure Land seriously: "It would seem clear that Takagi believes in the Pure Land as an actual realm (as opposed to simply a metaphor, existential condition, or ideal of a future society). . . . In other words, Takagi's Pure Land acts not only as a heavenly model and guide for those of us remaining in the fallen world; it is also a place where beings are able to act on their fundamental reorientation towards compassion by engaging with this world of suffering."[34]

In both Curley's and Shields's works, we see that the supernatural potency of the Pure Land functions as an important link between what exists in the present world and what exists in a better world whose status can be described neither in terms of transcendence nor immanence. This link impacts our understanding of how such a better world can be brought nearer or made present. If we imagine that we attain a better world through transcendence, then this suggests that we leave the present world behind (it perhaps implies leaving behind spatiotemporal life altogether). If we imagine that we attain a better world through immanence, then this implies that the Pure Land is simply already present, thus diminishing the drama of its power to transform existing conditions. Pure Land thought makes possible a third way. Contrary to either transcendence or immanence, Pure Land thought suggests that we might we reform the current world through supernatural force—or, in Pure Land terms, an "other-power" (*tariki*) greater than our "own-power" (*jiriki*).

2.4. Self-Power, Other-Power, and Environmental Preservation

In trying to make visible a force such as *tariki* for environmental philosophy, we benefit from philosophical attention to categories such as the supernatural that help us to think outside of the transcendent/immanent paradigm, with its roots in the philosophical, religious, and theological discourses of European intellectual history. To begin, we can draw an analogy between our self-defeating intentions to practice Buddhism (as Shinran discusses) and our intentions regarding environmental protection: When it comes to preserving so-called wilderness, intentional human intervention seems both necessary and problematic.

In a recent article on the history of the concept of "wilderness" in America, J. Baird Callicott raises the dilemma of human interference in wilderness conservation. He draws critical attention to the various models of "wilderness" in American history that have, in one way or another, imagined the wilderness to be cut off from humans and human cultures. On the one hand, this separation of humans and nature helps to uphold a colonial agenda: "In the postcolonial United States and Australia, the wilderness idea enabled non-indigenous Americans and Australians, self-deceptively, to erase from memory a genocidal heritage."[35] In other words, this concept of wilderness—as an untouched natural environment ripe for settlement—erases the intentional violence against indigenous inhabitants that made the advance of European "settlers" possible.

On the other hand, the human/nature divide also upholds an anthropocentrism indebted to an outdated teleological worldview that privileges human beings. A better model, Callicott suggests, is the current paradigm "firmly entrenched in twenty-first-century ecology," which holds that

> ecosystems have no developmental strategy or aim; they are not biological objects subject to natural selection (indeed, that they are robust biological entities at all is the subject of much dispute); they are open to fluxes of invasive organisms and ambient materials; they are subject to periodically recurring natural disturbances (disturbance regimes); they may be affected for better or worse by distant forces and processes; and nearly all have been subject to human influence or disturbance for many hundreds of years.[36]

Maintaining such ecosystems requires, Callicott stresses, the recognition that indigenous peoples and the environments they inhabit cannot be understood in isolation from each other. Given that the human/nature divide often has no direct counterpart outside the Eurocentric worldview, it is a mistake, as Callicott says, to allow ecological preservation to come at the expense of indigenous habitation. He concludes: "In twenty-first-century international wilderness thinking, wilderness preservation is not only compatible with the presence of indigenous peoples and their cultures, it *requires* either the continuation of such presence or the simulation thereof by professional wilderness managers." As this makes clear, the goals of environmentalism cannot be understood apart from the concerns and interests of indigenous peoples.

My own thesis echoes the above and adds what may appear to be an untenable, or at least odd, qualification: In many cases, the goals of environmentalism cannot be understood apart from the concerns and interests of *supernatural* forces. That is to say, any given ecosystem may include plant, animal, human, and supernatural components, all with overlapping and potentially conflicting interests. Given that this claim may sound at first implausible, I take my conclusion in two steps, beginning with a limited, perhaps more agnostic appeal to supernatural other-power that I am making in the context of Pure Land thought and Japanese environmental philosophy. This more limited point boils down to the issue of humbleness and the insights that the Pure Land tradition can offer us regarding how to cultivate and practice humbleness in environmental management. But this limited point opens out onto more speculative considerations at the end, regarding the importance of the supernatural in environmentalism.

2.5. Conclusions

The first step of my conclusion is, I hope, uncontroversial. Few would argue against the claim that humans must tread carefully when interfering in natural environments, even when such interference is for the sake of environmental management and protection. The impact of such intervention is often unpredictable, despite copious planning and the best of intentions. Part of the unpredictability results, of course, from the fact that human agency is not the only force at play—animal, plant, as well as mineral and chemical aspects of a given ecosystem are all active factors in determining the outcome of human meddling.

Pure Land Buddhism is, if anything, a robust set of guidelines for managing one's own meddlesome agency. Despite impressions that Pure Land practices are "passive"—that is, the submissive inactivity of the self before the other-power of Amida—TACHIKAWA Musashi stresses the active resoluteness of Pure Land adherents: "Thus, the attitude of Pure Land Buddhists is indeed active. Before they have made their crucial resolution, they are not Pure Land Buddhists. The term Other Power is used because they have entrusted completely to the personal Buddha. Because they constantly negate the existence of the self by entrusting to the other, it is said that they abandon all personal designs and calculative thinking."[37] As we saw earlier, Shinran equates the natural world with Buddha-nature. In this sense we can take Tachikawa's advice to "negate the existence of the self by entrusting to the other" to mean an attitude toward both Amida and the natural environment. Hence, we can say that Pure Land practices help us cultivate the active resoluteness needed to interact with the environment as unselfishly as possible. In putting aside our "calculative thinking" we do not stop thinking critically or strategically about environmental issues; rather, we attain the selfless and noninterfering action that expresses the activity of other-power.

Tachikawa elaborates: "Since action is always a function of time, cessation holds the significance of transcendence of time. Through the cessation of action, action is sacralized. For us today, action means work. . . . Fundamentally, however, the traditional Buddhist method of the sacralization of action through cessation remains valid. Although we seek to realize our desires to the widest possible extent and ignore the effects of our actions on later generations, Buddhism offers a critical stance."[38] As Tachikawa says, the cessation of action results not in inaction but in sacred action, and the action is sacred because it happens outside of time—here Tachikawa uses the word "transcendence," but Curley's sense of "supernatural" might be more appropriate. That is to say, this sacred action is noninstrumental (i.e., not work) and nonselfish (i.e., not in the service of our own desires); but rather, as Tachikawa goes on to explain, it is the activity of Amida:

> Thus, the most important theological problem facing us today is the demonstration of the "fulfilled body" Buddha (Buddha who possesses a body as the result of fulfilling practices in the past, such as Amida) not as merely a mythical sublimation of Shakyamuni but as a living, active Buddha. . . . we must confront the issue of how this world of ignorance can be the sacralized world. This is to face the problem of history and time. The question of how Amida Buddha or Vairochana act is the question of how Dharma manifests itself in time and how, in the history of Dharma, Buddha has functioned.[39]

This is indeed an interesting problem to face. The cessation of (selfish) action that makes (sacred) action possible is not a skill that I develop through practices of self-cultivation. In other words, selfless action does not arise because I have cultivated mindfulness, or moral insight, or compassion. On this point, Pure Land is clear—it is Amida who is really acting. It is the dharma manifested in time with the ability, to quote Curley again, to "trouble the real social order."[40]

This leads me to the more speculative portion of my conclusion, which takes us beyond an agnostic acknowledgment of the Pure Land tendency to conflate the natural world with the actual, active Amida Buddha. Returning to our opening example, in the 2002 dispute between the University of Hawai'i and native Hawaiians, the College of Tropical Agriculture and Human Resources at the Mānoa campus first patented several varieties of hybridized taro seeds, and farmers using these seeds were prohibited from selling or breeding the plants without paying royalty fees. Shortly after, UH researchers engineered varieties of the patented seeds spliced with rice, wheat, and grapevine genes.[41] Native Hawaiians and supporters of native Hawaiians expressed concern on two fronts: On the one hand, researchers justified the genetically modified taro seeds as solutions to ongoing issues of crop disease. But, as Hawaiians pointed out, commercial planting practices, which entirely disregard centuries of traditional taro-growing methods, were responsible for the disease-prone cultivar that dominated the market. On the other hand, the patenting and genetic modification of the plant was itself an affront to the agency of the taro, which, as we saw earlier, is the elder brother Hāloa. As a contingency of native Hawaiians argued, you cannot patent or own your elder brother.[42]

After a series of protests, the University acquiesced to Hawaiian demands and offered to transfer the patents to members of the native Hawaiian community.[43] This, of course, misses a crucial point. As one news source recounts: "UH Vice Chancellor for Research Gary Ostrander had previously offered to assign its patents to a Hawaiian organization, but opponents said that was insufficient. 'We rejected that because we object to anyone owning kalo, even ourselves,' said Moloka'i activist Walter Ritte Jr."[44] After further negotiations, the University agreed simply to terminate the patents. Currently, state legislation is in place that recognizes the sacred status of *kalo* and prohibits genetic modification. Meanwhile, in the agricultural community, renewed energy has been directed toward recovering the diversity of native Hawaiian cultivars and promoting traditional farming methods.[45]

In this example, the goals of Ritte and fellow activists cannot be separated from the concerns and interests of Hāloa. Or, in the example of Pure Land activist-priests mentioned earlier, the goals and strategies of their activism cannot be separated from the ability of Amida's compassion to effect change. What is the appropriate attitude of scholars in Japanese philosophy toward the existence of the Pure Land and the activities of its presiding Buddha? I suggest that agnosticism or friendly skepticism is nonproductive at best and condescending at worst. Such agnosticism does little to challenge the Eurocentric worldviews that threaten to constrain environmental activism by shutting out some indigenous voices. We need an attitude of active support that does not merely tolerate beliefs in supernatural entities as expressions of local cultural customs. Such *active* support may mean, to borrow Tachikawa's language of Pure Land resoluteness, negating our personal designs and entrusting ourselves to the other-power. For environmental philosophers, this does not necessarily require conversion to a different worldview, but it does mean, as I have argued here, rendering the "supernatural" visible as a philosophical category worthy of sustained engagement.

Ecological accomplishments carried out in the name of Hāloa or Amida are, if anything, philosophically interesting. The dispute between local Hawaiians and the University problematizes our understanding of "agency" and our conception of the sorts of entities who bear legal rights and are afforded legal protections. We see very similar issues arise in movements to grant personhood status to dolphins and primates or, in the case of Bolivia, to grant legal rights to the earth itself. Expanding these existing questions over the human/nature divide to include questions about the human/natural/supernatural divide complicates our philosophical discourse in productive ways by forcing us continually to re-examine the often-Eurocentric assumptions at play in such distinctions. In the case of Pure Land Buddhism in Japan, the notion of enacting Amida's paradise on earth has influenced the revival of traditional Buddhist "mutual aid societies" in the form of leftist-leaning credit unions dedicated to causes of social justice and environmental protection.[46] In this way we see Pure Land discourse intervening productively not only in political philosophy but in concrete economic practices.

As stated at the outset, in both cases the palpable forces of Hāloa and Amida in environmental activism are diminished if we insist on fitting them into the categories of transcendence and immanence. For this reason, the visibility of the "supernatural" as an important philosophical category is key to providing productive support to progressive environmental movements emerging from, as in our examples, Japanese and Hawaiian contexts. Within the study of Japanese environmental philosophy in particular, Pure Land thought stands out as a resource for taking the supernatural seriously in philosophical discourse.

Notes

1. OMINE Akira, "Probing the Japanese Experience of Nature," trans. Dennis Hirota, *Chanoyu Quarterly* 51 (1987): 32.

2. See, for example, the chapters by Berque, Yamauchi, and Kagawa-Fox in this collection (especially Berque's discussion of subjectivity and nature, and Yamauchi's and Kagawa-Fox's discussions of the relation between nature and culture).

3. Simon P. James, *Environmental Philosophy: An Introduction* (Cambridge: Polity, 2015), 3–4.

4. James, *Environmental Philosophy*, 4.

5. Rebecca Jacobs, "Kalo Is More Than a Native Hawaiian Plant—It's an Ancestor to Hawaiian Culture," *Indian Country Today Media Network* November 21, 2011): http://indiancountrytodaymedianetwork.com/2011/11/21/kalo-more-native-hawaiian-plant-its-ancestor-hawaiian-culture-63402.

6. Melissa Anne-Marie Curley, *Pure Land / Real World: Modern Buddhists, Japanese Leftists, and the Utopian Imagination* (Honolulu: University of Hawaiʻi Press, forthcoming in 2017), 23. Curley borrows this sense of supernatural from Gayatri Spivak's application of the term in the article "Moving Devi," where Spivak comments: "The polytheistic imagination negotiates with the unanticipatable yet perennial possibility of the metamorphosis of the transcendent as the supernatural in the natural." See Gayatri Chakravorty, "Moving Devi," *Cultural Critique* 47 (Winter 2001): 123.

7. Duncan Ryūken Williams, "Buddhist Environmentalism in Contemporary Japan," in *Handbook of Contemporary Japanese Religions*, ed. Inken Prohl and John K. Nelson (Leiden: Brill, 2012), 381. The priests mentioned are ŌKŌCHI Hideto and AOKI Keisuke. As Williams notes, Aoki discusses the possibility of Amida's compassion transforming current conditions to nurture an "ecology of the Pure Land" on earth. See especially the section *Jōdo no ekorojii* 浄土のエコロジー ("Ecology of the Pure Land") in AOKI Keisuke, *Edo to kokoro: Kankyō hakai kara jōdo e* 穢土とこころ—環境破壊から浄土へ (Tokyo: Fujiwara Shobō, 1997), 229–258.

8. Tomoko MASUZAWA, *The Invention of World Religions: Or How European Universalism Was Preserved in the Language of Pluralism* (Chicago: University of Chicago Press, 2005). See especially chapter 3.

9. Robert Ford Campany, "On the Very Idea of Religions (in the Modern West and in Early Medieval China)," *History of Religions* 42, no. 4 (2003): 287.

10. Campany, "Very Idea of Religions," 287–288.

11. Jason Ānanda Josephson, *The Invention of Religion in Japan* (Chicago: University of Chicago Press, 2012), 72–73.

12. Josephson, *Invention of Religion*, 28.

13. Jason Ānanda Josephson, "When Buddhism Became a 'Religion': Religion and Superstition in the Writings of Inoue Enryō," *Japanese Journal of Religious Studies* 33, no. 1 (2006): 144.

14. This is a better approximation of the Chinese *rujia* (儒家), or "scholarly lineage."

15. Josephson, "Buddhism Became a Religion," 160. The last names of the two scholars mentioned in the quote have been capitalized for clarification.

16. Josephson, "Buddhism Became a Religion," 160.

17. Josephson, "Buddhism Became a Religion," 159.

18. Josephson, "Buddhism Became a Religion," 161.

19. Griffith T. Foulk, "Ritual in Japanese Zen Buddhism," in *Zen Ritual*, ed. Steven Heine (Oxford: Oxford University Press, 2007), 23.

20. Foulk, "Ritual," 64.

21. Shinran, "Wisdom as Light," trans. Mark L. Blum, in *Japanese Philosophy: A Sourcebook*, ed. John Maraldo, Thomas Kasulis, and James Heisig (Honolulu: University of Hawaiʻi Press, 2011), 257.

22. Omine, "Probing the Japanese Experience," 26.

23. Omine, "Probing the Japanese Experience," 29–30.

24. Christoph Harbsmeier, "Toward a Conceptual History of Some Concepts of Nature in Classical Chinese: *Zì Rán* 自然 and *Zì Rán Zhī Lǐ* 自然之理," in *Concepts of Nature: A Chinese-European Cross-Cultural Perspective*, ed. Mark Elvin, Gunter Dux, and Hans Ulrich Vogel (Leiden: Brill, 2010), 220.

25. Shinran, "Naturalness as Sacred," trans. Mark L. Blum, in Maraldo, Kasulis, and Heisig, *Japanese Philosophy*, 255.

26. Shinran, "Naturalness as Sacred," 255.

27. Shinran, *The Collected Works of Shinran*, vol. 1: *The Writings*, trans. Dennis Hirota et al. (Kyoto: Jōdo Shinshū Hongwanji-ha, 1997), 427.

28. Shinran, *The Writings*, 93.

29. Omine, "Probing the Japanese Experience," 31.

30. Here, of course, I do not mean "not properly religious" to mean that the supernatural is outside the scope of the contemporary academic study of religion. Indeed, the field of contemporary religious studies has taken steps to explicitly resist the various dichotomies that serve to uphold Christianity as the paradigm case of "proper" religion.

31. Curley, *Pure Land / Real World*, 23.

32. Curley, *Pure Land / Real World*, 28.

33. James Mark Shields, "Zen and the Art of Treason: Radical Buddhism in Meiji Era (1868–1912) Japan," *Politics, Religion, and Ideology* 15, no. 2 (2014): 8.

34. Shields, "Zen," 9–10.

35. J. Baird Callicott, "What 'Wilderness' in Frontier Ecosystems?," *Environmental Ethics* 30 (Fall 2008): 244.

36. Callicott, "What Wilderness," 244.

37. TACHIKAWA Musashi, "Mandala Contemplation and Pure Land Practice: A Comparative Study," in *Toward a Contemporary Understanding of Pure Land Buddhism: Creating a Shin Buddhist Theology in a Religiously Plural World*, ed. Dennis Hirota (Albany: SUNY Press, 2000), 112.

38. TACHIKAWA Musashi, "The World and Amida Buddha," in Hirota, *Pure Land Buddhism*, 233.

39. Tachikawa, "World and Amida Buddha," 232.

40. Curley, *Pure Land / Real World*, 28.

41. Jacobs, "Kalo Is More."

42. Susan Essoyan, "Activists Tear up 3 US Patents for Taro," *Star Bulletin* 11, no. 172 (June 21, 2006): http://archives.starbulletin.com/2006/06/21/news/story03.html.

43. "Two Patents in Native Hawaiian Hands," *Hawaii News Now*, http://www.hawaiinewsnow.com/story/4985450/taro-patents-in-native-hawaiian-hands.

44. Jan TenBruggencate, "UH Expected to Abandon Controversial Taro Patents," *Honolulu Star Advertiser*, June 20, 2006: http://the.honoluluadvertiser.com/article/2006/Jun/20/ln/FP606200342.html.

45. Jacobs, "Kalo Is More."

46. Williams, "Buddhist Environmentalism," 382–83. The institution Williams discusses is the Mirai Bank, but the newer AP Bank is another interesting example.

CHAPTER 3 | From *Kyōsei* to *Kyōei*
          | *Symbiotic Flourishing in Japanese*
          | *Environmental Ethics*

JAMES MCRAE

KYŌSEI, OR SYMBIOSIS, is a Japanese philosophical paradigm that is the cornerstone of the Caux Round Table Principles of business ethics. Though this notion comes from the idea of mutualistic symbiotic relationships in the biological sciences, it has only recently been applied to the discipline of environmental ethics. This chapter first investigates *kyōsei* as a normative ethical principle and then draws from contemporary Japanese philosophy and J. Baird Callicott's interpretation of Aldo Leopold's land ethic to demonstrate how the adoption of *kyōsei* (symbiosis) by individuals, corporations, and governments can promote *kyōei* (mutual flourishing). Particular emphasis is placed upon the concept of noninterference (*jū*), which promotes ethical conduct by encouraging respect for others and minimizes waste through the promotion of maximal efficiency. By using *kyōsei* as the guiding principle for international business and politics, we can create policies and laws that allow us to live sustainably and flourish, both economically and ecologically.

3.1. Kyōsei as a Normative Paradigm in Applied Ethics

The concept of *kyōsei* 共生, or symbiosis, is part of the foundation for international business ethics. This section discusses the concept of symbiosis in biology, the history of its use in business ethics, and the more recent application of *kyōsei* to the field of environmental ethics.

3.1.1. Symbiosis in Biology

Anton de Bary originated the concept of symbiosis in 1879 to explain the ways in which different organisms live together. Symbiosis can take various forms, as illustrated in Table 3.1.[1]

This table shows how two organisms (or species) can be benefited or harmed through their interaction. The second column indicates the extent to which each organism's fitness is increased (+), decreased (–), or not affected (0) by its relationship with the other. This produces six types of symbiotic relationships:

1. *Competition* between species over resources leads to harm to both species, such as the green anole, a lizard indigenous to the southern United States, and brown anole, a closely related species introduced from Cuba.
2. *Amensalism* takes place when one species negatively impacts the other without being harmed itself. For example, the black walnut tree exudes a toxic chemical from its roots and foliage that prevents the growth of other plants, such as ferns, around its base.
3. *Agonism* (also called "antagonism") occurs when one species is harmed by the relationship while another is benefited. A dog with fleas experiences discomfort and health problems, while its parasites get a home and constant food source.
4. *Neutralism* refers to two species that, for the most part, do not affect each other, even though they live in the same area. Because all species are, to some extent, interdependent, it is difficult to provide examples of completely neutral relationships, but one possible case would be a rabbit and a trout; even though they live in the same forest, they do not directly interact, so neither is benefited or harmed.

TABLE 3.1 Types of Symbiosis

TYPE OF SYMBIOSIS	INCREASE/DECREASE OF ORGANISMS' FITNESS	EXAMPLE OF THIS TYPE OF SYMBIOSIS
Competition	–/–	Green anole / brown anole
Amensalism	–/0	Fern / black walnut
Agonism	–/+	Dog/flea
Neutralism	0/0	Rabbit/trout
Commensalism	0/+	Cow / cattle egret
Mutualism	+/+	Boxer crab / anemone

5. *Commensalism* describes a relationship in which one organism benefits while the other is neither harmed nor benefited. For example, cattle egrets eat the insects that are stirred up by livestock, which are in turn unaffected by the egrets' actions.
6. *Mutualism* is a symbiotic relationship in which both organisms benefit. The boxer crab clenches a small sea anemone in each of its pincers, which it uses to threaten predators and collect food. The anemones benefit from the relationship because the crab waves them through the water to collect food particulates, providing them with a constant source of nourishment.

3.1.2. Symbiosis in Business Ethics

Though *kyōsei* has its origins in ecology, it is readily applicable to the type of competition and adaptation that takes place in the corporate as well as the biological world. In business ethics, it has been used as a paradigm to promote harmonious relationships between human beings and nonliving entities such as corporations. One of the earliest applications of *kyōsei* to business ethics occurred in 1991 when HIRAIWA Gaishi, chairman of Tokyo Electric Power Company, urged Japanese businesses to promote symbiotic relationships with their shareholders.[2] In 1987, on the fiftieth anniversary of the founding of Canon, chairman KAKU Ryūzaburō applied the biological concept of *kyōsei* to corporate social responsibility.[3] *Kyōsei* is composed of the characters *kyō* 共, "working together," and *sei* 生, "life," and means "living and working together for the common good." Kaku argues that when *kyōsei* is adopted as a central business paradigm, it promotes happiness, fairness, and the value of community.[4]

Kaku credits the seventeenth-century Confucian scholar FUJIWARA Seika with developing the roots of *kyōsei*. A contemporary of TOKUGAWA Ieyasu, Seika cultivated a Confucian philosophy of business that emphasized the right of merchants to profit as long as they did so fairly with the goal of helping others. This philosophy was adopted by the Suminokura family, which developed a house code called the *shūchū kiyaku* (舟中規約), which stated that trade should be mutually beneficial and not driven by greed, and that trading partners should be treated as equals regardless of background.[5] This philosophy reflects seven core Confucian ethical principles: (1) one should seek reciprocity (treat others as you would have them treat you); (2) virtue, not profit, is the goal of the exemplary human being; (3) self-interest should be balanced by altruism; (4) we do not exist as isolated individuals, so we must promote harmony through appropriate action; (5) acting according to the golden mean can minimize risk; (6) filial piety is important; and (7) one must value learning and constantly seek the tutelage of experts.[6]

Kaku also parallels *kyōsei* with the Buddhist concept of *tomoiki* (共生), which is written with the same characters as *kyōsei* and refers to living together with other beings in harmonious, unified relationships.[7] In business, there must be "harmony between profit and social justice": a corporation should cultivate synergistic relationships that maximize the good of all parties involved.[8] *Kyōsei* encourages the firm to take all stakeholders into account when making business decisions with the goal of promoting mutually beneficial coexistence with all members of the global community, including the environment. The Caux Round Table has adopted *kyōsei* as one of the Seven Point Principles for Business Conduct, and the Keidanren (Japan's Federation of Economic Organizations) has promoted the principle since 1992 as a way to reduce international trade conflicts.[9]

Often corporations operate on a model that is primarily competitive rather than synergistic. Heidi Von Weltzien Høivik argues that contemporary civilization is a tension between two distinct spheres: a sociocultural sphere in which life is lived and a professional sphere devoted to research, business, and politics. The former is characterized by moral norms, while the latter is expected only to be efficient and calculating. However, businesses should be concerned with more than just efficiency and profit maximization. They are an essential part of our moral lives—we exist in a reciprocal relationship with them—so they cannot be considered amoral entities.[10] Empirical studies (such as those conducted by Peters and Waterman) have indicated that virtually all firms that have performed well over time are grounded in a well-articulated set of shared values.[11] According to stakeholder theory, it is in a firm's enlightened self-interest to promote the interests of all those who have a stake in the firm. Though it might be more costly in the short term, it will pay off financially in the long run while benefiting society at large.[12] Kaku's *kyōsei* model argues that the separation of ethics and business is an artificial dichotomy that reflects the traditional Western separation of the good from the material realm. Ethics and business should be fundamentally interrelated because the true purpose of business is to promote the common good through a harmonious relationship with all stakeholders. *Kyōsei* is grounded on the idea that business and society have an "integrated coexistence" so that employees cannot act as if they are not citizens with social responsibilities. Business and ethics cannot be compartmentalized, but must rather complement one another as interdependent spheres of human existence.[13]

YAMAJI Keizō, who succeeded Kaku as president of Canon in 1989, continued to promote *kyōsei* as the corporation's central business philosophy.[14] He argues that no corporation can succeed if it is universally despised. The "Kyosei Initiative" views a good company as one that coexists harmoniously with the world, earning the respect of everyone by promoting a better future for all.[15] The chaos of contemporary times is caused by both economic and ecological turmoil. Shortsighted, small-scale thinking has promoted conflict between groups of people who have squandered the planet's natural resources in an attempt to achieve economic prosperity. This has damaged the environment and created an enormous gap between the world's rich and poor.[16] Yamaji argues that the Kyosei Initiative involves two philosophies of management: Sensitivity Conscious Management (SCM) and Ecology Conscious Management (ECM). SCM promotes fair competition between businesses by adhering to stakeholder theory. Ultimately, the corporation exists to benefit society, not the other way around. ECM respects the natural environment upon which humans and businesses depend for natural resources. Ecological sensitivity should be a key element for competition, along with quality, cost, and delivery. Corporations should operate with a minimal environmental impact.[17] Yamaji argues that management must "create the main stream of the times." Managers must reform business culture so that stakeholders and the environment are considered essential to the good of the corporation.[18]

3.2. From *Kyōsei* to *Kyōei*

Kyōsei (共生, symbiosis), is closely related to another concept in Japanese ethics, *kyōei* (共栄, mutual flourishing), which was developed by KANŌ Jigorō, who was one of the key figures in the modernization of Japan during the late nineteenth and early twentieth centuries. He was arguably the most important educator in the history of modern Japan: he held a graduate degree in philosophy and economics from Tokyo University, spent his life as a teacher and administrator in the Japanese school system, was the father of Japan's physical and music education programs, served the government as a member of the House of Peers and a spokesman for the Japanese Olympic committee, and was the founder of the martial art judo.[19] Kanō was born in 1860 at the end of the Tokugawa era and raised during the Meiji Restoration. He was educated by YAMAMOTO Chiku'un, a noted

Confucian scholar and master of several traditional Japanese arts.[20] Kanō adopted core principles from both Western and Eastern philosophical systems[21] to develop an ethic grounded in two core principles: *jita kyōei* (自他共栄, mutual flourishing) and *seiryoku zenyō* (精力善用, maximum efficiency).

3.2.1. *Jita Kyōei*: Mutual Flourishing

The kanji for *jita kyōei* (自他共栄) literally means "self-other together-prosperity," and the term can be best translated as "mutual flourishing."[22] Kanō argues that human beings are social creatures: we cannot live meaningful lives if we are separated from other people. Cooperation with the goal of mutual benefit is essential for humans to interact harmoniously with one another so that they can achieve common goals that promote flourishing. Each person is a moral exemplar who models ideal conduct to those around him or her. By acting in ways that benefit others as well as oneself, each person encourages others to act accordingly, so that all may continually develop.[23]

The first character in *kyōei* (共栄, flourishing) is identical to the first character in *kyōsei* (共生, symbiosis), which indicates an etymological parallel between the two terms based on the idea of *kyō* (共, together or mutual). By acting in a manner that promotes mutualistic relationships, we can bring about an environment in which we maximize flourishing for all parties. As an educator, martial artist, and politician, Kanō was primarily interested in conflict resolution, and he viewed the philosophy of mutual flourishing as the mechanism through which such resolution could take place.[24] Human interaction is not a zero-sum game in which one's prosperity is contingent upon others' failure; we can interact synergistically to resolve disputes in ways that promote one another's good.[25] Just as two judo competitors can engage in *randori* (free sparring) or *shiai* (competition) with the goal of helping each other to achieve each person's maximum potential, corporations can compete in a business environment while promoting the flourishing of all of their stakeholders.

One of Kanō's judo students, SUZUKI Masaya, was the third director general of the Sumitomo Conglomerate, one of the largest commercial concerns of Japan. Suzuki made *jita kyōei* his business philosophy and endeavored to secure good pay, housing, pensions, healthcare, and other benefits for his workers at the beginning of the twentieth century, a time when such measures were unusual. He also initiated reforestation efforts to repair areas damaged by earlier Sumitomo mining projects.[26] Suzuki was

living Kanō's vision that the philosophy of *jita kyōei* could allow capitalism and social responsibility to work together to promote an economically
stable, flourishing society.[27] This business philosophy anticipates *kyōsei*
by emphasizing the value of all stakeholders and interpreting prosperity in
a mutualistic sense.

3.2.2. *Seiryoku Zenyō*: Maximum Efficiency

Seiryoku zenyō comprises the characters for "energy" (精力) and "good
use" (善用) and is typically translated as "maximum efficiency."[28] Kanō
despised wastefulness, insisting that in any endeavor, one should strive
to achieve the best possible results while minimizing wasted effort and
resources. The name of Kanō's martial art, *jūdō* (柔道) is written with two
kanji. The latter character, *dō*, comes from the Chinese term *dào* and refers
to a "way" of self-cultivation. The former character, *jū*, comes from the
Daoist term *róu*, which means "suppleness" or "yielding strength." Green
bamboo exemplifies *jū*: in a winter storm, bamboo bends under the weight
of the ice and snow and the force of the wind, while the rigid trees around
it snap. A judo practitioner mimics this suppleness: when pushed, she does
not push back, but rather pulls her opponent off balance, channeling the
energy of the shove into a throw.[29] This reflects a central notion in Daoist
philosophy, *wú-wéi* (無為), which means "noninterference" or "nonassert-
ive action." One should not work against the way things are in nature, but
should instead harmonize oneself with one's context to achieve maximum
efficiency and a flourishing existence. Following the descriptions of old
Tokugawa texts, Kanō describes judo as "the path that follows the flow of
things" to promote "the most efficient use of energy."[30]

Kanō believed that maximum efficiency was a principle that could
lead to the resolution of all types of conflict, both on and off the tatami.
Seiryoku zenyō entails self-cultivation (making the most of one's talents
and opportunities) and mutual cooperation between individuals, organizations, and political systems, all of which promote success and human welfare.[31] Kanō summarizes this principle as follows: "Don't waste anything.
Use it efficiently."[32] The concept of efficiency as the avoidance of waste
is essential for both business ethics and environmental ethics. Waste is
abhorrent in both fields because it represents a poor use of resources. For
example, recycling an aluminum can is good not only because it promotes
environmental sustainability, but because it costs only 5 percent of what it
takes to make a new aluminum can.[33] Thus, recycling is "green" not only
in the environmental sense, but in the monetary sense as well. Waste is

foolish. We should adopt a philosophy of frugality at the level of personal ethics, business policy, and national/international law to promote a world in which waste is minimized.[34]

Taken together, *jita kyōei* and *seiryoku zenyō* form a philosophy of life in which one strives to efficiently promote the flourishing of everything with which one interrelates. *Kyōsei* (mutualism) promotes *kyōei* (flourishing) by encouraging people to view interactions with others not in competitive terms, but as an opportunity for mutual benefit and welfare. Interference must follow the principle of *jū*: it should be minimal and should promote the flourishing of all parties involved.

3.3. *Kyōsei, Kyōei*, and the Land Ethic

While *kyōsei* and *kyōei* are valuable normative paradigms, they need to be grounded in a viable environmental ethic if they are to have cash value in helping us to resolve the current environmental crisis. The land ethic was originally articulated by Aldo Leopold in his 1949 book, *A Sand County Almanac*, and later developed into a rigorous philosophy by environmental ethicist J. Baird Callicott. According to Leopold, human beings mistreat the environment because they consider themselves to be conquerors of the wilderness, which they view as little more than raw material meant to serve human interests. The land ethic involves a paradigm shift from the idea that humans are conquerors of the land to the notion that we are "plain members and citizens of the biotic community."[35] The central paradigm of the land ethic is the notion that "a thing is right when it tends to preserve the integrity, stability, and beauty of the biotic community. It is wrong when it tends otherwise."[36] This parallels the *kyōsei* model of stakeholder theory articulated above: when humans consider their species as just one of a myriad number of biological stakeholders in the environment, they will cease to focus exclusively on human concerns and begin to act in ways that promote the flourishing of the biosphere as a whole.

Arthur Tansley (1871–1955) introduced the concept of the "ecosystem," uniting living organisms with their abiotic environments into a unified systemic whole.[37] Raymond Lindeman (1915–1942) further developed the ecosystem in ecology as a thermodynamic flow model in which energy is trophically exchanged: energy is the "currency" that drives the "economy of nature."[38] Leopold's "Land Pyramid" is based on this concept: producers, consumers, and decomposers form an energy network that maintains the continual flow of energy through the system.[39] Integrating the then new ecosystem idea in ecology with the older "community concept," Leopold conceived plants and animals to be related to the whole "biotic community" in the same way that citizens are related to the social community. Each member has a *niche* or function in the context of which it cooperates with and contributes to the whole. The food chain is a *biotic pyramid* in which producers absorb sunlight and are eaten by herbivores, which are prey for carnivores, all of which are eventually broken down by decomposers. A biotic system is essentially an energy conduit consisting of hydrogen, carbon, oxygen, nitrogen, and other "nutrients," which are synthesized into complex organic molecules by green plants powered by radiant energy from the sun. Herbivores use atmospheric oxygen—a waste product of photosynthesis—to "burn" the chemical energy stored in the tissues of the plants they consume for their own metabolic processes and movements from place to place.[40] Evolution is a protracted series of changes that lengthen and stabilize the energy conduit. These changes are typically slow and local: natural extinction occurs when a new, more adaptive species replaces an older, less adaptive one. Human beings can injure the biotic pyramid faster than evolution can repair it: species become extinct in a geological instant, leaving other species to take over their niches in a simplified ecosystem or, more dangerously, for those niches to remain unoccupied. Thus, a core maxim of the land ethic is "Thou shalt not extirpate or render species extinct."[41] Removing a species from an ecosystem is like driving a type of business or industry out of a community: when such evictions accumulate, the community functions less and less well until it becomes like a ghost town or the abandoned and decaying core of a Rust Belt metropolis. Unlike cities and towns, nature does not have any rural redevelopment or urban renewal programs. To be sure, we have restoration ecology; and "de-extinction" is currently a matter of biological speculation, but once a species has become extinct its recreation is highly improbable if not altogether impossible, and the restoration of degraded biotic communities is both expensive and hardly ever fully successful.[42]

Much of Western ethical and political theory since the Enlightenment has tended to be psychocentric, individualistic, and atomistic: it is grounded in the interests of the individual, so the community is nothing more than a social contract between individual rights-bearers.[43] Ecology, by contrast, is the study of *relata*: organisms related to one another through their interdependent participation in the natural environment. Individual organisms are determined by their ecological relationships, the ways their species have adapted to particular niches in the ecosystem. The biosphere is a superorganism, a concatenation of ecological processes enveloping the earth, in which all the living and nonliving components participate. Therefore, we can meaningfully talk about ecology in terms of the *health* or *disease* of the land based on the extent to which its vertically integrated ecosystems are fully functional.[44] Multicelled organisms are composed of cellular parts and microbial symbionts that operate together to form a second-order whole. An ecosystem can be understood as a "third-order organic whole," which is "a unified system of integrally related parts."[45] The duties toward self-preservation (the maintenance of organic integrity) and noninterference that we endorse on the individual level can be extended to the biotic community. Over time, the boundaries of moral considerability have grown from family to community to country to all humankind. Leopold calls this the "ethical sequence": the progressive extension of value to all of the groups in relation to which one is interdependent. The sequence can be further extended to the biotic community because of the realization that the land itself is part of our community (which is a fact of ecology). Eventually, this will become part of the collective cultural consciousness, once we have achieved "universal ecological literacy."[46] The more we learn about science and ethics, the more we view ourselves as interdependent beings. This is why, as Kanō argues, education is such as essential part of flourishing: it is only when we internalize these values as habits that we can practice them in our daily lives.

In his book *Nonzero: The Logic of Human Destiny*, Robert Wright develops the thesis that both biological and cultural evolution are driven by "nonzero-sumness." According to game theory, zero-sum games are contests in which there can only be one winner: a victory for one opponent entails defeat for the other, which makes the relationship inherently antagonistic. In non-zero-sum games, the interests of the players overlap, which makes a win-win outcome possible if they cooperate to achieve a common objective. The evolution of life on the planet and the development of human culture are propelled by nonzero-sumness: environmental pressures force individuals and whole species into mutualistic relationships that promote survival and prosperity. Life evolved on this planet as a means of storing sunlight as "structured energy," and all living beings cooperate at the ecological level to maintain this structure. Ethics evolved as a type of "reciprocal altruism" that encouraged non-zero-sum relationship between human beings. Even conflict between groups of people can promote non-zero-sum relationships: for example, warfare forces the members of a community to unite against a common enemy and develop creative solutions to their predicament.[47] Wright's theory closely parallels Callicott's Humean foundation for the land ethic: moral sentiment evolved because it is adaptive. Ethics promotes mutualistic relationships, which in turn promote flourishing.

Kyōsei is the key philosophical paradigm of nonzero-sumness. When human beings think of themselves as interdependent with other people and with the environment as a whole, they will strive to develop creative ways that promote the mutual benefit of all things. The Caux Round Table has demonstrated that *kyōsei* can allow businesses to be profitable while promoting the good of all stakeholders. If we extend this philosophy beyond the business world to apply to all human endeavors, it can have tremendous implications for the way we interact with the natural environment. Perhaps nature itself can be considered a stakeholder. Of course, it does not have any interests, but that does not mean that it lacks *best interests*, which might best be described by Leopold's criteria of the "integrity, stability, and beauty of the biotic community."

Whether we admit it or not, human beings exist in a symbiotic relationship with the environment because we depend upon it as a life-support system. *Kyōsei* addresses anthropocentric concerns within an ecocentric framework. Human beings can only flourish if they look after the good of the whole life-support system. All beings have niche roles to keep the energy circuit open. The niche role for human beings is stewardship of the environment. As Leopold and Callicott point out, we have historically considered ourselves to be conquerors of the planet rather than plain citizens of the biotic community. Kanō's principle of *jū* is a philosophy of noninterference. Maximum efficiency means that one should interfere only minimally by nudging things in the right direction without opposing them. Mutual flourishing means that one should minimize injury and maximize benefit for both oneself and others.

But can a policy of noninterference be practicable? Don't we have to interfere with the environment to some extent just to live? Considering the Daoist notion of *wú-wéi*, Karyn L. Lai argues that the goal is for both parties to attain the "maximum compossible state of affairs": the outcome that promotes the good of both parties to the greatest extent possible.[48] It will not always be possible for both parties to get everything they want, but this does not make every interaction into a zero-sum game. Just because some interference might be necessary does not mean that we cannot act in ways that minimize such interference.

Law enforcement officers, security personnel, and martial artists use the idea of a force continuum to minimize injury to both oneself and one's attacker. The idea behind the force continuum is that an individual has a moral obligation to use the least amount of force necessary to neutralize

TABLE 3.2 Continuum of Noninterference

TYPE OF SYMBIOSIS	BENEFIT/HARM TO SELF/OTHER	LEVEL OF NONINTERFERENCE
Mutualism (*kyōsei*)	+/+	Ideal (both benefit)
Commensalism	0/+ or +/0	Acceptable (neither is harmed)
Neutralism	0/0	
Agonism	–/+ or +/–	Unacceptable (one is harmed)
Amensalism	–/0	
Competition	–/–	Worst-case scenario (both suffer)

an attacker. For example, a law enforcement officer should first use verbal commands, then empty-hand submission techniques (e.g., joint locks and pressure point control tactics), then less-than-lethal weapons (e.g., pepper spray or baton), and finally lethal force (e.g., handgun). Each level of the force continuum interferes progressively more with the suspect's bodily integrity, and thus the higher levels should be avoided if at all possible. Using too little force might result in injury to the officer (and legal problems for the assailant); using too much will lead to legal problems for the officer (and injury to the assailant). The right amount of force maximizes the good of both parties while minimizing negative outcomes.

This idea of a force continuum can be applied to Lai's notion of noninterference as maximum compossibility (see table 3.2). *Kyōsei* reflects the drive to promote mutualistic relationships between human beings, non-human animals, and the natural environment. Ideally, one should strive for mutualistic, non-zero-sum relationships that benefit all parties to the greatest extent possible. When this is not possible, one moves to the next level of the continuum, where one tries to promote commensal or neutral relationships that at least do no harm to others (even if they are not benefited). One should avoid agonistic or amensal relationships that cause harm to other beings if at all possible. Competitive relationships should be eschewed because they result in harm to both parties.

3.4. Conclusion

By using *kyōsei* as a guide, human beings can exist in their environment with minimal interference. The ecosystem is an energy circuit developed over millions of years of evolution, and anthropogenic changes can disrupt its delicate balance with catastrophic consequences. *Kyōsei* allows us to simultaneously promote human goals while respecting the integrity, stability, and beauty of the biotic community. This ecocentric outlook has long-term anthropocentric benefits because sacrifices made for the community good will indirectly benefit oneself. Carpooling might be inconvenient, but saves the individual money in the long run and reduces carbon emissions that contribute to climate change (and might help to cultivate rewarding friendships among the carpoolers). Eating a bit less ahi tuna protects the population of an apex predator in the ecosystem while guaranteeing that future generations of fishermen have something to catch. As a business ethic and a philosophy of life, *kyōsei* encourages us to approach all of our relationships as creative opportunities for mutualism. It is only by living symbiotically with other people and the environment that we can all truly flourish.

Notes

1. Table 3.1 is based primarily on D. H. Lewis's article "Symbiosis and Mutualism: Crisp Concepts and Soggy Semantics," in *The Biology of Mutualism: Ecology and Evolution*, ed. Douglas H. Boucher (New York: Oxford University Press, 1985), 29–39. See also Surindar Paracer and Vernon Ahmadjian, *Symbiosis: An Introduction to Biological Associations*, 2nd ed. (New York: Oxford University Press, 2000), 6–8; Jan Sapp, *Evolution by Association* (Oxford: Oxford University Press, 1994); Steven A. Frank, "Models of Symbiosis," *American Naturalist* 150 (1997): S80–S99; and ABE Hiroshi, "From Symbiosis (Kyōsei) to the Ontology of 'Arising Both from Oneself and from Another,'" *Environmental Philosophy in Asian Traditions of Though*, ed. J. Baird Callicott and James McRae (Albany: SUNY Press, 2014).

2. Calvin M. Boardman and Hideaki Kiyoshi Kato, "The Confucian Roots of Business Kyosei," *Journal of Business Ethics* 48 (2003): 317–318.

3. Richard E. Wokutch and Jon M. Shepard, "The Maturing of the Japanese Economy: Corporate Social Responsibility Implications," *Business Ethics Quarterly* 9, no. 3 (1999): 536–537. See also James McRae, "Triple-Negation: Watsuji Tetsurō on the Sustainability of Ecosystems, Economies, and International Peace," in *Environmental Philosophy in Asian Traditions of Thought*, ed. J. Baird Callicott and James McRae (Albany: SUNY Press, 2014), 368–369.

4. Henri-Claude de Bettignies, Kenneth E. Goodpaster, and MATSUOKA Toshio, "The Caux Roundtable Principles for Business: Presentation and Discussion," in *International Business Ethics: Challenges and Approaches*, ed. Georges Enderle (Notre Dame, IN: University of Notre Dame Press, 1999), 131–142. See also Boardman and Kato, "Confucian Roots," 318.

5. Boardman and Kato, "Confucian Roots," 318–319, 322–323.

6. Boardman and Kato, "Confucian Roots," 320.

7. Bettignies, Goodpaster, and Matsuoka, "Caux Roundtable Principles," 133.

8. Bettignies, Goodpaster, and Matsuoka, "Caux Roundtable Principles," 133–134.

9. Wokutch and Shepard, "Maturing of Japanese Economy," 536–537. See also McRae, "Triple-Negation," 368–369.

10. Heidi Von Weltzien Høivik, "A Joint Stakeholder Learning Process in Participatory Environmental Ethics: A Case Study," *International Journal of Value-Based Management* 10 (1997): 148–149.

11. Von Weltzien Høivik, "Joint Stakeholder Learning Process," 153.

12. Wokutch and Shepard, "Maturing of Japanese Economy," 528–529.

13. Von Weltzien Høivik, "Joint Stakeholder Learning Process," 153–154.

14. YAMAJI Keizo, "A Global Perspective of Ethics in Business," *Business Ethics Quarterly* 7, no. 3 (1997): 55. Yamaji holds a degree in physics with a concentration in the natural sciences, and has used this scientific understanding to expand Kaku's notion of *kyōsei*.

15. Yamaji, "Global Perspective," 56.

16. Yamaji, "Global Perspective," 57.

17. Yamaji, "Global Perspective," 59–61.

18. Yamaji, "Global Perspective," 68.

19. John Stevens, *The Way of Judo: A Portrait of Jigoro Kanō and His Students* (Boston: Shambhala, 2013), 9, 20, 77–78, 94.

20. Stevens, *The Way of Judo*, 13.

21. Kanō was influenced not only by Japanese Confucian ethics, but modern Western philosophy, including the work of John Dewey, whom he befriended when the latter visited Japan (Stevens, *The Way of Judo*, 91, 76).

22. Stevens prefers to use "mutual well-being and benefit," but I have chosen a translation that is closer to the literal meaning of the original Japanese characters (see Stevens, *The Way of Judo*, 313). Flourishing is a central concept for most systems of virtue ethics (e.g., Aristotelian and Confucian approaches), so this translation resonates with Kanō's emphasis upon character development.

23. KANŌ Jigoro, *Kanō Jigoro Chosakushu* (Tokyo: Gogatsu Shobo, 1992), section 75.

24. Stevens, *The Way of Judo*, 99.

25. Stevens, *The Way of Judo*, 307. This parallels Robert Wright's refutation of the notion that competition is always a zero-sum game, which is discussed in greater detail in section 3.3.

26. Stevens, *The Way of Judo*, 248–249.

27. Stevens, *The Way of Judo*, 308. This fusion of capitalism and socialism seems to anticipate John Rawls's notion of "welfare capitalism."

28. Stevens uses the translation "concentrated effort, maximum efficiency," but I use only the latter part of the phrase in an attempt to stay faithful to the literal translation, "good use of energy" (see Stevens, *The Way of Judo*, 312–313).

29. James McRae, "Conquering the Self: Daoism, Confucianism, and the Price of Freedom in *Crouching Tiger, Hidden Dragon*," in *The Philosophy of Ang Lee*, ed. Robert Arp, Adam Barkman, and James McRae (Lexington: University Press of Kentucky, 2013), 32. Kanō often made use of the analogy of "willow branches yielding, but not breaking, under the weight of heavy snow" (Stevens, *The Way of Judo*, 59).

30. McRae, "Conquering the Self," 32; Stevens, *The Way of Judo*, 37.

31. Stevens, *The Way of Judo*, 90–91.

32. Stevens, *The Way of Judo*, 306.

33. "The Price of Virtue," *Economist*, June 7, 2007, http://www.economist.com/node/9302727.

34. Stevens, *The Way of Judo*, 61.

35. J. Baird Callicott, *In Defense of the Land Ethic* (Albany: SUNY Press, 1989), 92, 96.

36. Callicott, *Defense of Land Ethic*, 21.

37. A. G. Tansley, "The Use and Abuse of Vegetational Concepts and Terms," *Ecology* 16, no. 3 (1935): 284–307.

38. J. Baird Callicott, *Thinking Like a Planet: The Land Ethic and the Earth Ethic* (Oxford: Oxford University Press, 2013). See also Raymond L. Lindeman, "The Trophic Dynamic Aspect of Ecology," *Ecology* 23, no. 4 (1942): 399–417.

39. Callicott, *Defense of Land Ethic*, 84–90.

40. Callicott, *Defense of Land Ethic*, 89–91

41. Callicott, *Defense of Land Ethic*, 90–91.

42. John A. Wiems and Richard J. Hobbs, "Integrating Conservation and Restoration in a Changing World," *BioScience* 65 (2015): 302–312; Beth Shapiro, *How to Clone a Mammoth: The Science of De-extinction* (Princeton, NJ: Princeton University Press, 2015).

43. This type of thinking is common in Western social contract theory, deontology, and utilitarianism, though it is not the case in virtue ethics and care ethics, which tend to view human beings as contextual (defined by their roles and relationships).

44. Callicott, *Defense of Land Ethic*, 84–90.

45. Callicott, *Defense of Land Ethic*, 22–23.

46. Callicott, *Defense of Land Ethic*, 80–82.

47. Robert Wright, *Nonzero: The Logic of Human Destiny* (New York: Vintage Books, 2000).

48. Karyn L. Lai, "Conceptual Foundations for Environmental Ethics: A Daoist Perspective," in *Environmental Philosophy in Asian Traditions of Thought*, ed. J. Baird Callicott and James McRae (Albany: SUNY Press, 2014), 190–191. By "compossible," Lai means "co-possible" or "possible for both to be true at the same time without contradiction."

PART II | Human Nature and
the Environment

CHAPTER 4 | Kūkai and Dōgen as Exemplars of Ecological Engagement

GRAHAM PARKES

AT A TIME when the world is facing an unprecedented environmental crisis in the form of human-caused global warming, most politicians in the developed nations (especially, and crucially, in the United States) seem to be unable or unwilling to take action to prevent disastrous consequences for millions of people (for the most part in the developing world). One factor behind this passivity is that the general public is disinclined to believe the findings and predictions of the climate sciences, and is happier to continue with "business as usual" in the hope that, if anything is in fact going wrong, some new technology will be able to set it right.

There are many reasons (psychological, social, and political) for this pathological behavior, but it ultimately stems from a particular basic conception of the human relationship to nature that is central to anthropocentric traditions of thought in the West, and which understands the human being as separate from, and superior to, all other beings in the natural world. Traditional East Asian understandings of this relationship are quite different and relatively unanthropocentric, especially as exemplified in the ideas of Chinese Daoism and Japanese Buddhism—even though these have now been to a large extent replaced by Western conceptions in present-day China and Japan. Nevertheless, these ideas and understandings are experientially accessible to any contemporary person who has full contact with the natural world, regardless of which tradition that person stands in.

The focus of this chapter is on the human-nature relation that we find in the philosophies of Kūkai (空海, Kōbō Daishi, 774–835) and Dōgen (道元, 1200–1253), from whom we can learn a great deal that is beneficial in the context of our current environmental predicament.[1] The ideas of both thinkers are firmly rooted in practice (*shugyō* 修行), and especially bodily or somatic practice, designed to bring about a transformation of experience. The argument is not that we should appropriate their conceptions of nature in order to solve our environmental problems; rather, since they both practice "philosophy as a way of life," I am suggesting that we can learn from the practices they advocate in the light of what they say about natural phenomena—and would benefit from emulating their ways of engaging the world ecologically.

Two ideas central to Japanese Buddhism (in part thanks to Kūkai and Dōgen) merit a brief discussion at the outset, since they are the source of some revealing misunderstandings, which will be dealt with in the last section. These are *hongaku* (本覚), usually translated as "original enlightenment," and *busshō* (仏性) or "Buddha-nature." The idea of original enlightenment, or "radical awakenedness," is implied by the basic idea in Mahayana Buddhism that "form is not different from emptiness, emptiness is not different from form" (the *Heart Sutra*), or that "nirvana is not different from samsara" (Nāgārjuna). Śākyamuni Buddha realized that the unsatisfactory condition of existence derives from ignorance, that things don't go well because our experience is distorted by our desires and cravings, and that it's possible to become aware of this distortion and thereby clarify our experience. This insight becomes radicalized in the Mahayana tradition into the realization that there's no need to transcend the world of samsara to the other shore, since we've been standing on it right here all along, but without realizing it. This shift focuses our attention on this present existence as the only one, and on affirming and working to improve it. *Hongaku* thus means that we can awaken to the condition that we've always been in, but unawares, and also that *any* human being—not just the saint or the bodhisattva—may attain enlightenment.

However, further consideration of the central Buddhist doctrines of *anatman* (no-self) and *pratītya-samutpāda* (dependent arising) led Mahayana thinkers to question the assumption that only humans have the capacity for enlightenment, or "Buddha-nature." What one realizes, after all, is that the idea of the self is illusory and that one is what one is, or becomes what one becomes, only in—and as—an infinitely complex network of interconnections. This is the context for the bodhisattva's vow to realize enlightenment "for the sake of all sentient beings." The term *hongaku* (or its Chinese precursor, *benjue* 本覺) makes its first significant appearance in a Chinese text from the sixth century, the *Awakening of Faith in the Mahayana*.[2] When Buddhism was transplanted from India to China, some thinkers there began to ask—no doubt under the influence of Daoist ideas—whether the extension of *hongaku* to include "all sentient beings" was sufficient. Jizang, who founded the Chinese Madhyamaka (Sanlun, or "Three Treatise") school at the end of the sixth century CE, was the first to speak of the "attainment of buddhahood by plants and trees."[3] Some two hundred years later the Tiantai patriarch Zhanran used the term *Buddha-nature* in arguing that not only plants, trees, and earth but even particles of dust are originally enlightened.[4]

When Buddhist ideas from China began to arrive in Japan, they found fertile ground prepared by the indigenous religion of Shinto, according to which the natural world and human beings are equally offspring of the divine. In Shinto the whole world is understood to be inhabited by *kami* (神), which include not only divine spirits and spirits of the ancestors but also any phenomena that occasion awe or reverence: the sun, wind, thunder, lightning, rain, mountains, rivers, trees, and rocks. Such an atmosphere was naturally receptive to the idea that the earth and plants participate in Buddha-nature. As William LaFleur has pointed out, whereas the Chinese proponents of the extension of *hongaku* to all beings, sentient and nonsentient, were concerned primarily with "the logic of Mahayana universalism," the Japanese philosophers who adopted the idea were more interested in the special role played by the natural world in the Buddhist concern with enlightenment. Although the first Japanese thinker to use the phrase *mokuseki busshō* ("Buddha-nature of trees and rocks") was apparently Saichō, founder of the Tendai school, the first to make the ideas of *hongaku* and the buddhahood of all phenomena central to his thought was Kūkai.[5]

4.1. Kūkai on Nature as Sermon and Scripture

Kūkai's best-known idea is probably *sokushin jōbutsu* (即身成仏), the idea (predicated on *hongaku*) that it's possible to attain enlightenment in this present body—by contrast with earlier Buddhist views that it can be achieved only after many lifetimes. What one realizes through the somatic practices that Kūkai recommends for this endeavor has to do with a larger body belonging to Dainichi Nyorai (大日如来, the Great Sun Buddha: Mahāvairocana in Sanskrit), the Dharmakāya or cosmic embodiment of the Buddha. In his "Introduction to the Mahāvairocana Sutra," Kūkai writes that "Mahāvairocana is the One whose own nature is the Dharmakāya ... which is intrinsic and original enlightenment."[6] Kūkai's second great idea, *hosshin seppō* (法身説法), means that Dainichi as the

Dharmakāya is constantly engaged in expounding the Buddhist teachings, or dharma. This contrasts with the traditional understanding of the cosmic embodiment of the Buddha as "formless and imageless, and totally beyond verbalization and conceptualization."[7] It also exemplifies one of Kūkai's major innovations in the development of Buddhist doctrine, which was to bring the idea of the Dharmakāya "down to earth" by identifying what had been customarily regarded as the formless and imageless Absolute with the actual world we presently inhabit.

If we think about what it means for Kūkai to say in the Heian period Japan that all phenomena (dharmas) are expounding the dharma, we realize that by far the greater part of this elucidation is being done by natural phenomena. After all, the extent of the human imprint on the natural environment was far smaller then than it is now, and Kūkai pursued the earlier phases of his thinking, during the third decade of his life, while living a nomadic existence in the mountains of his native Shikoku. And in a poem written much later, explaining his decision to remain in the retreat he established up in the Kōga mountains (in what is now Wakayama Prefecture), he writes:

> I have never tired of watching the pine trees and the rocks at Mt. Kōya;
> The limpid stream of the mountain is the source of my inexhaustible joy.[8]

The world, for Kūkai, is constantly creating itself through the Five Great Processes (*godai* 五大) of earth, water, fire, wind, and space interacting with each other and with a sixth process, awareness—so that he also speaks of the Six Great Processes constituting the cosmos.[9] At one point he discusses the Buddha-nature of vegetation in this cosmological context:

> The explanation of the buddhahood of insentient trees and plants is as follows: the Dharmakāya consists of the Five Great Processes within which space and plants and trees [*sōmoku*] are included. Both this space and these plants and trees are the Dharmakāya. Even though with the physical eye one might see the coarse form of plants and trees, it is with the buddha-eye that the subtle color can be seen. Therefore, without any alteration in what they are in themselves trees and plants may unobjectionably be referred to as buddha[-nature].[10]

The awakened nature of vegetation isn't going to be clear to the ordinary eye, but requires practice in a different kind of seeing, through the "buddha-eye." In a poetic excursus in his essay "On the Meanings of the Word *Hūm*" (*Unji gi*), Kūkai twice alludes to the awakened nature of vegetation (*sōmoku*):

> If trees and plants are to attain enlightenment,
> Why not those who are endowed with feelings? . . .
> If plants and trees were devoid of buddhahood,
> Waves would then be without wetness.[11]

When the cosmic embodiment of the Buddha preaches the dharma, this takes place through both sound (as in a sermon) and signs (as in a scripture). Indeed, for Kūkai reality consists of nothing but sounds and signs, as he explains in his treatise "The Meaning of Sound, Sign, Reality" (*Shōji jissō gi*), where he describes the process whereby sounds become signs and signs become things.

Taking the elucidation of the teachings by sound first: this means on the one hand sounds we can ordinarily hear, such as the wind blowing through the grass, the crashing of waves on the shore, the roaring of a forest fire, the song of birds, and the cries of mammals. Even for the uninitiated among us, such sounds can seem, if we attend to them with an open mind, in some way meaningful (though we may have no idea what it is that they mean). On the other hand, Kūkai is talking about sounds that are ordinarily inaudible: vibrations emanating from the sun, the resonances of clouds, and the voices of rocks. The key to understanding this enigmatic idea is his notion of *sanmitsu* (三密), the "Three Mysteries" or (in the more illuminating translation suggested by Thomas Kasulis) the "Three Intimacies."[12] This triad is based on the traditional Buddhist conception of the individual as consisting of "body, speech, and mind," and working karmically as "acting, speaking, and thinking." Corresponding to these three aspects of the individual are three aspects of Dainichi as the cosmic Buddha: the sounds of the world as his speech, the signs of the world as images of his thought, and the things of the world as his body. Although Kūkai emphasizes that Dainichi's elucidation of the Buddhist teachings is "for his own enjoyment" and thereby a communication "between the Buddha and the Buddha," it is also true that "he deigns to let it be known to us."[13] Insofar as Dainichi preaches the Buddha-dharma with his voice, through the sounds of the cosmos, the student of Shingon will be able, by chanting mantras, to attune his or her hearing to the cosmic resonances and thereby understand the sermon.

Just as every phenomenon is basically a vibration that we can learn to hear "with the third ear," as it were, so everything is also a sign inscribed in the great scripture that is the world. As Kūkai writes in one of his longer poems:

> Being painted by brushes of mountains, by ink of oceans,
> Heaven and earth are the bindings of a sutra revealing
>   the Truth.
> Reflected in a dot are all things in the universe;
> Contained in the data of senses and mind is the sacred book.
> It is open or closed depending on how we look at it;
> Both [Dainichi's] silence and His eloquence make incisive tongues
>   numb.[14]

This sutra bound by heaven and earth won't be readable by the uninitiated—even though striations on rocks or patterns in water or vegetation may appear, to an open mind, to mean something. A full reading of the world's signs will require the Shingon practices of visualizing mandalas and settling the mind in meditation (samādhi)—an opening of the third eye, as it were—to be comprehensible.

Finally, to experience all things as constituting Dainichi's body, the somatic practice of mudras is necessary. As Kūkai puts it, in "Attaining Enlightenment in this Present Body":

> If there is a Shingon student who reflects well upon the meaning of the Three Mysteries, makes mudras, recites mantras, and allows his mind to abide in the state of samādhi, then, through grace, his three mysteries will be united with the Three Mysteries [of the Dharmakāya Buddha].[15]

These three kinds of practice allow one to realize one's participation as body, speech, and mind in the body, speech, and mind of the cosmos—and thereby experience the Dharmakāya elucidating the dharma.

If we ask, in the case of natural phenomena, what is to be learned from them, which aspects of the Buddha-dharma they teach, we find that Kūkai gives no explicit answer. But presumably they would include the impermanence of all things, the interdependence of their arising and perishing, the necessity for limits, the infinity of perspectives in the world, and the beauty of natural and spontaneous unfolding. In any case, insofar as the world is what Kūkai calls the "wondrous" and "fulfilled" body of the cosmic Buddha, it is worthy of our reverence and respect.[16] And insofar as natural phenomena are delivering sermons and scriptures in the primordial natural language, they are worthy of our careful attention as valuable sources of understanding. Naturally, as beings that have to eat and find shelter and protection from the world's dangers, we are going to have to consume vegetation at the very least, even though this goes against the Buddhist precept against killing. But it would seem that, for Kūkai (and in line with the Buddhist precepts), to kill capriciously, or exploit what we call "natural resources" unnecessarily, would be to desecrate the body of the Buddha and destroy opportunities for learning and understanding.

Some difficult ecological questions arise, however, when it comes to animal life that threatens humans (whether saber-toothed tigers or deadly microbes): Is it good to wipe out dangerous predators in order to enhance the safety of human beings? Or to exterminate lethal viruses and bacilli to the extent that we can? What is more, as mentioned earlier, Kūkai understands the Dharmakāya as all phenomena, which would include not just things of nature but also things made by humans. Thus, not only temples and ritual instruments but also secular constructions and artifacts would be part of the cosmic body of the Buddha and engage in preaching the dharma. If we can look to Kūkai as a guide for ecological behavior, we might wonder what his attitude would be toward such things as chemical pollution and plutonium waste. Are these human-made products also worthy of our reverence and respect? Or on what grounds, by contrast, might we want to eliminate them? But let us postpone answering these questions until after the discussion of Dōgen's ideas, since a consideration of those will prompt similar questions.

4.2. Preparing Food and Sailing Boats

Moving from the ninth century to the thirteenth, and from Shingon Buddhism to the beginnings of the Sōtō school of Zen, we find that Dōgen maintains Kūkai's emphasis on the centrality of somatic practices, and has similar ideas about the world as the body of the Buddha. Just as for Kūkai there is a distinction without a difference between body and mind (since the five processes comprising the physical world are always interfused with mind, or awareness), so in Dōgen's *Shōbōgenzō* (*Treasury of the True Dharma-Eye*) the distinctions between body and mind, and between self and world, are consistently minimized. Whereas philosophical texts that talk of, and speak only to, the mind tend to draw us away from the body into a realm of abstraction, his emphasis on the body connects us to the natural world in which it participates. If so many people in today's world appear unfazed by the prospect of our destroying the natural environment on which we depend, the reason may be that they subscribe to some kind of mind-body dichotomy, and identify themselves with an immortal soul rather than a body destined for death. By contrast, Dōgen advocates the nonduality of body and mind, which encourages the concomitant realization of the intimacy between self and world, and by emphasizing our embodiment he recalls our utter dependence on the well-being of the natural world for our own well-being.

Another factor behind our environmental predicament is our poor relationship with *things*, insofar as rampant consumerism encourages using things up—thereby promoting a certain disregard for them. Dōgen's *Shōbōgenzō* is unique among the masterpieces of world philosophy in devoting chapters to the preparing and eating of food, as well as to the making, washing, and wearing of clothes, and the proper care of eating bowls (which he calls "the body and mind of buddha ancestors").[17] Careful attention to the things we handle on a daily basis leads, for Dōgen, to care for the wider environment in which we live. When, in "Recommending Zazen to All People," Dōgen says, "Do not try to become a buddha," he is affirming the oneness of "practice and realization"—and thereby highlighting the limitations of the "means-ends" schema that structures ordinary experience.[18] When we stop discriminating between the fulfilling ends we aim at and the burdensome "chores" we are required to perform in order to attain those ends, preparing meals (for example) becomes just as important as eating them: both activities can be consummate expressions of full awakening. Dōgen therefore advises monks who work in temple kitchens to use the polite forms of language when referring to meals and their ingredients: "Use honorific forms of verbs for describing how to handle rice, vegetables; salt, and soy sauce; do not use plain language for this."[19] He also stresses the importance of treating the kitchen utensils as well as the ingredients with the utmost care and respect:

> Put what is suited to a high place in a high place, and what belongs in a low place in a low place. Those things that are in a high place will be settled there; those that are suited to be in a low place will be settled there. Select chopsticks, spoons, and other utensils with equal care, examine them with sincerity, and handle them skillfully.[20]

Gratitude and reverence for what is given us to eat, and for what we use to prepare and ingest our food, dictate that we take care to keep the kitchen clean and well ordered. But the order doesn't derive from an idea in the head of the cook, but rather from careful attention to suitabilities suggested by the things themselves. This allows us to situate the utensils so they may be settled and thus less likely to fall down or get damaged. And once we get down to cooking, we find that the creative interplay between activity, utensils and ingredients is a paradigm case of what Dōgen calls "turning things while being turned by things."[21] For his ideal of fully engaged activity, or total dynamic functioning (*zenki* 全機), full attention is crucial—for a sense of both how things are turning so that we can align ourselves aright, and how our turning is in turn affecting what is going on.

When it comes to eating, the activity that sustains all human life, the practice becomes all the more important. Dōgen begins an exposition of regulations for the serving and eating of meals in monasteries (*Fushuku hampō*) by citing a line from the *Vimalakirti Sutra*: "When we are one with the food we eat, we are one with the whole universe."[22] From this it follows, Dōgen says, that food is also the dharma and the Buddha. After a thousand or so words on how monks are to enter the hall, where the various monastery officials are to sit, and on how and where the monks are to sit down and arrange their robes, Dōgen finally gets to the regulations concerning the bowls and utensils.

> In order to set out the bowls one must first make *gasshō*, untie the knot on the bowl cover and fold the dishcloth to an unobtrusive size, twice crosswise and thrice lengthwise, placing it, together with the chopstick bag, just in front of the knees. Spread the pure napkin over the knees and put the dishcloth, with the chopstick bag on top of it, under the napkin.
>
> The cover is then unfolded and the farther end is allowed to fall over the edge of the tan, the other three corners being turned under to make a pad for the bowls to be placed upon. The lacquered-paper table-top is taken in both hands, the under-fold being held in the right hand and the top one in the left, and is unfolded as if to cover the bowls.
>
> While holding it in the right hand, take the bowls with the left and place them in the centre of the left end of this table-top, thereafter taking them out from the large one separately, in order, beginning with the smallest. Only the ball of the thumb of each hand is used for removing them so as to prevent any clattering.[23]

The practice of this ritual at every mealtime inculcates care and reverence for the things that accompany this central necessity of human existence.

While we are learning, it obliges us to become acutely aware of how we are handling these things, and of the joy, when the food is served, of harmonious interaction with others. Once the ritual has been incorporated and made "second nature," the actions flow spontaneously—so that it's not that a subject of consciousness uses the body to unfold the lacquered paper, but rather that my hands guide the papers unfolding and help it on its way to where it needs to be. In the course of these activities there is ample opportunity to appreciate that the food we eat is "the dharma and the Buddha."

Another discussion of the use of artifacts, in the chapter on "Total Functioning," broadens the context of our activity to cosmic dimensions. Dōgen invokes as his prime example a product of basic technology:

> Life is just like sailing in a boat. You raise the sails and you steer. Although you maneuver the sail and the pole, the boat carries you, and without the boat you couldn't sail. But you sail the boat, and your sailing makes the boat what it is. Investigate a moment such as this. At just such a moment, there is nothing but the world of the boat.[24]

The sailboat is the consummate nature-friendly product of technology, one that—by inserting a human artifact (in the form of sails) into the interplay of the powers of heaven and earth—makes use of natural forces without abusing them or using them up. Since winds are by nature variable, a sailboat functions properly only if it can also be propelled by human action mediated through a pole or oars. And yet these implements only work in conjunction with a boat. The activity of sailing is thus another prime example of "turning things while being turned by things."

> When you sail in a boat, your body, mind, and environs together are the dynamic functioning of the boat. The entire earth and the entire sky are both the dynamic functioning of the boat. Thus, life is nothing but you; you are nothing but life.

Regarded from our customary anthropocentric perspective, a boat, as something made by human beings, is in our world, in my world, but lacks a world of its own; whereas for Dōgen the context of total functioning allows the world to be construed by any particular focus of energy, or pivot of force, or dynamic function within it.[25]

4.3. Dōgen on Landscape as Scripture and Sermon

Dōgen quotes Śākyamuni Buddha's saying, "When the morning star appeared, I attained the way simultaneously with all sentient beings and the great earth," and takes this as a ground for holding that the earth and all that it produces engages in enlightened activity (Buddha-nature) and thereby preaches the dharma.[26] In one of his earliest works, "On the Endeavour of the Way," he writes:

> Earth, grass, trees, walls, tiles, and pebbles in the world of phenomena in the ten directions all engage in Buddha activity.... Grasses, trees, and lands that are embraced by this way of transformation [the *samādhi* of zazen] together radiate a great light and endlessly expound the inconceivable, profound dharma. Grass, trees, and walls bring forth the teaching to all beings, including common people and sages; all beings in response extend this dharma to grass, trees, and walls.[27]

Again we can see Dōgen move from the interconnection of practice and realization on the part of all phenomena to the ideal of total dynamism as exemplified in zazen.

Two fascicles of the *Shōbōgenzō* in particular, "Voices of the Valleys, Shapes of the Mountains" and "Mountains and Waters as Sutras," echo Kūkai's idea of *hosshin seppō* in showing that the natural world can be experienced and understood as a spoken and written elucidation of the Buddhist teachings.

"Mountains and Waters as Sutras" is one of the most profound and poetic chapters in the *Shōbōgenzō*.[28] Its main thrust is summed up in these admonitions: "Do not view mountains from the standard of human thought," and "Do not foolishly suppose that what we see as water is used as water by all other beings.... You should not be limited to human views when you see water."[29] While there is a brief allusion to words of wisdom being inscribed "on trees and rocks, on fields and villages," the main aim of this talk is to prepare the listener for reading landscape (*sansui*, "mountains waters") as a scripture rather than to argue that it is expounding the dharma. Such a reading is possible only if we abandon our customary anthropocentric way of regarding mountains and waters as insentient beings. Only then can we appreciate that, as the opening sentence puts it, "mountains and waters right now actualize the ancient buddha expression."[30]

Dōgen goes on to quote a Zen master's saying, "The green mountains are always walking." He urges his listeners not to doubt that mountains can walk, "even though it does not look the same as human walking." If we think about our actual experience of walking in the mountains, we realize that when we walk, the mountains appear to move, and when we stop they appear to stop moving—unless of course we turn our head, in which case they move again. What is immediately given in the experience of walking are mountains in motion; but because we (think we) know that mountains don't really move, we construe them mentally as standing still. But that is a prejudice of thought and not our actual experience. Moreover, contemporary geologists tell us that mountains do indeed move, only too slowly for the human eye to perceive.

But Dōgen wants to make another, more significant point, when he writes:

> "In the mountains" means the blossoming of the entire world. People outside the mountains do not notice or understand the mountain's walking. Those without eyes to see mountains cannot notice, understand, see, or hear this reality.[31]

When he says that the blossoming of the entire world is *sanchū* (山中), "in the mountains," Dōgen is talking not only about the experience of being up among mountains but also about experiencing from *within* the heart of the mountains themselves. Everyday experience of mountains is based on how they appear to human beings, and as long as we maintain our anthropocentric standpoint that's all we get: how they appear to us, rather than how they are "in themselves." We need to go beyond "merely looking through a bamboo pipe at a corner of the sky" and open up to a broader view of the world.[32] Dōgen helps us do this by going on to talk about waters.

Indian Buddhist thinkers had used the image of water, as the source and sustainer of life, to elaborate a perspectivism based on karmic conditioning. A philosopher from the sixth century, Asvabhāva, formulated the "four views on water," alluding to four of the Six Realms of samsara: celestial beings, humans, hungry ghosts, and fish all regard water differently because of their different karma and the different realms they inhabit. Dōgen elaborates a radical perspectivism based on this traditional idea, in which he invites the reader to entertain the perspectives of a variety of different beings.[33] This leads to the realization that each particular phenomenon, occupying a unique locus in the complex web of interrelations that is the world, construes the world while abiding in its own dharma-position (*jū hō i* 住法位). If, then, we can get ourselves into the "dharma-position" of a mountain, or a body of water, this will allow us to read them as letters in a sutra.

Just as for Kūkai the inscription of the teachings "by brushes of mountains and ink of oceans" makes the world a sutra, so Dōgen insists that sutras are more than ancient texts and scrolls containing written characters. In the chapter "Buddha Sutras" (*Bukkyō*) he writes:

> The sutras are the entire world of the ten directions itself. There is no
> moment or place that is not sutras.... . The sutras are written in letters
> of heavenly beings, human beings, animals; fighting spirits, one hundred
> grasses, or ten thousand trees.[34]

Since the words and letters of plants and animals differ from those employed by humans, they constitute "natural language" in the deeply literal sense.

Like "Mountains and Waters," "Voices of the Valleys" begins with an encouragement to go beyond anthropocentrism, recommending "slipping out of your old skin and not being constrained by past views" so as to attain "experience beyond the realm of human thinking."[35] Dōgen then discusses some lines from a poem by the eleventh-century Chinese poet Su Dongpo (SU Shi), who became enlightened after hearing the sounds of a valley stream one night:

> Valley sounds are the long, broad tongue [of the
>   Buddha],
> Mountain shapes are the unconditioned body.
> Eighty-four thousand verses are heard through the night,
> What can I say about this in the future?

> On seeing this verse, [Zen master] Changzong approved his understanding.... .
> Dongpo had this awakening soon after he heard Changzong talk about insen-
> tient beings preaching the Dharma.[36]

Instead of *hosshin seppō*, Dōgen uses the expression *mujō seppō*, which means that even insentient beings (*mujō* 無情) expound the Buddhist teachings. He goes on to discuss two other cases of sudden enlightenment in natural settings. A monk named Xiangyan, after practicing for many years, built himself a hut in the mountains and planted bamboo beside it "for company." One day, he was sweeping the path when a pebble flew up and struck a bamboo, triggering instant awakening. Another monk,

Lingyun, who had practiced for thirty years, went into the mountains, and "on seeing peach blossoms in full bloom by a distant village he was suddenly awakened."[37] As Dōgen remarks, there are many such stories in the Zen tradition; and while some of them involve artifacts such as the broom Xiangyan was using, these are all made of natural materials. Working with today's tools is less likely to conduce to satori: the roar of a motorized leaf-blower would render the sound of a pebble striking bamboo inaudible.

4.4. Shallow Readings, Deeper Ecology

Dōgen has not been well treated in recent discussions of ecology. In the course of borrowing some Zen Buddhist ideas from him, the deep ecology movement, unfortunately, missed the point—in a way that exposed his ideas to subsequent and misguided criticism, which in turn mistook what is at stake. The mistakes are, however, instructive.

Deep ecology promotes an "ultimate norm" of "biocentric equality," which evidences its narrower focus as compared with Zen, where the so-called inorganic world of mountains and waters is as worthy of reverence as the vegetal and animal realms.[38] The principle, or "intuition," of biocentric equality is based on the idea that "all nature has intrinsic worth" and states that "all things in the biosphere have an equal right to live and blossom and to reach their own individual forms of unfolding and self-realization."[39] Peter Harvey's paraphrase of Dōgen's idea of Buddha-nature comes perilously close to this formulation: "Each aspect of nature has an intrinsic value as part of ultimate reality, and to let go of oneself in full awareness of the sound of the rain or the cry of a monkey is to fathom this in a moment of non-dual awareness."[40] But to adopt the deep ecology principle as an ultimate norm would mean abandoning the work of human culture altogether: if, on discovering the tubercle bacillus, we had upheld its equal right to live and flourish, tuberculosis would have decimated our best artists long ago. And there are numerous viruses that, if given encouragement to "reach their own individual form of unfolding and self-realization," would bring the human race to a gruesome finish in very short order.

Whether or not influenced by the deep ecology reading, other scholars have argued more recently that Zen Buddhist ideas aren't of much help when dealing with environmental problems because they entail not only acceptance, but even celebration, of the all-devouring power of radical impermanence.[41] In a brief but incisive essay, Yuriko Saitō calls into question "the alleged Japanese love of nature" by examining its three "conceptual bases," and finds these lacking in their ability to "engender an ecologically desirable attitude" toward the natural world.[42] She argues that the attitude of *mono no aware* ("the pathos of things") that has informed so much of Japanese culture is too fatalistic to promote salutary ecological awareness, pointing out that deforestation or pollution can on this view be accepted as yet another instance of transience.[43] This is true, but let us focus on the role of impermanence, as understood in Zen, which provides Saitō's third basis for the love of nature.

"As respectful of and sensitive to nature's aesthetic aspect as [Zen Buddhism] might be," she writes, "it still does not contain within it a force necessary to condemn and fight the human abuse of nature." The reason for this has to do with Dōgen's insistence that "impermanence is itself Buddha-nature."[44] Saitō continues: "If everything is Buddha-nature because of impermanence, strip-mined mountains and polluted rivers must be considered as manifesting Buddha-nature as much as uncultivated mountains and unspoiled rivers." She concludes by observing that the notion of "responsive rapport" among all things, which is likewise found in Dōgen, "makes it impossible for any intervention in nature to be disharmonious with it."[45] This is a powerful objection, which we might as well intensify by invoking the phenomenon of radioactive contamination (sadly topical in Japan since the meltdown of the reactors at Fukushima): if everything human beings do is natural-manifesting, and in tune with, Buddha-nature—then plutonium waste, which remains lethal for at least ten thousand years and is so deadly that a tiny amount can vastly devastate life around it, would be a natural product that positively hums with Buddha-nature.

In a similar context, another commentator, Ian Harris, invokes John Stuart Mill's argument against the idea of "natural law" in order to show that the "extreme holism" advocated by Mahayana Buddhism is incoherent when it comes to questions of value. Mill argues that if natural law implies a conception of nature as "the sum of all phenomena, together with the causes which produce them, there is no mode of acting that is not conformable to nature in this sense of the term."[46] Harris argues that since Mahayana Buddhism holds just such a view of nature, there is no essential difference between the proposition that "all things are equally valuable" and the view that "everything is devoid of value." This would be an argument against the deep ecology principle of "biocentric equality," but it doesn't apply to the philosophy of Kūkai or Dōgen, as we shall see shortly.

Harris levels a similar criticism against "the Hua-Yen doctrine of the mutual interpenetration of all things" when used to promote reverence toward the natural world:

> The intention here is to show that since all things are inter-related we should act in a spirit of reverence towards them all. However, the things category of "all things" includes insecticides, totalitarian regimes and nuclear weapons and the argument therefore possesses some rather obvious problems.

Since ethics, for Harris, is in the business of generating "judgments about those states of affairs that are valuable and those that are not," this kind of Buddhism "suffers from a certain vacuity from the moral perspective." It's not at all clear that Huayan Buddhism would be making any ethical arguments in this context, and it's certain that neither Kūkai nor Dōgen would. But since Harris invokes in support of his argument the work of HAKAMAYA Noriaki, one of the primary exponents of "critical Buddhism" in Japan, it will be instructive to consider the critical Buddhists' criticisms before showing how they all miss the mark.

Hakamaya and his colleague MATSUMOTO Shirō argue that several apparently central ideas in Mahayana and Vajrayana Buddhism—*hongaku* and *busshō* prominently among them—are "not really Buddhist."[47] This seems rather narrow-minded, but our present concern is not with Buddhology and the history of Buddhist thought but rather with an interpretation of Kūkai and Dōgen that makes philosophical and practical sense without violating the historical context. Hakamaya claims that if "grasses, trees, mountains, and rivers have all attained Buddhahood, and sentient and non-sentient beings are all . . . included in the substance of Buddha," this leaves no room for the moral imperative (implied by *anatman*) to act selflessly to benefit others. But Kūkai and Dōgen certainly hold this view of grasses and trees, mountains and rivers, *and* are fully committed to promoting selfless activity that benefits others—though not just other humans, as the critical Buddhists would have it. That commitment is obvious throughout the writings of both thinkers. Apparently, the critical Buddhists fail to see this because their perspective is so anthropocentric, as evidenced in the distinction Matsumoto insists on "between two types of *tathāgata-garbha* thought":

> The first type could be considered the original type, that is, the idea of Buddha-nature as "immanent" [仏性内在論] or as "Buddha-nature in one's body." The second type is the more extreme type, and could be called

the "theory of the manifestation of Buddha-nature" [仏性顕在論] and is expressed in sayings like "Buddha-nature manifested as phenomenal existence such as trees and stones."[48]

The gloss "Buddha-nature in one's body" says it all: Matsumoto's extreme anthropocentrism prevents him from seeing that for Kūkai "one's body" participates in the Dharmakāya, and that for Dōgen "the true human body" is similarly "the entire world of the ten directions." What Matsumoto calls "the more extreme type" is simply the more expansively selfless and more comprehensively compassionate understanding.

In the context of a diatribe against the appropriation of the "enlightenment of grasses and trees" by *Nihonjinron* enthusiasts such as UMEHARA Takeshi, Matsumoto overstates his case:

> It is simply not logically possible to derive environmental ethics from an Eastern naturalism expressed in such phrases as "mountains, rivers, plants, and trees are all enlightened." Such "naturalism" leads nowhere but to the "natural state of doing nothing. . . ." In order to acknowledge the "wrongs" brought about by destruction of the natural world and to right these wrongs by changing our way of living, we need to think and to act.[49]

While Matsumoto's criticisms of the *Nihonjinron* proponents are well taken, they completely misunderstand the role of "mountains, rivers, plants, and trees" in the philosophies of Kūkai and Dōgen. There's no need to try to "derive an environmental ethics" from their thought: one simply has to appreciate their perspectives and ask what kinds of activity these would lead to in the contemporary context. Both figures were energetic and vigorous actors as well as thinkers, and they encouraged their audiences to behave in a similar way. They certainly relegated conceptual and logical thinking (of the kind praised by the critical Buddhists as the only thinking worth the name) to a secondary role, acknowledging its usefulness in certain contexts and pointing out its limitations in others. In its place, they advocated subtler, more responsive (because more deeply embodied) modes of seeing and hearing and engaging the particular emerging situation.

If we go back to the question left open at the end of our consideration of Kūkai, we need to ask how something like plutonium waste can be part of the cosmic embodiment of Dainichi Nyorai. It's admittedly hard to see how it would fit: as the Great Sun One who has "Thus Come" (the literal meaning of his name), Dainichi is certainly radiant—but also lethally radioactive? Since the Dharmakāya comprises awareness as well as the Five Great Processes, it must include artifacts—and even synthetic products such as plastics, chlorofluorocarbons, and radioactive waste. But the human introduction of nonbiodegradable elements that disrupt the dynamics of natural ecosystems is something unprecedented in the history of the biosphere, and the injection of such pathogens into the body of the earth is surely making it sick. We know now that the biosphere is only a minuscule part of the universe, and so this process can hardly be doing harm to the body of the cosmos, but from Kūkai's perspective it would surely constitute a desecration of, if not bodily injury to, the Dharmakāya, We can in any case ask, assuming the Dharmakāya is expounding the dharma, just what these newly introduced components are teaching us.

If natural phenomena demonstrate the ideas of impermanence and interdependence—in broad terms, the lessons of contemporary ecological science—what is the nonbiodegradable plastic with which we have littered the world's oceans telling us? It tells us that our carelessness is killing many kinds of marine life and thereby disrupting the fabric of interdependence on which our own existence depends. And since plastic takes longer to decompose than the life cycles of seabirds and fish, it shows us the dangers of making such relatively permanent things. Plutonium waste teaches a more extreme version of the same lesson: being the result of highly complex technological manipulations, it is infinitely more disruptive to ecological relationships than any naturally occurring radiation, and is again relatively nonimpermanent, remaining far more deadly for far longer than any natural toxins.

The deep ecology appropriation of Dōgen and the criticisms of Zen as quietist because it affirms the equal worth of all phenomena (and therefore the status quo) misunderstand his philosophy in two respects. Dōgen's perspectivism, which is similar to—and no doubt influenced by—the Daoist thought of Zhuangzi, undermines anthropocentrism by relativizing the human perspective with respect to those of other beings, both animate and inanimate.[50] But to show up the arrogant pretensions of our ego-based discriminations between pleasant and painful, good and bad, beautiful and ugly, and so forth, is not to deny that there is a certain patterning (which Zhuangzi calls *dao* and Dōgen "Buddha-nature") to the ways the world unfolds, such that all phenomena abide in their particular "dharma-positions."

In his discourse "Buddha-Nature," Dōgen says not just that human beings (or all sentient beings, or all phenomena) *have* Buddha-nature, but they all *are* Buddha-nature—or better, since, Dōgen views everything as activity: they all *do* it, or enact it.[51] Buddha-nature turns out to be not only "mountains, rivers, and the great earth ... the fins of a donkey and the beak of a horse" as well as "grass, trees, land and earth ... the sun, moon, and stars," but it's also "walls, tiles, and pebbles."[52] But when Dōgen equates impermanence with Buddha-nature, the focus is not on any particular phenomenon per se but rather on its interactions with other phenomena. Nor is it a matter of the simple sum of all impermanent phenomena: it's rather the organized totality of their dynamic interactions (which he calls *shitsu-u* 悉有, or "whole-being") that's important. As with Kūkai, human activities and artifacts participate too; but since what's crucial is *zenki*, the dynamic functioning of all phenomena together, there would be every reason to eliminate, rather than celebrate, something as toxic as plutonium waste. Indeed, Dōgen would want to ask the deeper question concerning the desires that drive us to consume so much energy that we think such contrivances as nuclear power plants, with all the dangers and problems that they involve, are a worthwhile component in the whole.

So, although for Mahayana Buddhists such as Dōgen the whole world is to be affirmed in its suchness—*nyo* (如)—at every moment, this means neither that every phenomenon is perfect nor that we shouldn't exert ourselves to improve things in the next moment. The world, as impermanent, is different every next moment—and this is what can give us some reason for optimism no matter how bad things become. They could get worse, but they can also improve; and if they are constantly changing anyway, it only takes a small nudge from us to affect the direction of that change for the better.[53] But does Dōgen offer any guidelines for our actions?

One thing is clear: our motivations, and our choice of what to do, had better come not from our egotistical desires—and especially for gain and fame—but rather from the energies and activities of the whole, to which the practice of entertaining multiple perspectives will have opened us. Kūkai powerfully evokes the salutary effects of confronting impermanence, and similarly for Dōgen what most effectively eliminates selfishness, profit, and fame as motives is the confrontation with, and embrace of, the world's impermanence—and our own.[54] When talking to the "Students of the Way" in his monastery, he says:

> When you truly see impermanence, egocentric mind does not arise, nor does desire for fame and profit. Out of fear that the days and nights are passing quickly, practice the Way as if you were trying to extinguish a fire enveloping your head. . . .

It goes without saying that you must consider the inevitability of death. . . .
You should be resolved not to waste time and refrain from doing meaning-
less things. You should spend your time carrying out what is worth doing.
Among the things you should do, what is the most important?[55]

The activity that responds to that question will be different for every one
of us, but for those who have incorporated Dōgen's teachings, the style of
the engagement will surely be ecological.[56]

The way of life, then, that Kūkai and Dōgen advocate involves energetic participation in the dynamic functioning of the whole world. Their
discourses on natural phenomena encourage a respectful and reciprocal
engagement with artifacts and things of nature and an attitude open to the
wisdom expressed in their words and letters. And their ideas give every
warrant for promoting (though it was unnecessary in their times) an overcoming of the hubris of our anthropocentrism in order to preserve and
enhance the workings of Buddha-nature all over this green and blue planet.

Notes

1. I have treated some of these themes before, in two essays that I would not now
recommend, since the attempt to reconcile the notions of *hosshin seppō* and *busshō* with
environmental toxins was, in retrospect, misguided. More worth reading is "Body-Mind
and Buddha-Nature: Dōgen's Deeper Ecology," in *Classical Japanese Philosophy*, ed.
James W. Heisig and Rein Raud, Frontiers of Japanese Philosophy 7 (Nagoya: Nanzan
Institute for Religion and Culture, 2010), 122–147, even though the discussion of
Buddha-nature is still flawed.

2. Jacqueline Stone, *Original Enlightenment and the Transformation of Medieval
Japanese Buddhism* (Honolulu: University of Hawai'i Press, 1999), 5.

3. William R. LaFleur, "Saigyō and the Buddhist Value of Nature," in *Nature in Asian
Traditions of Thought: Essays in Environmental Philosophy*, ed. J. Baird Callicott and
Roger T. Ames (Albany: SUNY Press, 1989), 184.

4. LaFleur, "Saigyō," 184–185; Stone, *Original Enlightenment*, 9.

5. LaFleur, "Saigyō," 185–186; see also Stone, *Original Enlightenment*, 11.

6. Kūkai, "Introduction to the Mahāvairocana Sūtra," cited in *Kūkai: Major Works*,
trans. Yoshito S. Hakeda (New York: Columbia University Press, 1972), 86. Subsequent
references will be abbreviated as *KMW*.

7. "The Difference between Exoteric and Esoteric Buddhism" (*Benkenmitsu nikyō
ron*), *KMW*, 154.

8. "Difference," *KMW*, 52.

9. "Attaining Enlightenment in This Very Body" (*Sokushin jōbutsu gi*), *KMW*, 228–
229. I translate *godai* as the Five Great Processes, rather than the customary "Five Great
Elements," since for Kūkai they are in constant dynamic transformation, and on the

assumption that they are modeled on the Chinese idea of *wuxing* (五行), the "five goings" or "processes" or "phases of transformation."

10. "Record of the Secret Treasury" (*Hizō ki*), cited in LaFleur, "Saigyō," 186–187; trans. slightly modified.

11. *KMW*, 254–255.

12. See Thomas P. Kasulis, "Reality as Embodiment: An Analysis of Kūkai's *Sokushinjōbutsu* and *Hosshin Seppō*," in *Religious Reflections on the Human Body*, ed. Jane Mane Law (Bloomington: Indiana University Press, 1995), 166–185. This essay is an exceptionally lucid exposition of these two key texts of Kūkai's.

13. Kūkai, "Exoteric and Esoteric," *KMW*, 152; "Introduction to All the Sutras," trans. Kasulis, in "Reality as Embodiment," 174.

14. *KMW*, 91.

15. *KMW*, 230–231.

16. "Introduction to All the Sutras," cited in Kasulis, "Reality as Embodiment," 174.

17. Dōgen, "Eating Bowls" (*Hou*), in *Treasury of the Trite Dharma Eye: Zen Master Dōgen's Shōbōgenzō*, 2 vols., ed. and trans. TANAHASHI Kazuaki (Boston: Shambhala, 2010), 2:720. Subsequent references to the *Shōbōgenzō* will be to this edition, by the volume and page number.

18. "Recommending Zazen to All People" (*Fukanzazengi*), *Shōbōgenzō*, 2:908.

19. "Instructions on Kitchen Work" (*Ji kuin mon*), *Shōbōgenzō*, 2:764.

20. "Instructions for the Tenzo" (*Tenso kyōkun*), in *Moon in a Dewdrop*, ed. and trans. TANAHASHI Kazuaki (San Francisco: North Point Press, 1987), 55.

21. "Instructions for the Tenzo," 56.

22. "Regulations for Eating Meals," in Roshi Jiyu Kennett, *Zen Is Eternal Life* (Emeryville, CA: Dharma Publications, 1976), 97.

23. "Regulations for Eating Meals," 100–101.

24. "Undivided Activity" (*Zenki*), *Shōbōgenzō*, 1:451 (trans. modified).

25. On the centrality of practice as activity (*gyōji*) to Dōgen's thinking, see Hee-Jin Kim, *Eihei Dōgen: Mystical Realist* (Boston: Wisdom Publications, 2004), chap. 3, esp. 67–76.

26. Dōgen, "Arousing Aspiration for the Unsurpassable" (*Hotsu mujō shin*), *Shōbōgenzō*, 2:650; see also "Continuous Practice" (*Gyōji*), part 1, *Shōbōgenzō*, 1:334.

27. "On the Endeavour of the Way" (*Bendōwa*), *Shōbōgenzō*, 1:6.

28. Although the title is usually translated as "The Mountains and Waters Sutra," Dōgen surely wasn't presuming to write a sacred text. It makes more sense to see it in the context of his idea of *mujo seppō* as introduced above.

29. "Mountains and Waters as Sutras" (*Sansuikyō*), *Shōbōgenzō*, 1:163, 161.

30. "Mountains and Waters as Sutras," 1:154.

31. "Mountains and Waters as Sutras," 1:155.

32. "Mountains and Waters as Sutras," 1:156.

33. "Mountains and Waters as Sutras," 1:158–159.

34. "Buddha Sutras" (*Bukkyō*), *Shōbōgenzō*, 2:538.

35. Dōgen, "Voices of the Valleys, Shapes of the Mountains" (*Keisei sanshoku*), *Shōbōgenzō*, 1:85.

36. "Voices of the Valleys," 1:86–87.

37. "Voices of the Valleys," 1:87–88.

38. Bill Devall and George Sessions, *Deep Ecology: Living as If Nature Mattered* (Salt Lake City: Peregrine Smith, 1985), 66, where the norm is attributed to the "founder" of deep ecology, Arne Naess. The authors refer to and quote from Dōgen several times: 11 (where he is invoked as a representative of Daoism), 100–101, 112–113, and 232–234.

39. Devall and Sessions, *Deep Ecology*, 69, 67.

40. Peter Harvey, *An Introduction to Buddhist Ethics* (Cambridge: Cambridge University Press, 2000), 177.

41. See, for example, Yuriko Saitō, "The Japanese Love of Nature: A Paradox," *Landscape* 31, no. 2 (1992), 1–8, who uncharacteristically misses the deeper point of Zen thought here. Also Ian Harris, "Getting to Grips with Buddhist Environmentalism," *Journal of Buddhist Ethics* 2 (1995), 173–190.

42. Saitō, "Japanese Love of Nature," 3.

43. Saitō, "Japanese Love of Nature," 5.

44. Dōgen, "Buddha-Nature" (*Busshō*), *Shōbōgenzō*, 1:243 (citing Huineng, the sixth patriarch of Chan Buddhism).

45. Saitō, "Japanese Love of Nature," 8.

46. John Stuart Mill, *Three Essays on Religion*, cited by Ian Harris in "Getting to Grips," 177–178.

47. See the essays in Jamie Hubbard and Paul L. Swanson, eds., *Pruning the Bodhi Tree: The Storm over Critical Buddhism* (Honolulu: University of Hawai'i Press, 1997).

48. MATSUMOTO Shiro, "Comments on Critical Buddhism," in Hubbard and Swanson, *Pruning the Bodhi Tree*, 162.

49. Matsumoto, "The Lotus Sūtra and Japanese Culture," in Hubbard and Swanson, *Pruning the Bodhi Tree*, 402–403.

50. For a more detailed discussion of this topic, see the section "Waters and Waters," in my essay "Body-Mind and Buddha-Nature: Dōgen's Deeper Ecology," 134–138.

51. Dōgen, "Buddha-Nature," 1:234–236.

52. Dōgen, "Buddha-Nature, 1:238, 250, 259.

53. See, in this context, Peter Hershock, *Chan Buddhism* (Honolulu: University of Hawai'i Press, 2004), 18; *Buddhism in the Public Sphere: Reorienting Global Interdependence* (New York: Routledge, 2006), 57.

54. See, for example, Kūkai's magnificent prose poem "Impermanence," *KMW*, 131–133.

55. "Points to Watch in Practicing the Way" (*Gakudō-yojinshu*), in *Dōgen Zen*, trans. Shōhaku Okumura (Kyoto: Soto Zen Center, 1988), 1; *Shōbōgenzō-zuimonki*, trans. Shōhaku Okumura (Kyoto: Soto Zen Center, 1987), 2–17, 97.

56. See the eloquent account of acting through "no-self" in the chapter "Self and No-Self," in James W. Heisig, *Nothingness and Desire* (Honolulu: University of Hawaii Press, 2013).

CHAPTER 5 | Sensation, Betweenness, Rhythms
Watsuji's Environmental Philosophy and Ethics in Conversation with Heidegger

INUTSUKA YŪ

We had a remarkable sunset one day last November.... When we reflected
that this was not a solitary phenomenon, never to happen again, but that it
would happen forever and ever, an infinite number of evenings, and cheer
and reassure the latest child that walked there, it was more glorious still.

—HENRY DAVID THOREAU, "Walking"[1]

5.1. What Is "Environment"? Watsuji on Environmental Philosophy and Ethics

"Environment"—a key word in today's society—is a relatively new concept. It is said that the English word was invented by Thomas Carlyle in
1827 in its modern meaning of "the aggregate of external circumstances,
conditions, and things that affect the existence and development of an individual, organism, or group."[2] In the case of the Japanese, research has
shown that the word *kankyō* (環境) appeared in the early twentieth century
as the translation of the imported words "environment," *Umgebung*, and
"milieu" in the Western sciences (these words were first translated as *tori-
maku koto* (取巻ク事) or *kanshō* (環象) at the end of the nineteenth century).[3] A contemporary dictionary will define *kankyō* as "external world"
or "outside entity," as seen from the perspective of its interaction with
humans or organisms.[4]

The definition we choose informs the direction that the discussion over
the environment takes. For example, since the emergence of the field of

environmental ethics in the 1970s, the debate between "nonanthropo-centric" and "anthropocentric" positions has been at the core of the discipline. The former, typically holding to the intrinsic value of "nature"[5] independent of human beings, has been criticized by the latter, whose representatives regard this value as the product of the investment by human beings. No end to this debate is in sight, and the theoretical orientation of researchers has been criticized as ill adapted to respond to real-world challenges. Many researchers have accordingly taken a more practical orientation in the field, notably in the form of the "environmental pragmatisms" popular since the 1990s. The real problem, however, does not lie in the theoretical nature of the discussion, but rather in the perceived dichotomy between humanity and nature that informs it. In *Environmental Ethics*, David Richard Keller defines nature as "nonhuman,"[6] but this may represent an inadequate point of departure. Might we not bring the environment into the realm of human ethics by re-examining concepts such as "nature," "environment," and "humanity"?

In this chapter, the thoughts of the Japanese philosopher WATSUJI Tetsurō (和辻哲郎, 1889–1960) will provide us with the necessary bearings. His writings, especially on the concept of *fūdo* (風土), have recently attracted attention in the context of the attempt within environmental ethics to overcome the dichotomy of humanity and nature.[7] To re-examine our concept of environment is at the same time to re-examine our concept of humanity. In brief, this chapter will demonstrate that Watsuji proposes the environment as an entity that is not external to human existence, but rather internal; to be precise, it is internalized through one medium of sensation and action. To bring this continuity into view, this chapter will look at the development of Watsuji's philosophy while tracing his reading and criticisms of Martin Heidegger. Both philosophers criticize the view that the environment is outside of human beings. Watsuji's philosophy, however, follows a different path, and examining his stand against Heidegger is useful when it comes to understanding the whole picture of Watsuji's analysis of humanity and the environment.

5.2. Discussing "Sensation" in Watsuji's "Consideration of National Character"

Is the dichotomy between humanity and nature valid? If not, what alternative model might we envisage? This section will address these questions by looking at Watsuji's notes for his lectures given at Kyoto Imperial University just after his stay in Germany from 1927 to 1928. While these lecture notes are relatively neglected in scholarly research even in Japanese, their significance lies in Watsuji's interpretation of Heidegger during his early phase, and they are also interesting in the context of environmental philosophy.[8]

The title of the lecture notes is "Consideration of National Character, 1928–1929: The First Draft of *Climate: On the Study of Human Being*."[9] At the time when he returned to Japan from Germany, Marxism was attracting increasing attention from intellectuals.[10] In these lecture notes written in a mixture of Japanese and German, Watsuji criticizes Marxism, more precisely the work of Heinrich Cunow, for focusing exclusively on the historical effect of human productivity and labor systems on national character.[11] He then seeks to add to this perspective the significance of the "natural base" of the latter.[12] It is in this context that he cites Heidegger's analysis of Dasein (literally "being-there") in *Being and Time* (*Sein und Zeit*, 1927), which Watsuji encountered during his stay in Germany.[13]

Watsuji begins the theoretical section of his notes by saying, "I think that the significance of weather [*Wetter*], climate [*Klima*], soil [*Boden*], and landscape [*Landschaft*] in their most fundamental state can be revealed by Heidegger's analytic [*Analytik*] of Dasein."[14] Following Heidegger's discussion in sections 12 to 18 in *Being and Time*, Watsuji first rejects the naturalistic view that considers climate or soil as the outside world that influences human beings.[15] Dasein as "being-in-the-world [*In-der-Welt-Sein*]" is more fundamental than the opposition of human beings and the outside world or the opposition of subject and object. "Knowing" (the outside world) is a "mode [*Modus*]" in which "concern [*Besorgen*]" holds itself back from any kinds of practical activities so that Dasein lacks its essence, which is "care [*Sorge*]." Here the "opposition of human and the environment" is regarded as "opposition of human and nature," which is a false point of departure in conventional ontology.

Natural objects are things merely abstracted from everyday practice. The "world [*Welt*]" is not a thing external to Dasein, but is rather inherent to Dasein.[16] In the world, our "dealings [*Umgang*]" with the "entities within-the-world [*innerweltlich*]" diverge according to the different modes of "concern [*Besorgen*]." Within them, the closest sort of dealings to us are not perceptual cognition but "the concern that manipulates things and puts them to use [*das hantierende, gebrauchende Besorgen*]." The closest things that reveal our existence are therefore not the objects of "knowing" but "equipment [*Zeug*]." Dealings with such equipment are conceived as an appropriation of the "in-order-to [*Um-zu*]." For example, the hammer is used "to hammer." The equipment itself, however, does not appear as the main focus of our action but is rather encountered in its usability, the "towards-which [*Wozu*]," as, for example, "to produce a shoe." The produced shoe is also discovered as equipment "to be worn." At the same time, the production practice guides us to the "whereof [*Woraus*]," materials like leather, threads, and nails. Thus "Nature" is consequently discovered at the same time through the use of equipment: the forest as the collection of wood, and the wind as that which fills a sail. In addition, the product does not only refer to the usability and materials, but also to others as a carrier or user of the product (for example, a wearer of shoes). Also, the "environing Nature [*Umweltnatur*]" is discovered through equipment. A sheltered railway platform takes account of potential bad weather, a lamp indicates the transition from light to darkness, and a clock refers to the position of the sun. On the other hand, there are things that are missing in our dealings with the world, not in the sense of being nonfunctional, but rather insofar as they are not "to hand [*zur Hand*]." Thus the world appears through the harnessing of equipment. At the same time, Dasein assigns itself to the equipment, that is to say, it assigns itself in such a way that a "for-the-sake-of-which [*Worumwillen*]" is understood as the "with-which of an involvement [*Womit einer Bewandtnis*]," which becomes self-understanding of Dasein. This is the phenomenon of the world in which Dasein becomes absorbed in harnessing equipment, and it is in these terms that Watsuji focuses on Heidegger's analysis of Dasein and the world.

Here Watsuji raises the following three questions.[17] First, are our dealings with the world to be defined exclusively in terms of "the concern that manipulates things and puts them to use [*das hantierende, gebrauchende Besorgen*]"?[18] For example, it is difficult to consider this concern in the case of "clothing and involvement [*Bewandtnis*] to wear." The real involvement in this case must be "to shelter from coldness." It does not come from "potentiality-for-Being [*Seinkönnen*]" of Dasein, but "entities within-the-world [*innerweltlich Seiendes*]." The same goes for "climate [*Klima*]," "soil [*Boden*]," and "landscape [*Landschaft*]."

Second, is it valid to regard "entities within-the-world [*innerweltliches*]" only in their "character as equipment [*Zeugcharakter*]"?[19] While "coldness" and "rain" can be sometimes used as the "equipment [*Zeug*]" for food processing and agriculture, it is clear that there are closer forms of dealings if we look at the plentiful production of equipment like clothing and umbrellas. Wind is more fundamentally "a strong wind," "a breeze," or "a mild wind" than "a wind to fill a sail" or "a wind to turn a windmill." It can be said that Heidegger only considers nature from the point of view of equipment, dismissing that aspect of nature which is given and exceeds our control.

Third, is it valid to consider "concern [*Besorgen*]" as the only mode of Dasein?[20] Heidegger chooses this word to indicate that the being of Dasein is to be made visible as "care [*Sorge*]." From this viewpoint, those without the "concern" are considered as the modes (*Modi*) that fall or deteriorate (*verfallen*). However, what are called "concernful [*besorgend*] dealings" should include not only care but also moments of "enjoyment [*Geniessen*]" or "sensation [*Fühlen*]." In the case of clothing, "involvement [*Bewandtnis*]" not only fulfills the function of shelter from the cold, but clothing must also be comfortable to the touch; we choose wool or cotton. It can be said that "clothing" is the equipment that is to satisfy our sensation of touch; yet in this case "the concernful [*besorgend*] dealings become the enjoying [*geniessend*] dealings."[21]

> If we say that enjoyment [*Geniessen*] (sensation [*Fühlen*]) is a mode [*Modus*], here one must clearly accept the two aspects of concern [*Besorgen*], namely *the active side [aktive Seite] and the passive side [passive Seite]*. This is important for matters like weather [*Wetter*], climate [*Klima*], or landscape [*Landschaft*]. In everyday dealings, a wind is "a cold wind," "a pleasant wind," or "a fresh wind" more generally than "a wind that turns a windmill": they are what Dasein *passively* enjoys in the form of being "given."[22]

While in our dealings with equipment we only encounter the things that we seek (which are, thus, those we lack), in nature we encounter the things that we do not seek but which are already given. If we do not accept this aspect, it will be difficult to explain the notion of "aesthetic empathy [*ästhetisches Einfühlen*]."[23]

Considering these points, Watsuji concludes as follows:

> If we notice that, in the structure of Dasein, the environing Nature [*Umweltnatur*] is discovered not only in its character as equipment [*Zeugcharakter*] but also in enjoying [*geniessend*] (sensing [*fühlend*]), it will be revealed how determinative [*bestimmend*] the climate [*Klima*], landscape [*Landschaft*], etc. as the *environing Nature* [*Umweltnatur*] are for Dasein. Now the *burdensome character* [*Lastcharakter*] that is important for Heidegger's Dasein must include one new moment [*Moment*].[24]

According to Heidegger, "state-of-mind [*Befindlichkeit*]," or "mood [*Stimmung*]" experienced in everyday existence, is the first way the existence of Dasein is disclosed as *Da*.[25] Dasein discovers itself already in a certain mood. We know nothing of where it comes from or where it goes because it occurs by itself. Watsuji here insists on the need to highlight the participation of the "environing Nature [*Umweltnatur*]."[26] In the case of a "fresh mood in the morning," there is a unity of "fresh air" and "feeling of freshness." Although we cannot admit any causality between a certain air condition and the "freshness" of the mental situation, one must accept the power of "entities within-the-world [*innerweltliches*]" to burden Dasein in "finding itself in the mood that it has [*gestimmtes Sich-befinden*]." Heidegger indeed recognizes this relationship in the case of "fear." If we allow this, we must admit all climatic and landscapic "entities ready-to-hand [*Zuhandenes*]" that can participate in the mood being actively involved in the "Being-attuned [*Gestimmtsein*]" of Dasein. The "burdensome character [*Lastcharakter*]" of Dasein bears not only the past ("Being-already [*Schon-Sein*]") but also the "environing Nature [*Umweltnatur*]."

Hence, Watsuji's claim is to propose what is generally understood as "sensation" as a key aspect of the self-understanding of Dasein. In fact, in his subsequent article "Climate [*Fūdo* 風土]" based on these notes, he redescribes the analysis above as "sensational interaction [*kanjuteki na kakawari* 感受的なか > はり]."[27] While one may find the concept "sensation" and the distinction of "active aspect" and "passive aspect" as retrograde to subject-object dualism, Watsuji's intention is otherwise. Watsuji's claim above is probably informed by the discussion of aesthetic empathy (cf. Theodore Lipps and ABE Jirō: Watsuji, however, judges that the theory of empathy could not escape from subject-object dualism)[28] as mentioned above and also his study of Buddhism carried out before his journey to Germany. In the lecture notes titled "History of Buddhist Ethical Thought [*Bukkyō rinri shisōshi* 仏教倫理思想史]" (1925–1926), Watsuji considers the problem of sensation (感受) in the concept of *ju* (受), which is the translation of Sanskrit *vedanā* (sensation, feeling) of the five aggregates.[29] He evaluates this translation positively for including the passive aspect of the meaning of the original word: the passivity existing in sensational contact (受 literally has the meaning of "receiving," and the word "passive" in Japanese is written as *judōteki* 受動的). This is a form of situation that is both physical and psychological and not merely a psychological situation. While feeling is generally considered a "subjective state," there is no subject that feels from the Buddhist viewpoint of "no-self" (*anātman*): only "something sensed" exists. Not somebody seeing a flower and sensing joy but only the impression of a flower exists in the form of *ju* (受), or "sensation." Watsuji relates this position of "no-self" to the philosophies of Kant and Husserl.[30] After encountering Heidegger's *Being and Time*, Watsuji reinterprets sensation as the basis for the self-understanding of Dasein.

5.3. Conceptualizing Betweenness in Watsuji's *Ethics as the Study of Human Being* and *Climate*

The previous section showed Watsuji's analysis of how sensation determines our self-understanding. Now the question is, when one discovers oneself in a certain sensation, is one alone? We can attain the means to respond to this question from the following works of Watsuji, which address the sociality of human existence and the repetitive nature of climate.

After returning to Japan, Watsuji started his research in ethics and published *Ethics as the Study of Human Being* (*Ningen no gaku toshite no rinrigaku* 人間の学としての倫理学) in 1934. His analysis in the notes "Consideration of National Character" was partially published with some modification as an article titled "Climate" (*Fūdo* 風土) in 1929 and completely as a book titled *Climate: On the Study of Human Being* (*Fūdo: Ningengakuteki kōsatu* 風土：人間学的考察) in 1935. What Watsuji obtained through this research in ethics is the understanding that human existence is marked by individual-social duality.[31] He notes that the word *ningen* (人間), meaning "human being" in Japanese, had originally meant "society" in Chinese and that the words *seken* (世間) and *yononaka* (世の中) mean not only "world," but also "society" and "public."[32] Watsuji then tries to examine these facts by taking the word *aidagara* (間柄) as a key. Our action and self-understanding are determined by a certain human relationship or "betweenness [*aidagara*]" and at the same time such betweenness is formed through our actions.[33] From such a viewpoint, Watsuji distinguishes "human existence in 'public [*yononaka*]'" from Heidegger's "being-in-the-world [*In-der-Welt-Sein*]," saying that the point of departure for the latter is the relationship between things and me and not between human beings.[34] While Watsuji acknowledges Heidegger's notion of *Mitdasein*, he regards it as "juxtaposition of individuals" discovered through equipment.[35] The world or public (*seken*) formed through human actions presupposes a certain transience and locality.[36] The article "Climate" and the book *Climate* were written within the framework of this project.

In the preface to *Climate*, Watsuji criticizes Heidegger for overemphasizing temporality and underestimating spatiality.[37] Watsuji sees the reason for this in Heidegger's limiting of Dasein to individuality and his overlooking of individual-social duality. Although we can observe continuity here with Watsuji's criticism at the end of the last section, now his criticism is further developed into the problem of spatiality and temporality, and the notions of individuality and sociality appear anew. The analysis of *fūdo*, or "climate," provides the connection between these different elements.

Before turning to the text, however, let us consider the meaning of *fūdo* (風土). Literally, it is "wind" (*fū* 風) and "soil" (*do* 土). One encyclopedia states that "the word originated in China, and has signified the fertility of the earth corresponding to the seasonal circulation. . . . Because people assume different outward appearances according to the differing fertility of the regions, despite the same nature of human beings, the word came to take on the meaning of regional difference in the *Book of the Later Han*."[38] "Climate," the usual translation for *fūdo*, is problematic, as noted by Augustin Berque, who translated Watsuji's book *Fūdo* into French.[39] Berque and some other researchers prefer "human milieu," which avoids the naturalistic notion of the word "climate" and emphasizes Watsuji's rather phenomenological view. The word *fūdo* is, indeed, different from "climate," as the former is typically used in the relation to human beings and the latter gives the impression that it is related to meteorological phenomena. But it must be cautioned that it is also different from "milieu" in the sense that *fūdo* implies the repetitive or rhythmic aspect of weathers, seasons, or human activities. In this chapter, the word "climate" is used as the translation of *fūdo* to emphasize this notion.

Now, let us look at the text. Watsuji himself describes *fūdo*, or climate, as follows:

> What I call here climate [*fūdo*] is the general term for weather, meteors, the nature of rocks and soils, topography, landscape, etc. of a certain land. . . . There is a good reason to examine it [nature as the environment of human beings] as "climate" rather than to problematize it as "nature." To gain a clearer understanding, the phenomenon of climate must first be outlined.
>
> We all inhabit a certain land. Therefore, regardless of whether we wish it or not, the natural environment of that land "environs" us. . . . However, our problem is whether the climate as everyday direct reality can be regarded *exclusively* as natural environment.[40]

In the earlier article "Climate," the corresponding paragraph states that its objective is to question the common understanding of climate as our "outside."[41] While this parallels Heidegger's challenge to the view of an "outside world," Watsuji's focus is not on the "world" of Heidegger but "climate" (*fūdo*) and "public" (*seken*).

To understand the "phenomenon of climate," Watsuji provides the example of "coldness."[42] What is "coldness"? He rejects the view that it is the atmosphere characterized by a certain temperature that results in us feeling cold. Rather, the phenomenon of coldness first occurs and then we discover ourselves feeling cold and the cold atmosphere around us. The distinction between subject and object, or the distinction between "us" and "cold atmosphere" in this case, is a misunderstanding. In the phenomenon of coldness, we reside in the cold atmosphere. That is to say, borrowing a term from Heidegger, our state is characterized as "being out [*soto ni deteiru* 外に出ている] (*ex-sistere*)." Watsuji identifies this state with the "intentionality" of phenomenology.

Here proposed is human existence, which extends outward from the individual body. Yet Watsuji further claims that we are still operating here from the perspective of individual consciousness.[43] In reality, as there was no problem using the term "we" (*wareware* 我々) instead of "I" (*ware* 我れ) in the analysis above, who experiences this coldness is not just "I" but "we." We feel the same coldness together. We can therefore talk about the weather in our daily greetings. Here is observed a state of "I as we" and "we as I."

> Thus the structure of "being out" also exists as *being out among other I's* already before being out among "things" such as cold atmosphere. This is *not an intentional relation* but "betweenness [*aidagara*]." Therefore, it is primarily "we" as betweenness that discover our selves in the coldness.[44]

We experience such coldness in relation to a series of weather patterns in a certain land, that is, climate.[45] Thus we discover ourselves as betweenness in "climate." Yet this discovery or "understanding" does not necessarily lead to conscious self-reflection. Rather than engaging the consciousness of "I," it induces the practical action of keeping out the cold, which is directed not necessarily to oneself, but rather to the people around us. Furthermore, forms of action are not always produced spontaneously: they are rather determined by preexisting habits such as putting on clothes or seeking the protection of housing. "In the 'interaction' with coldness, we integrate ourselves individually and socially within various practices for keeping out coldness."[46]

It is here that the repetitive nature of climate comes into play:

> In coldness or hotness, storm or flood, we do not protect each other and work together simply among ourselves in the present. We possess the prolonged

accumulation of understanding from our ancestors. The style of housing is said to be a fixation of a *way of building houses*. This *way* cannot be realized without the interaction with climate.[47]

The accumulation over generations presupposes the reiteration of the same phenomena of climate in the region, resulting in the formation of "ways of self-understanding [*jikoryōkai no shikata* 自己了解の仕方]"[48] of human existence over individuals. Therefore, the environment must be not just static but repetitive climate.

This is what Watsuji calls the unity of "historicality [*rekishisei* 歴史性]" and "climaticity [*fūdosei* 風土性]" of human existence.[49] In such a unity, history acquires its body, and this is part of human existence. Watsuji criticizes the idea of individual "being toward death [*Sein zum Tode*]" and proposes the social "being toward life [*sei e no sonzai* 生への存在]."[50] This is because the extension to which human existence functions is over an individual body and across generations. Watsuji says climaticity and historicality emerge from the spatiality and temporality of human existence, but the latter are not explained in detail in *Climate*. The detail is rather in *Ethics*.

5.4. Understanding Rhythms in Watsuji's *Ethics*

In the previous section, we have seen the way in which human existence extends outward from individuality via the repetitive phenomena of climate. However, its description in *Climate* has confusing aspects, as the theoretical section is summary in character and the analytical sections on different climate types have been often criticized as environmental determinism. In reality, in the thought of Watsuji, even the seasons do not exist without human beings. As Watsuji himself noted in *Climate*,[51] the detailed analysis of human existence and its spatiality and temporality were provided in his later work *Ethics* (*Rinrigaku* 倫理学) (1937–1949), Watsuji's principal work further developed from *Ethics as the Study of Human Being*.

In *Ethics*, the problem of sensation is still addressed yet further developed as the interaction between human beings. My act of seeing you is already determined by your act of seeing me.[52] That is to say, at that time, our consciousnesses mutually affect and penetrate. "When you get anger, my consciousness is colored by the anger overall. When I get sadness, your consciousness is also affected."[53] When we see and sense "things," we are not alone but "see them together" and "sense them together."[54] Natural phenomena are not directly perceived by individuals but already embedded in human society.[55]

While Watsuji's stand against Heidegger remains the same from *Ethics as the Study of Human Being*, arguing that the German philosopher addresses principally the dealings between human and equipment and not relations between human beings,[56] in this book we can observe an interesting application of Heidegger's analysis of Dasein to "betweenness":

> The essential nature of the activity in betweenness [*aidagara*] is the fact that the subjects who find themselves in betweenness are in mutual determination *already beforehand*. In the case of the relationship between me and you, the simplest relationship, my action on you is already determined by you, and your response is already determined by me. In such mutual determination, betweenness unfolds. In simple dealings such as when I see and call you and you look back and respond to me, it is clearly indicated in what kind of betweenness is the relationship between me and you. . . . Thus we can say that the betweenness of me and you is nothing else but *mutual understanding* [*sōgo ryōkaisei* 相互了解性]. Of course, this understanding may be lacking in various ways, but its absence can cause various tragedies, as many literary works treat it as their theme. This shows that mutual understanding is a core element of betweenness. Various moods, affects, emotions, wills, etc. from me to you, or from you to me, stand on this mutual understanding and are not phenomena only within either my consciousness or yours.[57]

Here one can see Watsuji's strategy, which uses the same concepts of dealings, understanding, absence, and mood as he highlighted in "Consideration of National Character."

From such fundamental "betweenness," the spatiality of human existence is drawn. The unity and confrontation between me and you as practical subjects produce "inside" and "outside," which are different from naturalistic space.[58] The wider "public" also assumes certain spatiality—the spatiality that can be formed and deformed by traffic and communication systems. Human existence, which splits into multiple subjects and unifies them through actions, has such "subjective extent."[59] The space of the natural sciences results from the spatiality of human existence.

Furthermore, Watsuji's theory of space is closely interconnected with that of time. "Spatiality does not exist independently from temporality. The spatial character of human existence already implies its temporal character."[60] Taking the phenomena of traffic as an example, Watsuji analyzes the moment of "already beforehand."[61] Our walking is determined by a certain "way to go [*yuku kata*]" or "destination": a place of work, a friend's house, and so on, already exists in the walking action beforehand. Such "already beforehand" has its significance as the mode of existence of the walker beyond his consciousness. Here, the "beforehand" of "already beforehand" means the "possible betweenness" or possible human relationship that gives direction to any kind of practical action. It appears as the "future." Also, the human relationship that exists in the present act of walking "beforehand" cannot determine the act without existing "already" in some sense. Therefore, the past "betweenness" does not disappear but exists in the present action.[62] That is to say, a past human relationship as a possible future supports our present action. Thus the human relationship as revealed through simple traffic involves not just the subjective extension but also the temporal structure of the unity of past and future in the present.

As the spatiality of human beings produces space, time emerges from the temporality of human existence.[63] The most practically used concept of "time" signifies such moments of human relationships. There are, for example, the times when one is born, marries, or dies, or more ordinarily when people meet or separate. Such "times" are immeasurable, and they all imply the "opportunities" or serve as the "occasions" for human relationships.

> From such "times," however, we can choose the "times" that repeat daily the most frequently: the "times" from which the fateful crises have been excised as much as possible. The time to wake up, time to eat, time to sleep, and more widely, time to sow seeds, time to harvest, and so forth. Because of their regularizing, such "times" have been fixed *publicly* in human existence. Especially the labor relationships of human beings are determined by such public "times." They are the "hours" in small and the "seasons" in large. The hours are realized by bells or horns because they are public. Likewise, the seasons are realized by festivals, ceremonies, or holidays. The measurements are only possible in terms of such hours or seasons, but their standards were primitively the sun and the moon.[64]

With the advent of measurement, time comes to be considered as a continuous flux. The hours and seasons, however, do not leave the horizon of human existence. The hours are measured because they are fixed publicly and the seasons are measured according to the practices of collaborative farming and agricultural practices.[65] The naturalistic time only exists by virtue of the abstraction of human relationship from them.[66]

These "occasions" emerging from human relationships in turn provide the rhythms of human life. This is the origin of years and history in nations.[67]

> They [occasions] provide a certain rhythm to the subjective nexus in human organizations: the one deeply connected to this rhythm from the origin is the *alteration of day and night*. Usually activity is done *while it is light* and rest takes place while it is dark. Therefore, the subjective nexus consequently fixes the *daily* patterns of behavior according to this rhythm. It is true that the unit of *a day* indicates the revolution of the sun, but originally it is based on such *unity of subjective nexus*. . . . This rhythm of day and night is included in the rhythm of waxing and waning of the moon. . . . People set days of rest and days of festivals within a series of workdays and regulate their lives. This rhythm of the moon/month [*tsuki* 月] is further included in the rhythm of seasonal circulation. The time to sow seeds, the time to harvest, etc., have been central to human existence since the remotest past, and it is the seasonal circulation that allows us to determine such periods. . . . Then from one circulation of four seasons the unit of a "year" is created. Again it is also originally the *unity of human existence*, not a mere abstract unit of time.[68]

In *Ethics as the Study of Human Being*, Watsuji writes that just looking at "a part of our everyday experience in close proximity to us, a simple event such as waking up in the morning and eating meal" can reveal the collection of places and things connected to a certain form of collective life, such as our bedroom, pajamas, living room, dishes, and so on, and the shared understanding of people in using them.[69] We can observe certain rhythms inherent to them. There is no place in which humans live without rhythms. These rhythms do not exist independently from human existence but are born because of its "betweenness." The environment—here there is no distinction between natural and social—is integrated within human existence with rhythms that in turn support cooperative life.

In the end, even a relationship of mutual trust cannot exist without this foundation. Human relationships, which exist "already beforehand," enable trust in human society. Watsuji gives the following appraisal of trust:

> The ground of trust exists in the spatial and temporal structure of human existence. In other words, the law of human existence that develops spatially and temporally enables trust. Consequently, the plausible proposition "human relationships are built on trust" is actually the inverse of reality. The

ground on which human relationships stand is the law of spatial and temporal human existence, which is therefore the *ground* of trust. On this ground human relationships stand and so does trust. Thus, human relationships are relationships of trust at the same time, and trust is established simultaneously wherever human relationships are.[70]

Trust provides the criteria for the goodness and badness of human behavior, as betraying trust has been considered bad from the most ancient of times.[71] Relationships of trust are also the basis of a practical "sincerity/truthfulness [*makoto* まこと]" to be realized in our society, which is something that ethics have strived to achieve since the remotest past.[72] Here the environment involving rhythms is a part of our existence that supports our ethical life.

5.5. Environment *within* Human Existence

An attempt has been made in this chapter to trace the development of Watsuji's analysis of humanity and the environment following his encounter with Heidegger's *Being and Time*. First, from Heidegger's analysis of Dasein, Watsuji obtained the idea that underlining our practice and self-understanding is the sensation of relating to the environment. While conducting his research in ethics, he proposed the significance of climate for human existence by establishing the individual-social duality. Human existence extends out from the individual body as "betweenness" in the present and also over generations that are connected by the repetition of the phenomena of climate. This repetitive nature of climate is in fact discovered through the rhythms that emerge from the spatiality and temporality of human existence. In other words, the environment is not an entity external to human existence; it is rather integrated into this individual and social existence. Within this structure of human existence, trust and our ethical life are realized.

Our environment is integral to our life, understood not only in biological but also in ethical terms. This understanding provides a base for a new anthropocentric environmental ethics, which considers the environment a part of human existence and integrates it into human ethics. It opposes non-anthropocentrism, which claims that "human beings are a part of nature"; it rather proposes that "the environment is a part of human existence." Yet it also opposes modern anthropocentrism, which takes as its point of departure the independent individual. Watsuji's environmental philosophy and ethics provide the means for expressing the significance of the environment as an integral element of human existence with individual-social duality, and not just in terms of biodiversity or as a form of subjective pleasure, which tends to be interchangeable with other interests.

Today the environment is conceived as a mere "outside" entity and thus easily destroyed. Furthermore, the segmentation of industries and the development of mechanization, which possess particular rhythms, have made the rhythms of human life more and more inconsistent. The resulting unpredictability risks undermining trust relations in everyday life. We may find today's diverse antimarket movements sharing the intention to regenerate rhythms. Watsuji's thought provides us with the means to envisage the problem of our environment not just ecologically but more comprehensively.

There is a vast potential for further research on just such rhythms. Newly born human babies do not possess the distinction between day and night, yet soon adjust themselves to the rhythms of their surroundings after birth. Recently, the daily rhythm shared by living organisms generally—the circadian rhythm—has been investigated at the genetic level.[73] The rhythms that pertain to human life are more complex and include an ethical dimension. While the notion of rhythm has also been the focus of recent work in human geography,[74] the significance of Watsuji's theory drawn from the analysis of human existence lies in the ethical depth that it adds to such an understanding of the environment.

Last but not least, research in the field is of course important for environmental studies. This research does not obviate the need, however, to re-examine the concepts of "environment" and "humanity." The philosophical project of transforming current concepts, and the vision of the world that follows from them, shall be continued.

Notes

1. Henry David Thoreau, "Walking," in *The Natural History Essays* (Salt Lake City: Peregrine Smith Books, 1989), 134–135.

2. Robert Hendrickson, *The Facts on File Encyclopedia of Word and Phrase Origins*, 4th ed. (New York: Facts on File, 2008), 282.

3. SODA Osamu, "*Nihon ni okeru yōgo 'kankyō' no dōnyū katei*" ("The Introductory Process of the Word '*Kankyo*' in Japan"), *Waseda Studies in Social Sciences* 3, no. 3 (2003): 65–72; TAKANO Shigeo, "'*Tetsugaku-jii' no wasei kango: Sono goki no seiseihō, zōgohō*" ("Word Stems in '*Tetsugaku-jii*': Word Stems of the Japanese-Made Chinese Words and the Method of Word Creation and Formation"), *Bulletin of the Institute of Humanities, Kanagawa University* 37 (2004): 105.

4. *Kōjien*, 6th ed. (electronic version) (Tokyo: Iwanami Shoten, 2008).

5. Here the word "nature" is often used interchangeably with "natural environment" or simply "environment."

6. "Introduction: What Is Environmental Ethics?" in *Environmental Ethics: The Big Questions*, ed. David Richard Keller (West Sussex: Blackwell, 2010), 1.

7. e.g. Augustin Berque, *Être humains sur la Terre, principes d'éthique de l'écoumène* (*Being Human on the Earth: Principles of Ecumenal Ethics*) (Paris: Gallimard, 1996); KAMEYAMA Sumio, *Kankyōrinri to fūdo: Nihonteki shizenkan no gendaika no shiza* (*Environmental Ethics and Fūdo: A Perspective on Modernization of the Japanese View of Nature*) (Tokyo: Otsuki Shoten, 2005); James McRae, "Triple-Negation: Watsuji Tetsuro on the Sustainability of Ecosystems, Economies, and International Peace," in *Environmental Philosophy in Asian Traditions of Thought*, ed. John Baird Callicott and James McRae (Albany: SUNY Press, 2014), 359–375.

8. About these lecture notes, also read INUTSUKA Yū, "*Fūsui to kankyōrinrigaku o saikō suru: Watsuji no Heidegger dōguron hihan o tegakari ni*" ("Rethinking Feng Shui and Environmental Ethics: Watsuji Tetsurō's Critique of Heidegger's Analysis of Tools"), in *Kaze o kanjiru: Kotonaru discipline to deau toki* (*Feeling the Wind: When We Encounter a Different Discipline*), ed. MURAMATSU Shin, ZHAO Chi, and KONDO Ryosuke (Tokyo: University of Tokyo, Integrated Human Science Program for Cultural Diversity, 2015), 9–22.

9. The Japanese title of this work is *Kokuminsei no kōsatsu, Shōwa* 3-4 nen, "*Fūdo*" *Ningengakuteki kōsatsu no daiikkō* 国民性の考察 昭和3-4年 "風土"人間学的考察の第一稿. WATSUJI Tetsurō, *Watsuji Tetsurō Zenshū Bekkan 1* [(*Complete Works of Watsuji Tetsurō*, supplementary volume 1) (Tokyo: Iwanami Shoten, 1992), 373. Hereafter cited as "WTZ B1." The other volumes from the *Complete Works* will also be cited as "WTZ" with the number of the volume. While I use my own translation for Watsuji's quotes in this chapter, there are also other versions of translated works of Watsuji: e.g., WATSUJI Tetsurō, *Climate and Culture: A Philosophical Study*, trans. Geoffrey Bownas (New York: Greenwood Press, 1988) (translation of *Fūdo: Ningengakuteki Kōsatsu*); WATSUJI Tetsurō, *Watsuji Tetsurō's Rinrigaku, Ethics in Japan*, trans. YAMAMOTO Seisaku and Robert Edgar Carter (Albany: SUNY Press, 1996).

10. KARUBE Tadashi, *Hikari no ryōgoku: Watsuji Tetsurō* (*The Realm of Light: Politics and Humanity in the Thought of Watsuji Tetsurō*) (Tokyo: Sōbunsha, 1995; reprint Tokyo: Iwanami Shoten, 2010), 183–186.

11. WTZ B1, 376–378.

12. WTZ B1, 378.

13. In this section, I refer to Martin Heidegger, *Being and Time*, trans. John Macquarrie and Edward Robinson (New York: Harper and Row, 1962) for English translation of Heideggerian terminology.

14. WTZ B1, 380.

15. WTZ B1, 380–382.

16. WTZ B1, 382–388.

17. WTZ B1, 388–392.

18. WTZ B1, 388.

19. WTZ B1, 389.

20. WTZ B1, 390.

21. WTZ B1, 391.

22. WTZ B1, 391.

23. WTZ B1, 392.

24. WTZ B1, 392.

25. WTZ B1, 392. The corresponding sections are 29 to 31 in *Being and Time*.

26. WTZ B1, 393.

27. WTZ B1, 399.

28. WTZ B1, 392.

29. WTZ 19, 51–52.

30. WTZ 19, 56. Watsuji says that the philosophies of Buddhism, Kant, and Husserl see the empirical self as an empirical object like other phenomena. Yet, in his view, the Buddhist "no-self" rejects all notions of "I," including logical principles like Husserl's "the pure ego [*das reine Ich*]."

31. To be precise, in *Ethics as the Study of Human Being* the duality of human existence is first described as "individuality" (個人性 *kojinsei*) and "worldliness" (世間性 *sekensei*) (WTZ 9, 27) but later transformed into "individual-social duality" (個人的・社会的なる二重性格 *kojinteki shakaiteki naru nijūseikaku*) (WTZ 9, 39). In *Climate*, it was understood as the "individual-social dual structure" (個人的・社会的なる二重構造 *kojinteki shakaiteki naru nijūkōzō*) (WTZ 8, 2).

32. WTZ 9, 13–28.

33. WTZ 9, 25. The word 間柄 *aidagara* has been translated as "betweenness" in research on Watsuji in English to attain the meaning of 間 *aida* meaning "between" (柄 *gara* means "character"). Therefore, the more precise translation of Watsuji's 人間 *ningen* would be "human being in betweenness" to imply the meaning of *aidagara* (I thank Prof. NAGATOMO Shigenori for his advice on this issue). On the other hand, Watsuji himself placed *Verhältnis* in German for *aidagara* (WTZ 9, 122). I would like to discuss these words on another occasion.

34. WTZ 9, 158.

35. WTZ 9, 161.

36. WTZ 9, 27.

37. WTZ 8, 1–2.

38. SUIZU Ichirō, "*Fūdo*," in *World Encyclopedia* (electronic version) (Tokyo: Hitachi Digital Heibonsha, 1998).

39. Augustin Berque, "*Préface à la traduction française*" ("Preface to the French Translation"), in WATSUJI Tetsurō, *Fûdo, le milieu humain* (*Fūdo: The Human Milieu*), trans. Augustin Berque, Pauline Couteau, and KURODA Akinobu (Paris: CNRS Éditions, 2011), 14–21.

40. WTZ 8, 7.

41. WTZ B1, 395.

42. WTZ 8, 8–12.

43. WTZ 8, 10.

44. WTZ 8, 10.

45. WTZ 8, 11.

46. WTZ 8, 11.

47. WTZ 8, 12.

48. WTZ 8, 14.

49. WTZ 8, 16.

50. WTZ 8, 16.

51. WTZ 8, 14.

52. WTZ 10, 73.

53. WTZ 10, 73.

54. WTZ 10, 76.

55. WTZ 10, 78.

56. WTZ 10, 19 and 185.

57. WTZ 10, 527–529.

58. WTZ 10, 163–164.

59. WTZ 10, 173.

60. WTZ 10, 189.

61. WTZ 10, 190–192.

62. WTZ 10, 192.

63. WTZ 10, 199.

64. WTZ 10, 200.

65. WTZ 10, 200–201.

66. WTZ 10, 202.

67. WTZ 11, 16.

68. WTZ 11, 16–17. Here Watsuji uses the word *toki* 時 (time, hour, opportunity, occasion, when, while) in the Japanese specific manner.

69. WTZ 9, 163–164.

70. WTZ 10, 285–286.

71. WTZ 10, 286, 302.

72. WTZ 10, 286–298.

73. e.g. KUSHIGE Hiroko et al., "Genome-Wide and Heterocyst-Specific Circadian Gene Expression in the Filamentous Cyanobacterium, *Anabaena* sp. Strain PCC 7120," *Journal of Bacteriology* 195, no. 6 (2013): 1276–1284.

74. e.g. Tom Mels, ed., *Reanimating Places: A Geography of Rhythms* (Aldershot: Ashgate, 2004); Tim Cresswell and Peter Merriman, eds., *Geographies of Mobilities: Practices, Spaces, Subjects* (Farnham: Ashgate, 2011).

CHAPTER 6 | Climate Change
as Existentialist Threat

Watsuji, Greimas, and the Nature of Opposites

STEVE BEIN

THE AIM OF this chapter is to use WATSUJI Tetsurō's models of human existence (*ningen sonzai*, 人間存在) and climate (*fūdo* 風土) to clarify why climate change is not just an existential threat but also an existentialist one. I will take it as given that climate change is in fact an existential threat—or, put another way, that the latest report from the International Panel on Climate Change is accurate when it says that anthropogenic climate change is a reality, that the evidence for it is widespread and systemic, that it has already had serious deleterious effects on human welfare, and that these effects are likely not just to persist but also to multiply and intensify.[1] While all of this is lamentable, it is not my concern here. My focus is the threat not to our status quo but to our very mode of being-in-the-world.

According to Watsuji, culture and climate are mutually transformative of each other, defined not just in juxtaposition to the other but *by* the other. Culture does not simply carve out a space for itself in nature; it is always a response to nature—and not nature in the abstract, but always to a specific geohistorical context, which Watsuji calls climate. Climate is the lived-world, both of individuals and of collectives, and according to Watsuji—and to many existentialist thinkers—human existence is always existence in a lived-world. If global warming alters every climate, then it alters every possible lived-world, from which it follows that it alters human existence itself.

There is of course a sense in which *nothing* can threaten being-in-the-world: no matter how rapidly or violently the natural environment may change, humanity will either survive (in which case the lived-world continues) or else it will die out (and no lived-world exists to be threatened). But this is no cause for optimism, and indeed it veils a deeper and more significant threat: our relationship with the natural world, while oppositional, has long been stable, but that period of stability is nearing its end.

Watsuji accounts for such stability and instability in Hegelian terms, through a dialectical structure of double negation. In this case, climate and culture are opponents engaged in what I shall call *creative tension*, a stable, sustainable, mutually transformative style of opposition. He also envisions individuals and their communities as opponents engaged in this kind of creative tension. But there is another kind of opposition: *destructive tension*, which is neither stable nor sustainable. Thus to say culture and nature are "opposites" is ambiguous, and in fact the term "opposite" is itself ambiguous.

To resolve the ambiguity I will draw on the work of semiotician Algirdas Julien Greimas, who provides the conceptual framework necessary to elucidate the distinction between creative and destructive tension—that is, between a mutually transformative tension that is beneficial and sustainable, and a tension that is unsustainable because it is damaging to one or both sides. Having clarified this distinction, I will explain how Watsuji exposes climate change as an existentialist concern and close with some brief thoughts about what bearing this has for us.

6.1. Greimas's Semantic Squares

Algirdas Julien Greimas was a founding father of the Paris School of semiotics. He developed a conceptual tool called the semantic square, also called the Greimas square, which has taken on a degree of importance in semiotics similar to that of Aristotle's square of opposition in philosophy. (In fact, Greimas derived his square from Aristotle's.) Greimas himself applied the semantic square to such mundane objects as traffic lights; since then it has since been applied to everything from print advertisements to fairy tales.[2] In a particularly interesting case, the science fiction novelist Kim Stanley Robinson allows a character to apply semantic squares to the other characters' personality types, and semiotician William J. White then applies semantic squares to Robinson's application.[3] The fact that the Greimas square can be used this way is a testament to its versatility. I, too, will co-opt the semantic square, applying it to search for meaning not in the semiotic sense but the existential sense. Put another way, I am interested not in signifying but in significance.

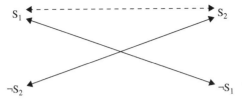

FIGURE 6.1 The Greimas Square.

The central insight behind the semantic square is that when we speak of "opposites," we speak ambiguously (see figure 6.1). Here Greimas does not have ambiguous homographs in mind (e.g., "light" being the opposite of both "heavy" and "dark"), but rather the ambiguous nature of opposition itself. Light is the opposite of darkness in the sense that it annihilates darkness, and the opposite of dimness in the sense that it is simply not-dimness. Dimness too has a pair of opposites: it is both not-light and not-dark. Semantically, we can parse out the meanings of these terms by using each to negate the others, such that, for example, light is *not*-dimness but *anti*-darkness.

Greimas couples these terms to create different kinds of binary relationships:

1. Opposition, or Contrariety: S_1 and S_2 (e.g., light and dark)
2. Contradiction: S_1 and $\neg S_1$ (e.g., light and not-light)
3. Complementarity: S_2 and $\neg S_1$ (e.g., dark and not-light)
4. Neutrality: $\neg S_1$ and $\neg S_2$ (e.g., not-light and not-dark)

This light/dark/dim analysis is an easy example, but not one of particular philosophical interest. Consider instead the distinction between masculinity and femininity, which is culturally dependent and which evolves over time. We can map this relationship with a Greimas square in figure 6.2.

Here masculinity has two opposites, the feminine and the effeminate. Effeminacy is destructive to masculinity: if you dub me effeminate, you

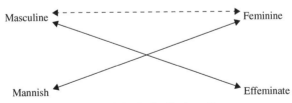

FIGURE 6.2 Masculinity and Femininity in the Greimas Square.

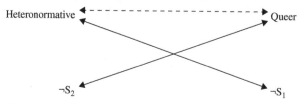

FIGURE 6.3 Heteronormativity and Queerness in the Greimas Square.

emasculate me. On the other hand, masculinity and femininity exist not in destructive tension but in creative tension: each is defined in contradistinction to the other in a relationship that constantly evolves. This works very well for Greimas's purposes as a semiotician. For any given set of cultural norms, we can study what is meant by the masculine and the feminine, and we can ask questions of semantics, such as, what is the difference between being manly and being mannish?

Of course there is much more to be said here. A college freshman in a 100-level Sex and Gender class will have acquired sufficient tools in the first week to dismiss this masculinity/femininity square as being overly simplistic. But this highlights the utility of the Greimas square, because the squares can be stacked to provide additional levels of analysis. Let us call the previous square "heteronormative," and let us designate it as a new S_1 in a new semantic square (see figure 6.3). In this new square, let us set the new S_2 as "queer."[4]

With the first two elements in place, we could then explore how best to define $\neg S_1$ and $\neg S_2$. Completing the square runs too far afield of any discussion of Watsuji and climate change, so I will go no further, except to summarize by highlighting two particular points. First, for any S_1 we can conceive of two opposites, S_2 and $\neg S_1$, and two kinds of opposition, creative tension (transformative, beneficial, sustainable) and destructive tension (damaging, unsustainable). Second, any Greimas square can itself be made a node in a new square.

6.2. Watsuji via Greimas

As I mentioned earlier, my purpose in co-opting Greimas's work is to investigate not signification but significance—that is, to shift from semantics to philosophical anthropology. Watsuji's model of understanding human being-in-the-world can be represented remarkably well with the Greimas square. This is because Watsuji sees us as having two inalienable, inseparable, interdependent modes of being, the private and the public, and because he sees these modes of being as being irreducibly and inextricably grounded both in the natural world and in what we might call the lived-world.

Watsuji presents us with two models for understanding our place in society and in nature, the most important of which is *ningen* (人間), the human being. It is an everyday word, but in Watsuji's usage it is packed with layers of meaning. The first of its two characters, *nin* or *hito* (人), means "person," and Watsuji takes it to signify our drives toward autonomy and individuality. The second character, *gen* or *aida* (間), means "between," and can also be read as *aidagara*, or "betweenness." Watsuji takes this to signify the interconnectedness inherent in the human condition, similar to Aristotle's contention that we are essentially political animals (*politikon zōon*). Betweenness represents our public, communal drives. These two aspects, *nin* (人) and *gen* (間), exist dialectically, each negating the other in order to assert itself.[5] This maps quite well onto the Greimas square in figure 6.4.

Here *nin* and *gen* are engaged in creative tension. Their struggle against each other results in their own self-transformation and self-discovery—and make no mistake, there is struggle. Employing Hegelian language, Watsuji describes it as a double negation: the individualistic aspect of our being cries out for independence, while the society in which we are embedded seeks to assimilate us into the whole. Each would subvert the other, and from this conflict emerges the socialized individual, a *nin* that has negated *gen* just as it was first negated by *gen*.[6]

I contend that we can see this double negation play out quite literally in developmental psychology. At birth we are the ultimate egoists, incapable of attending to others' needs: all we can do is scream until we get what we want. But society cannot tolerate this behavior for long. It quashes the selfish caterwauling as early as possible, socializing the child and exercising discipline when the child will not comply. As a teenager the child rebels again, compelled by hormones that literally change the shape of the brain, and once again the collective seeks to control the child. Ideally this process

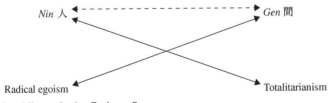

FIGURE 6.4 Ningen in the Greimas Square.

results in the emergence of a socialized individual capable of striking the right balance between private needs and public obligations.

Taken to its logical extreme, fully indulging *gen* with no respect for *nin* results in the totalitarian state. In this imbalanced relationship the individual is but a cog in the machine, to be ground up and spit out if the public sees fit. This presents a pair of Greimassian opposites to *nin*: there is *gen* in proper balance as a source of creative tension, and then there is *gen* taken to its totalitarian extreme as a source of destructive tension. Similarly, allowing *nin* to fully express itself with no respect for *gen* results in radical egoism (and ultimately in the worst excesses of American culture, if we put Watsuji's most propagandistic work on par with his most philosophical).[7] Thus there are two Greimassian opposites to *gen* as well: *nin* held in proper balance as a socialized individual and unfettered *nin* as a sociopathic anarchist. Here again we see the difference between creative tension and destructive tension.

One point worthy of note is that the radical egoist and the totalitarian state are pitted in the most destructive tension possible. Whereas properly balanced *nin* and *gen* can engage in some gentle push and pull in pursuit of self-discovery, the radical egoist and the totalitarian state must fight to the death. One must annihilate the other. We can modify the Greimas square as in figure 6.5, with vertical arrows showing S_1 and S_2, *nin* and *gen*, taken to their logical extreme, with dotted lines representing destructive tension and the dashed line representing creative tension.

Ningen, the first of Watsuji's models, always lives within his second model: *fūdo* (風土), or climate. *Fūdo* denotes much more than the literal meaning of its characters, wind (*fū* 風) and earth (*do* 土), and even more than the English word "climate." ("Acculturated climate" or "acclimatized culture" come closer.) For Watsuji, climate is "the agent by which human life is objectivized, and it is here that man comprehends himself; there is self-discovery in climate."[8] His book *Fūdo: ningengakuteki kōsatsu* (*Climate: An Anthropological Study*, 1935) is widely regarded as a philosophical featherweight, and the last four of its five chapters deserve that

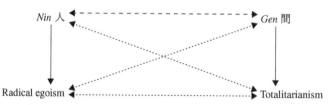

FIGURE 6.5 Ningen in the Modified Greimas Square.

criticism. To separate those four (primarily travelogue, heavily spiced with an implausible theory of climatological determinism) from the first chapter (a careful and nuanced existentialist treatment of being-in-the-world), I will draw a distinction between *fūdo* (風土) and *kokumin jikaku* (国民自覚), both of which feature prominently in Watsuji's thought.

Kokumin jikaku means "self-awareness of national character," and to put it frankly, it is a half-baked idea. As Bruce B. Janz observes, the idea that cultures have a specific character is not only a "vast over-generalization" but also falsely "sees those cultures as largely self-contained and self-sustaining over time."[9] Some of Watsuji's political opponents dubbed him as a rightist because of his advocacy of *kokumin jikaku*, which is fundamentally conservative in nature. David Dilworth points out that the idea of national character crops up elsewhere in Watsuji's thought, most importantly in *Nihon rinri shishōshi* (*History of Japanese Ethical Thought*, 1952), a distillation of some of Watsuji's more propagandistic wartime and prewar writings.[10] Dilworth argues that "there is therefore a consistent thread of thought stretching over twenty years that climaxed with the appearance of the *Nihon rinri shishōshi*."[11] I have argued elsewhere that Watsuji's political position was not quite so straightforward or univocal, but politics aside, it remains that the idea of national character fails to reflect what we know about social science.[12]

On the other hand, *fūdo* is the ground of experience, the mirror that serves as "a means for man to discover himself."[13] On the first page of his *Fūdo* he says, "All of us live on a given land, and the natural environment of this land 'environs' us whether we like it or not."[14] This is as true of cultures as it is of individuals. Clothing, architecture, and even basic vocabulary are all cultural responses to climatic conditions. In fact, that linkage is so tight that he says it is nonsensical to speak of culture and climate as if they exist independently of one another: "From the very first, climate is historical climate. In the dual structure of man—the historical and the climatic—history is climatic history and climate is historical climate. History and climate in isolation from each other are mere abstractions."[15]

Watsuji cites diet as an interesting case in point:

> It is not that man made the choice between stock-raising and fishing according to his preference for meat or fish. On the contrary, he came to prefer either meat or fish because climate determined whether he should engage in stock-raising or fishing. In the same way, the predominant factor governing the choice between a vegetable or a meat diet is climate, rather than the vegetarian's ideology.[16]

Written in 1935, these words still apply today. I myself am a vegetarian, and maintaining that diet has never been easier in mainstream American culture. In the 1990s, when I first became vegetarian, I could not take it for granted that a restaurant would have anything on the menu for me; today I can eat more or less wherever I like. Similarly, advances in farming technology have made it possible to raise beef cattle in places that were previously unworkable, and have consequently extended a meat-based diet to populations for whom that was once financially out of reach. But the deleterious effects of this two-way relationship are now far more visible than they were in 1935, including not just climate change (livestock being a major source of methane, a powerful greenhouse gas) but also water pollution, water shortage, topsoil degradation, and biodiversity loss.[17]

Unlike *kokumin jikaku*, which is ideally as unchanging as a Platonic Form, climate is "filled with tensions and oppositions. It is not static, it is not just a mutually interlocking and supporting system of puzzle pieces."[18] These tensions and oppositions are crystallized in the Greimas square in figure 6.6.

Here culture occupies one node of the square, and in a Watsujian context a culture can only be a community of *ningen*, that is, of contextualized individuals, each of whom has internal tensions that we have already seen diagrammed in a Greimas square. *Ningen*'s culture is always embedded in climate, with which it always exists in creative tension—and here I say *creative* tension because the crude eighteenth-century vision of the struggle between humanity and nature does not adequately describe our relationship with our environment. It is true that a necessary condition for human survival is our ability to carve out a safe living space for ourselves, but it is also true that we build such spaces out of nature. Culture *is* reappropriated nature. Everything we have we took from nature; this is our ongoing process of self-discovery.

Of course we do more than merely survive in our environment; we thrive in it, cultivate it, take our leisure in it, honor it, blight it, restore it, preserve it, and find new and ingenious ways of converting it into capital. When the

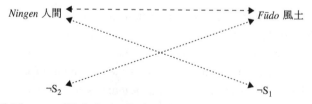

FIGURE 6.6 Ningen and Fūdo in the Greimas Square.

latter goes wrong, it often goes horrifically wrong. Accidents like the BP Deepwater Horizon spill of 2010 or the triple meltdown at Fukushima in 2011 are, in the most literal sense, inevitable. This is for several reasons. One is that, as sociologist and risk analyst Charles Perrow explains, when "complex nonlinear systems" interact (as they must in the operation of a nuclear power plant or a semisubmersible drilling rig), they tend to generate unpredictable failures, and when these systems are "tightly coupled" (as they must be in such complex systems), even trivial failures tend to cascade into ever more and ever greater failures.[19] A second reason is simple supply and demand. Ultra-deepwater drilling is difficult, expensive, and risky; the only reason to engage in it is that market forces reward it. So long as those forces reward it, companies like BP must either take part or lose market share.[20]

But strictly speaking, even spectacles like the Deepwater Horizon spill or the Fukushima meltdown are not threats to climate. These can devastate ecosystems, to be sure, but climate in the Watsujian sense is the ground of experience itself. It is that against which culture defines itself as culture, and the topos within which individuals discover themselves as individuals. It is so tightly connected to our being-in-the-world that we might call it world-in-the-being. So while philosophers have begun to distinguish between environmental ethics and climate ethics, even these distinctions are too abstract for *ningen* and *fūdo* as being-in-the-world.[21]

There is only one ecological crisis large enough to threaten being-in-the-world itself, and that is climate change. Because it portends change for every climate, it entails change for every culture. There remains a sense in which even climate change cannot threaten being-in-the-world: no matter how hostile the environment becomes, it is still *our* environment, until at last it eradicates us and there is no lived-world at all. But in a much more important sense, climate change fundamentally alters who we are. It forces cultures to change or die out, and that itself is a change to our very being. That is why, in the Greimas square in figure 6.7, climate and culture are contrarieties (S_1 and S_2), while climate change is the contradictory to both of them ($\neg S_1$ and $\neg S_2$).

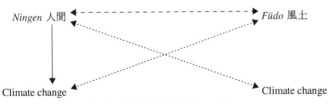

FIGURE 6.7 Ningen and Fūdo in the Modified Greimas Square.

When *ningen* disregards its relationship to *fūdo*, and behaves as if its lived-world is external to itself and therefore irrelevant, *ningen* and *fūdo* slip into destructive tension. This, fueled by a series of technological and economic developments, has resulted in climate change. Climate change, in turn, is the contradictory not just to cultures but also to individuals who comprise them. Indeed, it is destructive to both the private and the public aspects of the individual—that is, to both *nin* (人) and *gen* (間).

Watsuji writes primarily of cultures discovering themselves through creative tension with climate, but taking his thought to its logical conclusion, we can see that individuals must also discover themselves this way. For instance, I enjoy camping but my brother does not. Since we grew up in the same household and took the same childhood camping trips, it is not enough to say that our relationship with climate is entirely defined by our culture. People who find it invigorating to live close to the land are right to pursue self-discovery there; people who find it exhausting are right to seek self-discovery elsewhere. But in any case, my preference to cook over a fire and his preference to cook on a grill are both under threat if our culture is forced to undergo radical change for its own survival.

Radical change is coming. For some cultures it has already arrived. Martin Schönfeld highlights the case of the Darfur region of western Sudan:

> Darfur's lands used to support farmers and herders as long as the monsoon kept fields and pastures green. Rising temperatures over the Indian Ocean destabilized this rhythm and make the monsoon erratic. Consequently, the land dried out; the age-old cooperation of sedentary and nomadic tribes exploded in genocide, and as early as 2007, UN Secretary-General Ban Ki-moon blamed climate change as one of the culprits of Darfur's collapse. More failed states are to come.[22]

If that last sentence sounds alarmist, consider the fact that we have recently had to invent the term "water security." In 2009 that the Pentagon declared global water shortages a serious danger to American security interests over the next twenty to thirty years, and it was arguably overdue in that announcement.[23] The International Panel on Climate Change shares similar concerns; in the summary of its latest report it makes thirteen references (in just twenty-six pages of text) to heightened human vulnerability resulting from changes in the hydrological cycle, including not just armed international conflict but also economic recession and changes in waterborne disease vectors.[24] Armed conflict and economic collapse are the predecessors of failed states.

It is clear that when human interests are taken to be the only relevant interests, the result is egregious environmental and ecological neglect. Given the right technologies and the economic incentives to use them, the result is climate change. Whether we have reached the point of irreversibility is a point of some debate, but that we have allowed a previously sustainable relationship with the environment to fall out of balance is a certainty.

6.3. Conclusion: Climate Change as Existentialist Threat

If Watsuji is correct, we are always already grounded in a social network that is itself always already grounded in historico-climatic space, or *fūdo*. In the *Rinrigaku*, he suggests that our morality consists in striking the right balance between our private and public needs and obligations—that is, between *nin* (人) and *gen* (間).[25] He has very little to say about what happens when we pursue those two sets of needs exclusively, without regard for the *fūdo* against which *ningen* exists in creative tension. It is hard to know why he had so little to say about this. He has much to say about our spatiality in the *Rinrigaku*, but in these sections his goal is to address shortcomings he found in Heidegger's *Being and Time*. Watsuji accepts our thrownness (*Geworfenheit*) into time, but emphasizes that we are also thrown into space—and there he stops, at least in the *Rinrigaku*.[26] He has everything he needs to speak of *fūdo*—namely, space and time, correlates to geography and history—but he does not take this next step.

Perhaps ecological problems were not as easily visible in his day; perhaps the people of his day were not as ready to see them; perhaps his critics are right and his doctrine of *kokumin jikaku* blinded him to issues of broader ethical and philosophical import. In any case, he does not address the ethical import of balancing *ningen* against *fūdo*. That is a task left for us. What he does provide us with is exceptionally powerful models of the individual, the society, and the environment in which individuals and societies find themselves.

I think it is reasonable to surmise that just as *nin* and *gen* ought to be held in proper balance, *ningen* and *fūdo* ought to be held in proper balance. Watsuji allows that the balancing point is ever shifting. Selfish *nin* and selfless *gen* are both morally praiseworthy, provided only that they are expressed in the appropriate measure. What is most important is that the relationship must not slip out of a state of creative tension, for the only place left for it to fall is into destructive tension. This, clearly, is what has happened in the case of anthropogenic climate change (and also in hundreds of other ecological crises, to be sure). As Aldo Leopold argued, so long as we exist within an ethical framework in which we must mount an argument for the moral relevance of the nonhuman, harm to lands and species is inevitable.[27]

If Watsuji is correct, then climate change necessitates cultural change, and cultural change necessitates individual change. Therefore, climate change is an existentialist threat: it alters every aspect of our being, both *ningen* (人間) and *fūdo* (風土), *nin* (人) and *gen* (間). Nuclear meltdowns and multi-million-barrel oil spills are almost quaint by comparison.

Understanding climate change as an existentialist threat sheds some light on why climate change deniers are so adamant in their denial, even in the face of overwhelming evidence: to accept the reality of anthropogenic climate change is not simply to change one's mind, but to change one's place in the world. Denial is far more than a belief about the reliability of the data. It is a political commitment, and as such it affects how individuals vote, how they consume, how they choose which charitable organizations to support, and even how they choose their sources of news and entertainment. It has also become the third plank of religious antiscientism, which also rejects both evolutionary biology and physical cosmology. As such, it affects much more than one's political position and consumer habits; it becomes a facet of the central pillar of one's spiritual life, and often one's social life as well.

Thus if I am a climate change denier, accepting the latest IPCC report is not simply a matter of acknowledging the reliability of the data; it heralds tumultuous changes to some of the most important aspects of my personal life. If the report is true, then my favored political candidates are incorrect. Moreover, given the widespread availability of the evidence, my political candidates may even be guilty of lying to me, and if they are not lying, then at a minimum they are epistemically irresponsible. If I am religious, then my church may be guilty of the same offenses. I ought to find a new congregation, new political candidates, and perhaps even a new political party. This may precipitate confrontation with my family and friends. If I have chosen to home-school my children to shield them against false doctrine, I must revisit that decision. My basic consumer habits will also be subject to review, and the list goes on.

It is in this sense that our very beliefs about climate change are an existentialist concern: belief in it, or denial of it, affects our most basic sense of what we are and even *how* we are. It has everything to do with being-in-the-world, and the shift from denial to affirmation represents a shift in our understanding of that being. Climate change itself (as opposed to our beliefs about it) is a much greater existentialist concern, because it actually alters our experience within the lived-world.

Now, what is to be done about it? A first step is to acknowledge that asking deniers to change their minds is no small request. The most outspoken deniers have the most to lose; those politicians who have staked their careers on an antiscientist platform cannot change their minds and keep their constituencies. This is not to say that they ought not to change their minds, nor that the rest of us ought not to persuade them to do so. On the contrary, I would argue that those moral oughts are in fact binding. Nevertheless, we ought to recognize that changing one's mind about climate change is not as simple as flipping a switch. It is not comparable to changing one's mind about the permissibility of abortion; it is more closely akin to converting to a new religion.

The difference, of course, is that this conversion is supported by reams upon reams of data. To refuse to convert is to reject the evidence, or else to remain willfully ignorant of it. Rejecting it is warranted only on the condition that this rejection is supported by data gathered impartially through verifiable, reproducible methods. It is possible to search for such data in the name of healthy scientific skepticism, but that is not what we typically see. More often (at least in mainstream American politics) we see dogmatism, denial by rote, and sophistry, all in support of willful ignorance.

I will freely confess: I do not know what to do in the face of willful ignorance. Reasoned argument is ineffective. I do not think that climate change deniers are morally equivalent to Holocaust deniers—I do not perceive the former as being openly hateful—but epistemically speaking they are equally irresponsible, and perhaps more so. (All the evidence that the Holocaust took place already exists; the evidence for anthropogenic climate change is ever growing.) In the light of that irresponsibility, I think it is fair to make policy as if there are no climate change deniers. To crib from the Latin aphorism, *quis gratis asseritur, gratis negatur*: those who assert without evidence can be dismissed without evidence. Those who remain willfully ignorant of the evidence have left themselves only two logical possibilities: to assert without evidence or else to assert nothing at all—that is, to remain silent.

But this is not an argument for holding compassion in check. Even if we ought to hold the deniers to a higher standard epistemically, morally we ought to recognize the possibility of doxastic conversion and remain welcoming to those deniers who face a crisis of faith. Scorn has never been of much use in resolving existentialist crises, and perhaps showing support to those who are "on the fence" will yield more converts.

Notes

1. International Panel on Climate Change, "Climate Change 2014: Impacts, Adaptation, and Vulnerability" (http://ipcc-wg2.gov/AR5/images/uploads/IPCC_WG2AR5_SPM_Approved.pdf.

2. Algirdas Julien Greimas, *On Meaning: Selected Writings in Semiotic Theory*, trans. Paul J. Perron and Frank H. Collins (Minneapolis: University of Minnesota Press, 1976), 52–53; Luca Cian, "A Comparative Analysis of Print Advertising Applying the Two Main Plastic Semiotics Schools: Barthes' and Greimas,'" *Semiotica* 190 (2012): 67–74; Victor Laruccia, "Little Red Riding Hood's Metacommentary: Paradoxical Injunction, Semiotics and Behavior," *Modern Language Notes* 90, no. 4 (1975): 517–534.

3. Kim Stanley Robinson, *Red Mars* (New York: Bantam Books, 1993), 217–220; William J. White, "'Structuralist Alchemy' in Kim Stanley Robinson's *Red Mars*," *Extrapolation* 48, no. 3 (2007): 578–602.

4. I follow David Halperin's assessment of the meaning of "queerness": "Queer is by definition whatever is at odds with the normal, the legitimate, the dominant. There is nothing in particular to which it necessarily refers. It is an identity without an essence. 'Queer' then, demarcates not a positivity but a positionality vis-à-vis the normative" (Halperin, *Saint Foucault: Towards a Gay Hagiography* [Oxford: Oxford University Press, 1995], 62).

5. WATSUJI Tetsurō, *Rinrigaku: Ethics in Japan*, trans. Yamamoto Seisaku and Robert E. Carter (Albany: SUNY Press, 1996), 22–24.

6. WATSUJI Tetsurō, "The Significance of Ethics as the Study of Man," *Monumenta Nipponica* 25, nos. 3–4 (1971): 399–402.

7. *Amerika no kokuminsei* (1944). Watsuji was loosely associated with the expansionist imperial government during World War II. His true political allegiances have been the source of debate among scholars, and also of some hysterics; writing in the immediate aftermath of 9/11, David Dilworth goes so far as to liken Watsuji's politics to al-Qaeda's ("Guiding Principles of Interpretation in Watsuji Tetsurō's *History of Japanese Ethical Thought*," in *Neglected Themes and Hidden Variations*, eds. Victor Sōgen Hori and Melissa Anne-Marie Curley [Nagoya, Japan: Nanzan Institute for Religion and Culture, 2008], 101–112). For more measured treatments, see, for example, Steve Bein, *Purifying Zen: Watsuji Tetsurō's "Shamon Dōgen"* (Honolulu: University of Hawai'i Press, 2011), 8–9; David Gordon, "Watsuji Tetsurō's *Rinrigaku: Ethics in Japan*," *Philosophy East and West* 49, no. 2 (1999): 216–217; William R. LaFleur, "Reasons for the Rubble: Watsuji's Position in Japan's Postwar Debate about Rationality," *Philosophy East and West* 51, no. 1 (2001): 1–25.

8. WATSUJI Tetsurō, *Climate and Culture: A Philosophical Study* (Tokyo: Hokuseido Press, 1961), 14.

9. Bruce B. Janz, "Watsuji Tetsurō, Fūdo, and Climate Change," *Journal of Global Ethics* 7, no. 2 (2013): 180.

10. Dilworth cites *Nihon seishin* (*The Japanese Spirit*, 1934) and "Nihon shindō" ("The Way of the Japanese Subject," 1943), to which I would add some of the more egregious passages from the latter chapters of *Fūdo* and the second volume of the *Rinrigaku*.

11. Dilworth, "Guiding Principles," 107.

12. Bein, *Purifying Zen*, 7–9.

13. Watsuji, *Climate and Culture*, 8.

14. Watsuji, *Climate and Culture*, 1.

15. Watsuji, *Climate and Culture*, 10.

16. Watsuji, *Climate and Culture*, 10.

17. United Nations Food and Agriculture Organization, *Livestock's Long Shadow: Environmental Issues and Options* (Rome: Food and Agriculture Organization, 2006).

18. Janz, "Watsuji Tetsurō," 180.

19. See Charles Perrow, "Fukushima and the Inevitability of Accidents," *Bulletin of the Atomic Scientists* 67, no. 6 (2011): 44–52; and Perrow, *Normal Accidents: Living with High-Risk Technologies* (Princeton, NJ: Princeton University Press, 1999), 62ff.

20. As Martin Schönfeld puts it, in the market economy "economic stability is tied to economic expansion. . . . *Normal* business means to do *more* business, while doing the *same* business means to do *less* business" ("Plan B: Global Ethics on Climate Change," *Journal of Global Ethics* 7, no. 2 (2011): 130).

21. See Janz, "Watsuji Tetsurō"; Schönfeld, "Plan B"; and Stephen Gardiner et al., *Climate Ethics: Essential Readings* (New York: Oxford University Press, 2010).

22. Schönfeld, "Plan B," 131, citing Ban Ki-moon, "A Climate Culprit in Darfur" (2007).

23. John M. Broder, "Climate Change Seen as Threat to U.S. Security," *New York Times*, August 8, 2009. Lester R. Brown and the Earth Policy Institute had been making a similar prediction for many years prior to the Pentagon statement, and coalesced some of those findings in 2005 in a single monograph on water and food security (Brown, *Outgrowing the Earth: The Food Security Challenge in An Age of Falling Water Tables and Rising Temperatures* [New York: Norton, 2005]). Other environmental philosophers had issued earlier warnings; Vandana Shiva's *Water Wars* (Cambridge, MA: South End Press, 2002) is an aptly titled case.

24. International Panel on Climate Change, *Climate Change 2014: Impacts, Adaptation, and Vulnerability*, "Summary for Policy Makers."

25. Watsuji, *Rinrigaku*, 23, 145–148, 244.

26. For an analysis of Heidegger and Watsuji on spatiality, see Steve Bein, "Worlds Apart? An Analysis of Watsuji's *Seken* and Heidegger's *Welt*," *EASPAC: The Electronic Journal of the Association for Asian Studies on the Pacific Rim* (2003).

27. Aldo Leopold, *A Sand County Almanac* (New York: Oxford University Press, 1966), 201–214.

PART III | Environmental Aesthetics

CHAPTER 7 | # Whitehead's Perspectivism as a Basis for Environmental Ethics and Aesthetics

A Process View on the Japanese Concept of Nature

STEVE ODIN

ACCORDING TO ALFRED North Whitehead's process metaphysics, the aesthetic continuum of nature is an organization of *perspectives,* whereby each occasion is akin to a Leibnizian monad's perspective—that of a metaphysical point—each monad functioning as a living mirror that reflects the entire universe from its own unique standpoint as a microcosm of the macrocosm. Section 7.1 analyzes the metaphysical perspectivism underlying Whitehead's ecological concept of nature. In this section, there is also a brief consideration of how Whitehead's perspectivism illuminates the Japanese Buddhist religio-aesthetic concept of nature as visualized by the poetic metaphor of Indra's Net, wherein an event is likened to a brilliant jewel reflecting the whole cosmos from its own viewpoint. Section 7.2 examines Whitehead's Leibnizian perspectivism as reformulated by George Herbert Mead, and later by Lawrence Kohlberg and Jürgen Habermas, into an ethical procedure for moral perspective-taking, whereby free moral agents learn to put themselves into the perspectives of others in the community. Here it is shown how Japanese Buddhist as well as East Asian Confucian theories of "perspective-taking" can be applied to the formulation of an intercultural paradigm for ecological ethics. Section 7.3 sets forth my own thesis, whereby it is suggested that the above procedure for moral perspective-taking can be used as the basis for a new Japanese-Whiteheadian process model of environmental ethics and ecological aesthetics.

7.1. Whiteheadian Perspectivism

The metaphysical doctrine of perspectives was introduced into modern Western thought by the seventeenth-century philosopher-mathematician G. W. F. Leibniz (1646–1716). In his *Monadology*, Leibniz argues that the universe is not an absolute One, but is instead an irreducible plurality of monads, metaphysical points, or perspectives, each of which constitutes a "living mirror of the universe."[1] For Leibniz, each perspective mirrors the totality as a microcosm of the macrocosm from its own viewpoint, so that the divine glory of nature is "multiplied perspectively."[2] Leibniz suggests an ecological view of nature as a system of perspectives, writing that each monadic organism can be viewed "as like a garden full of plants, and like a pond full of fish. But every branch of a plant, every member of the animal, and every drop of the fluids within it, is also such a garden or such a pond."[3]

In the twentieth century, Leibniz's perspectivism was revived by the philosopher-mathematician A. N. Whitehead, so that the idea of perspectives was adopted as a key metaphysical principle in his categorial scheme.[4] Influenced by Leibniz, Whitehead articulates an ecological vision of nature as an aesthetic continuum wherein all relational events are self-creative occasions of experience that arise through interpenetration of disjunctive multiplicity into conjunctive unity so as to both contain and pervade the whole continuum as a novel aesthetic perspective of the universe.[5] Whitehead first explicitly outlines his concept of nature as an organization of perspectives in *Science and the Modern World* (1925). In this work, he cites the empirical testimony provided by Romantic nature poets as an argument on behalf of a philosophy of organism, which rejects the separation of facts from values in modern scientific materialism. The philosophy of organism instead holds that beauty or aesthetic value is intrinsic to the perspective framed by each occasion by virtue of the presence of the whole in each part: "Both Shelley and Wordsworth emphatically bear witness that nature cannot be divorced from aesthetic values, and that these values arise from the cumulation, in some sense, of the brooding presence of the whole on to its various parts."[6] Whitehead thus critically undermines the mechanistic Cartesian-Newtonian concept of nature as a meaningless flux of atomic substances devoid of value as held by scientific materialism based on the fallacy of vacuous actuality. In contrast, he articulates an ecological concept of nature as an organization of aesthetic perspectives with intrinsic value.

In Whitehead's organic process metaphysics, the Leibnizian idea of a monadic perspective, or metaphysical point, is described as an activity of prehensive unification:

> This unity of a prehension defines itself as a here and a now and the things so gathered into the grasped unity have essential reference to other places and other times. For Berkeley's mind, I substitute a process of prehensive unification.[7]

For Whitehead, the monad is no longer a windowless substance devoid of relationships, as for Leibniz, but is now conceived as an interactive event arising by a creative synthesis that unifies the given field of relationships from its own standpoint into a novel aesthetic perspective of nature through prehensive unification:

> In the first place, note that the idea of simple location has gone. The things which are grasped into a realized unity, here and now, are not the castle, the cloud, and the planet simply in themselves: but they are the castle, the cloud, and the planet from the standpoint, in space and time, of the prehensive unification. In other words, it is the perspective of the castle over there from the standpoint of the unification here.[8]

Tracing his idea of perspectives to Leibniz's monads, he writes:

> You will remember that the idea of perspectives is quite familiar in philosophy. It was introduced by Leibniz, in the notion of his monads mirroring perspectives of the universe. I am using the same notion, only I am toning down his monads into the unified events in space and time.[9]

Whitehead goes on to clarify how his reformulation of Leibniz's doctrine of monads as perspectives mirroring nature from their own standpoint involves the abandonment of the fallacy of simple location.

> My theory involves the entire abandonment of the notion that simple location is the primary way in which things are involved in space-time. In a certain sense, everything is everywhere at all times. For every location involves an aspect of itself in every other location. Thus every spatio-temporal standpoint mirrors the world.[10]

Whitehead's abandonment of "simple location" thus involves an ecological vision of nature as a web-like system of interconnected perspectives, whereupon each perspectival event both causally influences and receives influence from all other relational events from its own standpoint of unification within the aesthetic continuum of nature.

According to the categorial scheme articulated in *Process and Reality* (1929), an occasion of experience arises by a process of "concrescence," or creative synthesis of many into one, so as to unify the whole aesthetic continuum of nature from its own perspective standpoint. During the process of creative synthesis, alternate possibilities and irrelevant data are eliminated from the illuminated foreground into a remote dark background so as constitute a far-near perspective of the universe: "This fact of the elimination by reason of synthesis is sometimes termed the perspective of the actual world from the standpoint of that concrescence."[11]

Whitehead further clarifies how his theory of occasions as felt perspectives of nature is a reconstruction of Leibniz's monads in terms of his organic process metaphysics of becoming and perishing events:

> This is a theory of monads: but it differs from Leibniz's in that monads change. In the organic theory, they merely become. Each monadic creature is a mode of the process of "feeling" the world, of housing the world in one unit of complex feeling, in every way determinate.[12]

He then describes how each monadic occasion is a "perspective standpoint" that both pervades and contains the whole aesthetic continuum of nature, stating: "Thus the continuum is present in each actual entity, and each actual entity pervades the continuum."[13]

Whitehead further articulates his ecological concept of nature as an aesthetic continuum of overlapping multiple aesthetic perspectives in his penultimate work, *Modes of Thought* (1938). In chapter 4, aptly entitled "Perspective," he now asserts that each occasion of experience is a "perspective of the universe," adding: "This notion of perspective of the universe is discussed in my *Science and the Modern World*."[14]

The status of beauty as a value of all processes is presented in *Adventures of Ideas*:

> Beauty is a wider, and more fundamental, notion than Truth.... . Beauty [in the most general sense] is the internal conformation of the various items of experience with each other, for the production of maximum effectiveness.... Thus any part of experience can be beautiful. The teleology of the Universe

is directed to the production of Beauty. Thus any system of things which in any wide sense is beautiful is to that extent justified in its existence.[15]

As Whitehead articulates a metaphysics that challenges modern divisions between the true, the beautiful, and the good, he presents aesthetic value as, *one*, a basic feature of the world (not secondary to or merely a possible way of perceiving what exists in itself), and *two* as a "justification" for the existence of something. As the "production of beauty" is the telos of all processes, significance in the most general sense is connected to beauty, in its most general sense.

For Whitehead, each perspective arises through concrescence or prehensive unification as a process of creative synthesis of diverse multiplicity into novel unity, governed by an aim toward realization of intrinsic value as beauty or aesthetic importance: "The generic aim of process is the attainment of importance."[16] Furthermore, "Morality consists in the control of process so as to maximize importance."[17] It is then clarified how perspectival occasions aim toward realization of intrinsic value as *importance*, understood in the sense of "aesthetic importance."[18] He states:

Thus one characterization of [aesthetic] importance is that it is that aspect of feeling whereby a perspective is imposed upon the universe of things felt. . . . *The two notions of [aesthetic] importance and of perspective are closely intertwined.*[19]

Moreover, Whitehead identifies the aim of "[aesthetic] importance" with *beauty,* proclaiming: "Beauty is a grand fact in the universe."[20] There is also a moral dimension to Whitehead's ecological vision of nature as an aesthetic continuum of multiple perspectives: "Everything has some [aesthetic] value for itself, for others, and for the whole. By reason of this character, the conception of morals arises."[21] He adds that each aesthetic perspective of the universe as a feeling of the whole in each part is "the intuition of holiness, the intuition of the sacred, which is at the foundation of all religion."[22] Hence, insofar as each self-creative occasion is a novel aesthetic perspective of nature with the intrinsic value of beauty, it warrants poetic admiration and mystic reverence as well as moral concern. In Whitehead's idea of nature as an aesthetic continuum, everything in the continuum has some degree of aesthetic value, either more or less, but never zero.

Whitehead explains how a self-creative occasion of experience is a foreground/background or focus/field event that realizes intrinsic value as beauty or aesthetic importance by a process of composition, valuation, gradation, and elimination.[23] It is this valuation process of selective attention governed by pragmatic interests that sorts out given initial data into a novel aesthetic perspective of nature, whereby the most relevant data are discriminated in a clear foreground focus of attention, and the less relevant or irrelevant data recede into a vague undiscriminated background field of penumbral darkness.[24]

In my book, *Process Metaphysics and Hua-Yen Buddhism*, I argue that Whitehead's reconstructed Leibnizian doctrine of perspectives elucidates the perspectivism underlying Hua-yen (J. Kegon, 華厳) Buddhist philosophy, wherein nature is a system of perspectives reflecting totality from a point of view. This Sino-Japanese Kegon view of nature as a system of perspectives was itself incorporated into Zen (禅), Pure Land (浄土), and Shingon (真言) schools of Japanese Buddhism, as well as the modern Japanese philosophy of NISHIDA Kitarō (1870–1945) and the Kyoto school. The Kegon teaching of "nonobstructed interpenetration between the whole and the parts" (J. *riji muge* 理事無礙) is depicted by the poetic metaphor of Indra's Net, whereby all relational events are likened to shining jewels reflecting all the other jewels in the net from the standpoint of their own perspective. Indra's Net is described in the *Avatamsaka Sutra* as an infinite web in which at every intersection there is a perfectly reflective jewel. Each jewel reflects every other jewel (and each *reflected* jewel again reveals the entire, infinite web), and thus each part contains a reflection of the whole. In the tradition of Zen, *sumie* monochrome inkwash landscape paintings are characterized by the aesthetic ideal of *yūgen* (幽玄) or the beauty of shadows, and the Kegon teaching of interpenetration between part and whole is depicted by visible phenomena shading off into an invisible dark void of nothingness. Moreover, in Zen inkwash paintings, this part-whole, organism/environment, foreground-background, or microcosm-macrocosm patterning of events in nature is depicted by its characteristic three planes of depth: a clear foreground, vague middle ground, and dark background of enveloping pictorial space, technically called the "far-near perspective" (*enkinhō* 遠近法).

Whitehead gives a similar account of an aesthetic perspective of the universe and its imaginative expression in the penumbral beauty of art.

> The finite focus of clarity fades into an environment of vagueness stretching into the darkness of what is merely beyond. . . . In this way the immediacy of finite existence refuses to be deprived of that infinitude of extension which is its perspective.[25]

It is thus my view that both Whitehead and Japanese Buddhism articulate an ecological vision of nature as an aesthetic continuum of interpenetrating events, such that each aesthetic event mirrors the whole universe from its own unique perspective as a microcosm of the macrocosm.

The modern Zen philosophy of Nishida also views nature as a system of monads reflecting totality influenced by Leibniz's metaphysical notion of a "perspective" (パスペクテイブ). Nishida articulates an ecological view of nature as a web-like matrix of perspectives, which combines the perspectivism of Leibniz in the west and Zen/Kegon Buddhism in the east. Describing his concept of the individual self as a Leibnizian monad or metaphysical point constituting a perspective of the universe, Nishida asserts: "This is to be understood in the same sense as the individual which as monad, mirrors the world, and is at the same time a viewpoint of perspective."[26] However, like Whitehead, Nishida deconstructs Leibniz's reified notion of a monad or perspective as a windowless substance with no relationships, and instead sees the monad as a dynamic interactive event arising through creative unification of its given relationships into a perspective of nature as a microcosm of the macrocosm.

Elsewhere in his writings, Nishida describes his Leibnizian view of the monad or perspective as follows:

> Our selves are 'creative points' of this world. Leibniz called the monad a metaphysical point, but I think of each individual self as a creative point of the historical world, it extends to the eternal future and to the eternal past as the point of self-determination of the absolute present.[27]

According to Nishida's modern Zen philosophy of nothingness, a dependently co-arisen event is like the "metaphysical point" or monad of Leibniz's monadology, wherein each monad is conceived to be a living mirror that reflects the whole universe from its own perspective as a microcosm of the macrocosm. However, in contrast to the deterministic metaphysical point of Leibniz's perspectivism, Nishida's perspective is now conceived as a "creative point" (sōzōten 創造点) functioning to unify the many into the one in the Field (basho 場所) or matrix of absolute nothingness. Nishida's reconstruction of Leibniz's perspectivism with a notion of "creative points" thus approximates Whitehead's organic process metaphysics of creative advance into novelty, whereby each interactive monad co-arises through creative synthesis of multiplicity into unity producing a new perspective of the universe from its own unique standpoint in the continuum of nature.

7.2. Whiteheadian Ethical Perspective-Taking

In my book *The Social Self in Zen and American Pragmatism*, I have discussed at length how Whitehead's perspectivism has been developed by the American process philosopher George Herbert Mead, followed by Lawrence Kohlberg and Jürgen Habermas, into a procedure for ethical perspective-taking.[28] Through this procedure of ethical perspective-taking, the autonomous moral agent learns to enter the position of all others in the community to arrive at Kantian categorical imperatives of duty as universally valid ethical norms.

Mead developed his view of the person as a "social self" arising through individual-society relationships, based on a doctrine of "objective perspectives," derived primarily from the Leibnizian cosmology of perspectives as reformulated in the organic process metaphysics of Whitehead. Mead holds that what is most valuable in Whitehead's organic process metaphysics is the doctrine of perspectives worked out in *Science and the Modern World*. In an essay called "The Objective Reality of Perspectives," included in *Philosophy of the Present*, Mead explains his use of Whitehead's Leibnizian perspectivism as follows:

> What I wish to pick out of Professor Whitehead's philosophy of nature is this conception of nature as an organization of perspectives.[29]

Mead further explains that he intends to focus on Whitehead's "Leibnizian filiation, as it appears in his conception of the perspective as the mirroring in the event of all other events."[30] He continues:

> My suggestion was that we find in society and social experience ... an instance of that organization of perspectives ... of Professor Whitehead's philosophy.[31]

For Mead the person is a social self arising through organism-environment interaction in a focus/field situation, thus constituting a perspective mirroring both human society and the surrounding environment of nature. He thus speaks of the social self as "the organism and environment in the perspective."[32] According to this perspectival notion of the social self based on Whitehead's Leibnizian theory of perspectives, the social self is akin to a mirror reflecting its surrounding environment of nature from its own unique standpoint. Mead asserts:

Each individual self within that social process, while it reflects in an organized structure the behavior pattern of that [social] process as a whole, does
so from its own particular and unique standpoint ... just as every monad in
the Leibnizian universe mirrors that universe from a different point of view,
and thus mirrors a different aspect or perspective of that universe.[33]

Mead develops Whitehead's Leibnizian perspectivism into a procedure
of moral perspective-taking, whereby one can determine if a contested
ethical norm is right, fair, and just in a problematic moral situation, only
by putting oneself in the position of others in the community affected
by the norm. In mid-twentieth-century moral philosophy, Kohlberg and
Habermas have further elaborated Mead's notion of "role-taking" or
"perspective-taking" as a formal procedure for arriving at Kantian universally valid moral norms and categorical imperatives of duty.

Habermas builds upon the insights of Mead's Whiteheadian/Leibnizian
perspectivism in an effort to reformulate Kant's universalist deontological ethics by grounding moral norms in the dialogical process of intersubjective communication, thereby arriving at what he terms "discourse
ethics." In the method of perspective-taking formulated by Mead and further developed by Habermas, the categorical imperative of Kant, which
demands generalizability (or universalizability) for moral norms, cannot
be arrived at through a monological procedure conducted by a solitary
transcendental subject, but must instead be carried out as a dialogical
procedure mounted through open communication and public discourse
by an intersubjective community. Kant seems to anticipate this ethical
sociality in his concept of a kingdom of ends. Mead writes: "Kant's categorical imperative may be socially stated or formulated or interpreted
in these terms, that is, given its social equivalent."[34] According to Mead,
then, the categorical imperative of Kant, whereby an autonomous moral
agent legislates universally valid moral norms applicable to everyone,
is arrived at by the rational capacity for putting oneself into the perspective of all others in the community affected by those norms—which
is another way of stating Kant's second formulation of the categorical
imperative.

Mead explains how Kant's categorical imperative can be socially
reformulated through the principle of role-taking or perspective-taking,
whereby the rational autonomous moral agent takes on the roles, attitudes,
and perspectives of others in the entire community, altogether conceived
as the "Generalized Other":

The universality of our judgments, upon which Kant places so much stress, is a universality that arises from the fact that *we take the attitude of the entire community of rational beings.* We are what we are through our relationships to others. . . . Sociality gives the universality of our ethical judgments.[35]

Habermas's communication theory as developed in *The Theory of Communicative Action* is directly inspired by what he calls G. H. Mead's "paradigm shift" from Cartesian subjectivism to an intersubjective model of the social self arising through an I-me dialectic of communicative interaction between the individual and society. According to Habermas, communicative discourse ethics develops "the fundamental idea of moral theory that Lawrence Kohlberg borrowed from G. H. Mead's communication theory as the notion of 'ideal role taking.' "[36] Habermas goes on to cite Kohlberg's idea of a hierarchy of developing stages of moral consciousness based on G. H. Mead's principle of ideal role-taking or perspective-taking:

> Reasons for doing right are needing to be good in one's own eyes and those of others, caring for others, and because *if one puts oneself in the other person's place* one would want good behavior from the self (Golden Rule).[37]

As explained by Habermas, Kohlberg argues for an evolutionary scheme whereby moral consciousness is developed in hierarchical stages through perspective-taking, thus progressing from egocentrism to a decentered or multicentric viewpoint, whereupon one now learns to enter the diverse perspectives of others in the community. According to Habermas, "Kohlberg justifies the developmental logic of his six stages of moral judgment by correlating them with corresponding sociomoral perspectives."[38] Summing up Kohlberg's developmental scheme, Habermas clarifies that while the lower stages are characterized by egoism having only an individual perspective, higher stages of moral consciousness are characterized by perspectivism as the ability to put oneself in the position of others, which is itself a philosophical equivalent of the golden rule. Describing the third stage in his developmental scheme of moral perspective-taking, Kohlberg himself writes:

> This stage takes the perspective of the individual in relation to other individuals. . . . The person relates points of view through the "concrete Golden Rule," *putting oneself in the other person's shoes.*[39]

In his introduction to *Moral Consciousness and Communicative Action*, Thomas McCarthy clarifies this moral procedure of perspective-taking in Habermas's discourse ethics, writing that Habermas, "by requiring that perspective-taking be general and reciprocal, builds the moment of empathy into the procedure coming to a reasoned agreement: *each must put himself or herself into the place of everyone else* in discussing whether a proposed norm is fair to all."[40]

Here it is significant to note that while Habermas adopts Mead's ethical procedure for perspective-taking based on the metaphysical perspectivism of Leibniz and Whitehead, at the same time he takes up a postmetaphysical discourse that endeavors to critically *deontologize* or *deconstruct* the theory of perspectives, thus to articulate an ethics not grounded in metaphysics. Commenting on two passages cited above wherein Mead traces his procedure of moral perspective-taking to the metaphysical perspectivism of Leibniz and Whitehead, Habermas writes:

> Both of these passages do a good job of presenting the intuition that Mead wants to express; but the ontologizing connections with Leibniz and Whitehead distort its adequate explication, toward which Mead's own thoughts are pointing.[41]

According to Mead's Whiteheadian perspectivism, and its development by Habermas and Kohlberg, the evolution of moral consciousness beyond egocentrism to a *decentered* viewpoint involves an ethical procedure of ideal role-taking or perspective-taking, whereby one projects through sympathy, imagination, and rationality into the diverse multiple perspectives of others in the community, which Mead terms the "Generalized Other." The autonomous moral agent now arrives at moral decisions by viewing a universalized ethical norm *as if* to see it from the multiple perspectives of others. There is a hierarchy of developmental stages of moral consciousness based on a process of moral education whereby one learns to take on the roles, attitudes, or perspectives of others, and thereby to put themselves in the position of all others in the community affected by a contested ethical norm. Summing up Mead's development of Whitehead's Leibnizian perspectivism, Habermas thus argues that universally valid moral norms are achieved through a communication process of perspective-taking or role-taking, whereby the autonomous moral agent can "put himself or herself into the place of everyone else,"[42] "put oneself in the other person's place,"[43] or "[put] oneself in the other person's shoes."[44]

7.3. Whiteheadian Perspective-Taking and Environmental Ethics

In the Western philosophical tradition, the writings of Aldo Leopold are widely held to be the main inspiration for environmental ethics. Leopold defines ethics in terms of his key notion of "community." However, whereas ethics previously confined itself to the relationship between individuals and the human community, Leopold suggests that the field must now be expanded to include a land ethic or environmental ethic, which includes the relation of the individual to the "biotic community" of soil, waters, plants, and animals: "The land ethic simply enlarges the boundaries of the community to include soils, waters, plants, and animals, or collectively: the land."[45] Moreover, Leopold argues that the "land ethic" is itself grounded upon a "conservation aesthetic," stating: "A thing is right when it tends to preserve the integrity, the stability, and beauty of the biotic community."[46] As similarly argued by Whitehead, "All order is therefore aesthetic order, and the moral order is merely certain aspects of aesthetic order."[47] It can be said that for Whitehead, as for Leopold, the aesthetic continuum of nature warrants moral concern because it has the intrinsic value of beauty, so that the land ethic is itself based on a land aesthetic.

For Whitehead, as for Leopold, ethics is grounded upon the notion that the individual is a member of a community of interdependent parts. Also, similar to Leopold, he enlarges the notion of "community" or "society" so that it includes the surrounding environment of living nature. By extending the category of *the social* beyond human society to the wider society of nature, Whitehead thus formulates the metaphysical groundwork for an environmental ethics: "The Universe achieves its value by reason of its co-ordination into societies, and into societies of societies of societies."[48] Elsewhere he describes his ecological concept of nature as a "community" of interconnected occasions, each constituting an aesthetic perspective of the universe that both pervades and contains the whole community of living nature as a microcosm of the macrocosm:

> Then the actual world is a community of epochal occasions. . . . The epochal occasions are the primary units of the actual community, and the community is composed of the units. But each unit has in its nature a reference to every other member of the community, so that each unit is a microcosm representing in itself the entire all-inclusive universe.[49]

The ecological concept of nature as an organization of novel aesthetic perspectives articulated in Whitehead's *Modes of Thought* can be regarded as a prolegomenon to a new metaphysics of morals in general, and to an environmental ethics in particular. With the aim of overcoming the nihilistic concept of nature as a meaningless flux of lifeless substances posited by the Cartesian-Newtonian view of scientific materialism based on *the fallacy of vacuous actuality*, Whitehead articulates a profoundly ecological vision of living nature as a creative advance toward novelty, wherein each self-creative occasion produces as new aesthetic perspective of the universe with the intrinsic value of beauty. Similar to the Japanese Buddhist view of Dōgen (1200–1253) that "all beings are Buddha-nature," Whitehead formulates a panpsychism whereby all events in living nature are self-actualizing "occasions of experience." Whitehead here seeks to clarify how each occasion arises out of "concern" (prehension, feeling, sympathy) for all other occasions in the cosmos, so that moral concern is now expanded to include the whole community of interconnected events in the aesthetic continuum of nature:

> Each occasion is an activity of concern in the Quaker sense of the term. . . .
> The occasion is concerned, in the way of feeling and aim, with things that in
> their own essence lie beyond it. . . . Thus each occasion, although engaged
> in its own immediate self-realization, is concerned with the universe.[50]

For Whitehead, each occasion as a novel perspective of the universe warrants moral concern to the degree that it realizes the intrinsic value of beauty, or aesthetic importance. Based on his axiological criterion of realizing aesthetic importance in a perspective, he thus goes on to widen the circle of moral concern beyond human society to the whole community of living nature, including trees, plants, and animals, even insects:

> The destruction of a man, or of an insect, or of a tree, or of the Parthenon,
> may be moral or immoral. . . . Whether we destroy, or whether we preserve,
> our action is moral if we have thereby safeguarded the [aesthetic] impor-
> tance of experience.[51]

As indicated, Whiteheadian perspectivism has been reformulated by G. H. Mead, followed by Kohlberg and Habermas, into a stage-structured developmental scheme of moral perspective-taking.[52] My suggestion here is that if we add a new and yet higher stage of moral consciousness, then perspective-taking is enlarged to include all aesthetic value perspectives in the undivided continuum of nature, including the diverse multiple perspectives of both human and nonhuman animals. This ability to enlarge moral consciousness into the next evolutionary phase of an environmental ethics, thereby to widen the expanding circle of moral concern to all living creatures, is itself enabled by Whitehead's ecological concept of nature as an organization of multiple aesthetic perspectives.

Whiteheadian perspectivism further establishes the basis for an environmental ethics insofar as it signifies a paradigm shift from an egocentric or anthropocentric to the decentered viewpoint of an ecocentric or biocentric model of nature based on the moral procedure of perspective-taking. Using the technique of perspective-taking, one learns to project by sympathy and imagination into the diverse multiple perspectives, roles, and attitudes of all others in the community of nature. Hence, Whiteheadian perspective-taking overcomes the anthropocentric bias that animal liberationist Peter Singer calls *speciesism*, which extends moral consideration only to the human species, by now granting equal moral concern to the position of all animal species in nature, both human and nonhuman—even insects.[53] Further, an environmental ethics based on perspective-taking can be fully ecocentric, for it takes into account not only the perspectives of other persons, animals, or plants, but also the land itself. In *A Sand County Almanac*, Leopold urges us to "think like a mountain." One must learn to take the perspective of a mountain, to view the land from the standpoint of a mountain.

Elsewhere I have demonstrated how the Japanese religio-aesthetic concept of nature can be applied to the formulation of an environmental ethics.[54] But here I will focus on Japanese perspectivism based on the Zen/Kegon image of Indra's Net, whereby all events are living mirrors reflecting totality from their own perspective, thereby to develop the basis for a new environmental ethics through the method of perspective-taking.

D. T. Suzuki emphasizes that it is the Kegon/Huayan (Avatamsaka) Buddhist doctrine of *rigimuge* (理事無礙) or "interpenetration of one and many" that underlies the structure of the aesthetic continuum of nature as a web of relationships wherein all things are interdependent:

> The balancing of unity and multiplicity or, better, the merging of self with others as in the philosophy of the Avatamsaka (Kegon) is absolutely necessary to the aesthetic understanding of nature.... Aestheticism now merges into religion.[55]

According to Suzuki, it is this Zen-related Kegon Buddhist doctrine of harmonious interpenetration between part and whole, self and others, or unity and multiplicity that establishes the aesthetic pattern of nature as all in one and one in all. Moreover, this Japanese Buddhist Kegon doctrine of interpenetration between one and many is illustrated by the metaphor of Indra's Net, whereby all events are mirrors reflecting totality as a microcosm of the macrocosm. He goes on to say that it is this interpenetration between unity and multiplicity that underlies the Japanese reverence for all things in the aesthetic continuum of nature. I would further argue that it is this Japanese religio-aesthetic vision of nature as illustrated by Indra's Net that functions as the basis for an ecological practice of moral perspective-taking.

In Japanese philosophy and psychology, the notion of "perspective-taking" is rendered as *shiten-shutoku* (視点取得), or *kanten-shutoku* (観点取得). The Japanese technical term for "perspective-taking" as *shiten-shutoku* is often used in the fields of psychology and education, and is used more often than *kanten-shutoku*. The term "moral perspective-taking" as used by Habermas and Kohlberg in their development of Mead's Whiteheadian/Leibnizian perspectivism also has its literal Japanese language equivalent, as rendered by the technical term *dōtokuteki-kanten-shutoku* (道徳的観点取得). In Japanese philosophy, including traditional Japanese aesthetics, there are very specific theories, as well as practical techniques or spiritual disciplines of cultivation, for learning to put oneself in the position of others through aesthetic, moral, and religious modes of perspective-taking, or the ability of putting oneself in the position of others.

The Zen/Kegon teaching of interfusion between part and whole and its expression by the poetic metaphor of Indra's Net is depicted in Zen inkwash landscape paintings, wherein phenomena in the illuminated foreground shade into a dark background of nothingness, referred to in Japanese aesthetics as the "far-near perspective" (*enkinhō* 遠近法). Now I would like to illustrate the Whiteheadian technique of aesthetic and moral perspective-taking articulated by Mead and others with an example from Japanese theater. As I discuss in *Artistic Detachment in Japan and the West*, in the traditional Japanese art of Noh theater, the Noh actor aims to realize Zen satori (悟り) or "enlightenment" by cultivating an egoless meditative state of "no-mind" (*mushin* 無心), whereupon he puts on a symbolic mask and takes on the multiple roles and perspectives of others, including spirits of various gods, demons, ancestors, animals, and trees. Moreover, the Noh actor learns a dramatic technique for aesthetic and moral perspective-taking called *riken no ken* (離見の見), the "seeing of detached perception." In the words of ZEAMI Motokiyo (1363–1443):

> Your appearance as seen by the audience forms for you your detached perception (*riken*). What your own eyes see is your self-centered perception (*gaken*) and not the seeing of detached perception (*riken no ken*). When you exercise your *riken no ken*, you are of one mind with your audience.[56]

Hence, by shifting from the ego-centered standpoint of *gaken* (我見) to the egoless standpoint of *riken no ken*, or the "seeing of detached perception," the Noh actors learn to view themselves and the whole theatrical performance on stage from the diverse multiple perspectives of others in the audience.

Another vivid illustration of this kind of Whiteheadian procedure for aesthetic and moral perspective-taking, which itself leads directly to an ecological vision of nature, along with an environmental ethics and an acknowledgment of animal rights, is to be found in the 1982–1995 manga (graphic novel) series and 1984 anime (animated film), titled *Nausicaä of the Valley of the Wind* by MIYAZAKI Hayao.[57] Miyazaki's work is a cautionary tale of apocalyptic destruction in Japan due to biochemical and nuclear war leading to environmental collapse. In the opening scene, Miyazaki's shamanic ecofeminist heroine Nausicaä enters the toxic jungle to discover the empty shell of a giant tank-like insect called the "Ohmu." The empty shell of a giant Ohmu here makes reference to the ancient Japanese symbol of "impermanence" (*mujō* 無常) along with the "sad beauty" (*aware* 哀れ) of evanescence depicted by the poetic image of an "empty insect shell" (*utsusemi* 空蝉). When Nausicaä looks through a clear eye lens taken from the empty husk of an Ohmu, she views this toxic jungle from the alternate perspective of an insect, thus to now see the astonishing beauty of the polluted forest. Moreover, by viewing the toxic jungle through the eye of an Ohmu and taking on the perspective of an insect, she learns to have sympathetic moral concern for all living creatures in nature. Thus, while humankind declares war against the giant Ohmu insects, Nausicaä becomes their protector and has moral sympathy for their suffering. Here I quote from my essay "Down the Abyss: *Nausicaä of the Valley of the Wind*":

> At the very outset of the story, Nausicaa is under the transparent eye lens from the exoskeleton of an empty Ohmu shell, watching the deadly spores from the giant fungi in the toxic jungle fall like snowflakes, expressing sheer

aesthetic delight in their delicate beauty. Moreover, from an ethical standpoint, Nausicaä's view of the toxic jungle through the lens of an empty Ohmu shell, itself reveals her ability to arrive at moral decisions by seeing nature from the multiple perspectives of others, including the perspective of insects.[58]

An East-West intercultural parallel to the Whiteheadian method of perspective-taking as the basis for ethics is also to be found in the Chinese philosophical tradition of Confucianism, which later also flourished in Korea and Japan. The Confucian ethical principle of *shu* (J. *jo* 恕) has been variously translated by scholars as "reciprocity," "mutuality of human relations," "consideration," and "generosity." However, in his book *Confucian Role Ethics*, Roger T. Ames translates the principle of *shu* (恕) as "putting oneself in the other's place."[59] Ames emphasizes that in Confucianism, the idealized goal is that of establishing the *he*, or "harmony" (J. *wa* 和), of social roles and relationships constituting the self, the family, society, and the nation. In classical Confucian role ethics, social interactions governed by moral principles of *li* (J. *rei* 礼), or "ritual conduct," and *ren* (J. *jin* 仁), or "benevolence," require the principle of *shu* (J. *jo* 恕), understood as "putting oneself into another's position." Ames here cites from the Confucian classic *Zhongyong* (J. *chūyō* 中庸), or *Focusing on the Familiar*:[60]

> Putting oneself in the place of others (*shu*) and doing one's best on their behalf (*zhong*) is not straying far from the proper way. "Do not treat others as you yourself would not wish to be treated."[61]

In the passage cited above, *shu* is defined in negative terms as "Do not treat others as you yourself would not wish to be treated." This is a Confucian "negative" variant of the golden rule.[62] Ames also states, "*Shu* is a fundamentally aesthetic disposition."[63]

Here I would like to emphasize that the Confucian ethical principle of *shu* (J. *jo* 恕), understood as "putting oneself in the other's place," approximates Whiteheadian ethical-aesthetic perspectivism, as developed into a theory of moral perspective-taking through intersubjective dialogue by Mead, followed by Kohlberg and Habermas. It should be remembered that Habermas cites Kohlberg's idea of a hierarchy of developing stages of moral consciousness based on G. H. Mead's principle of ideal role-taking or perspective-taking:

> *If one puts oneself in the other person's place* one would want good behavior from the self (Golden Rule).[64]

This stage takes the perspective of the individual in relation to other individuals. . . . The person relates points of view through the "concrete Golden Rule," *putting oneself in the other person's shoes*.[65]

It is significant that in his account of successive phases of expanding moral consciousness through perspective-taking as the ability to "put oneself in the other person's place," Kohlberg identifies this stage with the golden rule, or the biblical injunction: "Do unto others as you would have them do unto you." It can thus be asserted that Confucian role ethics, on the one hand, grounded in the principle of *shu* (恕), and the Whiteheadian tradition of ethical perspectivism, on the other, running through Mead, Kohlberg, and Habermas, share a point of convergence in that the moral decisions governing our social interactions are based on the function of ideal role-taking, or perspective-taking, understood as the capacity for "putting oneself in the position of others."

Moreover, I would argue that the Confucian principle of *shu* (恕) can be applied to establishing the grounds for an environmental ethics and aesthetics, if one cultivates the ability to enter not only into the perspective of others in the human community, but also into the perspective of plants, trees, animals, soil, mountains, and waters in the biotic community. It is by learning to enter the perspective of all living creatures in the natural environment that one can realize the Confucian and neo-Confucian goal of achieving a unity of man, heaven, and earth. Thus both the Whiteheadian and Japanese Buddhist as well as Confucian principles of perspective-taking can be used as the basis for a new East-West environmental ethics based on the capacity for entering the perspectives of all sentient beings in the aesthetic continuum of nature.

7.4. The Upshot

In this chapter, I have endeavored to clarify Whitehead's ecological vision of nature as an organization of multiple aesthetic perspectives with the intrinsic value of beauty, thereby to warrant poetic celebration and religious contemplation as well as moral concern. I have pointed out that Whitehead's Leibnizian perspectivism was elaborated by G. H. Mead, followed by Kohlberg and Habermas, into a developmental scheme of moral consciousness, whereby one advances beyond the egocentrism of an individual perspective to higher stages characterized by ethical perspective-taking, or the technique of putting oneself in the position of others. My suggestion here is that if the procedure of perspective-taking is further developed into a new and yet higher stage of moral consciousness, it can function as the basis for a new environmental ethics and aesthetics. This chapter has also endeavored to clarify Aldo Leopold's idea of "thinking like a mountain" through the method of entering the perspectives of others.[66] An ethics based on perspective-taking is fully ecocentric insofar as one takes on not only the perspectives of other humans, plants and animals, but also that of the land itself, thus viewing the land from the standpoint of an ancient mountain.

Hence, my thesis is this: if Mead's Whiteheadian/Leibnizian perspectivism is extended into an environmental ethics and aesthetics, then by a process of moral education, one learns sympathetically to put oneself into the multiple perspectives of others—not only other persons in the human community, but also others in the whole biotic community of living nature, including the diverse perspectives of plants and animals, even insects.[67] Whiteheadian perspectivism as developed into a process of moral perspective-taking by Mead, Kohlberg, and Habermas, along with the Sino-Japanese and Confucian methods of perspective-taking, can be synthesized into a new transcultural paradigm of environmental ethics and land aesthetics based on the capacity for entering into the perspective of all others in the intersubjective community, including both the human community and the whole biotic community of living nature.[68]

Notes

1. G. W. F. Leibniz, *Discourse on Metaphysics / Monadology*, trans. George R. Montgomery (LaSalle, IL: Open Court, 1973), 263.

2. Leibniz, *Discourse on Metaphysics*, 263.

3. Leibniz, *Discourse on Metaphysics*, 266.

4. In his book *Perspective in Whitehead's Metaphysics* (Albany: SUNY Press, 1983), Stephen C. Ross argues that perspective is the key principle in Whitehead's metaphysical scheme of categories: "Among these principles is one which I believe to be the key to Whitehead's philosophy—*the principle of perspective*" (vii). Although Ross's study is significant in that it underscores the centrality of perspective in Whitehead's metaphysics, it has major shortcomings. To start, Ross's analysis of perspective focuses mostly on Whitehead's *Process and Reality*. Also, Ross's study completely neglects the relation between Whitehead's principle of perspective and the realization of aesthetic importance, intrinsic value, and beauty, as well as the function of foreground-background perspectives in Whitehead's philosophy of art. Also, Ross's book is in fact a sustained effort to radicalize Whitehead's perspectivism in the relativistic direction of Justus Buchler's 1966 work *Metaphysics of Natural Complexes*, 2nd ed. (Albany: SUNY Press, 1990). Ross's Buchlerian perspectivism abandons the notion of "ontological priority" for one of

ontological parity, whereby everything is equally real in the perspective that it is located. Hence, "processes" and "events" are real in one context or perspective, while "substance" and "matter" are equally real in other perspectives.

5. For a contemporary French postmodernist treatment of Leibniz's perspectivism and its relation to Whitehead's doctrine of perspectives, see Gilles Deleuze, *The Fold: Leibniz and the Baroque*, trans. Tom Conley (Minneapolis: University of Minnesota Press, 1993).

6. A. N. Whitehead, *Science and the Modern World* (New York: Free Press, 1967), 88.

7. Whitehead, *Science and the Modern World*, 69.

8. Whitehead, *Science and the Modern World*, 70.

9. Whitehead, *Science and the Modern World*, 70.

10. Whitehead, *Science and the Modern World*, 91.

11. A. N. Whitehead, *Process and Reality*, corrected edition, ed. David Ray Griffin and Donald W. Sherburne (New York: Free Press, 1978), 219.

12. Whitehead, *Process and Reality*, 80.

13. Whitehead, *Process and Reality*, 67.

14. A. N. Whitehead, *Modes of Thought* (New York: Free Press, 1981), 67.

15. A. N. Whitehead, *Adventures of Ideas* (New York: Free Press, 1967), 265.

16. Whitehead, *Modes of Thought*, 12.

17. Whitehead, *Modes of Thought*, 13–14.

18. Whitehead, *Modes of Thought*, 121.

19. Whitehead, *Modes of Thought*, 11; emphasis added.

20. Whitehead, *Modes of Thought*, 120.

21. Whitehead, *Modes of Thought*, 111.

22. Whitehead, *Modes of Thought*, 120.

23. Whitehead, *Modes of Thought*, 89.

24. Whitehead, *Modes of Thought*, 89.

25. Whitehead, *Modes of Thought*, 83.

26. NISHIDA Kitarō, *Intelligibility and the Philosophy of Nothingness*, trans. Robert Schinzinger (Westport, CT: Greenwood Press, 1965), 182–183.

27. NISHIDA Kitarō, *Nishida Kitarō zenshū*, 2nd ed., 19 vols. (Tokyo: Iwanami Shoten, 1965), 11:135.

28. Steve Odin, *The Social Self in Zen and American Pragmatism* (New York: SUNY Press, 1994).

29. George Herbert Mead, *The Philosophy of the Present*, ed. A. E. Murphy (Chicago: University of Chicago Press, 1932), 163.

30. Mead, *Philosophy of the Present*, 164.

31. Mead, *Philosophy of the Present*, 171.

32. Mead, *Philosophy of the Present*, 173.

33. Mead, *Philosophy of the Present*, 226.

34. George Herbert Mead, *Mind, Self and Society*, ed. Charles W. Morris (Chicago: University of Chicago Press, 1967), 379.

35. Mead, *Mind, Self and Society*, 379.

36. Jürgen Habermas, *Moral Consciousness and Communicative Action*, trans. Christian Lenhardt and Sherry Weber Nicholsen (Cambridge, MA: MIT Press, 1990), 121.

37. Habermas, *Moral Consciousness*, 123; emphasis added.

38. Habermas, *Moral Consciousness*, 128.

39. Cited in Habermas, *Moral Consciousness*, 128; emphasis added.

40. Habermas, *Moral Consciousness*, viii–ix.

41. Jürgen Habermas, *Postmetaphysical Thinking*, trans. William Mark Hohengarten (Cambridge, MA: MIT Press, 1992), 186.

42. Habermas, *Moral Consciousness*, ix.

43. Habermas, *Moral Consciousness*, 123.

44. Habermas, *Moral Consciousness*, 128.

45. Aldo Leopold, *A Sand County Almanac* (New York: Ballantine Books, 1966), 258.

46. Leopold, *A Sand County Almanac*, 262.

47. A. N. Whitehead, *Religion in the Making* (New York: Meridian, 1974), 105.

48. Whitehead, *Adventures of Ideas*, 264.

49. Whitehead, *Religion in the Making*, 89.

50. Whitehead, *Modes of Thought*, 167.

51. Whitehead, *Modes of Thought*, 14–15.

52. Habermas has responded to criticisms that his discourse ethics is anthropocentric, by arguing for a postmetaphysical, nonanthropocentric, Kantian universalist deontological ethics that recognizes our moral and legal duty to protect all vulnerable forms of life capable of suffering, including both human and nonhuman life, thus to support an ecological position for animal rights. See Jürgen Habermas, *Justification and Application: Remarks on Discourse Ethics*, trans. Ciaran P. Cronin, especially section 13 of his main essay, "Remarks on Discourse Ethics" (Cambridge, MA: MIT Press, 1993), 105–111. However, in this work Habermas does not develop the case for animal rights based on the notion of extending the procedure of moral perspective-taking so as to put oneself into all perspectives in the community of nature. This has been my own application of Mead's Whiteheadian/Leibnizian procedure of moral perspective-taking.

53. Peter Singer, *Animal Liberation*, 3rd ed. (New York: Avon Books, 2002).

54. Steve Odin, "The Japanese Concept of Nature in Relation to the Environmental Ethic and Conservation Aesthetics of Aldo Leopold," in *Environmental Philosophy in Asian Traditions of Thought,* ed. J. Baird Callicott and James McRae (New York: SUNY Press, 2014), 247–265.

55. D. T. Suzuki, *Zen and Japanese Culture* (New York: Bollingen, 1993), 354–355.

56. Quoted in Steve Odin, *Artistic Detachment in Japan and the West: Psychic Distance in Comparative Aesthetics* (Honolulu: University of Hawai'i Press, 2001), 115.

57. MIYAZAKI Hayao, *Nausicaa of the Valley of the Wind*, 7 vols., Studio Ghibli Library Edition (San Francisco: VIZ Media, 2004). The image is from vol. 1, p. 7. For the original Japanese manga (graphic novel) series, see MIYAZAKI Hayao, *Kaze no tani no Naushika*, 7 vols. (1982–1995). Also, for the anime (animated film) version, see *Nausicaä of the Valley of the Wind* (*Kaze no tani no Naushika*, 1984), Studio Ghibli, directed by Miyazaki Hayao.

58. Steve Odin, "Down the Abyss: *Nausicaä of the Valley of the Wind*," in *Manga and Philosophy*, edited by Josef Steiff and Adam Barkman (Chicago: Open Court, 2010), 261–262.

59. Roger T. Ames, *Confucian Role Ethics: A Vocabulary* (Hong Kong: Chinese University Press, 2011), 194–200.

60. Roger T. Ames, *Focusing on the Familiar: A Translation and Philosophical Interpretation of the Zongyong* (Honolulu: University of Hawaii Press, 2001).

61. Ames, *Focusing on the Familiar*, 197.

62. Ames, *Focusing on the Familiar*, 198.

63. Ames, *Focusing on the Familiar*, 196.

64. Cited in Habermas, *Moral Consciousness*, 123; emphasis added.

65. Habermas, *Moral Consciousness*, 128.

66. Leopold, *A Sand County Almanac*.

67. The extension of moral concern "even to insects" is of great significance to the field of ecology. The environmental movement was launched by the publication of Rachel Carson's *Silent Spring* (New York: Houghton Mifflin, 1962). In this book, Carson revealed how nature was being turned into a toxic jungle by the use of DDT and other deadly pesticides in the human war against the insects, developed through research in biochemical weapons of mass destruction during World War II. The final sentence of her book reads: "It is our alarming misfortune that so primitive a science [applied entomology] has armed itself with the most modern and terrible weapons, and that in turning them against the insects it has also turned them against the earth," 297.

68. Editor's note: many thanks to Benjamin Hoffman for his assistance in preparing this chapter for publication.

CHAPTER 8 | Japanese Gardens
The Art of Improving Nature

YURIKO SAITŌ

JAPANESE GARDENS ARE frequently appreciated for embodying the attitude of harmony with and respect toward nature, reflected in their informal and "natural" look. For example, one commentator finds in Japanese gardens "an attitude of humility and profound respect for [the] materials," while another sees in them "man's partnership with nature."[1] These observations are made in comparison with Western formal gardens, which are characterized by rigid symmetry, geometrical patterns, and strict order. The resultant design in Western formal gardens clearly reveals the human hand at work, commonly interpreted as the attitude of human dominance over nature, in contrast to Japanese gardens.[2]

In one respect, this alleged contrast between Japanese gardens and Western formal gardens can be misleading. The so-called natural look in Japanese gardens does not mean little human activity is involved in their production or maintenance. No matter how "natural" Japanese gardens may appear, they are still products of human artifice, resulting from extensive modification and manipulation of nature. Simply by virtue of being gardens rather than tracts of pristine nature, both Japanese and Western formal gardens share the same goal: representing an ideal image of nature by improving upon nature as it exists in its untouched state. They are created to deliver nature in its ideal form, something nature cannot accomplish by itself. In this regard, the difference in the styles of gardens is relatively insignificant because any garden, according to one commentator, "remains a statement of power" insofar as its art consists of rearranging and reshaping natural objects to achieve a desired end.[3]

However, within the realm of gardens, there is a sense in which Japanese garden-making respects nature in a unique and specific way, unlike the way in which Western formal gardens represent idealized nature. The difference between them is not simply that the former lacks those features such as rigid geometry and strict symmetry that are prominent in the latter. Japanese gardens, while avoiding symmetry or geometrical design, do consist of meticulously pruned trees and strategically and artistically arranged rocks. It is precisely through such manipulation of natural materials that nature is believed to express itself more eloquently in Japanese gardens than in untouched nature. Despite the variety of styles of Japanese gardens and some prominent disputes throughout the history of this art form in Japan,[4] I contend that there is one consistent manner in which nature is enabled to articulate itself forcefully in Japanese gardens. In what follows I specifically discuss how the voice of nature is heard more clearly and forcefully in Japanese gardens through extensive modification of natural materials.

8.1. Creation of Scenic Effect

From the earliest existing record on garden-making in Japan, the *Sakutei Ki* (作庭記, *The Book of Garden-Making*), by an eleventh-century aristocrat, TACHIBANA-no-Toshitsuna (橘俊綱), we can gather that Japanese gardens were never intended to be literal and indiscriminate copies or miniaturizations of nature. Although nature was generally regarded worthy of aesthetic respect, Toshitsuna[5] clearly states that not all parts of nature are appreciable:

> Some person has remarked that the stones placed and the sceneries made by man can never excel the landscape in nature. Nevertheless, traveling through many provinces I have noted on several occasions that when I was deeply impressed by the beauty of some famous scenic site, I also found some worthless views existing close by. . . . In the case of a man-made landscape garden, since only the attractive and best parts of the places are studied and modelled after, meaningless stones and features are seldom provided along with man's work.[6]

This passage clearly indicates that gardens, while representing nature, were regarded as improvements upon bare nature as a result of their selective design.

The representational function of a Japanese garden, even when it is created selectively, is meant to be neither literal nor conceptual, but rather emotive and atmospheric. Toshitsuna advises prospective gardeners to reproduce *the scenic effect* of a particular view: "Think over the famous places of scenic beauty throughout the land, and, by making your own that which appeals to you most, design your garden with the mood of harmony, *modelling after the general air of such places*."[7] For example, the mood associated with a craggy mountain adorned with gnarled pine trees differs from the atmosphere surrounding a winding river gently pouring into a vast ocean, both of which again differ from the ambience evoked by an inland sea with many scattered islands in the mist. The challenge to the Japanese garden designer starts with a careful observation of nature to define such essential characteristics of a particular scene, followed by reproducing a distilled scenic atmosphere by way of creative imagination.

This reproduction of scenic effect is made possible, at least partly, by closely observing the specific habitat of natural objects and adhering to this correspondence in garden-making. With respect to planting trees, for example, a fifteenth-century treatise, *Senzui narabi ni Yagyō no Zu* (山水並に野形図, *Illustrations for Designing Mountain, Water, and Hillside Field Landscape*), recommends "making their natural habitats your model."[8] That is, trees from tall mountains must be planted in the mountain part rather than in the seashore part of a garden. The scenic effect of a tall mountain cannot be obtained by planting trees that typically grow on the seashore because the mood associated with those trees does not harmonize with the desired effect of the tall mountain. Associations accompanying natural materials must be unified to give rise to the overall coherent impression. A Japanese garden, accordingly, is successful when it effectively evokes the mysterious darkness of a tall mountain, the gentle peacefulness of a slowly winding river, or the forbidding dynamism of a waterfall rushing straight down to the pool below.

However, such successful expression of scenic mood must involve "little touch of artificiality," according to Toshitsuna. For example, stones at the top of a waterfall should be "placed in a more casual manner *as if they were left there and forgotten*," while a garden stream "should be made in some interesting and natural manner *without the air of artificiality*."[9] In short, the considerable human design required for successfully reproducing the scenic atmosphere must be hidden behind the appearance of nature.

8.2. The Principle of "Following the Request"

How then is it possible to create such an illusion of casualness and natural-ness while selectively distilling and representing the atmosphere charac-teristic of a particular scene? How can "an artificial beauty" be achieved that is "calculated to look as natural as possible"?[10]

The answer can be found in the most important and intriguing design principle of Japanese gardens, *kowan ni shitagau* (乞はんに従ふ, follow-ing the request),[11] first proposed in the *Sakutei Ki* and faithfully adhered to since then. Originally proposed as a method of arranging stones, this principle requires the designer to select the principal stone by closely observing its native characteristics, and to choose and arrange other stones to complement the main stone. According to the *Sakutei Ki*, the gardener "should first install one main stone, and then place other stones, in neces-sary numbers, in such a way as *to satisfy the requesting mood* of the main stone."[12] The unity of the whole arrangement is achieved by the selection and placement that accentuate the characteristics of each stone through contrast rather than repetition. For example, the *Sakutei Ki* suggests that the "running away" stones should be accompanied by "chasing after" stones, a leaning stone by a supporting stone, a "trampling" stone by the "trampled" stone, a "looking-up" stone by a "looking-down" stone, and an upright stone by a reclining stone.[13] Similarly, the *Illustrations* recom-mends the vertical placement of "the never aging rock" (a sharp-edged rock with distinct, straight grain) complemented by the horizontal place-ment of "the rock of ten thousand eons" (a relatively smooth stone with a gentle, cushion-like upper surface).[14]

This aesthetic principle of "following the request," initially proposed for arranging rocks, was subsequently applied to designing other aspects, even including the functional aspects, of the Japanese garden. For exam-ple, in making a bridge, a long and flat rock marked by prominent grain was often selected. Its lateral orientation becomes enhanced both by its horizontal placement and by an accompanying rock or rock arrangement with a prominent vertical thrust. Similarly, stepping stones were arranged by juxtaposing rocks of different and often contrasting colors, shapes, and textures in order to mutually articulate the respective sensory qualities.

The same aesthetic consideration operates in placing stones that are themselves already modified by human design, such as ashlar rocks made for the construction of castles, foundation stones from ruined temples, old base stones from bridge piers, and discarded millstones and mor-tar stones. When arranged as a bridge or stepping stones, these stones' relatively geometrical shapes and smooth texture were accentuated either by nongeometrical placement or by being placed next to those rocks found in nature that exhibit more irregular shapes and rough texture. Through such juxtaposition, the contrasting characteristics of both kinds of stones are made prominent.

The principle of enhancing the individual characteristics of an object also governs the placement and handling of trees and shrubs. For example, when planting trees and plants, one important consideration is to create a contrast of color, shape, and texture, particularly derived from the difference between evergreen and deciduous trees.[15] Furthermore, instead of allowing unmitigated free growth, Japanese gardeners meticulously shape the trees and shrubs by extensive pruning, clipping, shearing, pinching, or plucking, or sometimes by stunting the growth of some parts by use of a retardant.[16] Indeed, one commentator even identifies the secret of Japanese gardens with clippers and scissors: "Ask a Japanese gardener the secret of gardening and he will hold up his pruning shears."[17] Sometimes various gears such as wires, ropes, poles, and weights are used to maintain the unique shape of a particular tree.

However, unlike topiary in Western formal gardens, where shapes—for instance, that of a screw or an animal—are designated regardless of the characteristics of the plant material used, the desired shape of a tree in a Japanese garden is defined by the particular form of the tree itself. For example, the *Illustrations* specifically recommends:

> When it comes to horizontal trees, observe the natural growth pattern of the tree, and then prune it to bring out *its inherent scenic qualities*. . . . Do not prune back the longer of those branches inherent to a tree's natural growth pattern. . . . Prune out only those branches that wander erratically or are long and unkempt, *so as to achieve a visually harmonious effect*.[18]

The gardener is thus required to distinguish between the essential features of the particular material and its adventitious, inessential, and irrelevant aspects. The pruning consists of eliminating these latter elements to make room for a clear and forceful articulation of the former. This design process by "elimination" or "subtraction" is also used in a number of Japanese art forms, ranging from bonsai, flower arrangement, and brush ink painting to theatrical and literary media, all of which seek minimalistic expression by distilling the essence of the subject matter.[19]

This design principle of bringing out the essential features of the plant materials can be clearly seen in the manner of emphasizing the horizontal branches of Japanese pine trees. This is achieved by clearing pine needles growing underneath those branches, as well as by inserting a support to ensure that the horizontal growth of the branch remains intact. Similarly, the branches of some cherry trees are supported to enhance the drooping effect of their blossoms. Again, the round, mound shape of azalea bushes created by meticulous pruning is intended to best bring out the innate growth pattern characteristic of this particular plant. Sometimes this roundness becomes further emphasized by being juxtaposed against a rigid square pattern, such as the raking pattern of the sand underneath.

Through these various techniques of arranging the stones and shaping the trees, the Japanese garden aims at assisting nature articulate its inherent characteristics more eloquently. Whether the materials be stones or trees, the Japanese gardener is thus required to be a good listener of what they "request," and modify or arrange them in order to "follow their requests." Some commentators call this aspect of Japanese garden-making "the aesthetic of discovery."[20] That is, the particular design, whether for a rock arrangement or shaping a tree, is determined after the latent aesthetic potential of the material is discovered; it is not something conceived beforehand and imposed upon the material.[21] The garden makers here, therefore, must possess, in addition to a keen sensibility and artistic discrimination, a deferential and respectful attitude toward nature's dictate. They are both discoverers and designers of each natural object's defining features, which are often obscured by distracting elements and accidental growths. The garden made in this deferential manner, with nature itself as its guiding principle, therefore, is said to appear "natural" because the defining characteristics of each object are distilled into their essential forms. The result is an improvement upon bare, untouched nature; however, it is an improvement *according to* nature's characteristics rather than *in spite of* or *irrespective of* them.[22]

8.3. Contribution of Zen Buddhism

In addition to the influence of Chinese geomancy, which dictates specific rules and taboos concerning the placement of stones, trees, and streams in relation to the directions, the influence of the Japanese indigenous tradition of Shintoism bears clearly on the design principles in the *Sakutei Ki*. The main tenet of Shintoism is its attribution of spiritual qualities to all natural objects, rendering nature worthy of our respect and appreciation. The celebration of this world by Shintoism helped the Japanese cultivate a keen sensitivity toward its beauty. Consequently, Japanese garden design is firmly rooted in the observation of empirical reality. This gives rise to the design principle of "following the request."

However, by far the most important philosophical basis that sustained and further developed this principle of "following the request" was Zen Buddhism, introduced to Japan toward the end of the twelfth century, a century after the publication of the *Sakutei Ki*. The influence of Zen Buddhism on Japanese garden-making is extensive and profound. Zen temples were always accompanied by gardens for facilitating meditation. Furthermore, even the gardens not associated with Zen temples were frequently constructed by Zen priests or those laypeople, such as tea masters, who were trained in Zen Buddhism.[23] However, Zen's philosophical influence on Japanese garden-making is what interests us here.

The teaching of Zen Buddhism is based upon the fundamental belief that everything whatsoever is Buddha-nature, loosely interpreted as reality. This starting point commits Zen Buddhism to a thoroughly egalitarian view concerning the value of objects, phenomena, and activities. In terms of Buddha-nature, a commonplace rock or broken teabowl is as valuable as a gorgeous painting or an expensive porcelain bowl. Similarly, activities generally regarded as mundane, such as eating and sweeping the ground, are equally as significant as studying Buddhist texts and meditating.[24] For example, a fourteenth-century Zen priest, MUSŌ Soseki (夢窓 疎石, also known as MUSŌ Kokushi 夢窓国師), who is also noted for the gardens he made, declares: "[All the things] the world contains—grass and trees, bricks and tile, all creatures, all actions and activities—are nothing but manifestations of this Law" (that is, Buddha-nature) and that "all those here present, including patrons and officials, the very eaves and columns of this hall, lanterns and posts, as well as all the men, animals, plants and seeds in the boundless ocean of existence . . . keep the wheel of the Law in motion."[25]

However, experiencing Buddha-nature as *everything* is difficult because of various distinctions and valuations necessary for organizing our everyday life. According to the noted Zen thinker of the thirteenth century, Dōgen (道元), our phenomenal world is guided by "the burden of self";[26] that is, it is organized by either personal or anthropocentric interests. However, the successful shedding of this all-too-human viewpoint facilitates our direct, unmediated experience of everything, transcending everyday concerns. In such an enlightened experience, it becomes possible that "the green mountains are forever walking," "a stone woman bears a child by night," and "water is not strong or weak, not wet or dry, not moving or still, not cool or warm, not existent or nonexistent, not delusion or enlightenment."[27] The ultimate reality is then describable only as simply being the way things are. Each object or phenomenon exhibits its Buddha-nature by simply and thoroughly being itself, exerting and asserting its "thusness."[28]

Furthermore, when each object is simply being itself by exhibiting its "thusness," the coexistence of objects and phenomena is made possible by mutual dependency. For example, the arrival of spring and the blossoming of flowers mutually sustain each other.[29] The assertion of individual "thusness" creates an ineffable harmony, or responsive rapport between and among various objects and phenomena. The harmony here is not pre-established; rather, it is given rise to spontaneously by the co-arising of various phenomena and coexisting of various objects, each of which is simply asserting its own "thusness."

Many Zen-inspired Japanese art forms are designed to help the audience engage in directly experiencing this Zen worldview. They do so by creating a microcosm in which the responsive rapport spontaneously brought about by the "thusness" of each object is given a sensuous expression. These art forms include chanoyu, gardens, Noh theater, haiku, linked verse, and calligraphy, as well as martial arts. Chanoyu is perhaps the most conspicuous example of providing an aesthetic environment for the layman's experience of Zen enlightenment. This art form celebrates the aesthetic value of the otherwise mundane activities of washing hands, eating, and drinking tea, as well as those commonplace objects such as ordinary-looking earthenware and flowering twigs. Furthermore, the participants are encouraged to appreciate the once-in-a-lifetime harmony created by the various ingredients constituting the occasion, ranging from such relatively obvious elements as the sensory qualities of the garden, hut, and tea utensils to less evident elements such as the weather conditions, placement of utensils on the tatami, and the conversation between the host and the guests.

The aim of many Japanese gardens can be compared to certain points underlying the Way of Tea. In gardens, the use of "found objects" indicates the commitment to discover aesthetic value in objects that are ordinarily considered aesthetically uninspiring. The particular way in which the rocks are arranged and the trees are shaped reveals that the overall harmony is generated by the mutual articulation and enhancement of each element's individual features, the "thusness" of each material. Harmony is never preconceived; rather, it is given rise to by the particular ingredients available at the time. One commentator remarks that the influence of Zen Buddhism is evident in Japanese gardens, where "the everyday stone and the commonplace pool [are] allowed to express their natures, [and are] allowed to whisper their meaning."[30] However, instead of merely presenting the "thusness" of an everyday stone or a freely growing, commonplace tree, the art of Japanese garden design creates an idealized microcosm of nature where each "thusness" becomes crystalized, giving rise to the overall harmony.

In this respect, one could find similarities, rather than differences, between Japanese gardens and Western formal gardens. The rigid geometrical patterns and symmetrical order of Western formal gardens, absent in Japanese gardens, also result from distilling the essence of nature, interpreted from the classical Western point of view. The Aristotelian legacy of viewing the essence of nature as order, unity, and coherence receives perhaps the most vivid visual representation in Western formal gardens. The logical order and coherence considered present, yet hidden, in nature becomes embodied in the geometrically laid-out ground and precisely clipped hedges and shrubs.[31]

Thus, both Japanese gardens and Western formal gardens give expression to idealized nature by distilling nature's essential features. The difference between them lies in the fact that the idealized form of nature in the Western formal garden is conceived in the intellect irrespective of nature's empirical manifestation, while the idealized form of nature in the Japanese garden is derived from the perceived features of empirical nature. Both gardens are attempts to give expression to the respective notion of idealized nature; however, only the Japanese garden pays tribute to nature as we experience it, rather than as we think of it.

As a result, the measure of artistic excellence in Japanese gardens can only be phrased in a paradoxical way: they are successful to the extent that human artifice seems absent. That is, the ideal gardener lets nature be the guide in determining the particular design, instead of imposing an overall scheme on individual materials and forcing them to conform to the preconceived plan, irrespective of their own characteristics. It should be a "space in which the art itself is so artless as to be totally unapparent," consisting of "the beauty of plants and stones that appear unaltered by human hands."[32] The hallmark of artistic success in Zen-related arts is spontaneity, artlessness, and freedom, without thereby meaning the absence of rule observance or human artifice. The highest artistic accomplishment within the Zen tradition is achieved when the artist has mastered and integrated the technique and rules of the medium so thoroughly that the end product, whether it be a tea-making procedure at a chanoyu gathering, a work of calligraphy, or a haiku, appears as if it is spontaneously and effortlessly generated. In the same vein, when the art of discerning and enhancing nature's essential characteristics becomes so accomplished, the garden looks as if it simply "became" rather than was "made into" one.[33]

8.4. Conclusion

Japanese gardens and Western formal gardens are commonly held in contrast. There is a need, however, to carefully define how they differ. We should keep in mind that both aim at presenting a sensuous expression of the essence of nature through extensive manipulation and modification. The difference lies in the way in which the essential features of nature get distilled. Western formal gardens, in general, rely on human intellectual analysis of nature's working, irrespective of its perceivable qualities. Japanese gardens, on the other hand, are designed to further emphasize and articulate the essential qualities of the natural materials, which are available yet obscured to our senses. If Japanese gardens embody a respectful attitude toward nature, it is in this aesthetic sense: to carefully observe nature and design its ideal form by "following the request."[34]

Notes

1. ITOH Teiji, *The Japanese Garden: An Approach to Nature* (New Haven: Yale University Press, 1972), 140. See also David H. Engel, *Japanese Gardens for Today* (Rutland, VT: C. E. Tuttle, 1959), 12.

2. For example, see Itoh's comparison between the Western garden that "represents ambition attained, nature subdued" and the Japanese garden, in which "there is no assumption that there is something better than nature" (*Japanese Garden*, 138). Or refer to KOJIRO Yūichirō's description of European formal gardens as "nature conquered by artificiality" in "The Japanese and Their Gardens," in *Tradition of Japanese Garden* (Tokyo: Kokusai Bunka Shinkōkai, 1963), 14.

3. Marc Treib, "Power Plays: The Garden as Pet," in *The Meaning of Gardens: Ideas, Place, and Action*, ed. Mark Francis and Randolph T. Hester, Jr. (Cambridge, MA: MIT Press, 1990), 93. The same point is made by Yi-Fu Tuan, a cultural geographer, in his interpretation of garden-making as one form of pet-making, an expression of human power over nature. See Yi-Fu Tuan, *Dominance and Affection: The Making of Pets* (New Haven: Yale University Press, 1984).

4. For example, a debate occurred during the sixteenth century concerning the treatment of the leaves and pine needles fallen over bridges, paths, and stepping-stones. The most noted sixteenth-century tea master, SEN Rikyū, preferred the natural atmosphere of the fallen leaves and pine needles. Some of his disciples, however, thought it best to clear the path or stepping stones. Yet another disciple, FURUTA Oribe, tried to find creative

uses of those leaves by using them for decoration. See TANAKA Seidai, *Nihon no Teien* (*Japanese Gardens*) (Tokyo: Kashima Kenkyūsho Shuppankai, 1967).

5. Editor's note: Although his surname is Tachibana, the landscape designer is often referred to by his given name, Toshitsuna.

6. TACHIBANA-no-Toshitsuna, *Sakuteiki: The Book of Garden [-Making], Being a Full Translation of the Japanese Eleventh Century Manuscript: Memoranda on Garden Making Attributed to the Writing of Tachibana-no-Toshitsuna*, trans. SHIMOYAMA Shigemaru (Tokyo: Town & City Planners, 1985), 32, slightly altered. This attitude toward nature (that while nature provides abundant materials for artistic representation, it also must be edited for such a purpose) is analogous to the way in which the eighteenth-century British picturesque writers "improved" actual sceneries either in their imagination or in their sketches during their travels in search of picturesque beauty.

7. Tachibana-no-Toshitsuna, *Sakuteiki*, 1, emphasis added.

8. Zōen, *Illustrations for Designing Mountain, Water, and Hillside Field Landscape*, in *Secret Teachings in the Art of Japanese Gardens: Design Principles, Aesthetic Values*, ed. and trans. David A. Slawson (Tokyo: Kōdansha International, 1991), sec. 10. Regarding rocks, for example, a contemporary commentator points out: "Rocks of sharp, rugged form found in the mountains conform most naturally and realistically as symbolic mountains of a garden. Similarly, rounded rocks and stones taken from a river bed are best used to make the course of a garden stream" (Engel, *Japanese Gardens for Today*, 29).

9. Tachibana-no-Toshitsuna, *Sakuteiki*, 11, 12, and 20 (emphasis added).

10. ITO Teiji, *The Gardens of Japan* (Tokyo: Kōdansha International, 1984), 84.

11. This principle can be compared to the Western notion of genius loci, particularly important in making picturesque gardens. It stresses the importance of designing a garden that respects and incorporates the topographical features of the land.

12. Tachibana-no-Toshitsuna, *Sakuteiki*, 20, emphasis added. An almost identical passage reiterates the importance of this point, saying that the gardener "should first complete the placing of the principal stone having a distinct character, and then proceed to set other stones complying to the 'requesting' mood of the principal stone" (23). This principle of following the request of the material may partly account for the absence of water fountains in Japanese gardens. The Japanese manipulation of water is always in accordance with its conformity to gravity, rather than in defiance to gravity in the form of a high jump into the air. For a discussion of the significance of water fountains, see chapter 4 in Yi-Fu Tuan and O-Young Lee, *Smaller Is Better: Japan's Mastery of the Miniature*, trans. Robert N. Huey (Tokyo: Kōdansha International, 1984), 86.

13. Tachibana-no-Toshitsuna, *Sakuteiki*, 25.

14. Zōen, *Illustrations for Designing*, sections 85–86. This design principle of complement, which rejects repetition and symmetry, is also supported by the rule of asymmetry established in *Sakutei Ki: Suji Kaete* (changing the axis) (Tachibana-no-Toshitsuna, *Sakuteiki*, 3, 27). The insistence on asymmetrical design becomes expressed later as a taboo concerning placing two rocks of the same size and same shape side by side. See *Hihon Sakutei-den* (*Secret Book of Garden Making*), included in MORI Osamu's *Teien* (*Gardens*) (Tokyo: Kondō Shuppansha, 1984), 58.

15. See pp. 85–96 of WATSUJI Tetsurō's *Katsura Rikyū* (*The Detached Villa at Katsura*) (Tokyo: Chūkō Bunko, 1991) concerning this point.

16. In section 59 of *Illustrations for Designing*, Zōen instructs the gardener to apply a mixture of rat droppings and sulfur to retard the growth of some branches.

17. Itoh, *The Japanese Garden*, 140.

18. Zōen, *Illustrations for Designing*, section 56, emphasis added. The same considerations guide the shaping of a bonsai tree. See pp. 96–99 of YAMAKAWA Midori's *Nihon Bunka no Tokushitsu* (*Characteristics of Japanese Culture*), a special edition of *Geijutsu Shinchō* 8, no. 8 (Tokyo: Shinchōsha, 1991).

19. The aesthetics of subtraction (*hikizan no bigaku*) are explored by KURITA Isamu, while the aesthetics of elimination (*kirisute no bigaku*) are discussed by WATSUJI Tetsurō. See KURITA Isamu, *Nihon Bunka no Kiiwādo* (*Key Terms of Japanese Culture*) (Tokyo: Shōdensha, 1993) 124–125, and Watsuji, *Katsura Rikyū*, 84.

20. ITOH Teiji, *The Japanese Garden* (Tokyo: Kōdansha International, 1984), 35. Similarly, David Engel points out: "By *discovering* the hidden artistic potentialities in a plant, the Japanese gardener can emphasize these qualities, eliminate distracting elements, simplify its lines, and thus reveal its true nature to the world" (*Japanese Gardens for Today*, 4, emphasis added).

21. This absence of a predetermined overall design to which parts are made to conform is also a feature of the way in which typical Japanese cities, such as Tokyo, have been created. Instead of the geometrical scheme used to create cities such as Paris, Beijing, and Kyoto (which was modeled after an ancient Chinese city), Tokyo is marked by "the centrifugal character of buildings or cities that start with individual parts and expand, the proliferation of parts defining the shape in a random manner." See ASHIHARA Yoshinobu, *The Hidden Order: Tokyo through the Twentieth Century*, trans. Lynne E. Riggs (Tokyo: Kodansha International 1989), 54–55. See also Augustin Berque, "The Sense of Nature and Its Relation to Space in Japan," *Journal of the Anthropological Society of Oxford* 15, No. 2 (1984): 100–110.

22. This commitment to site-specific and object-specific design makes possible the construction of Japanese gardens outside of Japan, where plants and rocks indigenous to Japan are seldom available. For example, a leading twentieth-century landscape gardener, IWAKI Sentarō, studied the indigenous rocks and trees along the Rhine for two years before constructing a Japanese garden in Düsseldorf in 1976. All the materials used in this garden, except for three stone lanterns and some bamboo trees for the fence, came from the areas around Düsseldorf (dialogue between IWAKI Sentarō and SUZUKI Hiroyuki in *Teien no Bi* (*The Beauty of Gardens*), ed. TSUBOTA Itsuo [Tokyo: Akatsuki Kyōiku Tosho Kabushikigaisha, 1980], 53). Similarly, NAKANE Kinsaku, another celebrated garden designer, studied the New England topography and vegetation extensively, both on land and from the air, before constructing the Japanese garden for the Museum of Fine Arts in Boston. The challenge posed by Japanese gardens outside of Japan, however, seems to lie in their constant maintenance. It requires somebody with a keen intuition and artistic sensibility who is also well-versed in the art of "following nature's request."

23. One reason for this close relationship between Zen Buddhism and Japanese garden-making is found in the Zen doctrine that any activity, including dirtying one's hands dealing with soil, is valuable. See ITOH Teiji, *Imperial Gardens of Japan* (New York: Walker/Weatherhill, 1970).

24. A full discussion of this Zen egalitarianism can be found in *Shōbōgenzō* (*The Storehouse of True Knowledge*) by a thirteenth-century Zen writer Dōgen. In

particular, see the chapters "Genjōkōan" ("The Issue at Hand") and "Hosshō" ("The Nature of Things"). See Dōgen, *Shōbōgenzō: Zen Essays by Dōgen*, trans. Thomas Cleary (Honolulu: University of Hawaiʻi Press, 1986).

25. MUSŌ Kokushi, "Sermon at the Opening of Tenryu Monastery," in *Sources of Japanese Tradition*, ed. TSUNODA Ryūsaku, Wm. Theodore de Bary, and Donald Keene (New York: Columbia University Press, 1964), 254.

26. Dōgen, "Genjōkōan," 32.

27. Dōgen, "Sansuikyō" ("The Scripture of Mountains and Waters"), in *Shōbōgenzō*, 89, 93.

28. See "Hosshō" ("The Nature of Things"), 38–41, and "Immo" ("Such"), 49–55, both in Dōgen, *Shōbōgenzō*.

29. Dōgen, "Kūge" ("Flowers in the Sky"), in *Shōbōgenzō*. Dōgen expresses the same point in "Zenki" ("The Whole Works").

30. Itoh, *The Japanese Garden* (1972), 139.

31. The long-held view that the beauty of nature cannot be found in empirical reality but only in its intellectual conception underlies artistic tradition in the West. For example, a sculpture of the human body, according to this tradition, realizes the ideal human body conceived in the artist's mind, which cannot be identified with any one particular person's body. It is interesting to note in this regard that the predominant medium of sculpture in Japan has historically been woodcarving, whereby the sculptor is supposed to bring out the potential form already latent in the particular piece of wood. The sculptural medium that requires the artist to construct an ideal mold out of clay never became a popular method in Japan.

32. HAYAKAWA Masao, *The Garden Art of Japan*, trans. Richard L. Gage (New York: John Weatherhill, 1973), 9–10; Itoh, *The Japanese Garden* (1972), 34.

33. Paul Reasoner discusses how the haiku master Bashō insisted that a good poet does not "make" a poem but rather lets the subject matter "become" a poem. See "Sincerity and Japanese Values," *Philosophy East and West* 40, no. 4 (1990): 471–488.

34. It is debatable whether this respect for nature in the aesthetic sense carries an ethical (ecological, to be specific) dimension. Although an ecologically desirable respect for nature is not incompatible with this aesthetic respect, it is not necessarily implied by the latter, either. I have argued elsewhere that this Japanese respect for nature, which is primarily aesthetic, does not necessarily lead to an ecologically desirable stance toward nature. See Yuriko Saitō, "The Japanese Love of Nature: A Paradox," *Landscape* 31, no. 2 (1992): 1–8.

CHAPTER 9 | KUKI Shūzō and Platonism
Nature, Love, and Morality

YAMAUCHI TOMOSABURŌ

9.1. Plato's Three Aspects of the Soul and Three Classes

KUKI Shūzō (九鬼周造, 1888–1941) was a unique figure in the philosophical circle known as the Kyoto school, which was led by NISHIDA Kitarō. Kuki was from a noble samurai family and well versed in traditional Japanese culture. He began his philosophical career by studying Western medieval and modern philosophies and later taught modern Western philosophy at Kyoto University. Kuki mastered French, German, and English and understood classical Chinese, Greek, Latin, Sanskrit, and Italian. He was well read and in a good position to compare Eastern and Western cultures. His first book, *The Structure of Japanese Taste* (*Iki*), has been widely read and become a classic of Japanese studies, having been translated into many Western languages. A careful examination of Kuki's aesthetics can reveal some of the problematic assumptions at the heart of Western environmental views, which are grounded in Platonic metaphysics.

One of the most influential critics of Platonism (and of Western Christianity) was Nietzsche, followed by Karl Popper and Ernst Topitsch, who were also known in Japanese academic circles. John Leslie Mackie and Richard Mervyn Hare, from the viewpoint of analytic ethics, rejected the existence of Forms. Val Plumwood also criticized Platonism from an environmental-ethics viewpoint. Today Platonism is a philosophy of the past. Yet the influence of Plato's view of humans and social ethics on Western thought and cultures is too immense to be neglected. Given that one of the central themes of today's environmental ethics is the problem of the relationship between human beings and nature, the human attitude toward nature in cultures that diverge from Western modernism is worthy of consideration.

Let us begin by examining the Platonic theory of love (erōs, philia) that underlies his psychology, anthropology, and politics. In arguing about justice in the *Republic*,[1] Plato divided people into three classes: rulers (philosophers), guardians, and common people. He argued that the virtue of the state (*polis*) consists in the unity or harmony of these classes, while justice consists of each class doing the work suitable for that class— philosopher-kings ruling, guardians enforcing the decrees of the rulers, and common people working at their trades and professions, together constituting the economic engine of the polis. Further, there are three elements of the soul (*psychē*): reason (*nous, logistikon*), spirit (*thymos*), and appetite (*epithymētikon*). Justice in individuals consists in the control of the appetitive element by reason helped by the spirit, each element functioning according to its nature—reason ruling the appetites, supported by the spirited faculty, while injustice in individuals inverts this natural order, the appetites ruling the other two faculties of the soul.[2]

There lies, in the three elements of the soul, Platonic "love" (*erōs*), since three types of people are called respectively "lovers of wisdom or learning" (*philosophos, philomathes*), "lovers of fame or victory" (*philotimos, philonikos*), and "lovers of gain or money" (*philokerdes, philoxrēmatos*). Here, love , or the desire of soul is, divided into three elements according to its object: wisdom, fame, and gain or self-interest. The three types of people issue from the three elements of the soul in each type.[3]

The ultimate object of Platonic *erōs* is in *the Form* of Truth, Good, or Beauty. Therefore, when, after Nietzsche, the theory of Forms was abandoned, only the shadowy, relative values of the sensible, phenomenal remained. Reason (*nous*), which yearns for and pursues the absolute ideal of the Form, loses its object of love; but its role as a steersman (*kybernētēs*) guiding the whole soul remains unaffected by the rejection of the theory of Forms.

In another of Plato's picturesque similes, the soul's three elements— reason, spirit, and desire—are respectively likened to a small human being, a lion, and a monster, the chimera, while their combination has the external appearance of a human being.[4] Then a good and right person is one whose small person within controls the monstrous beast by the aid of the courageous lion; and an evil, unjust person is one in whom the evil desires of the monster dominate his whole soul. If one compares a just and an unjust person in this simile, one finds that the former is most happy and the latter most unhappy.[5] In the Platonic individual-state parallelism, this simile is applicable to the types of state. The just state is one in which the three classes are in accord, philosopher-kings benignly governing common people with the aid of guardians, and an unjust state is one in which either the common people rule (democracy) or, worse still, an evil dictator dominates (tyranny).

In describing the ideal state (*polis*), Plato at first pictures a very simple state consisting of people with only the necessary food, clothing, and housing, all dividing the required labor, each doing what he or she is suited to by nature—some growing food, others making clothing, others building houses, and so on. Although he recognizes such a society as a healthy one, at the behest of his interlocutors, he proceeds to create a more luxurious state where an army is needed to seize the territory necessary to support such luxury and defend it against other states that might aspire to also become luxurious.[6] This foreshadows Plato's later discussion of desires, in which he did not denounce all human desires, but accepted those that are necessary for people to live. He espoused a minimal essential lifestyle; and certainly would have decried the excessive affluence of many of today's societies, particularly in comparison with the life of voluntary poverty embraced by his master, Socrates.

The best and most just states are those that are ruled by reason and thus by philosophers (the true *aristocracy*). The more unjust states are, in order of degradation, *timocracy*, governed by those who desire for fame; *oligarchy* or *plutocracy*, governed by those who love money; *democracy*, governed by hoi polloi, embodying all desires, chaotically liberated; and *tyranny*, governed by the worst desire: lust for power.[7]

In this classical ethico-politics, within the sensible world, all beautiful, right, and valuable things are of relative value; they are only a reflection of the objective and absolute value in the intellectual world. (The *Form of Good* is somehow the origin of being, knowledge, and value.) There is no space for the estimation of nature or love of nature here, neither in the ethico-politics nor in the mind of individuals.

It is noteworthy that Plato considered that "the essential mark, and internal motive force of the soul is *Erōs,* the stream of desire which may be directed into different channels." When the stream flows mainly into one channel, the flow toward other channels weakens.[8] In Plato's Form-oriented ethics, the restraint of the desire for fame or wealth can be attained by changing the flow of *erōs* toward the Form of the Good (that is, the very origin of the absolute truth, goodness, and beauty). Here one can see that the person whose three innate elements of soul are in order is to be called a just and good person; that is, it is the love of order in the soul (*ordo amoris*), not the order of objective values, that divides just from unjust people.

Then, if people in a Form-oriented society diverge from the belief in objective value (which was considered absolute, universal, and eternal), they tend, losing control over desire that was once controlled by reason, to pursue power for power's sake, money for money's sake. This can be seen as the source of the current problems of environmental ethics, where, in the time of our ecological crisis, we need to discover how to redirect desire toward preserving the order—its integrity, stability, and beauty—of nature. We must seek a way to channel desire away from fame and money and toward the integrity, stability, and beauty of nature, as a supremely well-ordered system of which we are a part. Like the citizens of the just polis, we must play our natural part and not the part of the evil and destructive tyrant.

9.2. *Ordo Amoris* in Plato and Kuki

In traditional Japanese thought and culture, nature was considered a living entity, a view expressed in such mottos as "Everything was born from *Yang* [陽, masculine principle] and *Yin* (陰, feminine principle]," "Heaven and earth are our great father and mother," "All things are one body," and so forth. Humans are, as a part of nature, inseparable from nature. So, the human-to-nature relationship was considered fundamental to being human. Nature is, in this sense, the very basis of human society, from which originated all sorts of culture, ideals, values, institutions, religions, thoughts, and so on. If everything was considered to have been born from heaven-earth-nature (天地自然 *ten-chi-shizen),* then personal love among humans might be considered a miniature of, or an imitation of, a cosmic love.[9]

Nature was, in this ecological sense, the basis of traditional Japanese culture. Japanese people's attitudes are, in a way, restricted by natural conditions, because people have to live on the small islands of the Japanese archipelago, nourishing a large population without destroying the natural environment. In Edo Japan, they not only maintained it, they enhanced nature, making it more productive, while creating a symbiotic culture based on nature. Hence *the welfare of humans and nature as a whole*—not only human or only natural welfare—was the supreme imperative of their morality. Thus, obedience to nature became second nature, so that people did not feel it as compulsory conformism and constraint, but only as natural, when they had to live simple lives, restraining themselves from surplus self-interest in order not to destroy the natural environment. Edo Japan might well be thought to exemplify some aspects of Plato's healthy state sketched in the second book of the *Republic*, although it was ruled by the shogun and samurai, so it also exemplifies some elements of Plato's ideal state portrayed in books 3 through 7 of the *Republic*.

Let us next examine Kuki's anthropological views. According to Kuki, all humans have three aspects: metaphysical (*homo meta-physicus*), historical (or social, *homo historicus*), and natural (*homo naturalis*). Humans have these three elements in a unitary fusion. In discussing Japanese character and culture, Kuki mentions three "moments" that are found in them: nature, (自然), spirit (意気), and resignation (諦念), corresponding to Shinto, Confucianism, and Buddhism.[10] One can surmise that these three moments originated from Plato, since Kuki referred to the three Platonic and Aristotelian aspects of the soul more frequently than to Augustine, Pascal, Maine de Biran, Buddhism, or Confucianism.[11] Kuki argued that Japanese culture originated from Shinto as the material cause and from Confucian idealism and Buddhist antirealism as formal causes.[12] The Australian philosopher Damon Young, in his article on *budō* (the way of the samurai), analyzed some aspects of Japanese culture expressed in the martial art judo. He attributed *budō* to its spiritual background of Shinto, Confucianism, and Buddhism. Considering that he did not refer to Kuki's philosophy, it is indeed a happy coincidence that his deep insights into Japanese culture resonate with Kuki's.

Kuki's generation did not anticipate the forthcoming environmental crisis; the fact that he founded his anthropology on the basis of nature may show the nature-oriented character of traditional Japanese culture. This may be seen more clearly in his analysis of traditional taste for *iki*, a mode of love born in the Edo era, a characteristic of Japanese culture expressed in refined, detached, heterosexual love. In Japanese, *iki* originally meant "breathing" (息), "anima" or "life" (生), "morale" or "high spirit" (意気), and "gallantry" (粋). The three moments of *iki* are, as rendered by Kuki, "coquetry," "spirit," and "resignation." *Iki* is created on the basis of "coquetry" (or amorousness) as material cause, with "spirit," originating from Confucian idealism (from which *bushidō*, the way of the samurai, originated), and "resignation," from Buddhist antirealism, both being used as formal causes. *Iki* comes,[13] in this sense, between celestial Platonic love and terrestrial *erōs* in Aristophanes's fashion, as portrayed by Plato in the *Symposium*.[14]

These three characteristics are seen also in his analysis of traditional aesthetics of *hū-ryū* (風流, etymologically meaning "wind flow"), expressed in a natural, elegant, and simple lifestyle. Three elements of *hū-ryū* are nature, unworldliness, and aestheticism. Love of nature is especially expressed in a wandering journey (*tabi* 、旅). Thus *iki* and *hū-ryū* are expressions of Japanese character and culture in the shape of a nature-oriented aesthetics and lifestyle.[15]

"In every Japanese art," Kuki writes, "in short poems [*waka*] and haiku, also in paintings, calligraphy, architecture, from the way of tea [*sadō*, tea ceremony] and the way of flowers [*kadō*, flower arrangement] to garden designing, the aim is the unified fusion of nature and the arts. Needless to say, this characteristic comes to the fore remarkably when one compares Japanese and Western flower arrangements or landscape gardens."[16]

Compare Kuki's view with Plato's in table 9.1.

We can see that Kuki's views are quite different from Plato's, though Kuki inherited Plato's critical framework on humanity. Comparing Platonic ethics with Kukian philosophy, one recognizes certain elements that are relevant to today's environmental ethics, as follows:

1. In the Platonic view, the world of *Forms* is primary and seems to dominate all beings. Kuki's view is the reverse; *nature* is the most basic source on which all beings are founded. This is most relevant to today's environmental ethics.
2. In Kuki's phenomenal worldview, in sharp contrast to Plato's, another world of objective values is not posited to exist. Thus all values are relative to each other, and it is basically the *love* (愛, 恋, desire, liking, or preference) of the valuer or moral agent, not objective values, that decides good and evil, right and wrong, beautiful and ugly, since the orders of objective values are different from culture to culture, from religion to religion, and from person to person.

TABLE 9.1 A Comparison of Plato's and Kuki's Philosophical Systems

PLATO	KUKI
Three aspects	Anthropology: Japanese culture—*Iki—hū-ryū*
Reason (*nous*): *erōs* for Forms	Metaphysical, resignation
Spirit (*thymos*)	Historical, spirit
Appetite (*epithymētikon*)	Natural, nature, coquetry

3. For one who posits Platonic absolute ideals and objective values, morality is not compulsion but pleasure. Likewise, one who loves ethics originating from a love of nature (a sort of unification of humans with nature) does not feel morality as compulsion but as joyful expression, just as deep ecological self-realization brings joy.

4. Kuki shares utilitarianism at the social and ethical level with Plato. In creating his ideal polis, Plato wished people to devote their efforts to making the whole polis happier, instead of single-mindedly pursuing their own happiness.[17] Indeed happiness (eudaemonia—literally "well-spirited"—for Plato is found in having a well-ordered soul, found in virtue, that is, *aretē*, or excellence of character).

In Kuki's anthropology and social ethics, the valuer or moral agent is concerned with human society, along with nature. A sort of holism also colors Kuki's view of society and nature, so that he aims for the welfare of humans and nature as a whole, because it is a presupposition of his ethics that human society and thought are founded on the basis of nature. Kuki's philosophy is, in this sense, informative for the integration of social ethics and environmental ethics. Our stream of love may be limited to a certain degree, such that if it flows more toward, say, love of money and fame, energy flows less toward love of nature. To make nature greener and to make more money at the same time would be ethically impossible, since no one can serve two masters, both Pan and Mammon.

If Japanese people are qualified to take any role in conserving this planet, as Fritjof Capra suggests,[18] it might be found in the traditional Japanese character and culture that Kuki described, which is unique and different both from other cultures of the East and those of the West. Let us examine next Kuki's view of nature.

Environmental ethics is embedded in Kuki's lifestyle in the love of nature, or *hū-ryū*. Kuki's aesthetic of *hū-ryū* reflects that of traditional wandering poets such as Saigyō (西行, 1118–1190) and Bashō (芭蕉, 1644–1694), and their followers,[19] whose lives were filled with love for nature. We can liken Kuki to the wandering poets, especially during his stay in Paris, where he composed many poems. *Hū-ryū*, characterized by Kuki as nature (自然), unworldliness (脱俗), and aestheticism (耽美), the very opposite of "fame-and-gain" (名利 *myō-ri*), which permeates the spirit and lifestyle of ambitious people.

If we trace his spiritual background to Buddhist resignation, we find it in the traditional Zen Buddhism of such thinkers as Dōgen (道元, 1200–1253) and Ryōkan (良寛, 1757–1831). Whereas Dōgen has been given fresh consideration by Western environmental philosophers and has had many of his poems translated into English, Ryōkan, nicknamed "Great Fool" (*tai-gu*), though most popular among Japanese people, is virtually unknown elsewhere. He was a first-rate calligrapher and poet, renowned for having led a very simple life in a hermitage on the mountainside. He often played with village children, having no worldly goods except clothing and a bowl for begging. This is a model of perfection in the religious life of *hū-ryū*—an ascetic aesthete who is not worldly and leads a life that is symbiotic with nature. In his later years, he communicated and exchanged poems with a nun called Teishin-ni, a sort of Platonic love with a flavor of *iki*. The Buddhist analog for St. Francis, the Christian paragon of environmental virtue, would have to be Ryōkan. When Kuki was young he was an admirer of St. Francis. Although Kuki was not a very religious person in the customary sense of the word, his philosophy of resignation and love of nature originated from Japanese Buddhist traditions.

On the other hand, Kuki was of an amorous character and, both in Paris and in Kyoto, enjoyed philosophy, music, arts, literature, dance, and *iki*. He wrote, in a short poem, "I am from the country where cherry blossoms and people die for love." He might have thought that to live is to love. He showed a protean aspect in his life: sometimes as Stoic, sometimes Epicurean, according to the changing channels of his love. One can imagine the distress in which Kuki found himself as an eccentric philosopher in a conventional academic circle.

He mentioned in an essay that the first of all his favored books is the *Symposium* of Plato, in which the ascent of Eros toward the Form of Beauty (which is also equated with the Good, explicitly in the *Symposium* and implicitly in the *Republic*) is the central theme; Kuki writes that in the *Symposium* "the core of morality, arts, religion, and philosophy is captured straightforwardly and shown."[20] One can reverse the direction of love: that is, to redirect the love for money and fame toward love of the beauty and goodness—or more generally, the order—of nature. For however much one may be intelligent and hold a prestigious position, once a person clings overmuch to fame, he is, by a nature-oriented standard, nothing but a worldly minded snob. A philosopher must, as stated by Plato, set himself apart from money and fame.[21]

Kuki once wrote in a short essay titled "On Form and Content" that those who are ardently attached to fame and position, and those who wish for social success, cannot be free. Though free people will stumble and be rejected, "The axis of the earth goes round the free person. . . . To cling to the ready-made *forms* is the common way of snobbish people. To proceed earnestly toward the living *substances* is the task of the philosophers. How lamentable it is when the majority of philosophers are merely snobbish people."[22] Attachment to fame and gain was often despised by people in the Edo society; while merchants pursued money, bureaucratic samurai were mostly poor but honored and prepared to die for honor's sake. They strikingly resemble Platonic guardians.

So far we have seen that if one controls the monstrous desires within, one can change the direction of flow of the central erotic desire toward a disinterested love of nature, much as modern environmental philosophers such as Muir, Leopold, Naess, and Callicott recommend we find joy in union with nature.

9.3. The Structure of *Iki* and Environmental Ethics

Today, given the critical situation of the global environment, one of the urgent tasks for our ethical deliberations must be what we ought to do to make our society sustainable, and how we are to live for that purpose. This task seems difficult, because the difference between rich and poor is too great. The excess consumption of the rich has resulted in the enormous political and economic suppression of lower classes and nature itself.[23]

Today's Platonic monsters take the shape of industrialization, multinational corporations, hegemonic power states, and a self-interest-oriented economy. Although the Platonic individual-as-state is no longer applicable in today's environmental ethics, these environmentally destructive monsters originate from the desires in each person's psyche. What today's environmental ethics should address is, at least theoretically, such situations. But in doing so, we can no longer rely on the Platonic Form or the Christian God.

What we may instead find in Platonic ethics that is relevant to today's social ethics for creating the framework of new environmental ethics is this: Plato considered the essential function of the soul to be love (*erōs*) and the role of reason to be a steersman that controls or orders the desires of soul. Of course for Plato, order and harmony in the human soul are nourished by seeking the Forms and the Forms are considered the very origin of order and harmony. One can, however, absent the Forms, find the epitome of order and harmony in nature. Nature, like the Forms, is universal, common to all cultures. In the absence of Forms, reason can control and order the whole soul and, via a well-ordered soul, live a well-ordered—that is a good, beautiful, and happy—life. To judge rightly, one has to know the facts about oneself, society, the world, and especially nature. In the case of environmental ethics, such knowledge is an aspect of the faculty of reason. In order for reason to guide the soul, it must determine the right course of action according to facts and logic. In cases where there is no objective value, the moral agent can decide which course of action is right or wrong on the basis of love of universal nature. Doing so brings us closer to the environmental ethics embedded in traditional Japanese environmental thought and culture.

One of the most urgent problems for our environmental ethics is, as stated earlier, the global environmental crisis: that is, how are we to change our course of action in order to create a sustainable society? A viable answer to this question must be ethical. Suppose the alternative courses of action we confront are A and B. A is to continue the present state of affairs headed toward the transmogrification of the earth, in such a way that we are no longer well adapted to its new and unprecedented state. B is to change course and head toward a sustainable future. Certainly we will choose B if we are impartial and prudent enough to imagine the earth and its future denizens. That which prevents us from choosing B is mainly the desire for money, fame, and conveniences—all unnecessary desires compared with our basic needs for foods, clothing, and living joyously with others. If Plato saw today's situation, the global village dominated by monstrous powers and money, he would certainly see it as diseased, corrupt, and most unjust. If one reduces it to the individual level, it looks like weakness of will; as, say, in an addicted person who cannot but continue unhealthy habits, in spite of knowing a better course.

Concerning the human-to-nature relationship, Kuki's philosophy is suggestive for today's environmental philosophy. It could be safely said that Kuki founded his philosophy on the basis of this relationship. He considered the characteristic of traditional Japanese morality to be naturalness:

> In Japanese morality, "spontaneous nature" is very meaningful. People dislike what is intentional and esteem what is natural. Morality is not considered perfect if it does not reach the stage of naturalness. In this respect it is quite different from Western morality. In Western philosophy at large, nature and freedom are often considered to be in opposition. In Japanese practice-experience, contrarily, nature and freedom tend to be embodied in a harmonious fusion. Freedom is what breaks forth naturally in spontaneity. Freedom is not what is born as the result of confined deliberation. What was brought forth naturally, according to the heart of heaven and earth as it is, is freedom.[24]

Here one can find that the image of morality for Kuki is oriented by nature. "Nature," *shizen* (自然) in Japanese, translates in two ways: external nature that is different from "environment," a living macrocosmos on the one hand, and a naturalness that means something like "automatic behavior," "spontaneity," or "self-so" on the other hand. If nature is considered a sort of living organism that is the origin of all life, these two aspects of nature presumably coincide.

Although ethics was not Kuki's main concern, he agreed with utilitarianism in his social ethics, mentioning "the greatest happiness of the greatest number."[25] Besides utilitarianism, what Kuki took from modern Western ethics was the Kantian idea of duty for duty's sake,[26] which for Kuki resembled the strong-willedness shared with Confucian morality and seen in common people like farmers, craftsmen, and, especially, samurai. These moralities are, on the social and ethical level, concerned with historical (or social) humans, in Kuki's terminology. Yet Kuki's ethics did not conflict with the care for nature, since human society was considered "only a member of the land community."[27] Human society was, in mainstream Japanese thought, considered to exist on the basis of nature, and nature considered to be precious and miraculous, but fragile and transitory, since it emerged by chance from nothingness. Hence, the culture of restraint before nature emerged, which was mingled with Western modernism after Japan opened its doors to the West in the Meiji era (1868–1912), but was replaced by Western modernism in the postwar era.

Today's self-interest-oriented economy and culture may be too deeply rooted in and dominant over the modern mind to convert attitudes to nature-oriented thought and lifestyle. However, a person may think, if he does not avoid confronting his own death, what is most important for him to do—that is, the ultimate object of his love; and he will, resigning other desires, prepare for death by accomplishing his last will. If people confront the environmental crisis squarely, and are terrified by the horrifying changes that the earth is undergoing, they will sincerely consider the matter. They will consider, if they are prudent and impartial, the survival of the global village and its future denizens, reigning in their worldly desires, which have today swelled out of control, and paring them down to those that are necessary.

9.4. The Philosophy of Contingence: Being and Nothingness

Platonic metaphysics expressed in the theory of Forms is akin to the philosophy of being (有 *u, on*), compared with the so-called Buddhist philosophy of nothingness (無 *mu, ouden*). In comparison with the world of Forms, which is supposed to exist eternally, this phenomenal world is like a reflection (*eikōn*) of real being, not nonbeing but a world of becoming (*genesis*), fluctuating between being and not-being (*mē on*). Accordingly, human society is valuable as long as it participates in the ideals originating from Forms. While the *kosmos* (beautiful order) is invaluable and immutable, because it is created by the demiurge and modeled on Forms, the natural environment is largely ignored by Plato.

The traditional Western religions have centered on the problem of death and salvation of the soul, emphasizing salvation from the mortal fear of death. In the Platonic myth the human soul goes into another world, subsequently to be reincarnated in this one, while in Christianity and Islam the soul punches a one-way ticket to Heaven/Paradise of Hell. The Homeric Greeks yearned to leave descendants or posthumous honor, out of love for eternal existence in this world. Likewise today, non-religious people often see the continuity of life in terms of genetics. All these forms of salvation or consolation are concerned with the death of the individual person, not with the mass die-off of many of the species that Leopold characterized as "our fellow voyagers in the Odyssey of evolution."[28] In case of anthropogenic mass extinction, the human species may well also become extinct. This very real possibility could not have been imagined, nor can it be coped with, by traditional religions. Once the sixth mass extinction in the 3.5-billion-year biography of the earth, exacerbated by global climate change, begins to cascade toward its nadir, terror will strike all global villagers, being faced with hunger, disease, crime, war, and deprivation.

Confronting such a catastrophe, people must face the prospect of nothingness—that is, not just personal annihilation, but the annihilation of humanity or at least human civilization. While traditional religions taught us to face personal death squarely, and asked us to think of the transience of life—saying, "Remember that you have to die" (*memento mori*) or "All is vanity of vanities" (*vanitas vanitatum*)—traditional religious thought cannot cope with the enormity of the death of so many other species and perhaps even that of our own species. We face the annihilation of the world as we have known it, ever since we have known anything.

In response to these enormities, let us next look at Kuki's philosophy of contingency, a sort of philosophy of nothingness that is typical of the Kyoto school. The question of being and nothingness is this: what is being, why does something exist at all, and why not nonexistence? It was in answer to this metaphysical question that Kuki developed his philosophy. His discussion of metaphysical humans is shadowed by the philosophy of nothingness and his exhortation for resignation, originating from Buddhism, is also backed by the philosophy of nothingness.

In everyday life, people usually think that everything occurs necessarily, as a falling object moves according to the law of gravity. It may be considered only natural and a matter of course, not just a chance happening, that I live here and now thinking and writing, since everything has its own cause. I was born in Japan and raised as a matter of course. I worked as a public servant, sustaining my family with a salary I duly received from the government; and then I retired from the job in accordance with my age. It is only natural that I had the right to live in health, to work, and so forth.

On the other hand, if we imagine the distress of others, we see the matter from another perspective. There are more than eight hundred million starving people in this global village. And, thanks to forthcoming environmental catastrophes, the future residents of this village are destined to suffer from all sorts of miseries before humankind will finally be reduced to a state of barbarism or perish outright. Is it a matter of course that this will occur necessarily? One can imagine another unfolding of events. Indeed we can imagine ourselves in other circumstances.[29] For instance, I could have been born one of the poverty-stricken people in the third world, dying from hunger or waterborne disease. But if everything occurs by necessity, according to the law of nature, then we cannot change our own circumstances by an act of will, let alone that of the whole world. Citing a passage from the Buddhist classics, Kuki wrote,

It is contingent that we are born as Japanese. It is even thinkable that we were born insects, birds, or animals. It is contingent that we are human beings, not insects, birds, or animals. In the depth of a great ocean, a blind pelagic creature comes up to the surface once in a hundred years. And there is a piece of floating wood that has only one hole, drifting on the sea at the mercy of the wind toward now toward the East and now the West. To be born human can be likened to the event that the blind sea creature, when he raises his head, meets by chance this hole in the wood. This parable has inexhaustible metaphysical meaning.[30]

Opposing the law of necessity, if I look at the matter from another perspective, this world is full of contingency (偶然 *guzen*) and luck (運 *un*). Although it is possible that I might die from hunger, be killed by war, or live in a refugee camp, it is only by chance that I myself exist here and now thinking and writing. There was always a possibility that the earth might have perished before my birth (e.g., by the sun becoming an astronomical red giant). Now I exist. And sooner or later I will slip into nonexistence. Of course, in retrospect, we can detect the cause of our existence: our ancestors and the sound nature that supported them, and before that the earth from which everything else emerged, and before that the cosmos. Thus tracing the ultimate cause and origin of everything, we reach the basic fact that something, not nothing, exists, and we are astonished; as Aristotle said, philosophy was born from wonder.[31] To the question of why something, rather than nothing, exists, there is no answer. It is only contingent fact, according to Kuki, that there occurred being, not nonbeing—as if by a throw of the dice. It was hard to exist (有 *aru*). Hence originated the Japanese concept of *arigatai* (有難, meaning "thankful"). It just happened that existence came about, happily. Kuki calls this fact "original contingence" (*Urzufall*), following the German philosopher Schelling.[32]

According to Plato, this sensible world of becoming originated from "the Form of Good" as eternal being (*ontōs on*) with eternal objective value. Therefore, Plato's is a philosophy of being. In the philosophy of nothingness, the world of becoming emerged from nothing, is shadowed by nothingness, and will be reduced to nothing. In this world of becoming and disappearing, being and nothingness are two sides of the same coin. "Being has meaning," according to Kuki, "relative to nothingness. Being is nonnothingness as the negation of nothingness. Nothingness is nonbeing as the negation of being."[33] The possibilities for humans and nature to shape other ways of existence are innumerable; it was possible that they would not exist at all, and it is miraculous and wondrous that they actually do exist. For something to exist means that it happened to exist along with the possibility that it might not exist. Thus existence is contingent; and therefore existence is, so to speak, supported by nonexistence.

Nothingness as the negation of being, so to speak, threatens being and calls it into question. The other sciences presuppose being as something self-evident and start to explore and develop under this presupposition. It may safely be said that they don't call being itself into question and explore it. Philosophy as metaphysics cannot, however, presuppose being as self-evident and start to explore from this presupposition.[34]

TABLE 9.2 Plato and Kuki on the Role of Nature

PLATONISM	KUKI'S PHILOSOPHY
Forms (being)	Becoming and nothingness
Necessity	Contingency
Objective values (ideals)	Relativism (resignation)
Humans apart from nature	Humans as a part of nature
Form-oriented reason	Nature-oriented reason
Erōs for Forms (eternity)	Love of nature (transitoriness)

Inheriting from Platonism, Kuki replaced the Platonic Form with nature, changing the order of love in a direction the reverse of Plato's, thus establishing love as the basis of values. Table 9.2 compares Kuki and Plato on this point.

While this phenomenal and sensible world is, compared with the world of being, not as valuable or meaningful, when this world is founded on the basis of nothingness, it has a high degree of being-ness (*ousia*). For being—that is, something that has the possibility to be or not to be—existence means contingency: it is quite difficult to exist. For the philosophy of nothingness, the world of becoming is certainly a transient and ephemeral world. Yet compared with nothingness, it is incomparably valuable. While humans and nature are, from the perspective of eternal being, not so valuable, they are, from the perspective of nothingness, invaluable. In this world of "secular as sacred,"[35] everything in nature is ordered and beautiful so that the transient life in this valley of the shadow of death is inexhaustibly meaningful. In traditional Japanese paintings the painted objects are balanced by vacant space, and sound in Japanese music must be complemented by silence. Shadow is as important as light in Japanese culture.[36] So being is supported by nothingness. As it is said that beauty is in the eye of the beholder, the view from the vantage of nothingness may be more valuable, more beautiful, than that from vantage of celestial value and beauty.

In conclusion, people in Edo society lived in a culture of restraint with respect for nature. Kuki introduced resignation, spirit, and nature as the three defining characteristics of Japanese culture; each corresponding with the cognitive, affective, and conative functions of mind, which respectively correspond with Japanese 知 (intellect), 情 (emotion), 意 (volition).[37] In order to redirect society toward a more sustainable future, it will not be enough merely to cultivate a love for nature; it will be necessary to allow love for nature, by sheer stoicism, to override excessive human desire, such that we retain only what Plato identified as the necessary desires. Kuki's three motives of Japanese culture are pertinent: we must nourish love for nature (affective) with a strong will to survive (conative) under the guidance of rational resignation of surplus desire (cognitive).

If we compare the philosophy of being with that of nothingness, we find that the hierarchical order of value in the former philosophy is reversed in the latter; the hierarchy of value in the philosophy of being and nothingness may be formulated thus:

Platonism:
> being
> becoming (nature/society)
> nonbeing

Kuki's philosophy:
> nature
> society
> nothingness

In the hierarchical order in Plato's philosophy of being, nature is superior in value to human society because the demiurge created nature by modeling it on the Forms and thus it reflects the absolute value of Forms, while human society more often than not deviates from the Forms, as it rarely manifests Plato's sense of aristocracy (as in Edo Japan), but far more often timocracy (military rule, as in Egypt today), some mix of plutocracy and democracy (as in the United States today), and tyranny (as in Hitler's Germany, Stalin's Russia, or Gaddafi's Libya). In Kuki's philosophy of nothingness, nature also occupies a position superior to that of human society—but, in sharp contrast to Plato, because nature is considered the foundation of human society, not a "moving image of eternity," that is, the image of the Forms. Thus in the philosophy of Kuki, the social value of fame and money (*myōri*) can be resigned as inferior to the natural value expressed in *hū-ryū*. Accepting this idea can facilitate people's love of nature and their resignation of selfish desires.

Today, Western environmental ethics as represented by Naess and Callicott and humanist and humane social ethics as represented by Hare and Singer are regrettably in conflict with one another—so much so that they are considered as separate specialized fields, even different disciplines. This unfortunate situation is certainly a deterrent to progress; it would seem a combination of both tendencies would be more influential and effective. I hope we have found at least one possibility for such a synthesis in Kuki's philosophy, as I have interpreted it so far, wherein

social and environmental ethics are not separated. When one does not presuppose objective values, one need not judge whether the human being
or nature is more valuable, only what one is to love and in which order.
Environmental ethicists will, for love of nature, restrain surplus desires,
not only because of a love of nature for nature's sake, but also because
nature sustains human life. On the other hand, humanists will refrain from
surplus desires in order for humanity to survive, because humanity cannot exist without the support of nature. Thus both camps must, for the
purpose of a sustainable future, coincide. What is at stake today is neither
humans nor nature alone, but the inseparable unity of humans and nature
as a whole.

Notes

1. Plato, *The Republic*, in *Complete Works of Plato*, ed. John M. Cooper and D. S. Hutchinson (Indianapolis: Hackett, 1997), 368–369.

2. Plato, *Republic*, 434–435.

3. Plato, *Republic,* 581.

4. Plato, *Republic*, 588–589.

5. Plato, *Republic*, 576–577.

6. Plato, *Republic*, 372–373.

7. Plato, *Republic*, book 8.

8. Plato, *Republic*, 485.

9. Plato, *Symposium*, in *Complete Works of Plato*, 188–189.

10. KUKI Shuzo, *Complete Works* (Tokyo: Iwanami Shoten, 1980), 3:18.

11. Kuki, *Complete Works*, 3:18.

12. Kuki, *Complete Works*, 3:281.

13. Kuki, *Complete Works*, 1:22.

14. Plato, *Symposium*, 227.

15. Kuki, *Complete Works*, 4:60–61.

16. Kuki, *Complete Works*, 3:277.

17. Plato, *Republic*, 420–421.

18. J. B. Callicott, *Earths Insights: A Multicultural Survey of Ecological Ethics from the Mediterranean Basin to the Australian Outback* (Berkeley: University of California Press, 1994), 208.

19. W. R. LaFleur. "Saigyo and the Buddhist Value of Nature," in *Japan: A Modern History*, ed. James L. McClain (New York: Norton, 2002).

20. Kuki, *Complete Works*, 5:45–46.

21. Plato, *Phaedo*, in *Complete Works of Plato*, 68 and 82.

22. Kuki, *Complete Works*, 5:6.

23. See chapter 3 of Peter Singer's *How Are We to Live? Ethics in an Age of Self-Interest* (Melbourne: Text Publishing Company, 1993).

24. Kuki, *Complete Works*, 3:276.

25. Kuki, *Complete Works*, 3:102.

26. Kuki, *Complete Works*, 3:196–197 and 5:22.

27. This parallels the language Aldo Leopold uses in *A Sand County Almanac* (New York: Oxford University Press, 1949).

28. Leopold, *A Sand County Almanac*, 109.

29. R. M. Hare, *Moral Thinking: Its Levels, Method, and Point* (Oxford: Clarendon Press, 1981), 113–114.

30. Kuki, *Complete Works*, 3:140.

31. Kuki, *Complete Works*, 3:176.

32. Kuki, *Complete Works*, 3:162.

33. Kuki, *Complete Works*, 3:119.

34. OBAMA Yoshinobu, *The Philosophy of Kuki Shuzo: A Wandering Soul* (Kyoto: Showado, 2006), 165ff.

35. Tu Wei-Ming, *Confucian Thought: Selfhood as Creative Transformation* (Albany: SUNY Press, 1985), 24.

36. Obama, *Philosophy of Kuki Shuzo*, 18ff.

37. Kuki, *Complete Works*, 3:288; Hare, *Moral Thinking*, 93.

PART IV | Nature and Japanese Culture

CHAPTER 10 | Recollecting Local Narratives on the Land Ethic

TOYODA MITSUYO

A VARIETY OF indigenous narratives about the land and its relation with human societies have been handed down from generation to generation as guides for appropriate human conduct. Different stories have been created in different areas of the world. Japan is one of the countries possessing a rich culture of nature narratives. There are stories associated with incomprehensible natural phenomena and unforeseeable frightening disasters such as earthquakes, thunderstorms, and floods. Mythological narratives about *kami* (神, deities), *hotoke* (仏, Buddha-nature), and *yōkai* (妖怪, goblins), for example, signify that people wish to live safely and comfortably in harmony with their surroundings.

People in the past have created folk stories using imagination to make sense of incomprehensible natural phenomena and to share local knowledge about wise living. Indigenous narratives, full of metaphors and analogies, teach us how to acclimate ourselves to surrounding environments, and provide us with crucial hints for getting ready for unforeseeable dynamic happenings in nature. They are the source of wisdom gradually developed for strengthening a community's risk management and enriching its people's lives.

The story-based source of wisdom, however, began to be neglected as a result of the expansion of modern epistemology, primarily based on scientific reasoning. Local narratives, which lack scientific foundations, began to be interpreted merely in the realm of myth: stories are just stories, not facts. Yet such a modern view began to be questioned when we realized that scientific and technical solutions are not sufficient for coping with a variety of environmental issues that involve unforeseeable events and axiological concerns.

If we need to develop land ethics as guides to share values and knowledge about how we should live in accordance with the natural environment, we will be able to find important teachings in indigenous narratives. Whereas scientific investigation and reasoning play crucial roles in foreseeing the future and responding to its challenges, it is also urgent to recollect wisdom transmitted from the past in various formats.

The focus of this chapter is to examine the value of indigenous narratives in light of land ethics. I first summarize the idea of the land ethic introduced by Aldo Leopold and explore a traditional view of nature that he criticizes. I then introduce some traditional accounts of nature developed from indigenous stories in Japan and examine the features of those accounts. Many stories handed down from people in the past contain important implications of how we should live in this world. I then consider the meanings of recollected narratives for developing the land ethics rooted in Japanese tradition.

10.1. Leopold's Land Ethic: Overcoming the View of Nature as Human Property

Aldo Leopold's land ethic starts from an allusion to Homer's *Odyssey*, which might appear shocking to those of us living in a society that is built on the shared understanding of respecting human rights.

> When god-like Odysseus returned from the wars in Troy, he hanged all on one rope a dozen slave-girls of his household whom he suspected of misbehavior during his absence.
>
> This hanging involved no question of propriety. The girls were property. The disposal of property was then, as now, a matter of expediency, not of right and wrong.[1]

What Odysseus did to his slave girls is not permissible from the modern ethical viewpoint. Indeed, owning other human beings as property, no matter how mercifully they are treated, is impermissible. Although hierarchical relationships no doubt exist in human societies, many of us think that no one can possess other human beings like objects, not to mention murdering them. On the basis of the recognition of the inherent dignity of human beings, the United Nations Universal Declaration of Human Rights clearly states that all peoples and nations must remember, "Everyone has the right to life, liberty and security of person."[2] Accordingly, "No one shall be held in slavery or servitude; slavery and the slave trade shall be prohibited in all their forms."[3] Odysseus's conduct infringes this widely acknowledged moral code.

Leopold's intention is of course not to blame Odysseus for neglecting human rights. He relates this episode in the *Odyssey* as an analogy for reconsidering our relationship with the natural environment. Most people today agree that human beings possess inherent value. But what about other life forms? Do they also possess dignity? Leopold begins his land ethic with this Homeric vignette in order to challenge our assumption that humans can use other living forms in nature for our own benefit. Whereas Odysseus's conduct was not ethically controversial at the time, it surely is considered immoral from a modern perspective. What was once regarded as a property has acquired a dignity and is now valued in a completely different way. Leopold considers whether a similar change could occur in the prevailing valuation of things in nature. He accordingly emphasizes the importance of expanding the realm of moral consideration to include soils, waters, plants, and animals, which he collectively calls "the land."[4] This expansion of our moral community calls for the reconsideration of how we relate to the rest of the world. We should not adhere to the hierarchical relationship between humans and nonhuman beings. On the basis of his ecological worldview, Leopold states, "In short, a land ethic changes the role of *Homo sapiens* from conqueror of the land-community to plain member and citizen of it. It implies respect for his fellow-members, and also respect for the community as such."[5]

This idea, embedded in the Leopold's land ethic, implies the rejection of the traditional view of nature as property belonging to humans. To begin with, where did this traditional view originate? The idea that nature is human property is often associated with the book of Genesis in the Old Testament, which depicts how the world was created by God and turned over to human beings. Light; the firmament; the dry land; vegetation; sun, moon, and stars; and animals were created by God before the creation of humans. Then God said, "Let us make man in our image, after our likeness; and let them have dominion over the fish of the sea, and over the birds of the air, and over the cattle, and over all the earth, and over every creeping thing that creeps upon the earth."[6]

The creation story in Genesis has been significantly influential in the development of the foundation of the Judeo-Christian worldview. The belief that human beings have the authority over the natural world, for example, is the premise posited in the theory of property discussed by John Locke. In his *Second Treatise of Government*, he mentions that nature has been provided to human beings for the purpose of enriching their welfare. He writes, "God, who hath given the World to Men in common, hath also given them reason to make use of it to the best advantage of Life, and convenience. The Earth, and all that is therein, is given to Men for the Support and Comfort of their being."[7] He then discusses how such commons begin to be possessed personally and are turned into private property.

Human beings have power to use other living things because they have been given to us by God. Such a biblical interpretation of the human relationship with nonhuman beings has been criticized as the root of our current exploitation of nature. A blistering critique of such a worldview was presented by Lynn White Jr. in "The Historical Roots of Our Ecologic Crisis,"[8] in which he blames Christianity, which inherited its creation account from the Hebrew Bible, for affirming beliefs that justify the anthropocentric exploitation of nature. Although not all Christian teachings justify our exploitation of nature, White warns that the Christian dogma of creation had certain influences on the formation of the basic axioms of modern science and technology, which were developed in the Occidental tradition. Nowadays, science and technology are regarded as neutral disciplines that pursue secular and objective interpretations of the world. Yet the presuppositions underlying these disciplines were rooted in the anthropocentric dogma that justifies the control of the world by human beings who were placed by God in a higher position than the rest of the world. Accordingly, White warns, "We shall continue to have a worsening ecologic crisis until we reject the Christian axiom that nature has no reason for existence save to serve man."[9]

White's argument has been criticized as oversimplifying the complex causes of ecological crisis, such as capitalism, urbanization, individual resource ownership, and population growth.[10] Moreover, it began to be argued that more careful examination of biblical texts needed to be conducted before criticizing biblical teachings as the roots of the environmental crisis. For example, examining the Hebrew word *radah*, translated as "dominion," Lloyd H. Steffen argues, "*Radah* is not, contrary to the claims of many environmental exegetes, a strong word that appeals to physical force. Although it is true that one of the meanings of *radah* is 'to tread down,' the word is actually employed in contexts in which justice, freedom from oppression, and even *shalom* are pronounced themes."[11]

Likewise, Richard H. Hiers examines the descriptions in biblical texts and demonstrates that the Judeo-Christian tradition does not necessarily support the exploitation of the environment. With regard to the human relationship with other life forms, Hiers, for example, refers to the following teachings in the Deuteronomy and Proverbs: "Lost animals are to be returned, and those that have fallen are to be helped up, even if they belong to one's enemy (Deut. 22:1–5)," "A nesting bird be let go (Deut. 22:6f)," "Are the trees in the field men that they should be besieged by you? (Deut. 20:19–20)," and "Caring for one's animals, of course, is good husbandry as well as humane practice (Prov. 27:13–17)."[12] These teachings signify God's order to humans to be respectful to his creation. According to Hiers, what lies at the root of environmental exploitation is the spread of an anthropocentric valuation of the world that appears in secular scientism and humanism: biblical faith, which points to the transcendent God as source and valuer of things in the world, rather functions as a brake on the wanton use of nature. The biblical texts indicate that human beings are expected to cultivate the awareness and affirmation of other life forms as well as the attitude of active caring of all living beings.

Unlike White's argument, however, it is important to note that the need for controlling our desires and behaviors had been discussed a long time before the emergence of current environmental degradation. Locke, for example, identifies the limitation of privatizing the land on the basis of the notion of labor. Whereas the earth is a commons, gifted by God and provided equally to all human beings, it is appropriated when being used by a person for satisfying his or her needs. Labor, which belongs to each person, justifies one's appropriation of nature: yet, at the same time, it is a measure to limit one's share. He writes, "As much as any one can make use of to any advantage of life before it spoils; so much he may by his labour fix a Property in. Whatever is beyond this, is more than his share, and belongs to others. Nothing was made by God for Man to spoil or destroy."[13] Each of us, according to Locke, has the common right of gaining profits, but needs to remember that wasting nature is not permissible. In addition to this limitation, this right presupposes a law of nature, which obliges everyone to have respect for properties and benefits of others. Both religious and social limitations are described in Locke's account of property.

Locke's intention was to develop a political philosophy that could save the public from the oppression of the monarchy. Accordingly, he begins his treatise with the claim that all humans are naturally equal regardless of their positions in society. This idea underpins his interpretation of property. Nature is the commons provided by God; therefore, each person has a right to use this commons and to satisfy his or her needs for living. The injustice that Locke wanted to rectify was the unreasonable inequality of people that was dictated by monarchic authority. He thus insists that the enclosure of the land can be justified only through labor, which does not depend on one's social status.

The situation seems much different today. Equality of human beings has been respected and democratic forms of governance have been developing in various countries of the world. But even in a democratic society, we still have the problem of the use of the land. The notion of labor cannot be a solution of problems such as the depletion of natural resources and the rapid expansion of land development. Many parts of the land began to be developed using the power of capital. With the advancement of technology, human impact on the land has become enormous compared to the age of Locke. Therefore the emergence of a sense of care toward the land is an urgent issue. Leopold's land ethic has provided an important initiative in response to this issue. It is not embedded in a sectarian religious tradition, such as the Judeo-Christian worldview. Thus his ecological account of ethics contains an important message that can be shared globally. Nevertheless, it is also important to consider other forms of land ethic that accommodate various local perspectives toward the land, which resonate well with Leopold's land ethic.[14]

In the case of Japan, we find different stories of the land. In the next section, I explore the accounts of the land developed in the Japanese tradition and consider the land ethic embedded in them.

10.2. Japanese Narratives of the Land

A keen contrast can be found in the narratives of the development of the world between the Judeo-Christian and the ancient Japanese traditions. The former portrays the power of God as a commander who created the world according to his word, and emphasizes the power of human beings who were created in God's own image and have been ordered by God to fill and subdue the earth. Although the biblical narratives do not necessarily justify our control over nature, humans are separated from other life forms and have been placed in a higher position from the beginning.

The Japanese narratives of the emergence of the world, on the other hand, depict chaotic, complex, and organic processes of genesis. They do not assume creation controlled by a supernatural being but illustrate an unpredictable spontaneous power of nature that continuously generates life. Things in nature have been metaphorically used to describe the divinity and dignity of the process of becoming. In *Kojiki*, the *Records of Ancient Matters*, for example, the words *ashi* (葦, reeds) and *ashikabi* (葦牙, reed-shoot) appear repeatedly as an expression of the vital organismic force of deities and the world.[15]

Reeds are a type of plant commonly found in wetlands. When wetland covered most of the lowlands of Japan, the landscape of thick reeds swaying in the wind was symbolic of the prosperity of the country. In ancient times, Japan was known by the names of *ashihara no nakatsu kuni* (葦原中国), which means "the central land of reed plains,"[16] and of *toyoashihara no mizuho no kuni* (豊葦原の水穂国), which means "the land of abundant reed plains and rice fields." In spring, strong reed-shoots grow straight up from the web of roots hidden in the soil or in the water. The power of growth represented by reed-shoots is also a wish of further development of life and culture. In virtue of adoring such powers of nature, the word *ashi* is also used for the names of deities. *Umashiashikabihikojinokami* (宇魔志阿斯訶備比古遅神) is the name of a deity who arose at the early stage of the emergence of this world. *Ookuninushi*, the deity who governed the land of Japan, is also called *ashiharanoshikoo* (葦原色許男命).

Nature untamed is also portrayed in images in Japanese mythologies. The force of nature is so wild and so beyond human control that even deities in the narratives struggle with subduing it. One example of such a narrative is the story of Susanoo fighting a giant serpent with eight heads and eight tails. This story metaphorically expresses the struggle for flood control. Susanoo is a deity who is associated with rain and thunder, and is depicted as a violent figure in mythologies in sharp contrast with his sister Amaterasu, who represents light and hope. A serpent, on the other hand, symbolizes a river called Hii-Kawa, which flows across Shimane prefecture. The violent figure of the serpent stands for a raging floodwater running down and destroying things in its basin. If you visit Hii-Kawa River, you see beautiful sandbars that look just like scales of a serpent.

In the story, Susanoo played a trick to first get this serpent drunk, then kill it with his saber while it was asleep. Susanoo's success in killing the serpent symbolizes the divine power to control violent nature. Water is essential for sustaining our life. At the same time, water has terrible power to destroy life. The worship of Susanoo is the manifestation of the wish of ancient people to control water. The shrines sacred to Susanoo were built all over Japan to avoid the risks of both flood and drought. Yet, at the same time, they indicate that water is always beyond human control. The Japanese sensitivity to nature embraces such a bipolar awareness of the power of nature.

Susanoo is only one deity out of many that are associated with natural phenomena. A variety of things in nature, for example, springs, mountains, marshes, and the ocean, have been portrayed through the personas of deities. The Japanese tradition of narratives portrays people's awe and reverence toward both the furious and blessed aspects of nature. This characteristic of Japanese religious sensitivity to nature, according to WATSUJI Tetsurō, comes from the humid climate of Japan.

Watsuji articulates the deep connection of human existence with surrounding environments in light of the notion of *fūdo* (climate).[17] Each of us lives in a certain environment that has unique climatic features. Watsuji's argument is that how we sense the world and how we behave in it are essentially influenced by local climatic conditions. According to Watsuji, the weather pattern of Japan is classified under the category of monsoon, and is significantly influenced by seasonal winds that bring high humidity during summer. He states that whereas humidity brings people intolerable and inescapable discomfort, it does not necessarily generate antagonistic feelings toward nature. There are two reasons for that: first, humidity also brings a blessing of nature essential to our survival—plant growth; and second, nature becomes extremely violent beyond human control because of high humidity—thunderstorms. Blessing and violence are the two sides of nature in a monsoon climate. Watsuji says that people in the monsoon region tend to be submissive to nature because of this two-sidedness.[18]

In addition to monsoon-type climatic features, Japanese people periodically experience devastating earthquakes, which are far beyond their control. Although it is important to prepare for unforeseen happenings and to attempt to reduce damages from them, it is not possible to prevent them or to keep them under control. In that sense, people might feel hopeless and become submissive. However, it is crucial to remember that this passivity is not the negation of positive actions in response to natural phenomena. Japanese narratives teach us that ancient people were actively working on their ways of coping with the enormous power of the natural world. They were trying to reduce risks and enhance the opportunities of survival by employing the power of narratives.

The shrines of Susanoo, for example, are located in safe places that have not been damaged even in the case of flooding. That is, the location of the shrine tells people where they should go in the case of a disastrous flood. The shrine and the deities are not mere objects of worship, but social devices for informing people how to survive. Many shrines sacred to Susanoo on the coastal areas of the Tohoku region escaped the devastating blows by the tsunami following the Great East Japan Earthquake in

March 2011.[19] Those shrines are located in hilly areas that have remained safe through the experiences of repeated tsunami disasters in the past.

Narratives of deities are thus not mere stories. They contain important implications concerning how we should live in accordance with the natural world around us. The collection of these narratives, therefore, is an important source of land ethics built upon the unique cultural sensitivity of this country. However, as a result of the development of scientific interpretations of natural phenomena, indigenous narratives about nature began to be neglected as mere superstitions.[20] This neglect had considerable impact on how people relate to their natural surroundings. As we forget to listen to messages embedded in the narratives, we began to lose a potential source of knowledge about how to accommodate ourselves to the land and live safely and wisely. We gradually came to think that we could control nature with human intelligence and power.

The object of control has, however, changed significantly. Whereas our predecessors attempted to control not only the environment but also their conduct in accordance with the conditions of nature, after the advent of the scientific worldview and the increasing power of technology, more focus began to be placed on keeping the environment under control. This shift has brought to Japan a considerable shift in the relationship between humans and the natural environment. If the land ethic is about how one should live in accordance with the environment, it presupposes one's keen awareness of the human connection with surrounding nature. However, our lifestyles have been changing in the opposite direction: we have less opportunity to actually recognize a connection with nature in our everyday lives. The rapid development of urbanization has influenced the ways that people relate to their environments. The consideration of how we cope with the vagaries of nature has been put into the hands of a few people, such as governmental officials, scientists, and engineers.

The separation with nature has resulted in people's apathy toward nature. How to retrieve our sensitivity to the environment is an essential question that needs to be considered for the development of land ethics.

10.3. Revitalizing Sensitivity to the Land

One of the difficulties for the restoration of a harmonious human relationship with nature is the physical separation of our lives from natural surroundings. Technological advancement has brought about the considerable alteration of Japanese landscapes that were once depicted in beautiful images of nature. For example, thick reed plains have been disappearing through the rapid development of waterfront areas. They began to be replaced by concrete and metal structures that are considered safer and more efficient for management. The loss of reed plains at the waterfront has resulted in the disappearance of gentle slopes of the bank and, thus, the degradation of the habitats of a variety of life forms. These structures also prevent people from coming close to the shore. The waterfront has become a dangerous area that children should avoid. It is difficult to find traces of life and sense the vitality of nature in such an artificially constructed waterfront.

I have observed these changes through the environmental restoration projects that I coordinate on Sado Island, Japan. Although this island still retains abundant natural resources, it is undergoing degradation due to excessive and inappropriate development of the land. The most serious issue is the lack of interest in their environments on the part of the local people. As a result of the modernization of our lifestyles, even those who live in rural areas have become indifferent to the conditions of surrounding nature. The development of infrastructure and the market-based distribution of commodities made it possible for many people to live without paying much attention to their environments. They direct their attention to the surroundings only when their lives are threatened by severe natural disasters. In short, people's sensitivity to nature has been significantly declining.

The lack of sensitivity to the environment is a serious problem when we attempt to give root to the ideas embedded in the land ethic. For Leopold, the interdependence of human beings and surrounding nature was what he experienced everyday through his work first as a forest conservationist and then a wildlife manager. By observing ecosystemic interactions from day to day, he deeply recognized the importance of the composition of biotic communities and the processes of their associated ecosystems and attempted to preserve their healthy functioning.

Leopold's call for a paradigm shift concerning the human relationship with nature will not provoke a strong objection in Japan, where the spontaneous power of nature has been respected as the source of life. However, if people do not feel connected with the land through their everyday experiences, this ethic might remain merely abstract. In addition to sharing Leopold's ecological worldview, which is applicable at the global level, creating opportunities to identify particular features of one's local surroundings and to consider how each of us is connected with the environment is also important.

A variety of approaches have been attempted for the cultivation of our sensitivity to local environments. One of them that I conduct in my environmental projects is a field workshop called *furusato miwake* (ふるさと 見分け), which aims at discovering and understanding unique regional features embedded in present landscapes. The word *furusato* means "home place," whereas *miwake* means "to identify." It is a style of workshop designed for land development in which people in various positions walk a targeted district together, share their findings and experiences, and build a plan cooperatively.

KUWAKO Toshio, who proposes this method, explains that there are three basic dimensions that characterize a place: space (geographical and climatic features), time (historical happenings), and value (interests of local residents).[21] These three dimensions should not be apprehended separately. Examples of spatial characteristics of the land are the location of mountains, valleys, and rivers; elevation; and distance from the ocean. These geographical features determine the climate of each region and significantly influence local lifestyles, community formation, industry, and so on. Thus, space regulates what has been happening there. In the framework of time, one examines not only cultural but also natural history and happenings. Natural disasters in the past, for example, have been influencing the interests of people who live there concerning how to survive and stay safe. The development of residential areas and farmlands is also related to the history of flooding and landslide disasters that actually happened in the past.

In order to uncover the messages from predecessors, Kuwako especially focuses on the location of shrines. As mentioned in section 10.2, information about where shrines are located and which deity is sacred to each is an important source for understanding both the geographical features and the historical events of that area. It is crucial to actually visit shrines and observe their surrounding landscapes carefully—for example, the direction of the altar, the shapes of mountains and rivers, and the shrine's positional relationship with neighboring communities. Standing on the actual locale, workshop participants use their imagination and attempt to uncover important environmental messages transmitted to them from their predecessors.

Underlying this methodology is Kuwako's deep criticism of the neglect of the traditional knowledge concerning land development accumulated through Japan's long history. The style of land development has been significantly influenced by the industrial approach, which pursues the efficiency of labor and cost by promoting the mechanization and standardization of production processes. Whereas civil engineers before industrialization needed to observe and examine the specific features of each place extremely carefully, those in the present age build infrastructure without keen observation at the site—because they think they can. By applying the power of modern engineering, people come to believe that they are able to construct large facilities without considering the constraints of local environments. Furthermore, the standardization of building materials has ignored the uniqueness of each place and has resulted in monotonous landscapes. The careful observation of the ecology and history of each site is not possible in such an industrial approach.

In order to change the modern framework of civil engineering and community development, Kuwako has coined the term *kūkan no rireki* (空間の履歴, spatial resume), and he insists on the importance of examining regional and climatic features carefully by uncovering the knowledge handed down from predecessors in the past. The workshop of *furusato miwake* mentioned earlier is a method invented for this examination. This workshop facilitates the participation of people in diverse social positions and generations, and promotes the sharing of discoveries about a region from different perspectives. This sort of participatory process began to be employed more often because of the increasing necessity of public participation in community and infrastructure development. This trend is an important opportunity to direct people's attention to their environments. In some cases of community development, local narratives about the land have been regaining their practical implications. These cases will generate further attempts to restore human connections with the environment and to cultivate a land ethic at regional and individual levels.

10.4. Conclusion

Through the alteration of lifestyles and living conditions after the development of industrialization and urbanization, many people seem to have disconnected from the natural environment, and thus are becoming apathetic to what is happening in their surroundings. This shift in the human relationship with nature might be what our ancestors hoped for because it can be interpreted as the sign of liberation from the constraints of nature. Having the power to control the natural environment for efficient and safe living, people believed that they would not be threatened by nature anymore. Mechanization has certainly helped to relieve people of the hard physical labor formerly required for developing the land. A person today can cultivate and take care of a much larger piece of land than during the time when handwork was the main means of doing so. Urban infrastructure, on the other hand, has helped to expand residential areas by directing the flow of water and changing the shape of hills as we desire.

There has been an assumption that our living becomes more sophisticated if we are free from the burden of caring for the land and worrying about the threat of natural disasters. This assumption, however, has begun to be questioned. First, we experience a variety of environmental problems: the pollution of air, water, and the land itself; the exhaustion of natural resources; and the degradation of biodiversity, due to the lack of care to the land. Second, we see the tragic results of a lack of observation of our natural surroundings in the case of natural disasters. As our everyday lives become further separated from nature, we have become insensitive to surrounding conditions and unaware of the degree of degradation and threat. What seems problematic is that many of us are not truly aware of these issues until we are actually hurt by environmental degradation and natural disasters. Although nature provides the essential foundation of our existence, it has been given little attention.

As discussed in this chapter, our predecessors have passed down important knowledge about nature through narratives. A variety of messages concerning how one should live in accordance with the natural environment are hidden in the stories and other forms of indigenous culture. But they are not adequately recognized. In addition to Leopold's ecological interpretation of the land, we need to re-examine local narratives as the source of vernacular land ethics and to consider how to retrieve our sensitivity to the blessing and beauty of nature, while never forgetting or ignoring its potential threats.

There is a growing recognition that a mere scientific account of nature does not necessarily result in understanding the richness of nature and conserving its aesthetic value. Observing current environmental degradation, civil engineers began to recognize the limitation of a merely technology-oriented understanding of nature and began to adopt the traditional aesthetic perception of nature in the design of infrastructure. One such engineer is SEKI Masakazu, who worked as a government official for the Ministry of Construction from 1972 to 1995. He emphasized the value of Japanese aesthetics based on *sanshi suimei* (山紫水明), and attempted to change orthodox ways of proceeding in the development of modern land infrastructure. The word *sanshi suimei* literally means "purple hills and crystal streams" and expresses the beauty of mountains that glow purple when reflecting sunlight and of clear water flowing down a river. The depth of nature aesthetics, he believed, cannot be measured or conserved merely by numerical expressions. His view is that engineers should broaden their aesthetic sensitivity to look qualitatively at the natural world.[22]

Seki argues, for example, that while borders that exist in the natural world are hazy and curved, lines drawn in public works for city planning and land management are mostly straight. He even claims that civil engineers should refrain from using rulers and drawing typical cross-sections because they result in ignoring the characteristics of the land. They should instead observe natural outlines and features of each region carefully and consider the most appropriate way to reshape the land. His philosophy has been employed in the government's guiding principles of river engineering in Japan.

Japan has developed a unique cultural tradition deeply inspired by the power and beauty of nature: accordingly, the integration of both scientific and nonscientific accounts is crucial in the development of land ethics rooted in this country. Indeed, Leopold himself also had a keen interest in nonscientific views of the world—aesthetic, historical, and even inspirational perspectives. He tried not only to understand complex ecological reality, but also to depict the inspirational scenes of the natural world through his everyday observation. His aesthetic sensitivity to nature is presented in the summary moral maxim of the land ethic: "A thing is right when it tends to preserve the integrity, stability, and *beauty* of the biotic community. It is wrong when it tends otherwise."[23]

Although industrialization and urbanization have negatively affected Japanese sensitivity to nature, several attempts have begun to be made for overcoming the postindustrial detachment from nature. By paying more attention to local environments and sharing voices with others, one will have deeper understanding of his or her surroundings. Such experiences lie at the foundation of the growth of practical and uniquely Japanese land ethics.

Notes

1. Aldo Leopold, *A Sand County Almanac and Sketches Here and There* (New York: Oxford University Press, 1949), 201.
2. The Universal Declaration of Human Rights, Article 3.
3. The Universal Declaration of Human Rights, Article 4.
4. Leopold, *A Sand County Almanac*, 204.
5. Leopold, *A Sand County Almanac*, 204.
6. The Holy Bible, Revised Standard Version, 1–2.

7. John Locke, *Two Treatises of Government*, ed. Peter Laslett (Cambridge: Cambridge University Press, 1988), 296.

8. Lynn White Jr., "The Historical Roots of Our Ecological Crisis," in *Ecology and Religion in History*, ed. David Spring and Eileen Spring (New York: Harper and Row, 1974), 15–31.

9. White, "Historical Roots," 15–31.

10. Lewis W. Moncrief, "The Cultural Basis for Our Environmental Crisis," in Spring and Spring, *Ecology and Religion*, pp. 76–90.

11. Lloyd H. Steffen, "In Defense of Dominion," *Environmental Ethics* 14 (1992): 63–80.

12. Richard H. Hiers, "Ecology, Biblical Theology, and Methodology: Biblical Perspectives on the Environment," *Zygon* 19 (1984): 43–59.

13. Locke, *Two Treatises of Government*, 290.

14. J. Baird Callicott conducted a multicultural examination of land ethics in *Earth's Insights: A Multicultural Survey of Ecological Ethics from the Mediterranean Basin to the Australian Outback* (Berkeley: University of California Press, 1994). In this book, Callicott explores ecological teachings that can be found in a variety of indigenous traditions around the world, and discusses the importance of developing culturally unique accounts of the human relationship with nature. *Earth's Insights* includes the examination of Japanese Buddhism and its influences on gardening. The purpose of this chapter is to supplement the understanding of the Japanese land ethic by examining mythological accounts of the land.

15. *Kojiki* begins with the story of emergence of the world and deities: When *ten* (天, heaven) and *chi* (地, earth) began to be separated, three deities were born alone and hid their persons. After this first emergence of deities, two deities appeared "from a thing that sprouted up like unto a reed-shoot when the earth, young and like unto floating oil, drifted about medusa like."

16. The central land signifies the land between the land of gods and of dead, and refers to the human world.

17. WATSUJI Tetsuro, *Fūdo: Ningengakuteki Kosatsu* 風土—人間学的考察 (Tokyo: Iwanami Bunko, 1979).

18. Watsuji, *Fūdo*, 29–31. Watsuji's characterization of ethnicity based on climate has been criticized as a stereotype of culture. However, it is important to recognize that his consideration of human existence in light of climate has presented a serious challenge to the Cartesian understanding of the self as a being independent from its surroundings, which had enormous influences upon the modern epistemology developed in the Western philosophical tradition. Watsuji's philosophy of climate, which explains the fundamental connection of human existence with surrounding nature, also permeates his theory of ethics; that is, his ethic encompasses the human-nature relation. According to Steve Odin, Watsuji's view tracks a similar perspective in Aldo Leopold. Odin writes, "Hence, Watsuji clearly formulates an ethics in which the individual must be conceived as being situated in a spatial field of relatedness or betweenness not only to human society but also to a surrounding climate (*fūdo*) of living nature as the ultimate extension of embodied subjective space in which man dwells. Watsuji's ethical philosophy is, therefore, one of the most suggestive Asian resources for environmental ethics as outlined by Aldo Leopold, in which morality is enlarged so as to include not simply individual/individual

and individual/social relations, but also the encompassing human/nature relation as a major extension of practical ethics." Steve Odin, "The Japanese Concept of Nature in Relation to the Environmental Ethics and Conservation Aesthetics of Aldo Leopold," *Environmental Ethics* 13 (Winter 1991): 345–360, 351.

19. TAKADA Tomoki, UMETSU Kimio, and KUWAKO Toshio, "A Study of the Deity and Spatial Arrangement of Shrines in the Tsunami Disaster Caused by the Tohoku Earthquake," *Journal of the Japan Society of Civil Engineers* F6 (Safety Problems), 68 (2012): 167–174 (in Japanese). According to the field research conducted by Takada et al., only one shrine out of seventeen that are sacred to Susanoo was destroyed by the tsunami.

20. INOUE Enryo (1858–1919) examined a variety of superstitious beliefs and rituals in light of the notion of *yōkai* (妖怪), and attempted to elucidate their meanings using a scientific approach. His understanding of *yōkai* includes all sorts of mysterious things that people believe without scientific evidence—climatic phenomena, disease, indigenous religions, and superstitions. His work signifies a modern attitude that aims to eradicate the unscientific interpretation of incomprehensible phenomena. INOUE Enryo, *Yōkai Gendan*, ed. TAKEMURA Makio (Tokyo: Daito, 2011). See also KOMATSU Kazuhiko, *Yōkai Bunka Nyumon* (Tokyo: Kadokawa, 2012), 22–23.

21. KUWAKO Toshio, "Houhou toshite no Kūkan-gaku" (方法としての空間学), in *Nihon Bunka no Kūkan-gaku* (日本文化の空間学), ed. KUWAKO Toshio (Tokyo: Toshindo, 2008), 13. See also Kuwako's chapter 15 in this anthology.

22. SEKI Masakazu, *Daichi no Kawa: Yomigaere Nihon no Furusato no Kawa* (大地の川−甦れ、日本のふるさとの川) (Tokyo: Soshisha, 1994).

23. Leopold, *A Sand County Almanac*, 224–225.

CHAPTER 11 | The Crucial Role of Culture
in Japanese Environmental
Philosophy

MIDORI KAGAWA-FOX

THE ORIGINS OF an environmental philosophy in Japan lie in its social
construct: empirical knowledge, time-honored traditions, and religious
beliefs that influenced the Japanese thinkers who built up a code of environmental awareness. Japanese philosophy is not just an academic discipline; it also extends beyond that into culture, which plays an important
role in Japan's environmental philosophy. Japanese thinkers, who can be
described as practical philosophers, expanded on both cultural convention
and academic thought to articulate a guide for Japanese moral principles
that express a healthy relationship with others, including the natural world.
Western environmental philosophy developed as an academic discipline
based upon Western ethical codes and theories from Western intellectuals
and philosophers. As a result, Japanese philosophy offers a unique perspective on environmental ethics that differs significantly from Western
approaches. The purpose of this chapter is to articulate the essential role
that the culture of Japan has played in the development of its environmental thought.

This chapter is divided into five sections plus a conclusion. The first
section analyzes what Japanese environmental philosophy is, how it
developed, and who the main architects have been in its evolution. The
second section examines three instances of historical crises caused by a
breakdown in environmental governance that resulted in catastrophic environmental pollution. The third section explores Japanese environmental
philosophy—the theories of Japanese ethics expounded by Japan's early
thinkers that are the foundation of environmental philosophy and how they

emerged from a cultural background. The final two sections explore and evaluate the importance of *kami* (神 spiritual deities), the meaning of the Shinto faith, and especially the spiritual role *kami* have played and play in Japanese environmental philosophy.

11.1. A Brief History of Japanese Philosophy

The word "philosophy" derives from the Greek word *philosophia*, meaning "love of wisdom"; it originally covered all intellectual quests, and whoever sought wisdom (or knowledge) was called a philosopher.[1] The prominent nineteenth-century Japanese thinker NAKAE Chōmin (中江兆民,1847–1901) said that there is "no philosophy in Japan." This statement became famous because it questioned what the term "Japanese philosophy" signified; what Nakae meant was that there was not a philosophy in Japan according to the Western definition.[2] The classical Japanese wisdom tradition was built on indigenous cultural values—but also, to a large extent, appropriated Chinese cultural values, including those characteristic of Buddhism—and thus has a different quality than what is found in the West. Therefore, in contemporary Japan, "philosophy" refers to an academic study of Western philosophies, such as those of Kant, Mill, Hegel, and Heidegger, all of whom influenced the relatively recent development of a distinctive Japanese philosophy (conforming to the Western definition of philosophy). Those thinkers who adopted Western ideas and theories into a Japanese framework are the founders of contemporary Japanese philosophy. While Western philosophy developed as a discipline of theories created by intellectuals, Japanese philosophy was developed from empirical teachings based on cultural and spiritual traditions. For the West, the first point of contact for Japanese philosophy today is the Kyoto school, founded by NISHIDA Kitarō (西田幾多郎, 1870–1945) in the early twentieth century just as "professional philosophy" was emerging in the West. James Heisig points out that the emergence of this school not only was a watershed in Japanese intellectual history; its thinkers also made original contributions to Western philosophical thought by fusing it with their distinctively Asian conceptual resources.[3] In this opening section, I first look at the great thinkers of Japan's past who contributed their wisdom to the development of today's distinctively Japanese philosophical systems, and then explore what environmental attitudes and values the Japanese school of thought embraces.

The Edo period, also known as the Tokugawa period, was one of Japan's most important from both historical and cultural perspectives. It was a time of intellectual awakening, and many of Japan's great thinkers were born in either the Edo period (1603–1868) or in the early Meiji period (1868–1912).[4] The Edo period was a culturally vibrant time, as Japan was isolated from much of world and had limited contact with foreign cultures (with the Dutch and Chinese as their only trading partners). This period provided the base for economic growth and increased prosperity, which led to a blossoming of the leisure arts. In literature, for example, novel writing and poetry became extremely important activities.[5] As Japanese Edo culture flourished, Japanese thinkers became extremely influential in the development of Japanese wisdom and moral guidance. Although there are few written philosophical works, the teachings of these thinkers about ethical principles became embedded in Japanese values and human relationships.[6] NAKAMURA Hajime pointed out that until the time of the Buddhist monk SUZUKI Shōsan (鈴木正三, 1579–1655), there was a strong inclination to believe that the Buddha's way of life was to live in the mountains, separate from the world.[7] Suzuki's teachings concerning how people relate to their mundane occupations were not only practical but also spiritual. Among the numerous great thinkers were ISHIDA Baigan (石田梅岩,1685–1744) and NINOMIYA Sontoku (二宮尊徳,1787–1856). These two, along with Suzuki, should be acknowledged for the wisdom they contributed to the emergence of a distinctive Japanese philosophy in the early twentieth century.

NISHI Amane (西周, 1829–1897) is known as an enlightened thinker who valued Western philosophy as well as Eastern Confucianism. He was the originator of the Japanese term *tetsugaku* (哲学, philosophy), and he first translated and introduced Western philosophy to Japan.[8] *Tetsugaku*, literally meaning "the study of wisdom," refers to an understanding of the research into Western philosophy at that time. According to Nishi there were famous moral philosophers in the West, but in the East there were followers of Confucianism; and although there are profound differences between the two, the fundamental concepts are the same for both: they seek reasoned regulations.[9] Along with Nishi, FUKUZAWA Yukichi (福沢諭吉, 1835–1901) presented himself as a thinker, educator, and samurai warrior and was a major influence on Japanese modernization during the Meiji period. Fukuzawa stated in his work *Gakumo no susume* (学問のススメ, *Encouragement of Learning*), the most famous (if not the most important) philosophical work of the Meiji period, that men and women are of equal stature.[10] Contrary to Nishi's thinking, Fukuzawa was critical of Confucianism during the process of Japan's modernization in the nineteenth century. He argued that if political policy followed the Confucian teaching of "letting people follow, keeping them uninformed," then Japanese modernization could not be accomplished.[11] He imported liberal Western notions into Japan, especially those relating to academic learning within society. This was crucial for the Japanese enlightenment of the nineteenth century. The third great thinker following Nishi and Fukuzawa was the aforementioned NAKAE Chōmin. Nakae was known as the "Rousseau of the East" because he introduced Rousseau's concepts into Japan by translating *Du Contrat Social, ou Principes du Doit Politique*.[12] Nakae was interested in foreign cultures and was involved in diplomatic missions to Paris. While he was there, he dedicated himself to learning the texts of Montesquieu, Voltaire, Rousseau, Mirabeau, Condorcet, Laboulaye, and Naquet.[13] Nakae was interested in the Western idea of democracy as well. According to HAMANO Kenzo, Nakae was one of the leading opinion-makers of the *Jiyū minkenundō* (自由民権運動, freedom and rights movements), and his appraisal of Confucianism was heightened by his encounter with Western ideas.[14] Nakae's theory is a fusion of Eastern and Western ideas that was a driving force in the Meiji Restoration (the end of feudalistic ruling and the emergence of a modern governmental system). The connection between Nishi, Fukuzawa, and Nakae was their exposure to Western thought; they traveled to the Netherlands, the United States, and France respectively. In the mid-nineteenth century their fusion of ideas provided the foundation of a twentieth-century Japanese philosophy.

Gerard Godart argued that "philosophy was an unstable and contested concept" in Japan during the Meiji period.[15] However, I believe that Japanese philosophy in that period was not unstable but rather in a stage of development, and that Japanese intellectuals were adopting new concepts from the West to introduce into Japanese culture and society. There are two prominent philosophers who made significant contributions to the foundation of Japanese philosophical concepts. The first is the aforementioned NISHIDA Kitarō, who is regarded as Japan's most important philosopher, a great Buddhist philosopher, and the founder of the Kyoto school. The second, WATSUJI Tetsurō (和辻哲郎,1889–1960), is highly regarded as a moral philosopher and is as significant as Nishida in the history of twentieth-century Japanese thought.

Nishida's philosophy was influenced, more particularly, by the teachings of Zen Buddhism, which is characterized by self-discipline. According to Robert Bellah: "It was Nishida, more than anyone else, who, with the help of Zen Buddhism and German idealism, contributed to the formation of the new position which strongly influenced all Japanese literature and culture from the period of the First World War."[16] Zen is a sect of Mahayana

Buddhism that has had an enormous influence upon Japanese culture. One of the reasons why Nishida was strongly influenced by Buddhism could well be because of his association with SUZUKI Daisetsu (鈴木大拙, 1870–1966).[17] Suzuki, who popularized Zen Buddhism in the West, was a close, lifelong friend whose works impacted Nishida's.[18] Nishida produced numerous works, including *Zen no Kenkyū* (善の研究, *An Inquiry into the Good*) in 1911 and *Shisaku to Taiken* (思索と体験, *Thinking and Experience*) in 1915. Although Nishida's philosophy has elements of Zen Buddhism such as self-consciousness and emptiness, his philosophy involves other Japanese social, cultural, and spiritual elements. Nishida believed in the coexistence of spirit and nature, and that God is the foundation of the universe.[19] The significance of spirituality is mentioned in his personal diary. In March 1905 during the Russo-Japanese War, he wrote, "Mere materialistic prosperity is worthless. We must attempt to develop the spiritual side of the people."[20] Following Eastern traditions, his philosophy developed the religious dimension of the well-being of individuals. Nishida's concept leans toward metaphysics (broadly defined as the fundamental nature of being and the world that encompasses it) in its endeavor to establish humankind's position within the universe. According to IWASAKI Takeo, the influence of Buddhism has implanted a metaphysical awareness in the Japanese mindset.[21] This fits in well with Nishida's ideas. Although his thought is based on Japanese religious traditions, he absorbed Western ideas and the thoughts of other scholars, especially those of Suzuki, to define his notion of self within Japanese society.

While Nishida sought "the self," Watsuji sought "self-control," especially in regard to society. Watsuji began the study of philosophy under the guidance of his teacher INOUE Tetsujirō (井上哲次郎, 1855–1944), who criticized the influence of Christianity on Japanese culture. At a later stage, Watsuji questioned Inoue's ideas and found spiritual elements and encouragement from the teachings of OKAKURA Tenshin (岡倉天心, 1862–1913), another Japanese scholar.[22] Watsuji's published works included a book on Nietzsche in 1913, one on Kierkegaard in 1915, and works on Greek philosophy, primitive Christianity, Indian Buddhism, and Buddhist culture in Japan. He visited Europe in 1927 for a year and studied Heidegger's *Being and Time* while he was in Berlin.[23] As a result of his overseas experiences, Watsuji not only developed as a philosopher but also constructed a philosophy that was uniquely his. I believe that his philosophy was always connected to Japanese cultural values; indeed, his exposure to European philosophy and culture enabled him to see the distinctive value of the Japanese way. Bellah states, "Watsuji was fully aware that early Japan was primitive, but he believed that Japan's primitiveness was the seed of its vitality, its sense of living community, and of the emperor system which provided the legitimization for the acceptance of foreign culture."[24] Watsuji identified efficient social interaction among the Japanese as central to Japanese *rinri* (ethics), which he interprets as self-regulated behavior within the society. He considered the value of respect, courtesy, and modesty in human relationships to be the defining attributes of Japanese ethical behavior.[25] Watsuji's important published works laid the foundation for Japanese ethical thought, especially in pre-war Japan. Many of his works have been translated into English, such as *Fūdo* (風土, *Climate*), which examines the relationships between climate, the environment, and humans. An analysis of Japanese philosophy reveals the influence of these two most respected and studied philosophers. Their theoretical concepts were developed from Japanese cultural values and particularly from those grounded in religion, both Buddhism and Shintoism—and as well Confucianism, if it can be denominated a species of religion. In sum and in short, the philosophies of Nishida and Watsuji fused traditional Japanese thought and culture with Western philosophy; Watsuji, especially, was influenced by foreign cultural values to which he added the essence of the more subtle Japanese *rinri* culture.

11.2. Japanese Environmental Problems: Historical Perspectives

It is instructive at this point when considering Japan's environmental philosophy to look at three episodes in the country's history when failed environmental governance resulted in catastrophic damage to Japan's environment. The first episode involves pollution from the Ashio copper mine, which was located alongside the Watarase River in Tochigi Prefecture from 1610 to 1973. The Meiji period was a time in which Japan was determined to develop and accelerate its nation-building aspirations. The Ashio copper-mining operation was important to Japan's domestic economy and crucial for foreign exchange. During the Edo period, Ashio Mining was an important exporter and bolstered foreign trade with the Netherlands and China.[26] Through excessive exploitation of natural resources, aimed at profit and export growth, the Ashio mining complex created widespread pollution. There were two major aspects to the devastation. The first was the deforestation of the surrounding area, which eventually totaled 12,000 hectares—caused by excessive logging for mine timbers. The second was the poisonous effects of sulfur-laden emissions from the refinery operations. The consequence of extensive deforestation was that the moderating and filtering effects that the forests afforded the Watarase River were lost. The resultant soil erosion and excessive runoff created massive buildups of silt within the river system. As pointed out by Notchelfer, the pollution problem was complicated by the acidic nature of Ashio ores and the inefficient copper-extraction techniques of the 1880s.[27] Mining practices always bring ecological concerns, but in Ashio's case the pollution problems were severe enough to kill the river's fish and so damage the local environment that agriculture was adversely affected. Thus, the livelihoods of the surrounding fishermen and farmers were destroyed. The Meiji government was finally forced to intervene, but falsely declared that the pollution at Ashio was caused by flooding, not copper extraction.[28]

The second case is Minamata disease, which first appeared in Minamata City in the 1950s. It creates a disorder of the central nervous system brought on by the effects of consuming water and fish that have been contaminated by methylmercury. Some of the symptoms are difficulty in speaking and listening, trembling of the legs and hands, becoming bedridden, and "crying out to die" after contracting the disease. Japanese authorities have officially recognized about three thousand patients who contracted the disease, but the number of victims is actually much greater. The Chisso Corporation, established in 1908 as a fertilizer-processing plant, discharged waste methylmercury into Minamata Bay. By the 1950s, about 50 percent of the town's residents were dependent on Chisso for their livelihood.[29] Even when the cause of the disease was known, vested interests within the company and the city council prevailed over human and environmental well-being.

The third case of environmental pollution caused by modern technology is the Fukushima disaster in 2011. On March 11, a magnitude 9 earthquake occurred off the northeast coast of Japan and triggered a huge tsunami that crippled the Fukushima Daiichi nuclear power plant owned by the Tokyo Electric Power Company (TEPCO). What is most troubling about this disaster is the fact that although the earthquake and resultant tsunami are natural occurrences and thus not preventable, the damage that occurred to the facility certainly was preventable. TEPCO had a profit-oriented outlook, and because of cost considerations and a perceived loss of face, it chose not to implement an adequate tsunami defense for the facility. The tsunami seriously damaged the Fukushima Daiichi nuclear power plant, causing a meltdown in some of the reactors. An overriding concern, in the aftermath of the disaster, is that the nuclear danger is not visible and remains deadly for a long time. The radioactive hazards take three forms: airborne pollution, waterborne toxicity, and nuclear contamination that has penetrated soils and buildings. As of the end of December 2013, nearly 94,000 people in Fukushima Prefecture alone were displaced.[30] Although the numbers include those affected by the natural disaster and the nuclear power event, the majority are from areas near the Fukushima nuclear facility. The Japanese government authorities and TEPCO stated that the tsunami was *sōteigai* (想定外, beyond their expectations), making the natural disaster the culprit for Japan's worst nuclear reactor calamity. The truth of the matter is that TEPCO's tsunami protection had prepared only for a worst-case scenario of a 5.5-meter-high tsunami, when the one that struck was in fact over 14 meters high. Like Fukushima, most of Japan's nuclear power plants have insufficient measures to deal with tsunamis.[31] Although TEPCO initially tried to deflect responsibility for the debacle by blaming nature, seven months after the incident, in October 2012, it acknowledged that human complacency and human error were to blame. The financial interests of the company and negligent government oversight overrode safety and environmental considerations.

11.3. Environmental Philosophy: The Japanese Understanding

Prior to the twentieth century, there was very little study of *kankyō tetsugaku* (環境哲学, environmental philosophy) in Japan. In contemporary Japanese philosophy, a number of Japanese scholars teach and write about environmental ethics, but for the most part they are content to reprise and interpret Western[32] environmental concepts and philosophy. There is as yet no distinct Japanese environmental philosophy.

Rather, an informal Japanese environmental philosophy has sprung up that reflects Japanese culture and social values. The developing environmental philosophy in Japan is a "bottom up" approach, while in the West, environmental philosophy was a "top down" development that resulted from a retooling of philosophical ethical theories in response to environmental problems and environmental sciences, such as ecology. Academic environmental philosophy, so constructed, then influenced cultural and social behavior. Japanese philosophers of the nineteenth century, such as Nakae, Suzuki, Nishi, Kitagawa, and Watsuji, developed their teachings and theories within a Japanese social construct. It is this social construct that has influenced the direction of policymaking regarding environmental protection and is reflected in an emerging, bottom-up environmental philosophy. J. Baird Callicott writes that in an emerging global environmental awareness, associated environmental ethics can be conveyed "in the vernacular of a particular and local cultural tradition."[33] I believe that the relationship between culture and social values is vital for environmental well-being, and thus culture and religious beliefs play key roles in a philosophical approach to the well-being of the environment. In this section, I explain the conceptual framework of Japanese environmental philosophy (see figure 11.1). The key elements of this are ethical/moral principles, Japanese thinkers, religion, and *kami* (神). The veneration of the latter is very important and is embedded in everyday Japanese living; belief in *kami* connects and shapes the Japanese attitude to the environment.

The Japanese word *rinri* (倫理) is usually translated into English as "ethics"; however, the Japanese understanding of the word differs from the Western understanding. While the concept of "environmental ethics" in the West has a close connection to moral and religious teachings, the Japanese understanding has a more cultural and social connotation. A more accurate rendition of *rinri* would be "the maintenance of a healthy relationship with other people in the community."[34] The philosophical essence of *rinri* has two main characteristics.

The first characteristic is that the concept of *rinri* has influenced social development within Japan. The Chinese character or kanji for *rin* (倫) refers to practical wisdom: a path that people should follow that sets a moral code by which people should live. Robert E. Carter argues

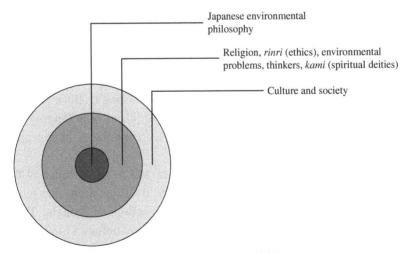

FIGURE 11.1 The Japanese Concept of Environmental Philosophy.

that Japanese ethics is an extensive application of the Buddhist theory of codependence, with a decidedly Confucian essence.[35] Although Confucianism is strictly not a religion, it teaches a code of moral behavior within society. Buddhism also teaches an inner discipline that cultivates wisdom for dealing with others and with the environment. Watsuji believed that the study of *rinri* is the study of human beings. In *Fūdo*, he argues that the primary role of a human is to be not only an individual but also a part of society.[36] The Japanese ethical consciousness has formed an inseparable tie between the individual and society. Watsuji also established that human existence has a dual structure of individuality and totality, which is always relational, and that the relationship with others is part of the totality.[37] The second characteristic is that *rinri* shapes the disciplinary code within society. The manner in which Watsuji explains the relationship between the individual and society illustrates how important Japanese social values are when *rinri* is involved. In Japan, "community" has a special significance as an all-embracing behavioral code that requires correct linguistic form between members, which expresses attitude and social standing, and is very demanding.[38] In Japanese primary schools there is a subject called *dōtoku* (道徳, ethics/morality); Japanese education emphasizes the importance not only of individual behavior but also how it fits within the community. In his study of ethics, Watsuji stresses that Confucianism has continued to have a place in Japan as *kokumin dōtoku* (national ethics/morality) especially in the early twentieth century.[39] Robert J. Wargo believes that, although Japanese culture has been greatly influenced by Confucianism and Buddhism, Japan does not have a Confucian culture like China, a Buddhist culture like Thailand, or a Western religious culture, despite the profound influence on Japan from the West.[40] However, since the introduction of Confucianism in the early sixth century, Japan has maintained the Confucian etiquettes of relationship within the society through the teaching of Japanese *rinri*. According to Befu Harumi, in Japan, Confucian ethics has reinforced the concept of belonging to a family.[41] The key element of Japanese *rinri* is the guidance of appropriate behavior within society.

The second characteristic of *rinri* is the historical significance of the Japanese thinkers who contributed to the ethical deliberations that led to the establishment of a Japanese philosophical school of thought. There are numerous early thinkers such as NIHOMIYA Sontoku (1787–1856) and MIYAZAWA Kenji (1896–1933) who taught a moral consciousness, particularly in relationship to farming practices and their embeddedness in the environment. A famous poem, "Amenimo makezu" (雨ニモマケズ, "Undefeated by the Rain") by Miyazawa in 1921, portrayed his caring, respectful, and modest approach to nature. There were two other scholars who studied morality and were influenced by their firm belief in Japanese religion: the aforementioned ISHIDA Baigan and SHIBUSAWA Eiichi (渋沢栄一, 1840–1931). Ishida was born in a farming village and later worked as a merchant in Kyoto. His theories were derived from the working class, not from the bourgeoisie, so they had a broad appeal the general public. He is known as the founder of *seki mon shin gaku* (石門心学, school of ethical teachings) and is greatly respected as a moral thinker. What is unique with Ishida's moral philosophy is its connection to cosmological notions. Ishida believed that every creature that lives between heaven and earth is created by the Will of Heaven (天命), and human beings, as one among them, must be able to understand that Will. He also taught that the appropriate way for a human to live is according to the Will of Heaven.[42] This vision is, in a modern sense, spiritual. From an environmental and philosophical perspective, Ishida's teachings connect nature, the environment, and cosmology, instructing people to care for all other living things. Like Ishida, Shibusawa valued Japanese tradition. He was one of the leaders of the Meiji Restoration, which restored imperial rule and fostered Japan's modernization process. He also played a significant role in the Japanese economic development of that period. Shibusawa's theory was named *Rongo to Soroban* (論語と算盤, Confucian Analects and the Abacus) and was based on the elements of morality and the economy.[43] He believed that good ethics and business should be in harmony. HORIDE Ichirō, a Japanese business expert, pointed out that in the Chinese classic *Da Xue* (大学) are the words 修身斎家・治国・平天下 (*Shūshin seika, chikoku, heitenka*), which mean that in order to control the whole country, you first you need to train yourself and make peace in your family.[44] Shibusawa achieved more in the field of economic development than philosophy, but he highly valued Confucian ideology and Japanese moral consciousness. Although Ishida and Shibusawa had different ideologies, their beliefs and philosophies were essentially Confucian teachings consonant with Japanese traditions.

Many sources of influence came together in the development of a Japanese environmental philosophy, but a common factor was the connection to the "community." Wasuji, Miyazawa, and Shibusawa all endorsed environmental philosophies that stressed the need for individuals to be of benefit to their societies.

11.4. The Position of *Kami* (神) in Japanese Traditions

Japanese religious beliefs have been of paramount importance in the development of Japanese environmental philosophy. During Japan's prehistoric Jōmon period (12,000 BCE to 300 BCE), the concept of *kami* took shape among the indigenous peoples of Japan, rooted in animism and animatism. The worship of nature spirits called *chi, mi,* and *tama* was common.[45] As the immigrant Yayoi population from the Asian mainland gradually spread north from Kyushu to Honshu, these beliefs evolved into regional Shintoisms (folk religions). A unique element of everyday Japanese life is the belief in and acceptance of myriad *kami* (spiritual deities or gods) who are ever present, existing, for example, in mountains, the sea, the sky, and cosmologically related divine beings. So ingrained is this belief that it is now more of a cultural conviction than a religious one; many Japanese who would claim to be nonreligious nevertheless believe in *kami.* The preservation of this belief is seen daily in contemporary Japan through the ancient practice of summoning the *kami* by hand clapping, and the propitiation of the *kami,* whatever their provenance, for the benefits of a this-worldly nature.[46] The prominent Japanese eighteenth-century classics scholar MOTOORI Norinaga (1730–1801), explained that *kami* exist in humans, natural phenomena, animals, plants, water, and mountains, and in entities that have feelings of reverence or exercise supernatural or holy powers.[47] The "belief in *kami*" in Japanese sociocultural traditions—with its origins in Shinto and folkloric religions, which are accommodating to those beliefs—has resulted in a deep-rooted spiritual presence. Shinto teaches that Japan is the land of the gods, where the deities dwell among the people and hover in the sky, forests, peaks, and hills.[48] In short and in sum, *kami* are spirits that play a significant role in Japanese society and culture, and belief in them plays an important role in the daily lives of its people.

Folk religions were unified with and accommodated by Buddhism when the latter was introduced into Japan in the sixth century. Confucianism was also introduced into Japan at that time as an ethical and philosophical system. Japan has many religions, but Shinto and Buddhism have been the most influential in shaping an ethical awareness. Shōtoku Taishi (聖徳太子, Prince Shōtoku) (574–622) was a leading figure who emphasized the importance of harmony within human relationships. He described Japanese religious life thus: "Shinto is the root, Confucianism is the flower, and Buddhism is the fruit of the one tree of life."[49] Japanese religion has woven these three traditions together. Although Confucianism is a more secular philosophy, the three have shaped cultural practices that have a bearing on the socioethical consciousness of the Japanese. In 1937, Father Leopold Tibesar argued that the Japanese by their nature are Shintoists, with the ruling class Confucianists, and the passive public Buddhists.[50] There are many Japanese who interchangeably practice Buddhism and Shinto in their rituals, ceremonies and customs; there is a Japanese saying that one is born in Shinto and dies in Buddhism. In *Japanese Buddhism*, GORAI Shigeru, one of Japan's leading folklorists, says that the relationship between the Japanese and Buddhism began through negotiations between the *kami* and the Buddha.[51] Gorai further explains that Buddhism spread widely in the country because it had memorial services for departed persons and repose for a vengeful ghost, similarities with Shinto doctrines based on Japanese mythology.[52]

11.5. *Kami* and Shinto

The literal meaning of *Shintō* (神道) is "the way of the *kami*." MITSUHASHI Takeshi points out that the term "Shinto" is found in the Chinese classic *Ekikyō* (易経), meaning "principles of nature's unexplained mysteries,"[53] which influenced the establishment of Shinto in Japan by building on the existing indigenous worship of nature. The Chinese concept was also applied to other religions. In China during the Chin Dynasty, Taoism and other related beliefs began to be called Shinto. The term was extended to apply also to Christianity as well as to a road leading to a cemetery or grave.[54] The first mention of Shinto in Japanese literature appeared in *Nihon Shoki* (日本書記, *Chronicles of Japan*),[55] the second oldest Japanese classic after the *Kojiki* (古事記, *Record of Ancient Matters*).

Within Shinto today, people pray to the *kami* for the fulfillment of their wishes, hopes, and dreams, asking for their support and protection in anything and everything. I believe that this deeply rooted belief in *kami* reflects the internal nature of the doctrine, whereas Shinto rites reflect the external. Shinto does not have written tenets but is commonly understood to teach the preservation of nature, the protection of animals, and a moral consciousness for the betterment of mankind. Japanese Shinto teaches that humans should possess the five virtues of purity (*kiyoi kokoro* 清い心), happiness (*akarui kokoro* 明るい心), right-mindedness (*tadashii kokoro* 正しい心), honesty (*sunao na kokoro* 直な心), and a sincere heart (*akaki kokoro* 赤き心). As long as people have these virtues, they live the way that the *kami* desire.[56] These virtues are not unique to Shinto, and some or all of these can be found in other religions and philosophical teachings, such as in Christianity and Confucianism. However, while Shinto differs from other religions in holding that *kami* exist not only within the Japanese psyche, but also in the natural environment—in water, stones, trees, and mountains. Paul Varley has stated that "a keen sensitivity to nature and a desire to find human identity with it in all of its manifestations are among the strongest themes in the Japanese cultural tradition."[57] The natural environment is the principal location of the *kami*.

The ancient cultural traditions in the Japanese mindset, a belief in *kami* and with it a strong link to nature, have shaped the development of Japanese environmental values. Shinto is the practice of rituals, and its concepts closely relate to animistic and naturalistic views found in the history and myths of Japan. It should be emphasized that Shinto is not a "religious faith" in the Western sense; it is a fusion of ideas, attitudes, and practices that has become the way of the Japanese people.[58] Shinto was built on the earlier beliefs in the *kami* and began to take shape in the Yayoi period (300 BCE to 300 CE) of Japanese history, particularly after rice farming was introduced.[59]

Japan's connection of their *kami* worship to agriculture has always been significant, and this is most apparent with rice culture. There is a term that refers to Japan as *mizuho no kuni* (瑞穂の国, "the land of abundance of rice"), which indicates an appreciation of this flourishing agricultural pursuit and its contribution to Japan's prosperity. Japanese rice is not only a food. As Emiko Ohnuki-Tierney puts it, rice grains have "soul," not simply as deities have soul, but closely associated with the Japanese word *nigitama* (和魂, "peaceful/positive power of the deity"), meaning the positive power of divine purity.[60] From the Japanese perspective, the production and consumption of rice, the ritual of harvesting it, and human reproduction all have a related meaning in that they facilitate the rejuvenation of the Japanese collective self by incorporating the divine power of *nigitama*.[61] Throughout Japanese history, there has been a religious significance to rice and to rice farming, demonstrated through the belief in the existence of the rice *kami* named Inari. Whether rice farmers today still have that belief is difficult to determine.[62] This faith is associated with Japanese Shinto. Peter Knecht states that Shinto has provided a strong incentive for Japanese rice farmers to care for their environment.[63] Japanese cultural traditions over the centuries confirm the existence of countless numbers of deities, and the rice deities are a positive power for Japanese rice farming.

Japanese environmental philosophy has developed through cultural traditions, and I argue that without that cultural role, it would have inadequate ethical content. Culture plays a crucial part in the evolution of an environmental philosophy, and I will discuss three elements that have made a contribution to the Japanese appreciation and respect of their natural environment: mythology, legends, and folklore. The geography of Japan with its abundant natural environment has been fertile ground for Japanese *kami*. Japan's highest mountain, Mount Fuji, is environmentally and culturally important to the Japanese. Central to Japanese mythology was the deity of the sun, the powerful Amaterasu Ōmikami (the sun goddess), who is believed to live on Mount Fuji and control the mountain.[64] Japanese mythology, with its expansively rich traditions, has had a natural influence on Japanese cultural identity. Michael Ashkenazi states that most Japanese are aware of their mythology, and although they may claim not to be religious, they nevertheless frequently perform religious rituals in their daily lives.[65]

In Japan, a divine mythology became enmeshed in society, and a consciousness of coexisting with the environment developed. In Japan it is not uncommon for people throughout their lives to pray to many different *kami*; it is the cultural belief in *kami* that identifies who the Japanese are. The conviction that Japan is "the land of *kami*" not only strengthens but identifies the relationship between land and deities. This legendary belief was bolstered when the Mongols attempted twice to invade Japan in the thirteenth century. It was believed that the two attempts were thwarted by the intervention of *kami* in the form of *kamikaze* (神風, divine wind) that wrecked the armadas. Ashkenazi puts it that the *kami* were ready to defend their land, but only if the Japanese were prepared to defend themselves without fear of death.[66] This is an illustration of how ancient Japanese history and mythology have influenced the development of a national psyche—so much so that the suicide bombing raids by Japanese pilots against the American armada in World War II took the name *kamikaze*.

Kami, in Japanese mythology, does not refer to a single deity, but rather to myriad deities that exist, as illustrated by the phrase *yaorozu no kami-gami* (八百万の神々, "eight million or numerous deities"). This signifies the pluralistic nature and mysticism of Shintoism. Japan's two oldest written classics, *Kojiki* and *Nihon Shoki*, were extremely influential in recording and cementing historic Japanese myths. In the *Kojiki* (AD 712), *kami* are described as *kakuremi* (隠身, unseeable figures).[67] Japanese *kami* have always been invisible figures in Japanese mythology as well as in the Japanese mindset. Japanese mythology relates the origins of who the

Japanese are, and the belief in *kami* has been central to the evolving myths and still remains central in the Japanese consciousness today.

Japanese legends are closely connected to the spread of folk stories that grew from Japan's many diverse regions. YANAGITA Kunio (柳田國男, 1875–1962), the "father" of Japanese folklorists and a very influential Japanese scholar, said that Japanese children are always loved by *kami* and *jizō* (地蔵, the stone guardian deity of children).[68] The animistic elements of Japanese legends have had both positive and negative significance for Japanese environmental thought. Children are frequently the audience during the telling of local legends that include ghosts and animals such as foxes or birds. These stories regularly teach a moral lesson and are significant elements in shaping Japanese values with respect to the environment: in time, the children become intuitively aware of and appreciative of the *kami* in the natural world. Although *kami* are invisible in nature, the children's belief in them is a significant part of their identity. In *Shinto, the Kami Way*, ONO Sokyo points out that the Japanese have a deep consciousness of *kami* and communicate with them directly, without there necessarily being a theological aspect to their acceptance of the *kami*'s spiritual existence.[69] In Japanese legend this perspective is often overlooked, as many myths are generally considered to be only traditional regional stories. It is, however, very important to examine this aspect of the Japanese identity when dealing with environmental awareness. Within Japanese legends that deal with the natural environment, the two most prominent spiritual figures are *kami* and *yōkai* (妖怪, often depicted as evil spirits). *Yōkai* are generally ominous, but can also be admired. The Japanese are intrigued by *yōkai* figures, which have been depicted in anime such as *GeGeGe no Kitarō* (ゲゲゲ の鬼太郎) and *Yōkai Ningen Bemu* (妖怪人間ベム). Even though they are popular cartoons, their story line and ideology point out that Japanese moral consciousness is an important part of cultural interaction with the environment. The Japanese film director MIYAZAKI Hayao's works are widely acknowledged and admired, not only by the Japanese but also by children and adults all over the world who place a value on human interaction with the natural world. One of Miyazai's films, *Spirited Away*, one of Japan's most commercially successful films, emphasized the significance of a spiritual existence in human society. These aspects were also seen in two of his other films, *Nausicaä of the Valley of the Wind* and *Princess Mononoke*, and the *totoro* of *Tonari no Totoro* is a type of *yōkai*. Yanagida once famously identified *yōkai* as "fallen *kami*."[70] Within Japanese culture, legendary spiritual figures can also be Japanese deities; although this might not have a close religious or philosophical connection, these figures are found in all Japanese regions. An example of this is a legend that I was told about when visiting the island of Kikai-jima, within the Amami archipelago in southern Japan. The islanders say that there is a *yōkai* named Kenmun who lives in the local banyan and fig trees and who protects their forests. According to them Kenmun is also a *kami*; in addition, they say that the *yōkai* in the Amami islands are not ghosts but are *kami* who understand humans and will guide them for their betterment. The description of Kenmun is that of a boy who has a plate on his head, a body covered with hair, webbed hands, and a face like a fox. There are innumerable legends in Japan that are regionally based and are accepted in those localities as a part of local lore. The close connection between the legends and the natural world reinforces the value that must be placed on the environment based on a holistic outlook within the community.

Finally, Japanese folklore reinforces the notion of the close spiritual relationship between humans and animals. John Knight pointed out that in Japanese myths, animals are often portrayed as being appreciative of human kindness and compassion, and that they have shown a reciprocal intent.[71] The spiritual element in Japanese folklore teaches moral consideration. An example is the tale of *tauejizō* (stone statue of rice planting), which tells how a young farmer paid respect to the stone deity figure that he passed each day on the way to his farm. His gentle and kind manner led the stone deity to repay his behavior by helping him when he was sick. This statue is a Buddhist symbol and a protector of children—another example of the flexibility of the accommodation of Buddhist and Shinto beliefs and practices. Children are taught through legend and folklore to respect the spiritual figures of *kami* at religious sites. In Japanese folklore, there is a strong element of morality in one's behavior toward and appreciation of nature; it is a combination of faith in the ever-present *kami* in nature as well as in oneself.

11.6. Conclusion

The seeds for Japanese environmental philosophy lay within religious, cultural, and social values. The philosophical concepts were developed by Japan's early thinkers, who were influenced by Shinto, Confucian, and Buddhist teachings. Western philosophers explored new areas of study that included environmental ethics and environmental philosophy, and they branched into many theories in these areas of study. On the other hand, Japanese environmental philosophy grew from within. During the

Japanese modernization period in the late nineteenth century, thinkers such as Nakae, Nishi, Watsuji, and Nishida drew inspiration from the new concepts and ideas of Western philosophies and cultures. Japanese philosophers established their own value systems, and Watsuji, particularly, articulated a Japanese environmental ethics. However, to the contrary, the Japanese government environmental policy did not reflect this orientation. Powerful national and business interests prevailed over traditional environmental wisdom and thus paved the way for Japan's devastating environmental disasters. Grass-roots empathy for the environment, which had become a part of Japanese culture and is exemplified in the teachings of Miyazawa, was either ignored or suppressed. Japan's environmental ethics and philosophy are built on social empirical principles, not on theory, as in the Western model. The key element to the Japanese vision is an ethical relationship between members of society and the environment. The wisdom of Japan's early thinkers shaped the Japanese environmental consciousness into a philosophical value system. The belief in the ever-present *kami*, with their power over humans and the natural world, makes these sprits a powerful influence in the Japanese worldview. The cultural influences of empirical knowledge, enlightened thinkers, and spiritual beliefs combine to exert a profound effect on Japanese environmental philosophy.

Early in the 1990s the term "environmental ethics" began to appear in Japanese government white papers on environmental policies, and it was a time when the government expressed its commitment to work with other nations on global environmental concerns. The principles for so-called environmental ethics were established within Western philosophy, so those teachings were somewhat foreign to the Japanese approach, wherein community initiatives had established a foundation from which to combat environmental problems. Acceptance of antipollution approaches at a grass-roots level is an effective, practical, and friendly way to reduce the impact of pollution. Although government policies are at times somewhat indefinite, the so-called cool-biz and warm-biz initiatives have been widely understood and accepted. These successful initiatives encourage individuals to dress according to the weather conditions and so reduce the reliance on energy-consuming air conditioners. The widespread belief in the *kami*, who are closely linked to the natural world, is so strong in Japan that it is now more a cultural belief than a religious one. The values expounded by contemporary Japanese environmental ethics are such that they can be readily accepted outside of Japan, and this acceptance is not conditional upon a belief in *kami*, although this belief was fundamental to the development of Japanese environmental philosophy.

Notes

1. Alistair Sinclair, *What Is Philosophy? An Introduction* (Edinburgh: Dunedin Academic Press, 2008), 1.

2. UEDA Shizuteru, "Contributions to Dialogue with the Kyoto School," in *Japanese and Continental Philosophy: Conversations with the Kyoto School*, ed. Bret W. Davis, Brian Schroeder, and Jason M. Wirth (Bloomington: Indiana University Press, 2011), 19.

3. James Heisig, *Philosophers of Nothingness: An Essay on the Kyoto School* (Honolulu: University of Hawaii Press, 2001), 3.

4. Editor's note: See the afterword for a fuller account of the transition from the Edo to the Meiji periods.

5. Hugh Cortazzi, *The Japanese Achievement* (London: Sidgwick and Jackson, 1990), 139.

6. Midori Kagawa-Fox, "Environmental Ethics from the Japanese Perspective," *Ethics, Place and Environment* 13, no. 1 (2010): 69.

7. NAKAMURA Hajime, "Suzuki Shosan, 1579–1655 and the Spirit of Capitalism in Japanese Buddhism," trans. William Johnston, *Monumenta Nipponica* 22, nos. 1–2 (1967): 5.

8. Gerard Clinton Godart, "'Philosophy' or 'Religion'? The Confrontation with Foreign Categories in Late Nineteenth Century Japan," *Journal of the History of Ideas* 69, no. 1 (2008): 74.

9. Shishen Xu, *Honyaku no Zōgo: Yan Fu to Nishi Amane no Hikaku* (*Coined Word of Translation: A Comparison between Yan Fu and Nishi Amane*), 2009, http://hamada.u-shimane.ac.jp/research/organization/near/41kenkyu/kenkyu17.data/17-03_xu.pdf.

10. Hansun Hsiung, "Women, Man, Abacus: A Tale of Enlightenment," *Harvard Journal of Asiatic Studies* 72, no. 1 (2012): 5.

11. HIRAISHI Nao'aki, "The Formation of Maruyama Masao's Image of Japanese Intellectual History during the War Period," *Social Science Japan Journal* 6, no. 2 (2003): 244.

12. Timothy Kaufman-Osborn, "Rousseau in Kimono: Nakae Chōin and the Japanese Enlightenment," *Political Theory* 20, no. 1 (1992): 56. In English, the title of Rousseau's book is *Of the Social Contract, or Principles of Political Right*.

13. Kaufman-Osborn, "Rousseau in Kimono," 56.

14. HAMANO Kenzo, "Human Rights and Japanese Bioethics," *Bioethics* 11, nos. 3–4 (1997): 329.

15. Godart, "Philosophy or Religion," 71.

16. Robert Bellah, "Japan's Cultural Identity: Some Reflections on the Work of Watsuji Tetsuro," *Journal of Asian Studies* 24, no. 4 (1965): 576.

17. Editor's note: Suzuki published in English under the name D. T. Suzuki.

18. HOJO Ko, "The Philosophy of Kitaro Nishida and Current Concepts of the Origin of Life," *Annals of the New York Academy of Sciences* 988, no. 1 (2003): 353.

19. Hojo, "Philosophy of Kitaro Nishida," 354. Nishida's concept has God as a part of, and integral to, the universe and not a separate creator figure, as in the Western tradition.

20. YUSA Michiko, *Zen and Philosophy: An Intellectual Biography of Nishida Kitaro* (Honolulu: University of Hawai'i Press, 2002), 78.

21. IWAWAKI Takeo, "Contemporary Japanese Moral Philosophy," *Philosophy East and West* 6, no. 1 (1956): 70.

22. Bellah, "Japan's Cultural Identity," 578.

23. Bellah, "Japan's Cultural Identity," 578.

24. Bellah, "Japan's Cultural Identity," 580.

25. Kagawa-Fox, "Environmental Ethics," 69.

26. F. G. Notchelfer, "Japan's First Pollution Incident," *Journal of Japanese Studies* 1, no. 2 (1975): 352.

27. Notchelfer, "Japan's First Pollution Incident," 365.

28. MIZUTANI Namiko, "Ashio kōzan ga motarashita engai to genzai he no kadai" ("Current Issues of Smoke Pollution by Ashio Copper Mining"), 2001, http://www.ritsumei.ac.jp/~oshima/kougi/2001/siryokenkyu2001/mizutani.pdf.

29. Dennis Normile, "Mercury Pollution: In Minamata, Mercury Still Divides," *Science* 341 (September 27, 2013): 1446.

30. *Fukushima Minpō*, "Hinansha sū' kennai 9-man 3846-nin, kengai 5-man 8608-nin" ("Evacuating 93,846 People within Fukushima Prefecture and 85,608 People Outside of Fukushima"), http://www.minpo.jp/pub/topics/jishin2011/2012/12/post_5761.html.

31. HIROSE Takashi, *Fukushima genpatsu meruto doun* (*The Fukushima Nuclear Power Meltdown*) (Tokyo: Asahi Shinsho, 2011), 39.

32. In this chapter, the "West" refers to the United States, Australia, New Zealand, and European countries that are grounded in the Judeo-Christian and Greco-Roman traditions.

33. J. Baird Callicott, *Earth's Insights: A Survey of Ecological Ethics from the Mediterranean Basin to the Australian Outback* (Berkeley: University of California Press, 1997), 12.

34. Kagawa-Fox, "Environmental Ethics," 68.

35. Robert E. Carter, *Encounter with Enlightenment: A Study of Japanese Ethics* (New York: SUNY Press, 2001), 124.

36. WATSUJI Tetsurō, *Fūdo* (*Climate*) (Tokyo: Iwanami-shoten, 2001), 166.

37. Anton Luis Sevilla, "Concretizing an Ethics of Emptiness: The Succeeding Volumes of Watsuji Tetsurō's Ethics," *Asian Philosophy* 24, no. 1 (2014): 83.

38. Carter, *Encounter with Enlightenment*, 124.

39. WATSUJI Tetsurō, *Watsuji Tetsurō Zenshū* (*Collected Works of Watsuji Tetsurō*), vol. 11 (Tokyo: Iwanami Shoten, 1979), 350.

40. Robert J. J. Wargo, "Japanese Ethics: Beyond Good and Evil," *Philosophy East and West* 40, no. 4 (1990): 499.

41. BEFU Harumi, *Ideologī to shiteno nihon bunkaron* (*The Theory of Japanese Culture as an Ideology*) (Tokyo: Shisō no Kagaku Sha, 2001), 28.

42. YAMAMOTO Shinkō, "Ishida Baigan no shisō to sono keizai rinri" ("Ishida Baigan's Thoughts and His Economic Ethics"), *Ningen Kaigi* (2003): 42.

43. KOGA Katsujirō, "Keizai to dōtoku, kigyō ka tachi no shisō" ("Economy and Morality: The Thoughts of an Entrepreneur"), *Ningen Kaigi* (2003): 24.

44. HORIDE Ichirō, "Hinhi aru keizai jin ni hitsuyō na kijun" ("The Necessary Standard of Being a Dignified Business Person"), *Ningen Baigi* (2003): 56.

45. MINAMOTO Ryōen, "Nihon ni okeru *kami* kannen no hikaku bunkaronteki kōsatsu" ("A Comparative Cultural Study of the Japanese Concept of *Kami*") in *Tōhoku Daigaku Bungakubu Nihon Bunka Kenkyūsho: Kami kannen no hikaku bunkaronteki kenkyū* (Tokyo: Kōdansha, 1981), 14.

46. John Breen and Mark Teeuwen, eds., *Shinto in History: Ways of the Kami* (Richmond, Surrey: Curzon Press, 2000), 5.

47. URYU Naka, *Shitte okitai nihon no shinwa* (*Japanese Mythology That You Should Know*) (Tokyo: Kadokawa Bunko, 2011), 25.

48. ANESAKI Masaharu, *The Mythology of All Races*, vol. 8 (New York: Copper Square Publishers, 1964), 247.

49. Leopold Tibesar, "Japanese Religion," *Primitive Man* 10, no. 2 (1937): 17.

50. Tibesar, "Japanese Religion," 18.

51. GORAI Shigeru, *Nihon jin no bukkyo* (*Japanese Buddhism*) (Tokyo: Kadokawa Shoten, 1989), 330.

52. Gorai, *Nihon jin no bukkyo*, 10.

53. MITSUHASHI Takeshi, *Shinto no jyōshiki ga wakaru shōjiten* (*A Small Book to Give You a Common Sense Understanding of Shinto*) (Tokyo: PHP Shinsho, 1996), 13.

54. Mitsuhashi, *Shinto*, 19.

55. Mitsuhashi, *Shinto*, 21.

56. TAKEMITSU Makoto, *Shitte okitai niho no kami sama* (*Japanese Deities You Should Know*) (Tokyo: Kadokawa Gakugei Shuppan, 2008), 165.

57. Paul Varley, *Japanese Culture* (Honolulu: University of Hawai'i Press, 1984), 51.

58. Kagawa-Fox, "Environmental Ethics," 59.

59. IWAI Hiromi, *Nihon no kami gami to hoteke* (*Japanese Kami and the Buddha*) (Tokyo: Seishun Shuppan-sha, 2002), 17.

60. Emiko Ohnuki-Tierney, *Rice as Self: Japanese Identities through Time* (Princeton, NJ: Princeton University Press, 1994), 55.

61. Ohnuki-Tierney, *Rice as Self*, 56–57.

62. Peter Knecht, "Rice Representations and Reality," *Asian Folklore Studies* 66, no. 1 (2007): 12.

63. Knecht, "Rice Representations and Reality," 7.

64. MIYAGI Naokazu, "What Is Shinto?" *Contemporary Religions in Japan* 7, no. 1 (1996): 49.

65. Michael Ashkenazi, *Handbook of Japanese Mythology* (Oxford: Oxford University Press, 2003), 65.

66. Ashkenazi, *Handbook of Japanese Mythology*, 21.

67. ŌNO Susumu, *Nihon jin no kami* (*Japanese Deities*) (Tokyo: Shinchō-sha, 2001), 17.

68. YANAGITA, Kunio, *Nihon no densetsu* (*Japanese Legends*) (Tokyo: Shinchō bunko, 1929), 147.

69. ONO Sokyo, *Shinto: The Kami Way* (Rutland, VT: Charles E. Tuttle, 1962), 8.

70. TADA Katsumi and ZOU Jimusho, *Nihon to sekai no yūrei, yōkai ga yoku wakaru hon* (*A Book That Explains Ghosts and Evil Spirits in Japan and around the World*) (Tokyo: PHP Kenkyū-sho, 2007), 19.

71. John Knight, "Feeding Mr. Monkey: Cross-Species Food 'Exchange' in Japanese Monkey Parks," in *Animal in Person*, ed. John Knight (New York: Berg, 2005), 234.

CHAPTER 12 | *Kagura*

Embodying Environmental Philosophy
in the Japanese Performing Arts

GODA HIROKO

THIS CHAPTER EXPLORES how *kagura* (神楽) folk dance plays reflect an environmental philosophy central to Japanese mythology. Environmental anthropology, which is an extension of the discipline of cultural anthropology, explores human culture and society from the viewpoint of the correlation of human beings and the environment. The field of environmental mythological studies, a subset of environmental anthropology, takes the embodied expressions and sensibilities of various peoples as clues that can illuminate their mythological beliefs. By analyzing *kagura* stage settings and concrete stage properties that symbolize parts of the natural environment, I pay attention to the body motions used by the performers to communicate with the audience. My research also focuses on the transmission of the art of *kagura* performance to future generations. I ask how the natural environment of a certain space has affected people's dispositions toward nature, and then try to understand the traditional attitudes passed down in each local space. By researching Japanese people's commitment to the environment in their local scenes, I hope to grasp the environmental philosophy at the core of Japanese mythology.

12.1. The Environmental Philosophy of Shintoism

According to Shintoism, the pedigree of the Japanese imperial line begins with Ninigi-no-mikoto (邇邇芸命) descending from the heavenly world to Hyuga as a grandson of Amaterasu Ōmikami (天照大御神), who is the sun goddess and the ancestor of the Japanese emperor's family. The land, islands, and nature gods, among them the fire god, the water god, and the clay god, were all born to the first couple of gods. After those births of nature gods, Amaterasu Ōmikami and her brothers were born. This fact that even the creation of the environment is narrated in the style of a pedigree clarifies how important the pedigree is in Japanese mythology. The pedigrees bestow political leaders with mythological authority by connecting their lineage with the founding emperors and the gods from whom the emperors were descended.[1]

Until the 1980s, scholars of religious studies and religious anthropology generally explained Shinto as a kind of polytheism that originated from animistic reverence for the power of nature, which thereafter developed into the worship of myriad anthropomorphic gods.[2] However, I prefer the term "animatism," defined by R. R. Marret, to the term "animism" used by E. B. Tylor, though ultimately both are insufficient to explain an archaic form of Japanese mythology later identified as Shinto. If I dare to clarify the difference between "animism" and "animatism," in the notion of the former Tylor uses a dualistic paradigm of body and soul to argue that spirits sometimes animate the substantial natural bodies of plants, animals, stones, and natural phenomena like thunder. On the other hand, "animatism" recognizes that power and energy are inherent in the objects themselves; Marret gives the example of *mana* in Melanesia.[3] Marret notes an episode in which a tribesman in South Africa asks a storm to change its route, thus recognizing that the storm itself has its own life, and is not being controlled by any spirits other than its own self.[4]

In *Manyoshu* (万葉集), which is the first poetry book edited in Japan, in the eighth century CE, there is a similar phrase, "Hey, this mountain, move!," in a love poem by a famous court poet, KAKINOMOTO Hitomaro (柿本人麻呂).[5] In a Japanese context, this represents an analog to the story of the South Africa tribesman as reported by Marret. In Japan, this power or energy is *ki* (気), which appears in many Japanese terms, such as *tai-ki* (大気, air), *gen-ki* (元気, healthy), *ki-ryoku* (気力, active power), *ki-bun* (気分, mental condition), *ki-mochi* (気持, feeling), and *ke-hai* (気配, feeling something to exist). It is interesting that these words combined together with *ki* are often used to express both mental states and invisible natural phenomena like air. Dr. OKADA Mamiko (岡田真美子) notes that the Japanese cognition of life, power, and subjectivity inherent in all things—whether they are animate or inanimate—is reflected in the Japanese Buddhist doctrine that "grasses, trees, and the lands all can attain Buddha-hood."[6]

Here I propose that this idea of embodied subjectivity is one characteristic that must differentiate environmental ethics from more traditional human-centered ethics. And I suggest that this embodied subjectivity is expressed in *kagura* performances. That such performances include natural materials that have sacred significance through their embodied subjectivity makes *kagura* a modality for expressing and implicit environmental ethic.

12.2. Environmental Themes in *Kagura* Performance

What follows are two case studies of *kagura*. The first deals with Takachiho and Gokase, while the second investigates a unique form of *kagura* found in Iwami.

The study of *kagura* can enhance the understanding of environmental thought in Japanese mythology. I experienced "the night *kagura*" in the Takachiho (高千穂) area of Miyazaki Prefecture in the central highland of Kyushu several times during the 2004–2006 winter seasons.[7] Takachiho *kagura* is performed annually in winter after the autumn rice harvest in every small village belonging to the township of Takachiho. Since the Edo (江戸) period (seventeenth–nineteenth centuries CE), the *kagura* tradition has developed from the ritual performances by religious groups belonging to the hamlet shrine center of the village where religious and cultural events take place.[8] Many of the rituals and habits supporting *kagura* performances have been preserved in the daily lives of village inhabitants. Takachiho is located in Hyuga and holds a special place in Japanese mythology: Hyuga is the place where Ninigi-no-Mikoto, as a grandson of the highest goddess, Amaterasu Ōmikami, descended from the heavenly world to earth.

The place where *kagura* is performed is the house of an ordinary person who takes a turn as host among the members of the shrine in a hamlet. Residents of this house and neighbors prepare the stage and other rooms, including a dressing room, a kitchen for serving supper, and a space for audience's seats. The number of visitors from outside, among them tourists, photographers, and researchers, has recently increased, so *kagura* stages are now often set up in the local public hall or constructed in the shrine yard. However, in Asakabe district of Takachiho town I visited in 2004, they still set the stage in an ordinary house. As village *kagura* groups conduct their performances almost every weekend during the *kagura* seasons in winter, heaters are prepared and campfires are burning in the yard. The audience is free to sleep or go home and return to see favorite programs.

A supper and snack are served to guests, who are obliged to bring a bottle of sake or a monetary gift to support the celebration.

The play is over fifteen hours long, taking place from early evening on the first day to late morning on the next. About twenty or thirty amateur performers play many times on a tight schedule throughout the night. The most important scene takes place at dawn and symbolizes the rebirth of the sun goddess, Amaterasu Ōmikami. KOBAYASHI Yasumasa, a folklorist, argues that there are two aspects to *kagura*: ritual and public entertainment.[9] The ritual role is fulfilled by the priest of the shrine, who prays for the villagers and the *kagura* performers, the latter of whom wear masks representing the gods. *Kagura* performers are called "servants of the gods" (*hosha-don* 奉仕者) in the dialect of Miyazaki. The public entertainment aspect is derived from the system of performance, which enables the interaction of the performers and the audience through the medium of the artists' bodies.

The stage properties and settings used by the performers have important spiritual and cultural implications.[10] The roof of the house used as the theater is decorated with a bow and arrow, meant to ward off evil spirits, and a *chigi* (千木), a special ornament on the roof showing that this house is regarded as a shrine for the duration of the *kagura* performance. Among the various elements of the stage-setting process, *kouniwa* (神庭) is the most important. It literally means "the gods' garden" and is regarded as just like the sanctuary of a real shrine. All the programs of *kagura* performances are played there. It is surrounded by four bamboo pillars with leaves standing at four sides and decorated with *erimono* (彫り物), which are white sheets of paper cut in various designs that symbolize the natural divinity sanctifying the space. At the back of *kouniwa*, there is an altar (*kami-dana* 神棚) for the gods where a priest from the local shrine prays during the opening ceremony of *kagura* performances. From the center of the ceiling above this sanctuary zone, a square shade called a *kumo* (雲) is hung. This is similar to the *tengai* (天蓋, literally "the shade of the heaven") hung from the ceilings of Buddhist temples. *Kumo* literally means "cloud" and symbolizes the heavenly world where the gods exist.

In the yard of the *kagura* house, a sacred place is constructed called *soto-jime* (外注連), which literally means "outside sanctuary." This corner is fenced with bundles of twigs from a special kind of tree, *sakaki* (榊), which convey the gods to this sacred space. In this corner, many bags, each containing seed rice and a pair of male and female snakes made of straw, are set out on the day of *kagura* performances. The snakes symbolize fierce gods who are regarded as terrible yet merciful, giving us both raging storms and the rainfall needed for rice farming. Beside this corner, one pillar called a *shime* (標) is constructed and decorated with colorful paper strings to show that this house is sanctified for *kagura* performances. *Shime* and *jime* are homonyms and represent marked objects or lines that are used to symbolize the border of sanctified space from secular space.

Among thirty-three programs, some deal with the theme of the right of land tenure. For instance, a new god who comes from the heavenly world needs to negotiate with the native gods about the use of the land. While the both sides are earnestly negotiating, they sit on square bags containing seed rice. These dramas transmit an important message for the farmers about the right of land tenure for rice farming. This program is different from the others, portrayed as a dialogue drama without dancing and music.

In the Iwami *kagura* of Shimane Prefecture, an important part of the performance features Susanoo-no-Mikoto (須佐之男命) slaying an evil eight-headed snake to save the life of the princess who later became the founder of Izumo. Scholars of mythological studies explain that this giant snake with eight heads symbolizes a fierce river that causes annual floods all over the Izumo plain.[11] The frequent floods caused by the river are regarded as a kind of environmental destruction resulting from poor maintenance of the mountains. Therefore, the figure of the eight-headed snake is considered to symbolize the retribution of nature itself. In the *kagura* performance, the snake is played by eight separate actors in snake costumes that seem to be overflowing from the stage.

12.3. Physical Materials and Living Power

The purpose of this chapter is to discuss environmental thought in Japanese mythology, not as a static description of the correlation between environment and religion, but as a dynamic presentation of how *kagura* connects the mythical events of the past to human life in the present. *Kagura* performances emphasize two elements: (1) the power of material objects such as props, costumes, and setting, and (2) the performers' body movements, through which they impact the audience. Once real material objects are utilized by performers who are alive in the present, the setting of the theatrical performance can be transformed into a kind of mythical scenery where performers and audience live together in the eternal past.

Eliade discusses the relation between mythology and reality in *Mythe de l'Eternel Retour*.[12] *Kagura* performances allow the mythology of the beginning times to be realized again as an eternal time when performed through the medium of the bodies of living artists. Michael Polanyi, a natural scientist, economist, and philosopher,[13] argues that dramatic performances contain "a tacit dimension of knowing." Human beings exist biologically in real vital bodies through the physiological mechanisms that allow them to survive and thrive. In this sense, human beings are no different from other organisms in the environment. Polanyi argues that there is a relationship between the human body and things outside:

> Our body is the ultimate instrument of all our external knowledge, whether intellectual or practical. In all our waking moments we are *relying* on our awareness of contacts of our body with things outside for *attending* to these things. Our own body is the only thing in the world which we normally never experience as an object, but experience always in terms of the world to which we are attending from our body. It is by making this intelligent use of our body that we feel it to be our body, and not a thing outside.[14]

Our embodied nature is affirmed by feelings and physical expression that can be realized only by utilizing our bodies in exercise or performance. This allows us to transform the "tacit dimension of knowing" into "formal knowledge." In *kagura* performances, actors use their body expressions as a means of communication. This nonverbalized "tacit knowing" parallels what takes place in other Japanese arts such as tea ceremonies (*chanoyu* 茶の湯) and judo (柔道) training. The term *kata* (型) refers to the structured patterns of exercises that lead learners first to imitate visible patterns and then to incorporate the patterns into themselves, thereby bridging the gap between "tacit knowing" and "formal knowing." Costumes, props, and stage settings help make up these structured patterns. Japanese arts have a tendency to use physical materials as main elements of the patterns that express tacit knowing.

The environmental philosophy of KUWAKO Toshio supports the bodily element shown in *kagura* performances. Kuwako argues that the extent to which humans view themselves as having a bodily existence determines whether or not environmental problems are essential for them. In the United States, for instance, environmental ethics, by those who know little about it, is categorized as a branch of applied ethics because ethics proper is a theoretical study. Applied ethicists then apply the theory generated by the proper philosophers to real-world problems, among them environmental problems. Or so the process is condescendingly perceived by "mainstream," "pure" analytic philosophers. But because ethics has traditionally been thought to be concerned only with humans, environmental ethics cannot be merely the application of anthropocentric ethical theory to things other than human. Environmental ethics is thus inherently theoretical as well as applied. Among the theoretical innovations necessitated by ethical concern for things other than human is abandonment of the long tradition in Western thought that regards human nature as more of a thinking thing than a bodily thing.[15]

Japanese beliefs about the divinity of nature are derived from the animatism of the Shinto tradition. This animatism is manifested in the costumes, props, and stage settings of *kagura* performances. According to archaeologists Kobayashi and Miyajima, ancient people set a high value upon the materials from which their regalia were constructed because of the eternal power these materials conveyed.[16] Regalia materials were precious because of the beauty, scarcity, and durability of the shells, stones, bronze, and iron components. Fukui, a social anthropologist,[17] also notes that among these three things—beauty, scarcity, and durability, which are essential qualifications for the materials of regalia—durability represents the durable succession of family's pedigree.

Kagura allows core concepts from the Shinto tradition to become embodied in the performances of the actors, and thereby become part of the lived experience of the community. This helps to reinforce the environmental sensibilities of the Shinto tradition within Japanese culture. *Kagura* is therefore a powerful vehicle for promoting environmental awareness because it can remind the community that environmental sensitivity is an integral part of what it means to be Japanese.

Notes

1. 次田真幸 (訳注),古事記 (中巻), TSUGITA Masaki, trans., *Kojiki*, vol. 2 (Tokyo: Kodansha, 1980), 58; 小島憲之編 (訳注), 日本書紀 (1), KOJIMA Noriyuki et al., trans., *Nihon Shoki*, vol. 1 (Tokyo: Shogaku-kan, 1994), 518. All English translations from Japanese sources in this chapter are the author's own.

2. 石川栄吉他編,文化人類学事典 ISHIKAWA Eikichi et al., eds., *The Encyclopedia of Cultural Anthropology* (Tokyo: Kobun-do, 1987), 385.

3. 合田濤編,現代社会人類学 GODA Tō, ed., *Current Social Anthropology* (Tokyo: Kobundo, 1994), 161–162.

4. 小口偉一, 堀一郎編, 宗教学辞典 OGUCHI Iichi and HORI Ichirō, eds., *The Encyclopedia of Religious Studies* (Tokyo: University of Tokyo Press, 1973), 7–8.

5. 中西進編, 万葉集 (1) NAKANISHI Susumu ed., *Manyoshu*, vol. 1 (Tokyo: Kodan-sha, 1978), 115–116, song number 2:131.

6. 岡田真美子, "山川草木の命", 小さな小さな生きものがたり, OKADA Mamiko, "The Lives of Mountains, Rivers, Grasses and Trees," in *The Story of Small Living Beings*, ed. OKADA Mamiko (Tokyo: Showa-do, 2013), 2–10.

7. This fieldwork was conducted as part of a project supported by the Japan Society for the Promotion of Science. The project title in English is "The Succession and Reconstruction of Japanese-Style Intellectual Property" (Project leader: Dr. KUWAKO Toshio; Group leader: Dr. OKADA Mamiko).

8. A hamlet is a small natural part of a village that originated during the Edo period (1603–1868 CE).

9. 小林康正, "花祭の誕生へ", 民俗芸能研究 (21), KOBAYASHI Yasumasa, "Toward the Birth of the Flower Festival," in *Studies on Folkloric Performing Arts*, vol. 21 (Tokyo: Waseda University Press, 1995), 5.

10. 後藤俊彦 (高千穂神社宮司) 他著, 神楽33番, GOTŌ Toshihiko (chief priest of the Takachiho Shrine) et al., eds., *Kagura 33 Numbers* (Miyazaki: Koumyaku-sha, 2008), 20–36.

11. *Nihon Shoki*, 91.

12. Mircea Eliade, *Myth of the Eternal Return*, trans. Willard R. Trask, translated into Japanese by HORI Ichiro with the title エリアーデ著, 堀一郎訳, 永遠回帰の神話：祖型と反復 (Tokyo: Mirai-sha, 1963), 93–101.

13. Michael Polanyi, *The Tacit Dimension* (Chicago: University of Chicago Press, 2009), vii–xvi, 17–21.

14. Polanyi, *The Tacit Dimension*, 15–16.

15. 桑子敏雄, 風景のなかの環境哲学 KUWAKO Toshio, *Environmental Philosophy in the Scenery* (Tokyo: University of Tokyo Press, 2005), 208–213. See also Kuwako's article in chapter 15 of this anthology.

16. 小林達雄, 宮島宏, 福井勝義他 "シンポジウム：古代日本の玉文化", 小林達雄編, 古代ヒスイ文化の謎を探る, KOBAYASHI Tatsuo, MIYAJIMA Hiroshi, and FUKUI Katsuyoshi, "Symposium," in *Searching the Mystery of Ancient Jade Culture*, ed. KOBAYASHI Tatsuo (Tokyo: Gakusei-sha, 2006), 126–127.

17. KOBAYASHI Tatsuo ed., *Searching the Mystery of Ancient Jade Culture*, 156.

PART V | Natural Disasters

CHAPTER 13 | Disaster Prevention as an Issue
in Environmental Ethics

TAKAHASHI TAKAO

13.1. The Age of Disaster

On Friday, March 11, 2011, eastern Japan was struck by an earthquake
with a magnitude of 9.0. It was the most powerful earthquake ever to have
hit Japan and one of the five largest earthquakes in the world since modern
record-keeping began in 1900. It sent tsunami waves over 10 meters high
onto the eastern shore of Honshu Island, causing a level-7 meltdown at
the Fukushima Daiichi nuclear power plant complex. As many as sixteen
thousand people were killed by the tsunami, and over two thousand people
are still missing. One hundred thirty thousand buildings were completely
destroyed, with a further 254,000 buildings half-destroyed, and 700,000
buildings partially damaged. The World Bank's estimated the economic
cost at US$235 billion, the most expensive natural disaster in world history.

It is said that Japan has entered a period of brisk seismic activity and
that we Japanese are facing an age of unavoidable disasters of which we
cannot help but become aware. On top of that, we are now also faced with
globally scaled disasters. Thus, to begin with, we have to be clear about
the concept of disaster. A disaster is "a sudden accident or a natural catastrophe that causes great damage or loss of life."[1] We can find two elements
that constitute the concept of disaster, that is, (1) accidents or natural phenomena, which cause (2) great damage or loss of life. Note well that the
cause of disasters can be separated into two categories: (a) anthropogenic
(human-made) accidents and (b) natural phenomena. Public pollution,
carbon-dioxide emissions, infectious diseases, and radioactive leaks are
anthropogenic or human-related accidents, whereas crustal movements,

large waves, strong winds, volcanic eruptions, droughts, floods, and mud or rock slides are natural phenomena. If (1) either (a) anthropogenic accidents or (b) natural phenomena cause (2) great damage or loss of life, then a disaster occurs. When the cause is (a), it may be called an anthropogenic disaster, whereas if (b) is the cause, it may be called a natural disaster. Sometimes (a) and (b) are difficult to isolate. A disastrous wildfire, for example, may be ignited by lightning (a natural phenomenon), but its fuel may have accumulated as a result of careless logging (an anthropogenic phenomenon).

Once more: the concept of a disaster consists of two elements, (1) accidents or natural phenomena, and (2) great damage or loss of life; therefore, disaster prevention also has two aspects, that is, preventing the occurrence of accidents or natural phenomena, if possible, and prevention of severe damage or loss of life. We cannot prevent the approach of typhoons, but if we do not prepare for them well, the consequences of such disasters will be at least partly anthropogenic. The characteristics of anthropogenic disasters are related to responsibility. Therefore, if there is any room in a disaster for blame or fault, the disaster is wholly or partly anthropogenic. One of the reasons for the globalization of disasters is that the total influence of human activity has drastically altered the earth's biosphere. Global warming, ozone depletion, air pollution, and radioactive pollution are all caused by an extension of human activities.

TERADA Torahiko (1878–1935), a Japanese physicist, says that as civilization develops, the damage caused by a disaster becomes more and more extensive; and in the twenty-first century, when Japan is interconnected and interdependent, a local disaster has effects all over the country.[2] Human beings are also interconnected and interdependent on a global scale. For example, the Great East Japan Earthquake caused a serious supply shortage of semiconductors, automobiles, and electronic components, followed by significant adverse effects on the production of cars and home electronics around the world. A global food crisis may occur when some large-scale food production area is devastated by drought or flooding. Because of the increase of interaction with people all over the world, infectious diseases are more easily becoming pandemic, yet another kind of disaster.

It may therefore be said that all of us live in the age of disaster. Many disasters are difficult to prevent, can occur at any moment, and often have global ramifications. Therefore, we have to learn to coexist with disasters. In what follows, I develop an idea of "co-disaster" that encourages us to reconsider the fundamental concept of ethics, the meaning of life and death, the relationships between humans and nature, the instability of the world, the nature of sciences, and the relationship of science to society, policy, and politics.

13.2. Hidden Anthropocentrism

Mainstream environmental ethics has focused on the conservation of nature or "wilderness" rather than on disaster prevention and mitigation. Part of the historical background of environmental ethics is the establishment of national parks in the United States during the century between 1850 and 1950. In 1890, the pronouncement of the "disappearance of the frontier" was made. Historically, the nature to be conserved in American environmental ethics was, above all, "wilderness"—namely, places that were believed never to have been greatly affected by humans. For a long time before this period in US history, "wilderness" was considered to be "wasteland" begging to be cultivated. For example, John Locke writes in *Two Treatises of Government*, book 2, chapter 5, after referring to the standard that every man should have as much as he can make use of, "This measure did confine every man's possession to a very moderate proportion, and such as he might appropriate to himself, without injury to anybody, in the first age of the world, when men were more in danger to be lost, by wandering from their company, in the then vast wilderness of the earth, than to be straitened for want of room to plant in."[3] In the United States the meaning of "wilderness" gradually changed, however, from "wasteland" to "sacred places to be conserved."[4] In the 1990s, the concept of wilderness was sharply criticized and American environmental ethicists are divided over legitimacy of its formerly uncontested role of the sanctum sanctorum of the American environmental movement.[5]

In the field of environmental ethics, one of the few essays that deals with disasters is "Disvalues in Nature" by Holmes Rolston III. Rolston admits that nature has violent forces, but, he says, "It is objective fact that the adverse, violent forces in dialectic with the prolific, enduring forces yield much of the romantic life. The violent forces of nature are as much to be celebrated for their creativity as for their destruction."[6] He quotes John Muir, who experienced the Inyo earthquake in Yosemite Valley in March 1872: "I ran out of my cabin, near the Sentinel Rock, both glad and frightened, shouting, 'A noble earthquake!'. . . a terribly sublime and beautiful spectacle."[7] For Muir, the earthquake is "wild beauty-making business."[8] According to Rolston, disasters appear to be disvalues individually, but to speak ecologically, they are not disvalues. "Floods, windstorms, lightning storms, and such violences would be more or less like wildfire in ecosystems, a bad thing to individuals burned and in short range, but not really all that bad systematically in long range, given nature's restless creativity."[9] From the point of view of mainstream environmental ethics, to pay attention to disasters and their prevention is to make too much of the individual lives that would be lost in a disaster. Decades after a disaster, such as the 1988 wildfire in Yellowstone National Park, a devastated area can become more vital and beautiful than before. But, suppose in several decades that northern Honshu becomes a more developed and comfortable place to live. Does that transform a disaster that cost a huge number of innocent individual human lives into good thing, "systematically" speaking?

In Japan, too, environmental ethicists have been mainly concerned with the conservation of nature, or more popularly, with a symbiosis between humans and nature, instead of with disaster prevention. The nature to be conserved in Japanese environmental ethics was never "wilderness," because it was more obvious in Japan than in North America that for a very long time no areas of wilderness existed. The situation is similar to that in Europe, as Aldo Leopold noticed during his trip to Germany in 1935.[10] In Japan, life in the *satoyama* (里山), which are undeveloped wooded areas near villages, has typified the good relationship between humans and nature—that is, human-nature symbiosis. In such a way of framing the relationship between humans and nature, the famous dichotomy in environmental ethics—namely, anthropocentric versus nonanthropocentric—is difficult to maintain.

Nevertheless, the Great East Japan Earthquake seems to have revealed a new agenda for environmental ethics: disaster prevention. However, very few articles on disaster prevention are found in the field of environmental ethics in the United States or even in Japan. Many disasters occur in the United States, such as hurricanes, tornados, forest fires, droughts, and earthquakes. Japanese people have experienced many earthquakes, typhoons, tsunami, floods, and volcanic eruptions. It is quite curious that American and Japanese environmental ethicists have not dealt with disaster prevention as an agenda of environmental ethics. Why? Do they think that it is not the agenda of environmental ethics, but that of policy and engineering? Taking a deeper and dialectical look at environmental ethics, we may notice the existence of its cryptic anthropocentrism. We human beings have seized power over nature; and *therefore* we have to conserve and protect it. We assume that we have a responsibility to or for nature. Mainstream environmental ethics assumes the active character of human agents and the passive and vulnerable character of nature. Human beings now have growing power over nature, and we have arrived at the stage of alteration of nature on a global scale. In such a situation, to preserve and conserve nature is the most important agenda because a radically altered nature can destroy us. Thus, at the very root of nonanthropocentric environmental ethics we can find cryptic anthropocentric attitudes. The main reason for not regarding disaster prevention as an agenda of environmental ethics is its forthright anthropocentrism.

13.3. A View of Nature Based on Old Japanese Myths

If we pay attention to the aspect of disaster prevention as well as nature conservation, what kind of view of nature can be adopted?

According to the modern view, the power of reason or science, in principle, precedes and can control the power of nature by knowing the causal rules that govern nature. Its fundamental principle, established also as an axiom of modern economics, is that we can utilize natural resources without limit; because when one resource becomes scarce a substitute will be found or invented by human ingenuity. However, we have begun to notice that nature does not have such infinite capacity. If we overexploit nature, the perilous destruction of natural capital—and various disasters—will follow. Disaster prevention, like nature conservation, is ultimately for the sake of human well-being. The positive relationship with nature that we human beings have been seeking is really only good for human beings. Here there can be no room for respecting nature, except in the way we "respect" something that has great power out of fear of the harm it can do to us.

Also, we can view nature as living being. According to this view, nature is not strictly determined by causal laws, but it is often capricious, and not only gives blessings but sometimes shows fury. We not only think, but also feel, that the behavior of nature is that of a living agent. We treat nature as having a life like animals and human beings—and thus having agency—and, therefore, we feel respect for nature. "Disaster" not only has the standard meaning as in the dictionary definition cited above, but also has significance for human beings: in principle, we can control only a small portion of the power of nature. This is a primitive, animistic view. It seems, however, to lie deep in our minds, at least in the minds of Japanese people. From this standpoint, cryptic anthropocentrism disappears and we understand the significance that disasters have for our lives and actions.

Additionally, our daily lives, our politics, and so on, are mutually related to disasters—that is, linked cosmologically. Disaster prevention and nature conservation is for the sake of nature as well as for human well-being.

There may be several possibilities for the basis of the position of nature as life. Here, it is worth visiting the characteristics of Japanese thought that appeared in old Japanese myths:[11]

1. Ontology

   a. *Animism*: All things are spiritual. Everything in the universe, including natural things such as mountains, seas, and rivers, has a life or an anima. They are interconnected and they essentially have a character that is uncontrollable by themselves or others (i.e., they have the character of otherness). In this framework, the powers of nature that we often feel are called gods (*kami*).

   b. *The biological world*: The process or the way of development of the world is similar to that of a biological world. Individuals might have purposes such as self-preservation, reproduction, or pursuing happiness, but not the world as a whole.

   c. *Gods as the base of human existence*: Most gods are powers of nature, and they produce the land where humans, animals, and plants grow.

   d. *Gods as beings who require worship*: Worship consists of two elements: praying to a god and taking care of a god (i.e., building a shrine, making an offering, etc.). Bad relationships between gods and humans, including insufficient worship, often cause disasters.

   e. *Gods and men as beings who worship*: It is not only men, but also gods, who worship, for the essence of personhood is to worship. The purpose of worship is, generally speaking, forming, maintaining, and restoring order. In several passages of *Kojiki* (the oldest book of myths, published in 712) we see the gods worship in order to form, maintain, and restore the order of the heavenly world. In Japan, even now, we are worshipful, for example, the ceremony of purifying a building cite. It is the ceremony of pacifying a local god by maintaining a good relationship with the god.

2. Epistemology

   a. *Empiricism*: The arts and patterns of the rituals of worship have been discovered throughout history. Here lies a kind of empiricism: whether we grasp the meaning of a god or not is confirmed by experiences.

b. *Reality of spiritual power*: At the base of religious experiences is the reality of spiritual power. Ancient people could not but feel power that is beyond reason. Experiences of spiritual power also support the metaphysics mentioned above.

c. *Disaster prevention*: The will of a god often reveals itself as a disaster, such as an earthquake, tsunami, massive fire, flood, famine, or epidemic. Only a part of the meaning of the god's will can be known through rituals (worship) and thereby listening with a selfless mind. Here, sensitivity or sympathy instead of reason is needed.

d. *Skepticism*: Skepticism about the rational transcendent world and the rational absolute, ultimate purpose of the universe comes as a result of the position of empiricism.

3. Morality

a. *Naturalistic morality*: Virtue and morality are based not on reason but on the primitive dynamic principle of the biological world. They are (1) self-preservation, (2) reproduction, and (3) the formation, maintenance, restoration of the order. These principles apply to both gods and human beings. Especially, the virtue corresponding to (3) is given much importance. It is called *kiyoku-akaki-kokoro* (清く明き心, pure and selfless mind).

b. *Good and evil*: Gods, in general, are not concerned with the categories of good and evil, which apply only to human beings (e.g., peace and quiet among us, rich harvest, famine, plague, etc.). Gods show us both blessings and violence, which are good or evil only for us human beings.

c. *Endurance as a value*: It follows from naturalistic morality that customs and old systems are respected because they have survived throughout history: they survived natural selection, as it were.

13.4. The Broad Meaning of Care

From the position described above we can see the fundamental relationship between gods and human beings. Gods are the foundation for human beings, and good relationships bring about blessings to humans, whereas bad relationships cause disaster. As gods are powers of nature, the same relationships apply between nature and human beings, that is, nature is the basis of human existence, and good relationships between nature and humans bring about blessings to humans, whereas bad relationships cause disaster. This supports the idea that ancient Japanese thought is worth considering as a possible framework for an environmental ethics that includes disaster prevention as an agenda.

One more step is needed to incorporate old Japanese myths into the framework of environmental ethics. I stated above that gods are beings who require worship, and worship consists of two elements: (a) praying to a god, (b) taking care of gods (i.e., building a shrine, making an offering). Slightly boldly, if we can interpret (a) as holding a god in memory or keeping a god in mind, then the two elements of worship are (a′) holding in memory or keeping in mind, and (b) taking care of. In childcare, patient care, and elderly care, elements of (a′) and (b) are required in order to achieve good care; therefore, such characteristics are those of care. If it is a possible interpretation, it can be said that Japanese gods require care.[12]

Unlike the notion of God in Judeo-Christian traditions, Japanese gods have only limited power and knowledge; and they are vulnerable. They can become fatigued or injured, and can even be killed. It is not so curious that gods of such character require care. In ancient Japanese thought, gods sometimes show violence and evoke a sense of awe; however, they are vulnerable and require worship, that is, care. The relationships between humans and nature can be understood as parallel to those between humans and gods; therefore, the most important relationships between humans and nature are also caring relationships.

How, then, can we understand the conservation of nature and the prevention of disasters in this framework? To consider it we need to refer to the meaning of the concept of care more closely. As Warren T. Reich writes in the *Encyclopedia of Bioethics*, "The term [care] had two fundamental but conflicting meanings. On the one hand, it meant worries, troubles, or anxieties, as when one says that a person is 'burdened with cares.' On the other hand, care meant providing for the welfare of another."[13] In bioethics, researchers have mainly focused on the second meaning, that is, taking care of others, helping others, caring for others, and sometimes caring for oneself. Similarly, when a god requires care, the required care is taking care of and keeping a god in mind, that is, the second meaning. However, the first meaning is also applicable to environmental ethics. The first meaning can be represented by the expression "care about," while the second can be represented by the expression "care for." Then the term "care" has two meanings: "care about" and "care for."[14] When we find ourselves or acquaintances to be in distress, we irresistibly feel worries or anxieties ("care about"); then we will help and support ourselves or others ("care for"). Japanese gods make people feel worries and anxieties. In response, they worship and care for the gods. "Care for" implies various actions; however, they can be regarded as behaviors for resolving the strong emotions of "caring about."

In environmental ethics, the relation of "care about" and "care for" can be applied to relationships between humans and nature as follows. Humans mainly have two strong feelings (i.e., caring about) about nature. One is the fear they feel when they face the violence of nature, especially the strong emotion we feel when confronting disasters; the other is the feeling of awe toward nature and the feeling of painfulness experienced when we see destruction of the environment. From such feelings of caring about, our behavior or attitude of caring for—that is, disaster prevention and conservation of nature—is forthcoming. The feeling of caring about in this context is worrying not only about ourselves, but about nature itself; therefore, for human beings, nature is neither simply the means of satisfying humans' desires, nor simply the object of conservation.

Contemporary care-based ethics can be traced back to the moral philosophy of David Hume, who argued that ethics flow not from dispassionate reason, but from moral sentiments. The concept of "care" or "caring" has been part of contemporary ethical debate since Milton Mayeroff wrote *On Caring*, in which he dealt with the concept from a philosophical viewpoint.[15] Similarly, Carol Gilligan's *In a Different Voice* distinguishes between an "ethic of care" and an "ethic of justice."[16] According to Mayeroff, the object of care includes not only a person but a philosophical or an artistic idea, an ideal, or a community,[17] but nowadays the object of care is limited to persons. We sometimes, however, use expressions such as "skin care," "hair care," "car care," "pet care," and "care for nature." It is reasonable to think that the concept of care has a broader meaning as well as a narrow meaning where the object being cared for is a person or a human being, and there is a mutual relationship between the person caring and the person being cared for.

The purpose of worship in old Japanese myths is forming, maintaining, and restoring order, which represents a kind of care. Therefore, it may be said that, in the broadest sense, to care is to form, maintain, and restore order or good relationships. When we find ourselves or our acquaintances in distress, we notice the destabilization of order or relationships. Then we feel worries and anxieties (caring about), and we want to help the troubled come back to ordinary life by forming, maintaining, and restoring good relationships (caring for).

I called attention to the cryptic anthropocentrism in environmental ethics in general, but an ethical framework based upon the concept of care is not a case of cryptic anthropocentrism. In this framework, human beings as well as nature are vulnerable, and nature appears to us as another being—which is, in principle, uncontrollable by human power and knowledge. We are in the age of co-disaster, and we have to prepare for the occurrence of disasters at any time. Cryptic anthropocentrism presupposes the agency of human beings as the base of ethics; however, an ethical framework based upon the concept of care acknowledges the agency of nature, in response to which humans experience feelings of worry and anxiety, which lie at the core of environmental ethics in the age of co-disaster.

13.5. Natural Spiritual Power and Integrity of an Ecosystem

Though this ethical theory might appear to be mystical, its metaphysics was supported by the everyday experiences of ancient people, which modern Japanese people sometimes still have. Moreover, nowadays we can apply the concept of natural spiritual power to the problem of environmental destruction. In other words, we can connect the old Japanese way of thought with some of the arguments in environmental ethics. The following sentences are from *Shugigaisho* by KUMAZAWA Banzan (1619–1691), a famous Confucian in the early Edo period who adopted Shinto elements into his thought. He made an effort to maintain good relationships, including maintaining so-called *satoyama*, for the sake of preventing disasters:

> In China they say "When the Wei River and Luoyang dried up, the Xia dynasty fell." Why did the Wei River and Luoyang dry up? As plants on the upstream mountains are cut down, the spiritual power (Shen qi) of the mountains becomes weak, and the current of the rivers decreases. Consequently sand piles up in the river when it rains heavily, and at last a landslide occurs resulting in the disappearance of the river. Recently we hear of mountain slides in many regions [of Japan], the process of which is similar to this.[18]

In this passage, the term "spiritual power" of mountains is crucial, because it plays the role of a touchstone indicating whether an ecosystem (in this passage, a mountain) is sound or not. Spiritual power is the driving force of the world. If that power is strong, the ecosystem is sound and healthy. In this respect, the "spiritual power" is not totally similar to that of Shinto, because in Shinto spiritual power has both positive and negative aspect for humans. Spiritual power will become weak when we cut down plants, but Kumazawa did not think that the more vegetation a mountain has, the more spiritual power it has. He writes, "Pine trees don't contribute to the enhancement of spiritual power of a mountain, but it will turn out to be worse, because on a mountain with pine trees underbrush doesn't grow, and it is not useful for the reservoir. Rain on a pine tree will become toxic to rice fields. Pine trees are suitable at the beach."[19] Here we can see that for the enhancement of the spiritual power of a mountain both the quantity and the quality of plant species are important.

The spiritual power in this context seems to be closely related to Aldo Leopold's famous declaration, "A thing is right when it tends to preserve the integrity, stability, and beauty of the biotic community. It is wrong when it tends otherwise."[20] Though these sentences are often cited as proposing a "land ethic," the concepts invoked—integrity, stability, and beauty—are not clear. After criticizing the view that a hard ecological theory can be judged on the basis of its ability to predict, Kristin Shrader-Frechette writes, "At the other extreme of the proposed ecological foundations for environmental philosophy, concepts such as 'integrity' demand too little of ecology because they are qualitative, unclear, and vague."[21] Ecological theory founded on a concept like "integrity" she calls "soft ecology." The same criticism applies to "balance of nature," "equilibrium," and "stability." Shrader-Frechette writes, "One reason for the under-determination of the theories of hard ecology and the untestability of the theories of soft ecology is that they rely, respectively, on concepts that are vague or incoherent, such as 'balance of nature,' 'equilibrium,' and 'stability.' "[22]

In the context of arguing for mutually sustaining and enhancing human-nature symbiosis, J. Baird Callicott refers to the irony, as he calls it, concerning two oases some thirty miles apart, one of which is a sanctuary and the other a place where people live and work: "At the A'ai Waipia bird sanctuary they [ornithologists] counted thirty-two species of birds; at the Ki:towak settlement they counted sixty-five."[23] The point of dispute is how to measure the health of an ecosystem. "Here, of course we must be cautious. Species richness is not the only measure of ecosystem health. The quality, so to speak, of species is also important."[24] I stated almost the same thing above in the context of Kumazawa's passage: for the enhancement of the spiritual power of a mountain both amount and quality of plants are important. However, "quality" of species is also vague, so the quality of species in addition to species richness does not seem to be sufficient for the measure of an ecosystem's health, integrity, balance, stability, and so on.

Concepts such as integrity, balance, equilibrium, stability, and health of an ecosystem seem to be, in principle, unclear and vague, because these criteria vary according to what ecosystem is being considered, what viewpoint we adopt, and what age we are in. To concentrate on the ecosystem of a mountain, some may, from a viewpoint of suitable use of forest resources, prefer timber management to the situation of being full of brush, and some may, from a standpoint of disaster prevention, oppose timber management, while still others may propose to conserve the mountain area as wildlife habitat.

We can say that the criteria of integrity and other similar concepts are determined by us, or, more correctly, that the criterion of integrity of an ecosystem reflects our view of the relationships between humans and nature. The relationship between humans and nature is interactive, and they have been coevolving, as it were, throughout history. In other words, the integrity of an ecosystem and the integrity of humans mutually reflect one another. Callicott says, "The human-nature relationship is an ongoing, evolving one. We can, I am confident, work out our own, post-modern, technologically sophisticated, scientifically informed, sustainable civilization just as in times past the Minoans in the Mediterranean, the vernacular agriculturists of western Europe, and the Incas in the Andes worked out theirs."[25]

If the integrity of an ecosystem and human integrity reflect each other, the two notions must have something in common, something that has a degree and can be perceived or, in a way, measured. For ancient Japanese people, at the core of the something in common was a spiritual power that could be perceived by many people in everyday life, and was the basis of metaphysics, epistemology, and morality. As Banzan stated, the spiritual power of mountains is closely related to disasters and the violence of nature. Callicott, who regards moral sentiments as the basis of Leopold's land ethic, writes, "And much of *A Sand County Almanac* is crafted to cultivate a love of nature in its readers, from which, Leopold hoped, benevolent and respectful actions toward nature would flow."[26] From the standpoint of "co-disaster" (i.e., the idea that we are in the age when we have to coexist with disasters), we, reviving the old Japanese myth, can interpret Leopold's terms "integrity," "stability," and "beauty" in a somewhat different way.

13.6. Environmental Ethics and Bioethics

Environmental ethics and biomedical ethics are two of the major branches of applied ethics, and they have not only different principles, but different issues to discuss. The principles of environmental ethics, in general, include things like the intrinsic value of individuals or species other than human beings, constraints on liberalistic rights, and responsibility to future generations. I propose in this chapter to add disaster prevention to this list of principles. In accordance with its principles, environmental ethics deals with issues such as the moral consideration of animals, plants, ecosystems, global warming, ecological destruction, energy issues, population issues, and disaster prevention. As is well known, the principles of biomedical ethics include respect for autonomy, nonmaleficence, beneficence, and justice. Biomedical ethics deals with ethical, legal, and social issues concerning medicine and biomedical sciences. While biomedical ethics is grounded in modern concepts of the individual, autonomy, and liberalism, environmental ethics is grounded on the ecological fact of the mutual interdependence of all living things and is skeptical about liberalism.

If we take the position that nature is life, environmental ethics and biomedical ethics will have a common task: to form, maintain, and restore good relationships between lives (both human and nonhuman). Conflicts are inevitable between lives; natural disasters and destruction of nature can be seen as conflicts between man and nature. Disaster prevention and nature conservation are instances of that common task. Furthermore, the task is the task of care in a broad sense.[27]

Notes

1. *Oxford Dictionary of English*, 2nd ed. (Oxford: Oxford University Press, 2005).

2. TERADA Torahiko, "Natural Disaster and National Defense," in *Collected Essays of Torahiko Terada*, vol. 5 (Tokyo: Iwanami Bunko,1948), 58–60.

3. John Locke, *Two Treatises of Government*, in *The Works of John Locke*, vol. 5 (Aalen: Scientia Verlag Aalen, 1963), book 2, chap. 5, 358.

4. For the standard account of this transformation see Roderick Nash, *Wilderness and the American Mind* (New Haven: Yale University Press, 1967).

5. See J. Baird Callicott and Michael P. Nelson, eds., *The Great New Wilderness Debate* (Athens: University of Georgia Press, 1999); and Michael P. Nelson and J. Baird Callicott, eds., *The Wilderness Debate Rages On* (Athens: University of Georgia Press, 2009).

6. Homes Rolston III, "Disvalues in Nature," in *The Ethics of the Environment*, ed. A. Brennan (Sudbury, MA: Dartmouth Publishing Company, 1995), 103.

7. Rolston, "Disvalues in Nature," 102.

8. Rolston, "Disvalues in Nature," 102.

9. Rolston, "Disvalues in Nature," 102.

10. Aldo Leopold, "Wilderness," in *The River of the Mother of God and Other Essays by Aldo Leopold*, ed. S. L. Flader and J. Baird Callicott (Madison: University of Wisconsin Press, 1991), 226–229. During a three-month trip to Germany in 1935, Leopold was strongly impressed by the lack of wildness in the German landscape. He "did not hope to find in Germany anything resembling the great 'wilderness areas' " (226), but he saw unnecessary outdoor geometry, and misguided zeal of the gamekeeper and the herdsman.

11. This summary is mainly based on Shinto. Other ways of describing the characteristics of Japanese thought, e.g., on Buddhism or Confucianism, might be possible, but the description stated here shows what is in the foundational layer of Japanese thought. It roughly corresponds to the features of Japanese thought or society proposed by several popular authors such as DOI Takeo, NAKANE Chie, and KAWAI Hayao.

12. This interpretation might seem curious because in worship we feel respect or awe for the gods, and yet it is possible to take care of someone without having feelings for him or her. To understand my interpretation more clearly, it is useful to consider what the essence of care is, i.e., the logic of care. Care is an interaction: it consists not only of the act of help or support based on sympathy, deliberation, and responding to the act of requirement for help, but also of the act of agreement or reception by those who are cared for. That is, the crucial point is that care, primarily, has the element of reception by the care receiver. The caregiver has to try to gain agreement with care receiver in order to provide appropriate care. Then, the initiative between the two may shift from caregiver to care receiver and vice versa. On the one hand, childcare is typical of the care where the caregiver has the initiative, though sometimes children come to have the initiative. On the other hand, caring for a god is the typical case where the care receiver has the initiative.

13. Warren T. Reich, "Care," in *Encyclopedia of Bioethics*, 3rd ed., vol. 1 (New York: Macmillan, 2004), 349.

14. The *Oxford Dictionary of English* says the following about the origin of "care": "Old English *caru* (noun), *carian* (verb), of Germanic origin; related to Old High German *chara* 'grief, lament,' *charon* 'grieve,' and Old Norse *kǫr* 'sickbed.' "

15. In "On Caring" (*International Philosophical Quarterly* 5, no. 3 [1965]: 462), Milton Mayeroff wrote, "Caring like knowing is a human activity that is intrinsically interesting, and also like knowing it is an activity whose understanding is central to the understanding of man. But, unlike knowing, it has been the subject of very little philosophical reflection." However, the history of care as the basis of ethics goes back to David Hume, though Hume used the term "moral sentiment" instead of "care." According to Callicott's interpretation, the intellectual forebears of Leopold's "land ethic" are the ecology of Charles Elton, the evolutionary biology of Charles Darwin, and the "moral sentiments" of Hume and Adam Smith. See J. Baird Callicott, "Can a Theory of Moral Sentiments Support a Normative Environmental Ethics?" in J. Baird Callicott, *Beyond the Land Ethic: More Essays in Environmental Philosophy* (Albany: SUNY Press,1999), 100.

16. Carol Gilligan, *In a Different Voice: Psychological Theory and Women's Development* (Cambridge, MA: Harvard University Press, 1982).

17. Milton Mayeroff, *On Caring* (New York: Harper Perennial, 1971), 2 and 262–263.

18. KUMAZAWA Banzan, *Shugigaisyo,* in *Nakae Toju & Kumazawa Banzan,* Japanese Classic Book Series, vol. 11 (Tokyo: Chuo Koro Shinsha, 1983), 399.

19. Kumazawa, *Shugigaisyo,* 400.

20. Aldo Leopold, *A Sand County Almanac and Sketches Here and There* (Oxford: Oxford University Press, 1949), 224–225.

21. Kristin Schrader-Frechette, "Ecology," in *A Companion to Environmental Philosophy,* ed. D. Jamieson (Malden, MA: Blackwell, 2001), 306.

22. Schrader-Frechette, "Ecology," 307.

23. J. Baird Callicott, "The Wilderness Idea Revisited: The Sustainable Development Alternative," in Callicott and Nelson, *Great New Wilderness Debate,* 356.

24. Callicott, "The Wilderness Idea Revisited," 356.

25. Callicott, "The Wilderness Idea Revisited," 357.

26. Callicott, "Theory of Moral Sentiments," 103.

27. For details, see TAKAHASHI Takao, "A Synthesis of Bioethics and Environmental Ethics Founded upon the Concept of Care: Toward a Japanese Approach to Bioethics," in *Taking Life and Death Seriously: Bioethics from Japan,* ed. TAKAHASHI Takao, Advances in Bioethics, vol. 8 (Linn, MO: Elsevier, 2005), 19–45.

CHAPTER 14 | Nondualism after Fukushima?

Tracing Dōgen's Teaching vis-à-vis Nuclear Disaster

ISHIDA MASATO

I do not believe that the original purpose of the rain dance was to make "it" rain. I suspect that that is a degenerate misunderstanding of a much more profound religious need: to affirm membership in what we call the *ecological tautology*, the eternal verities of life and environment.[1]

—GREGORY BATESON

14.1. Nuclear Waste, Evil, and Cleaning

14.1.1. Does Nuclear Waste Have Buddha-Nature?

It does not take much philosophical training to understand that humans and the environment form a single continuum—that we form part of a larger cosmic life. But in what sense are we supposed to be continuous with land waste? Or even with radioactive waste after the Fukushima nuclear power plant disaster in March 2011? Will not the Buddhist teaching of "nondualism" blur the distinction between harmony and disharmony with nature, action and nonaction on the human side, ought and ought not, and so on? Here the well-trodden Zen conundrum (*kōan* 公案) only needs to take a modern twist by asking, *Does nuclear waste have Buddha-nature* (*busshō* 仏性)? A simplistic response would deny the *Buddha-nature* of nuclear waste. However, this is not the way renowned Zen master Dōgen (1200–1253) thinks. As we shall see below, the only answer compatible with Dōgen's philosophy is that radioactive waste *is* Buddha-nature.

A partial account of this is not difficult to understand. It overlaps with common sense. Few people regard the presence of natural radioactivity as negative or evil, though it can damage biological cells.[2] Or take the radiotherapist's work. The therapist weighs the relative benefit of using radiation against its potential harm to the patient. The effect of radiation varies with organs and individuals, indicating that its toxicity is relative rather than absolute. Given the wide medical and industrial uses of radioactivity, it is pointless to ask whether uranium or some other radioactive element in nature is intrinsically good or evil. Air, water, mountains, and uranium ores are neither good nor evil in themselves. They are just what they are to constitute nature, though humankind can abuse them.

14.1.2. Buddha-Nature and Evil

The relational worldview of Mahayana Buddhism is not at odds with such commonplace observations. This tradition views things in the world as transient forms of interdependent origination, such that no entity has a fixed, stand-alone essence or identity. "Things do not originally have self-nature [*shohō motoyori jishō nashi* 諸法本無自性],"[3] in Dōgen's words. Further, it is the moment-to-moment *presencing* (*genjō* 現成) of the world as a whole, not isolated "objects," that Dōgen considers as manifestations of Buddha-nature. Therefore he suggests, "There is no Buddha-nature that is not presencing here and now."[4] Another point that becomes central to this chapter is that "Buddha-nature is not concerned with good or not-good [*busshō wa zenfuzen ni arazu* 仏性非善不善]."[5] It follows that debris, rubble, waste are all Buddha-nature. Dōgen writes: "Land, trees, grasses [*dojisōmoku* 土地草木], fences, walls, tiles and pebbles [*shōheki garyaku* 牆壁瓦礫], everything in the ten dharma directions engage in Buddha activity."[6]

Then is there any evil, or evil doing, in Dōgen's world? Yes, of course. There is no detached, otherworldly optimism in his philosophy. He is well aware that temptations of different sorts, inappropriate desire, and selfish need can easily lead us to wrong doings. Nonetheless Dōgen writes:

> The person who is just and right in the right moment [*shōtō'inmoji no shōtō'inmonin* 正当恁麼時の正当恁麼人] may live in a place where various evils are likely to occur, or the person may come and go to such places, or the person may appear to hang around with friends who do commit to

various evils, but despite such conditioned circumstances where evils are likely to occur, no further evil is committed by that [just and right] person.[7]

One point I wish to establish in this chapter is that there is a definite distinction between wrong or evildoing and nonevildoing for Dōgen, which must apply to environmental philosophy as well, if one wishes to live up to proper Buddhist standards.

14.1.3. Nondualism? No, We Must Clean Everything

When it comes to nondualism, however, the matter becomes more complicated. The great water cycle Dōgen describes in his "Mountains and Waters Sutra" (*Sansuikyō* 山水経) is beautiful—water forming clouds, rivers, landscapes, and penetrating into organic and inorganic realms—but does not the same cycle propagate radioactive particles all over the world? If that is not evil, why should we receive reproach for certain human activities? Perspectival or aspectual differences do not necessarily oppose each other, of course, but it seems legitimate to ask if we should distinguish between what counts as good and what as evil in general, and hence for the environment as a special case. I argue that, while nature has no intrinsic moral property, there are ways in which good and evil are not only distinguishable but are never collapsed into an indifferent continuum in Buddhism, which means little room remains for nondualism of morals.[8] What is going on in Fukushima is strictly our responsibility—we must clean everything inside and out, a theme concerning human *acts* that this chapter pursues from Dōgen's standpoint.

14.2 Washing and Physical Cleansing

14.2.1. Wash Your Face First

Whatever question we may start with, Dōgen's reply to it is likely to be quite simple: Wash your face first and clean your body properly. However, the instructions for washing ourselves—how to scoop water from the washbowl, where to place the hand towel, how to wipe oneself, and so on—will be extremely detailed. Not only that, lines from a canonical sutra will be cited to encourage the use of a toothpick after eating.[9] "Bathing your body and mind, anointing yourself with fragrant oil, and removing dust and dirt is the foremost of Buddhist teaching,"[10] he emphasizes. Further, "If you do not wash your face, then receiving a prostration of worship from others or making it to others involves a sin."[11] There is no uncertainty in his voice on this matter. "Not washing the face runs against Buddhist teaching,"[12] he says.

14.2.2. Washing inside the Body?

The meaning behind these words is deeper than it initially appears. To begin with, Dōgen reminds us that water is neither pure nor impure in and of itself, since it has no "self-nature." Accordingly, washing ourselves with water does not mean that we become pure and clean in the plain sense of the word. "In understanding this," Dōgen warns us, "you should not just think that you are pure and clean, having brought water and washed yourself with it. For why would water be originally pure or impure?"[13] He also observes that washing is not meant to just remove dirt. To those who contest his discourse, Dōgen responds as follows:

> Befuddled people who neither listen to Buddha's teaching nor practice Buddha's Way may contend, "Bathing ourselves barely washes the body's skin, while inside the body there are the five organs and six entrails. Without bathing each of them, we would not become pure and clean. Hence there is no overriding need to bathe the surface of the body." People who say such things do not know Buddha's teaching yet, nor have they met with a true teacher or a descendant of the Buddhist ancestors.[14]

True, washing will not remove impure elements inside the body. Taking a shower, for example, will not remove radioiodine accumulated in the thyroid gland. Yet if such thought is made into an objection to washing, Dōgen thinks that it simply misses the point. In the following passage, which is not altogether clear on first reading, Dōgen suggests that we wash ourselves *regardless* of the amount of dirt:

> Accordingly, the practice of washing and cleansing ourselves, when we have not even been polluted or have already reached great immaculacy, is maintained solely in the Way of Buddhist ancestors, which is beyond the knowledge of non-Buddhists. If things were just as the befuddled people say, we would have to grind the five organs and six entrails into particles of dust so minute as to become empty, and use up all the water of the great oceans to wash them, but unless we are washing inside the particles themselves, how could they become pure and clean?[15]

14.2.3. Washing as the Lifeblood of Buddhist Ancestors

There is, therefore, no end to physical cleansing. Complete removal of germs, chemicals, and radiation, as we might say today, is obviously impossible. Of course bathing leads to relative cleanliness, which is useful, but Dōgen considers that the Buddhist way of washing is not meant to result in anything like ultimate physical purification. It has a different meaning—washing cannot be concerned merely with the washing of the physical body, in his view. Reflecting this understanding, Dōgen moves on to suggest that washing "not only removes grime and grease but is the lifeblood of Buddhist ancestors."[16] His statement can be interpreted as describing a Buddhist practice or ritual, but as I explain below, considerable philosophical and practical insight lie in his words.

14.3. *Things* versus *Acts*: Dōgen's Philosophical Move

14.3.1. Past, Present, and Future: Washing Everything at Once

The larger framework of Dōgen's philosophy now starts to emerge. Dōgen boldly suggests that bathing ourselves cleans the entire environment at once: "As we bathe away dust and dirt and anoint ourselves with fragrant oil, it becomes clean inside and outside. When inside and outside are pure and clean, the agent and his environment [*ehō shōhō* 依報正報] are already pure and clean."[17] He further declares that cleansing ourselves in proper manner renders the world pure and clean in its entirety: "When incense and flowers are used to purify ourselves, achieved instantly is the purification of past, present, and future, causal relations, along with practiced deeds."[18] What he intends to say is that the purifying *act* qualifies the modes in which the world brings itself into being here and now, apart from which there is no independent reality. This certainly includes the three temporal modes of past, present, and future—there is no space-time "out there" in isolation from our *acts*, out of which the agent-and-environment arises.[19]

The kind of thought leading up to the above statements also relates to the question concerning good and evil. The question of immaculacy and dirt becomes a variation of the more general problem of good and evil—knowing what is good for the environment is to know what counts as "immaculate" for the environment. However, Dōgen's view of good and evil is not easy to follow and requires careful reading. A passage from his fascicle "Not Producing Evils" (*Shoakumakusa* 諸悪莫作)[20] may offer a first clue:

> Evils may be the same or not in this world and in other worlds; evils can be the same or not at previous times and at later times; evils in heavens above and in human worlds may be the same or not. Still greater is the difference between the Buddhist Way and the secular world with respect to what is called evil, good, and neither. For good and evil are times [*zen'aku wa toki nari* 善悪は時なり], but [conversely] time is neither good nor evil [*toki wa zen'aku ni arazu* 時は善悪にあらず].[21]

At first glance it might appear that the discernment between good and evil is made relative, what counts as evil differing from one world to another. But the real point of the passage surfaces as Dōgen moves toward the difference between the Buddhist and non-Buddhist views, where he starts to discuss *time* (*toki* or *ji* 時). To anticipate a cluster of notions that give rise to Dōgen's philosophical framework, we must note that good and evil are *times* for him, *arising events*, or better *ongoing acts*, as against *things*, where time is understood as neither good nor evil any more than "Buddha-nature" is. By saying that good and evil are *times*, he apparently brings *presencing* (*genjō* 現成) into focus, thus making a radical shift toward a form of *event ontology*. The idea of "self-nature" is dismissed in this way, but not the vital distinction between good and evil, since they are differently oriented *acts* for him, a view to be examined further.

14.3.2. Nonessentialism of Buddha-Nature

Dōgen's argument requires a clear understanding of the difference between *things* that are conceivably good or evil, on the one hand, and the *act* of *producing* or *not producing* them as such, on the other. It is important for Dōgen to turn away from the language of *things*. He thinks it is pointless to ask whether *evil things* —things with some evil nature—exist, since nothing has self-nature in the first place. A dense paragraph casts more light on his view:

> It is not that evil *things* [*shoaku* 諸悪] do *not* exist [*naki ni arazu* なきにあらず], for they are [in reality] only *acts,* not producing them as such [*makusa naru nomi nari* 莫作なるのみなり]. It is not that evil *things* do exist, for they are *acts,* not producing them as such. It is not that evil *things* are empty, for they are *acts,* not producing them as such. It is not that evil

things are phenomenal form, for they are only *acts*, not producing them as such. Evil *things* are not the same as the *acts* not producing them [*shoaku wa makusa ni arazu* 諸悪は、莫作にあらず], for they are themselves just the *acts*, never producing them as such.[22]

We should notice that the first two sentences taken together refute existence and nonexistence of evil *things*. The two middle lines declare that nothing is intrinsically empty or phenomenal, while the last sentence recommends the perspective of *act*, or *working*, as we may put it. If we reject essentialism altogether—the view that things have unchanging essences, which are grasped fully when we are enlightened—no act produces evil because nothing is able to have an evil essence as self-nature, while not every *act* is granted as morally permissible.

The consideration evokes parallels with Dōgen's interpretation of *Jōshū Kushi* (趙州狗子), a well-known koan, or Zen case, which he discusses in another fascicle, "Buddha-Nature" (*Busshō* 仏性). In one of its versions, two monks ask the same question to Master Jōshū, "Does a dog have Buddha-nature?" The master replies, "Yes, it does" to one monk, and "No, it doesn't" to the other. Leaving details aside, the main point for Dōgen is that Buddha-nature cannot be predicated of "having" or "not having" because everything is *presencing* in his world. "You must clarify the intent of this question," Dōgen thus remarks, continuing: "'*Kushi*' just means 'dog.' It asks neither whether a dog has Buddha-nature nor whether it does not have Buddha-nature."[23] For him, "Every sentient being without exception, every being *is* Buddha-nature."[24] The reason this matters is that the problem of good and evil, or immaculacy and dirt, transforms into a different kind of question by turning away from *properties* or *essences* of *things* to focusing on the *working* or *acting* in the present, a view that brings moral responsibility back into our hands in the end.

14.4. The *Presencing* of Good and Evil

14.4.1. Nondualism? What about Good and Evil?

Proceeding now to the heart of the problem concerning good and evil, Dōgen disapproves the view that no *act* counts as ultimately *evil* if it springs from one's pure and devout intention, presumably because it is part of the genuine *working* of the cosmos. In other words, the distinction between good and evil *acts*—not *things*—must be as clear and dyadic as that between, for example, killing and not killing. However, tendency toward nondualism of good and evil—often falling under the heading of *original enlightenment thought* (*hongaku shisō* 本覚思想)—is not as rare in the history of Japanese Buddhism.[25] In fact records indicate that a distorted interpretation of this sort entered Dōgen's temple as well. A slightly long dialogue between Ko'un Ejō (1198–1280) and Tettsū Gikai (1219–1309), who became the second and third heirs of Dōgen's temple, respectively, informs us how Dōgen reacted to such misunderstanding:

> The other year, I, Gikai, was listening to a group of monks in our own household, where I heard a discussion like this: "In Buddhist teaching, we say *not producing evils* and *producing innumerable goods*, such that wherever Buddhist truth prevails, evils are never produced from the beginning, which in turn means all deeds are the practicing of goods. It follows that whatever results from the arm or leg's behavior is the origination of the entire dharma, all of which are Buddhist truth, and so on." Is this view correct understanding?
>
> His reverence [Ejō] replied: "Among those who received teaching from our previous master [Dōgen], there were trainees of the kind you mention, who came up with this wicked understanding, as a consequence of which the master disowned them in his own time. It is clear that the master expelled them. For they upheld wicked understanding. If you belong to monks who desire to follow our previous master's Buddhist truth, do not talk or sit with them. This was indeed the last warning words of our previous master.[26]

It may appear obvious that the difference between killing and not killing, for instance, can never be collapsed in Buddhism, but confusions can arise easily and in different forms. One might argue, for example, that we have to persecute people insofar as this contributes to the greater good of the society. Taking life may be conceived permissible under specific circumstances when proper prayers are offered as last words to the victim. Perhaps building nuclear plants is just as good as any other industrial construction because advantages of nuclear energy might override or at least offset its harm in the long run.

14.4.2. Presencing of Innumerable Goods

Returning to the dialogue, Ejō and Gikai both received first-hand teaching from Dōgen. But from Gikai's perspective, the much younger of the two, the matter was worth verifying with Ejō, who reminded Gikai of Dōgen's resolute disapproval. Our acts do not give rise to things whose inner property allows us to distinguish between good and evil, as discussed earlier, but it does not follow from this that *all* modes of *presencing* promote the *good*. Any act is part of the world process, Dōgen will reassure, but it would be false to reason from this that all deeds are therefore the practicing of good. From Dōgen's point of view, nothing around us has a fixed essence, let alone an evil essence, but this by no means entails that every act arising from a genuine intention contributes to the presencing of the good, a point often poorly illuminated in crude "Zen" discourses.

"People today are also rash," Dōgen thus remarks, "because they do not inquire 'how [*ikanaruka* いかなるか] Buddha-nature is,' but ask whether things have or not [*umu* 有無] Buddha-nature and likewise questions upon hearing it."[27] He also notes, "If someone asked me, Eihei [Dōgen], 'Does a dog too have Buddha-nature,' I would say to the inquirer, 'Whether you say it has one or not, you commit slander.' "[28] Hence good and evil, considered in terms of *times, events*, and *ongoing acts*, as we saw in the previous section, must receive a different interpretation. As a clarificatory remark, some acts do lead to the presencing of innumerable goods in Dōgen's view: "The innumerable goods are not concerned with existence or nonexistence, having or not having phenomenal form, and so forth, but what we find instead [whenever innumerable goods are presencing] are nothing but devout acts."[29] Though Buddha-nature is neither good nor evil, there are many ways in which good and evil *presence* in each concrete context.

14.5. Don't Kill: There's No Way to Get Around Cause and Effect

14.5.1. Causal Connections Are Manifest and Unomovable

The main point I wish to derive from this, therefore, is that there remains a clear distinction between the *presencings* of good and evil brought about by our acts, deeds, and decision-making, although *things* do not have good or evil self-nature.[30] There is no room for Dōgen to endorse a nondualism of good and evil acts as modes of *presencing*, as if they were ultimately not opposed to each other from some higher perspective. On the Buddhist account, every act gives rise to interconnected consequences.[31] There is a telling narrative that Ejō records as part of an early conversation he had with the master. Ejō asks Dōgen, "What is the heart of the matter when it is said, 'Never being clouded about cause and effect [*fumai ingatei no dōri* 不昧因果底の道理]'?"[32] Dōgen's reply was, "Cause and effect are unmovable [*fudō inga nari* 不動因果也]."[33] Ejō advances, "Then how is it that casting off is possible?"[34] Dōgen responds, "In one glance cause and effect are manifest right in the present."[35] Then Dōgen proceeds, somewhat unexpectedly, to discuss the famous koan of Nansen Fugan (748–834) and a cat that he allegedly killed in front of his disciples.

14.5.2. Nansen Kills a Cat: Dōgen's Response

Disciples at a temple were fighting over a cat. Seeing this, Master Nansen steps in and shouts that he will take the life of the cat with his sword. He suggests, however, that the cat shall be spared if they could return a word to him. No word came out of the disciples, so Nansen killed the cat, an incident that has invited criticism from modern Western moralists. Although there is no settled interpretation of this koan—no koan receives a uniform interpretation—one common reading is that Nansen's act of killing the cat was pedagogy, an expedient means, to set the learners along the right path toward enlightenment. Dōgen, while not dismissing this traditional reading altogether, presents a different view in his conversation with Ejō, which includes a challenge to Nansen himself. He says:

> If I had been Nansen, I would have said immediately to the assembly: "Even if you can speak, I will cut the cat right away, and even if you cannot speak, I will cut it right away. Who fights for the cat? Who is there to save the cat?" I would then have represented the assembly by responding to Nansen: "We have already spoken. Please, master, go ahead and cut the cat." I would also have said to him on behalf of the assembly: "Master Nansen, you only know how to cut the cat into two halves in one stroke of the blade [*ittō ryōdan* 一刀両断], but you don't know how to use the stroke of the blade to cut it into one [*ittō ichidan* 一刀一段]."[36]

In the first part Dōgen makes clear that it would be pointless for the disciples to speak or not in order to save the cat—the cat will not survive either way. This will quiet the disciples fighting for the cat. Dōgen then faces Nansen and says that all has been spoken by the disciples, though not a single word has been uttered, which would mute Nansen too, since whether he cuts the cat or not, he is driven into contradiction: If all has been spoken, he cannot cut the cat, on the one hand, while if he cuts the cat, he would acknowledge his failure to hear that all has already been spoken, on the other. Dumbfounding both sides, Dōgen then poses a challenge to Nansen: Instead of cutting the cat into two halves, he should know better, that is, to cut the cat into one.

14.5.3. Don't Dispute over Buddha-Nature: Let the Cat Go

Naturally, Ejō asks Dōgen what it means to "cut into one [*ittō ichidan* 一刀一段]." A dialogue elsewhere offers a hint, which reflects Dōgen's take on Buddha-nature again. One day, Chōsha Keishin (d. 868), Nansen's disciple who later became his successor, and a government officer were discussing Buddha-nature, an anecdote Dōgen refers to after he considers *Jōshū Kushi* mentioned above. "A live earthworm is cut into two halves, and both parts are still moving," the officer says, continuing, "In which part does Buddha-nature reside?"[37] The master replies, "Do not delude yourself." Again the officer inquires, "But how should we understand the movement [of the separated parts of the earthworm]?" The master replies, "Wind and fire never dissipated." Dōgen's account, which employs a language very similar to that he used to discuss Nansen's cat, is that Buddha-nature cannot be predicated of one or two whether it is before or after the cutting. In Dōgen's own words:

> The officer here says that the earthworm is cut into two halves [*zan'i ryōdan* 斬為両段], but then can it be determined that it was one before it was cut [*mizanji wa ichidan* 未斬時は一段]? No, it is not so in the everyday practice of Buddhist ancestors. The earthworm was never one [*ichidan ni arazu* 一段にあらず], nor two [*ryōdan ni arazu* 両断にあらず] when it was cut.... When it was pointed out that both halves move, as they continue to move together, should one ask in which part of the two halves Buddhanature must reside? [no, of course not]. Hence the master replies, "Do not delude yourself."[38]

Though as present as wind and fire, it is wrong to ask where to locate Buddha-nature in the earthworm, or in anything dead or alive for that matter, when everything is *presencing* as a whole. This applies to Nansen's cat as well. By cutting the cat's body into two in one stroke (*ittō ryōdan* 一刀両断)—which body is ultimately "Dharmakaya [*busshin* 仏身]"[39] or the true body—we certainly do not cut Buddha-nature into two pieces. Dōgen was well aware of the many misguided disputes over Buddha-nature in those days and suggests we spare the cat by simply letting the stroke miss it. Dōgen is clear that the cat should have been released: "The assemblage could not say anything. If the absence of the response continued for a while, Nansen should have declared [himself], 'The assemblage has already spoken,' and saying this, he could have released the cat. An ancient said a great working becomes present and overrides stipulations."⁴⁰ The cat would leap away in one when the stroke misses the target.⁴¹ Nansen could then have provided the disciples with a convincing example of compassion, even if he did not literally go by his words.

14.6. Act Properly—Wrongdoing Is Wrongdoing

14.6.1. Killing the Cat Is Not Buddha's Practice

Not to completely dismiss traditional interpretations, on the other hand, Dōgen allows that the story of cutting the cat could be seen as a "great working of Buddhist dharma [*buppō-no daiyū* 仏法の大用]"⁴² or "Buddha's practice [*butsugyō* 仏行],"⁴³ while shifting the focus from the act of killing to Nansen's illocutionary act, as demonstrated in Dōgen's imaginary participation in the dialogue. When seen in this light, how Nansen *spoke* to the assemblage, not the act of killing, constituted the essential part of the koan, whence Dōgen also refers to it as the "great turning of words [*ittengo* 一転語]."⁴⁴ In his view, the act of killing carries little pedagogical value. Dōgen's intent is also mirrored rather clearly in the fact that, when asked by Ejō if the cutting of the cat was a sin, he affirms, "Yes, it is a form of sin."⁴⁵ Ejō asks again, "Then how is it that casting off is possible?"⁴⁶ "Buddha's practice and the sin are distinct [*betsu* 別], though they made appearance side by side [*narabi gusu* 並具],"⁴⁷ was Dōgen's reply. In Dōgen's view, two *distinct* acts can strike through a single event. What is particularly important here is that the killing is not absorbed or fused into "Buddha's practice" as if nothing had happened. Hence Dōgen also adds: "The best way, though, is not to work things out like that, however good it may seem."⁴⁸

Needless to say, Dōgen understands that it is possible to violate a precept while serving a different purpose, such as taking life to save other lives. This is why Buddhism and many other religions have different sets and varying levels of precepts. Yet Dōgen does not conflate wrongdoings with a second purpose as if the former becomes excusable if the latter "seemed good." The correct Buddhist view for him is that cause and effect are unmovable—killing is a cause, teaching and guiding trainees is another, each having its effect or consequence that does not hinder the other. What is insightful in Dōgen's interpretation is that the two acts remain *distinct* even if they constitute one and the same event right before the eye, which is different from thinking that the acts are, or become, indistinguishable in a continuum when seen from some "higher" perspective. The causal connection is never to be clouded for him.[49]

14.6.2. Whither Dōgen's Teaching?

All this prepares us to see where Dōgen's teaching would guide us in terms of environmental philosophy. As is commonly noticed, his nature-friendly aesthetic writings may give rise to ecological imagination and to natural compassion toward nonhuman creatures in the environment. As a result, it may cultivate a stronger sense of earth-human connection in the modern mind, reminding us that Mother Nature is not to be subordinated to self-centered human ends. But we may still face a basic question: How are we supposed to derive an *ought*, a normative incentive that guides us in a better direction, even if we accept the *fact* that we are part of the natural environment? Alerting people to human estrangement from nature, rectifying anthropocentrism, and blaming excessive human greed—these are all worthwhile efforts, for sure, but to what extent would this actually change people's present behavior and long-term habits? I might feel apprehensive of a serious nuclear reactor meltdown in Fukushima right after watching the television news, but my fear fades away in minutes. I walk out of my room without bothering to turn off the room lights.

It is here that Dōgen would encourage us to make a much desired difference. Were he around today, he would no doubt demand that I turn off lights whenever I leave the room. In his view this is precisely what makes the world pure and clean once for all, though the act is not meant to remove "dirty things" out of the way with a swing of a magic wand. As stressed in previous sections, there is nothing intrinsically dirty or unclean in the world, from urine and feces to nuclear energy. Only our *acts* can be conducive to the *presencing* of the good and clean. In the fascicle "Washing the Face," therefore, Dōgen goes as far as to define *washing* as the Buddhist practice itself. He starts by reminding us that water and the body it washes are neither pure nor impure:

> Water is not necessarily pure or impure originally. The body is not necessarily pure or impure originally. Everything in the world is alike. Water is neither sentient nor insentient, the body is neither sentient nor insentient, everything in the world is alike. This is how Buddha, the World-Honored One, has preached. Preached this way, it is not that we use water to cleanse

our body, for what the dignifying demeanor consists in is that we maintain the Buddhist law through practicing the Buddhist law. This is what is meant by washing.[50]

Now since everything is *time* for Dōgen—he famously writes, "Mountains are time, oceans are time"[51] and further "All being is time"[52]—the human body is nothing but a *flux* or *event* for him that unfolds into time, or better, unfolds *as* time. The body is said to be neither sentient nor insentient above because no *event* can be predicated of sentience or insentience in the ordinary sense of the word. Only the proper *act* of washing is conducive of the *presencing* of the good, which is why Dōgen identifies it with the *practicing* of the Buddhist Way. It is not abstract instruction, though, unrelated to general Buddhist practice. "Seated meditation, this is what Buddhist practice is,"[53] Dōgen says. And bringing it up as a practical matter, he also asks: "At the time of seated meditation, is there even one precept that we fail to obey?"[54] Simple as it is, there would be no time to commit evildoing if we are truly devoted to meditation. Although this needs a little further elaboration, especially with respect to *washing*, I wish to observe that the thrust of the argument consists in the nonduality of *acting, time*, and the *presencing* of the world, on the one hand, but with a proper discernment between *acts* that are conducive for the good and those conducive for the evil, on the other. Clearly, the second side concerning *acts* is no less important for Dōgen than the first side.

14.7. Purifying Acts: From Toilet to Environment

14.7.1. Washing as Common Fact

Buddhist practice interpreted along this line does not require a completely new lifestyle. In reality, the practice has been followed through for millennia according to Dōgen, each of us accomplishing some part of it. Going straight to the point, Dōgen says, "Do not neglect washing after relieving feces and urine."[55] He also writes, "If you do not clean yourself after relieving feces and urine, you commit a misdeed."[56] It is mere armchair thinking to say that we do not or might not "really know" what *washing* is or means, including how we should generally act in the natural environment. "Since monks started to live in temples, sheds have been built, which we call a toilet,"[57] Dōgen writes, but "when practicing under a tree in the woods or out in the open, there is no shed, so you wash yourself using pieces of soil or water from a valley or river."[58] One way or another *washing* is practiced, the act not stopping with our body but also taking care of the surroundings, including the bathroom. In Dōgen's words: "It is not that we purify only body-mind, we also purify under the tree and even the land of our country."[59]

14.7.2. Revisiting "Buddhist" Washing

To be cautious, though, it is not that the toilet bowl is "dirty" whereas the dining table is "clean." In Dōgen's philosophical framework, only *acts* in the *present* are *purifying* or *nonpurifying*. It is easy to call to mind that human excrement was widely used in Asia to increase harvests before chemical fertilizers were invented. Coprophagia is not uncommon in nature, such as dung beetles and scavenger fish feeding on biological waste of other organisms, rabbits eating their own droppings to extract more nutrients and energy from the same food source, and so on. In each of the myriad realms of nature, there are purifying and nonpurifying *acts* as part of the working of the world. Such acts are not limited to human activities but are revealed in all directions of the universe in Dōgen's view, including the worlds of Buddhas:

> This does not concern only Buddhas in this world but is the dignifying Buddhist demeanor in ten directions, the dignifying Buddhist demeanor in both the pure and impure lands. Poorly guided people entertain the thought that Buddhas do not have dignifying Buddhist demeanor in the toilet and that the dignifying demeanors of Buddhas in this world are not like those of Buddhas in pure land. This is not the learning of the Buddhist Way.[60]

Taken together with observable facts of nature, it is obvious that Buddhism does not start from scratch.[61] "Know that for Buddhas there are toilets,"[62] Dōgen writes, the toilet constituting "the training hall and temple of Buddhas. Never initiated by someone, it is the dignifying demeanor of Buddhas."[63] In the human realm efforts are made to meet Buddhist standards as well as common sense—when using the toilet, "Do not write on the walls,"[64] "Do not chat or joke with another person behind the wall in the next stall,"[65] and so on. From monastery rules to understanding how nature works, Dōgen makes no compromise in his interpretation of *washing,* which can be seen as a clear expression of his environmental philosophy.[66]

14.7.3. From the Body to Heart-Mind: The Direction of Change

As one may notice, there is a lot of practical thinking behind Dōgen's words, too. He is aware that it is difficult to change people's mindset without changing their behavior patterns first. It may sound counterintuitive to some Western thinkers, but the "mind" follows what the "body" does, not the other way around. "If you rectify your body in terms of dignifying demeanor," Dōgen thus suggests, "the heart-mind follows it and transforms itself."[67] There is no great surprise in this, however, if we accept the candid fact that the body and mind work together. In many cases changing our conduct works faster than trying to change our belief system. My feeling can become environment-conscious shortly after reading or hearing about environmental crises, but on a more fundamental level my mind does not change easily, not because I have an immoral nature, but precisely because my mind is entrenched in long accumulated body-mind habits from which *acts* continue to spring. In the end, of course, we wish to bring the mutual body-mind implication to perfection. In Dōgen's words, "Proper manners [of the body], this is nothing but the teaching [of the heart], and conversely, realizing the Way [i.e., the teaching of the heart], this is nothing but proper manners."[68] Undoubtedly, this last account speaks to the *oneness of practice and attainment* (*shūshō ichinyo* 修証一如), a view Dōgen is particularly well known for, according to which not a hairbreadth should lie between one's *act* in the present and *realization* in the Buddhist sense.[69]

14.8. Dōgen's Teaching in Present-day Context

14.8.1. The Theoretical Side of Dōgen's Teaching

There are several important points that I wish to draw from the considerations above. To begin with the theoretical side of Buddha-nature, the main implication is that what we commonly regard as "dirty" or "unclean"— from urine, to hazardous chemicals, and to nuclear waste—is not intrinsically so. The relatively fixed "nature" that things seem to possess—for example, uranium and H_2O reveal stable atomic and molecular weight in the natural environment—simply *arise* in the *present* from the Buddhist perspective as intermeshed karmic relationships determine the range of their *presencing*. This just means that modes of *presencing* are constrained in great measure by how things stand to each other in the world. But since things do not have self-nature, it is our *acts*, not separable from the world, that induce the *presencing* of what appears as dirty, unclean, impure, or the opposite of these. Radioactive material has always been part of nature, we may say, while human activities have condensed some portion of it into fuel pellets and burned them, which can anytime become an imminent threat to the environment in the usual sense. Seen under this light, the *cause* of the Fukushima nuclear plant disaster has lain in our *acts*, not in the material used to generate electricity, which simply places moral responsibility back in our own hands.

But we may also flash back to a broader and more fundamental question. If not through the production of massive toxic substance, does not nature take life, or even waste life? Insects, fish, birds, and other small creatures seem to reproduce in millions only to suffer predation by natural predators. Imagine a mother cheetah suffocating a young gazelle to feed her cubs. Is this the killing of the gazelle or the nurturing of the cheetah family? Do not delude yourself, would be Dōgen's reply. Just say that it is the killing of the gazelle *and* the nurturing of the cheetah family. The important insight he offers is that the two acts are not to be collapsed into one as if there was a privileged perspective in which distinctions disappear or become irrelevant. This may sound plain, but signs of confusions are not hard to find. Monks may have no trouble keeping a pet cat in the temple, eating whatever they like including meat, and so on, which Dōgen would have surely found problematic. It is true that life and death are not ontologically opposed to each other for him, because each is a *presencing* of the world, but I stress again that it does not follow from this that taking and saving life are not morally opposed to each other. Two things can arise from the same "ontological" stuff, if one pleases, but only some acts, clearly not all of them, achieve greater moral value. The consideration certainly has applications to environmental philosophy.

14.8.2. The Practical Side of Dōgen's Teaching

Dōgen writes that washing ourselves purifies the entire environment, a thesis stemming from his understanding of Buddha-nature and act-oriented event ontology that I examine in this chapter. To repeat, he does not mean that washing one's face works like a "magic ritual" that purifies the physical world. The message is twofold. First, the focusing into the present, aside which there is no origination or arising of events, makes it clear that "future predictions" are not what is at stake, while *everything* here and now matters, including the ongoing meltdown in nuclear reactors, toxicity moving and spreading in the air and water every millisecond, and the damages caused to biological cells in this very moment. The second important point is this: Our membership in the environment is a *fact* worth stressing, which expresses a form of ontological continuity with nature, but to make a further step, we must push ourselves beyond by drawing a stronger line between what we *ought* and *ought not* to do for the environment including ourselves. We work with one nature, of course, but no two *acts* have the same *effect* or *consequence*. Whatever "nondualism" means in this context, it is clear that relativizing environmental destruction, protection, and conservation does not help.

In making this claim, I do not intend to underestimate the complexity of the issue, which involves both human and nonhuman activities. Germs don't think they contaminate the environment, though we often think they do, and no species on earth works toward making the environment clean or unclean exclusively. We shall never stop eating, excreting, and cleaning, nature doing all of these things. Nonetheless when part of nature cleans itself, it does this in remarkable ways, and we generally know how to clean ourselves too, that is, unless we surrender to impulsive desires and make ourselves blind to moment-to-moment interactions with the environment.[70] If you think this is not the case, take a moment to reflect in the toilet, Dōgen would say. The best way to go, he would also add, is not to develop intellectual skepticism, not to consider things as "dirty" or "clean" in and of themselves, but to simply adopt proper dignifying manners here and now. This includes turning off lights when leaving the room—it is already a *purifying* act. When these things are practiced, the heart-mind shall find better guidance in his view. It is quite obvious, too, that if scientists, engineers, and policymakers had been able to foretell the 2011 earthquake and the tsunami that struck the northeastern coast of Japan, which led to the Fukushima nuclear plant disaster, they would have acted differently. The basic connection between cause and effect is not concealed, though our vision informed by modern science is still severely limited when it comes to *specific* causes and effects.[71]

14.9. Concluding Remarks—We Need Clear Thinking

We talk about "clean" energy, a useful metaphor in everyday life, but if examined in light of Dōgen's teaching, no energy is clean or unclean. The metaphor may become a source of confusion since it may distract us from taking into account the chances and opportunities to change our behavior patterns despite the causal—or "karmic" for the Buddhist—network that we are locked into. More specifically, what must be measured more prudently in view of the theme of this chapter is the actual balance between how well we can control our everyday conduct—in short, our *acts*—at the individual and social levels, on the one hand, and the form and amount of energy we decide to extract from the environment, on the other. In particular, if we cannot change our *habits*, we should know that we have much fewer—and worse—options for the environment and ourselves.[72] As mentioned in previous sections, the practical side of Dōgen's teaching is fairly straightforward: He encourages us to change our behavior from the simplest possible places, for example, from the toilet, the sink where we wash our face, and so on. Only then would one start *purifying* seriously, which Dōgen thinks must be expanded to the entire environment that is coarising with our own being.

Another point worth reiterating is that, though radioactivity is neither good nor evil, each *act* we take affects its *presencing* in the world and is therefore not neutral in the same way. For this reason I problematize "nondualism" in this chapter, a popularized notion that sometimes leaves moral and ethical questions poorly or inadequately answered. Some forms of nondualism are philosophically relevant, such as that of mind and body, self and world, mundane practice and enlightenment, and so forth. However, nondualism of good and evil, purity and nonpurity, or immaculacy and dirt in the current context, sounds more questionable. "Who said you may violate precepts and have no way-seeking mind?,"[73] as Dōgen says. Contemporary researchers have noticed that Dōgen greatly underscores the Buddhist law of causality in the last few years of his life: "When you are engaging in an evil act and do not consider it evil, and wickedly think that it shouldn't bring about retribution, this does not mean that you will not experience recompense."[74] I regard this as clear thinking rather than insistence on a mystical, premodern theory of karmic retribution. Facing Fukushima and tracing Dōgen's teaching from his early to late writings, I conclude that we must simply commit to cleaning.

Notes

1. Gregory Bateson, *Mind and Nature: A Necessary Unity* (Cresskill, NJ: Hampton Press, 2002), 197.

2. The sun supports life through heat and light, but being the most familiar source of cosmic radiation, it damages skin cells. Radium hot springs are generally considered beneficial to health despite higher levels of natural radiation that can increase cancer risk.

3. Dōgen, *Dōgen-zenji Zenshū* (*The Complete Works of Zen Master Dōgen*), 7 vols. (Tokyo: Shunjū-sha, 1988–1993), 4:16. All quotes from Dōgen's texts in this chapter are my original English translations based on this edition.

4. *Dōgen-zenji Zenshū*, 1:18. Prior to making this remark, Dōgen clarifies that there is no Buddha-nature realized *in* time as if some kind of potentiality were gradually brought to realization. This is because *Buddha-nature, time, being, self, act*, and the *world*—including the environment—are all inseparable for him, meaning that there is no *time* as a separate entity within which Buddha-nature becomes manifest (see also note 51 below).

5. *Dōgen-zenji Zenshū*, 4:16. The original idea appears in *Dainehangyō* (*Mahāyāna Mahāparinirvāṇa Sūtra*, T [Taishō Daizōkyō] 374, 12: 493c–494a). The phrase quoted by Dōgen derives from *Kataifutōroku* (*Jiatai Pudenglu*, ZZ [*Zokuzōkyō*] 137:22c), the interpretation of the sutra attributed to the Sixth Patriarch Huineng (638–713). Dōgen slightly modifies Huineng's words, "Buddha-nature is neither good nor evil [*foxing feishan feibushan*]" into his own wording here, in addition to the differences examined in ISHII Shūdō, *Dogenzen no Seiritsushiteki Kenkyū* (*A Study of the Formation of Dōgen's Zen*) (Tokyo: Daizōshuppan, 1991), chap. 2 (see especially 143–144).

6. *Dōgen-zenji Zenshū*, 2:463 (cf. 539 for a variant text). A helpful commentary on this passage can be found in AWAYA Ryōdō, "*Shōbōgenzō* ni okeru Shōheki Garyaku ni tsuite" ("On 'Shōheki Garyaku [fences, walls, tiles and pebbles]' in the *Shōbogenzo*"), *Journal of the Institute for Zen Studies Aichigakuin University* 18–19 (1991): 47–67. Whether trees, grass, walls, and the like engage in Buddhist activity (*butsuji o nasu* 仏事をなす) without human participation poses a subtle though important question discussed in relation to *original enlightenment thought* (*hongaku shisō* 本覚思想). For further information about *original enlightenment thought*, see notes 25 and 33.

7. *Dōgen-zenji Zenshū*, 1:344.

8. Nondualist *ontology* is worth stressing from a philosophical point of view, but I consider it problematic to proceed from this to a nondualist view of *morals* or *ethics*. As discussed in section 14.3.2, Dōgen devotes one of his *Shōbōgenzō* fascicles, "Not Producing Evils" (*Shoakumakusa* 諸悪莫作) to the interpretation of *The Common Precept Verse of the Seven Buddhas* (*Shichibutsu Tsūkai Ge* 七仏通戒偈), a popular verse that discourages evildoing and encourages serving the good. Including the original Pali verse in *Dhammapada* (traditionally known as appearing in *Hokkugyō*, T 210: 4.567b), the teaching has been accepted widely in Asian Buddhism, hence making it a central Buddhist claim.

9. *Dōgen-zenji Zenshū*, 2:43–44. The passage on the toothpick, which Dōgen refers to multiple times in his writings, can be found in *Kegongyō* (*Mahāvaipulya Buddhāvataṃsaka Sūtra*, T 278 9: 431a25–a26).

10. *Dōgen-zenji Zenshū*, 2:37. The fascicle "Washing the Face" (*Senmen* 洗面) containing this quote is known for textual divergences in two codices, *Tōunji bon* and *Kenkon'in bon*, the latter considered more definitive because of the extensive revisions Dōgen made to the text. In this chapter textual differences will receive attention insofar as they affect the main argument.

11. *Dōgen-zenji Zenshū*, 2:41.

12. *Dōgen-zenji Zenshū*, 2:52.

13. *Dōgen-zenji Zenshū*, 2:39. Following this remark, Dōgen suggests that we cast away the "either-or thinking" smuggled into "neither pure nor impure [*hijō hifujō*非浄非不浄]" (2:39). It would be a fallacy for him to seek for the original nature of water (which does not exist) and then declare that the two natures (pure and impure here) are in reality one, that is, "not-two [*funi*不二, i.e., nonduality]." Noteworthy in this

regard is Dōgen's statement, "How could Buddha-nature ever be concerned with *not-two*? Things do not originally have self-nature" (*Dōgen-zenji Zenshū*, 4:16).

14. *Dōgen-zenji Zenshū*, 2:37–38.

15. *Dōgen-zenji Zenshū*, 2:39. Dōgen's use of the word "non-Buddhist [*gedō* 外道]" in this passage indicates that the "befuddled people [*gujin* 愚人]" he has in mind are the "six heretical teachers [*rokushi gedō* 六師外道]" in ancient Indian philosophy around the sixth century BCE. The materialist tendency in the contesting perspective—under which the human body, including the five organs and six entrails, is nothing but an aggregate of physical particles—echoes this background and has solicited a response from Dōgen.

16. *Dōgen-zenji Zenshū*, 2:41.

17. *Dōgen-zenji Zenshū*, 2:37. As Dōgen revised his own text in the fascicle "Washing the Face" (see note 10), he expanded the effect of "bathing" from one's body-mind to encompass both the agent and the environment. ISHII Seijun observes that the idea was already contained in the earlier manuscript of *Tōunji bon* but was made clearer and more consistent in the revised version in *Kenkon'in bon*. For more detail, see ISHII Seijun, "Kenkon'in bon 'Senmen' to Tōunji bon 'Senmen' ni tsuite [part 1]" ("Contrasts between the Senmen Chapter of Shōbōgenzō within the Kenkon'in (temple) Manuscript and One within the Tōunji Temple Manuscript [part 1]"), *Journal of the Faculty of Buddhism of the Komazawa University* 48 (1990): 76–90.

18. *Dōgen-zenji Zenshū*, 2:39–40.

19. This is, of course, a complex idea. For Dōgen *acts* do not occur *in* space-time but rather *constitute* it—we might as well say that specific space-time coarises with specific acts. In outline he reasons as follows: If everything, including space-time, is mutually interdependent, as Buddhism teaches, then *space-time* is also interdependent and must *coarise* with the *acts* that constitute it from within.

20. A fascicle composed in Kōshōji Temple in August 1240, within a year from the deliverance of the fascicle "Washing the Face" at the same temple in 1239. As mentioned earlier in note 8, the purpose of the fascicle "Not Producing Evils" is to present an interpretation of *The Common Precept Verse of the Seven Buddhas*. More discussion about this follows in sections 14.4.1–14.4.2.

21. *Dōgen-zenji Zenshū*, 1:344. Note the one-way implication expressed in the last sentence, namely, the asymmetrical relationship between *time*, on the one hand, and *good and evil*, on the other. A parallel consideration appears elsewhere when Dōgen says: "Various goods [*shūzen* 衆善] are various things just as they are in the world [*shohō* 諸法], but [conversely] various things just as they are in the world are not [necessarily] various goods" (1:348). The "good" and "things just as they are in the world" are neither equivalent nor coextensive for Dōgen.

22. *Dōgen-zenji Zenshū*, 1:346. Italics in the translation are all my emphases—nothing corresponding to them exists in Dōgen's original text.

23. *Dōgen-zenji Zenshū*, 1:39.

24. *Dōgen-zenji Zenshū*, 1:14. This is Dōgen's famous reinterpretation of *issai shujō shitsuu busshō* 一切衆生悉有仏性, a phrase appearing in *Dainehangyō* (*Mahāyāna Mahāparinirvāṇa Sūtra*, T 374, 12: 522c24), whose traditional Chinese rendering is "All sentient beings without exception *have* Buddha-nature." Dōgen's alternative reading is of course intentional. For further explanation that comes close to mine in the current context, see Deane Curtin, "Dōgen, Deep Ecology, and the Ecological Self," in *Environmental*

Philosophy in Asian Traditions of Thought, ed. J. Baird Callicott and James McRae (Albany: SUNY Press, 2014), 268–270.

25. This chapter does not have enough space to discuss *original enlightenment thought* (*hongaku shisō* 本覚思想) in detail, a topic that has raised a number of issues in Japanese Buddhist studies, including Dōgen scholarship, over the past few decades. In rough outline the doctrine commits itself to supposing an all-inclusive whole, a generative continuum that transcends finite phenomenal distinctions and discriminations, as it were, in which everything, humans and nonhumans alike, is considered to be innately entitled to "original enlightenment [*hongaku* 本覚]." It thus undermines the importance of austere Buddhist practice and human effort, at times breaking down the distinction between what is strictly Buddhist and what is not. It is also viewed as a source of extreme "nonduality" claims. Most specialists agree that Dōgen eventually rejected such *original enlightenment thought*, hence not contradicting the viewpoint of this chapter, but how clearly and decisively Dōgen did so in his early to middle writings is a matter of scholarly debate. Interested readers will benefit from reading Steven Heine, "Critical Buddhism and the *Shōbōgenzō*: The Debate over the 75-Fascicle and 12-Fascicle Texts," in *Pruning the Bodhi Tree: The Storm over Critical Buddhism*, ed. Jamie Hubbard and Paul L. Swanson (Honolulu: University of Hawai'i Press, 1997), 251–285.

26. *Dōgen-zenji Zenshū*, 7:192–195. The dialogue between Ejō and Gikai, banal as it may sound, signifies a critical matter for Buddhist practice, particularly in the "Zen sect" tradition: Pure and devout acts do not justify themselves simply because they are pure and devout. TSUNODA Tairyū, who attends to the particular significance of this exchange between Dōgen's second and third heirs, observes that confusions of this sort were not rare in Song Dynasty China, when Dōgen undertook his apprenticeship. See TSUNODA Tairyū, *Dogen-zenji no Shisōteki Kenkyū* (*A Study of Zen Master Dōgen's Thought*) (Tokyo: Shunjūsha, 2015), 142–147 and 149–150 n. 13.

27. *Dōgen-zenji Zenshū*, 1:24.

28. *Dōgen-zenji Zenshū*, 3:214.

29. *Dōgen-zenji Zenshū*, 1:348. In preceding lines Dōgen makes it clear that the *presencing* (*genjō*) considered here is not *any* presencing but only that which is guided by an enlightened eye (*katsuganzei* 活眼睛). As briefly touched upon in note 21, *if* there is the presencing of good, *then* it is necessarily a devout act. Dōgen writes: "In the right moment of producing the good, there is no good that is not brought to realization [*kitarazaru shūzen nashi* きたらざる衆善なし]" (1:347). However, the *converse*—*if* an act is devout, *then* it is the presencing of good—does not always hold true. The latter portends a questionable attempt to describe the enlightened as morally infallible, a view that is assumptive at best.

30. The emphasis on *acts* or *deeds* is of course not unique to Dōgen's position. One may recall from *Suttanipāta*, the oldest known records of Buddha's teaching, that it is by *deeds*, not by birth or origin, that one becomes a farmer, a soldier, or a Brahman: "The wise perceive the deed. . . . The world Revolves by deeds, mankind revolves by deeds," as a verse chants in *Woven Cadences of Early Buddhists*, trans. E. M. Hare (London: Oxford University Press, 1945), 96–97.

31. On my reading Dōgen was unflagging about this from the beginning, that is, not just in his late writings, as some commentators contend. In the early years after he returned from China, Dōgen wrote: "It is an outrageous mistake for a Zen monk to prefer

evil acts, saying that there is no need [for a monk] to practice good or to accumulate virtuous merits. There is no traditional standard I have heard of [in Buddhism] where evil acts are favored in this manner.... Once it is realized through the body that everything is Buddha dharma [*shohō mina buppō* 諸法皆仏法], evil is decisive evil [*ketsujōaku* 決定悪], falling away from the Way of Buddhist ancestors, whereas good is decisive good [*ketsujōzen* 決定善] that serves as an occasion for the Buddhist Way" (*Dōgen-zenji Zenshū*, 7:110). The absence of ontological discrimination in the enlightened mind (where "everything" is perceived as "Buddha dharma," in Dōgen's words) demands all the more unclouded discernment between good and evil (as "decisive good" and "decisive evil").

32. *Dōgen-zenji Zenshū*, 7:67.

33. *Dōgen-zenji Zenshū*, 7:67. ISHII Shūdō interprets *fudō inga* in light of *karma over three time periods* (*sanjigō* 三時業) and of *believing deep in cause and effect* (*shinjin inga* 深信因果), which are two notions Dōgen emphasized in his late writings so that his followers would not take cause and effect—or one's act and its consequence—too lightly. The connection Ishii brings forth is important since some argue that Dōgen, conceivably influenced by the idea of *original enlightenment* (*hongaku*) mentioned earlier, failed to underscore the Buddhist concept of karmic retribution, especially in his early writings. See Ishii, *Dōgenzen-no Seiritsushiteki Kenkyū*, 514–524.

34. *Dōgen-zenji Zenshū*, 7:67. Ejō is wondering how anyone can be emancipated from karma through casting off body-mind, if cause and effect are indeed "unmovable."

35. *Dōgen-zenji Zenshū*, 7:67. Compare this with Dōgen's statement in his later fascicle "Not Producing Evils" (*Shoakumakusa*) that we have considered: "The original way in which cause and effect are, insofar as they are distinct and clear [*hunmyo* 分明], is the not producing [*makusa* 莫作] ... the not being unclear [*fumai* 不昧]" (*Dōgen-zenji Zenshū*, 1:345–346). "Not producing" (*makusa*) literally means "not being unclear about cause and effect" for him.

36. *Dōgen-zenji Zenshū*, 7:67.

37. *Dōgen-zenji Zenshū*, 1:41–42. Dōgen's examination of this exchange appears in two consecutive paragraphs, from which the next three short quotes are also taken.

38. *Dōgen-zenji Zenshū*, 1:42.

39. *Dōgen-zenji Zenshū*, 7:68. The appearance of the cat's body as Dharmakaya—a flowing *event* or unfolding *presencing* without fixed material form when seen under true light—is relative to the mode in which the experiencer coarises with it. Dōgen understands that Nansen's act was *originally* intended to help the disciples with such coarising, but he disagrees with Nansen as to what action had better be taken.

40. *Dōgen-zenji Zenshū*, 7:67.

41. This coheres with Dōgen's generally strict standards. Talking about cats, no pet should be allowed in temples in the first place, as Dōgen notes the words of his own teacher: "In recent times, abbots and others at many temples keep cats, but this is truly inadvisable. It is a deed of unenlightened people" (*Dōgen-zenji Zenshū*, 7:13).

42. *Dōgen-zenji Zenshū*, 7:67.

43. *Dōgen-zenji Zenshū*, 7:68.

44. *Dōgen-zenji Zenshū*, 7:67. As is the case with most koans, it is important to bring the *speech act* into focus, including the silence of the disciples. In this connection TERADA Tōru, an astute modern interpreter of Dōgen's work, presents a useful

reminder that words behave like verbs in Dōgen, the "great turning of words" offering a foremost example: "Compounds in the Chinese language [such as *ittengo* 一転語] appear as nouns to us [i.e., Japanese readers], but in Dōgen, the knowledge concerning the fact that they were used primarily as verbs [in Chinese] gains power in constructing his thought, let alone his expressions." Cf. TEREDA Tōru, *Dōgen no Gengo-uchū* (*Dōgen's Language Universe*) (Tokyo: Iwanami Shoten, 1974), 188.

45. *Dōgen-zenji Zenshū*, 7:68.

46. *Dōgen-zenji Zenshū*, 7:68. Ejō is now asking Dōgen how Nansen, who should have cast off body-mind as a master, can be free of karma if he indeed committed such a sin (this is a continuation of Ejō's wondering mentioned in note 34).

47. *Dōgen-zenji Zenshū*, 7:68.

48. *Dōgen-zenji Zenshū*, 7:68. For a study that advocates Dōgen on this last point, see James McRae, "Cutting the Cat in One: Zen Master Dōgen on the Moral Status of Nonhuman Animals," in *Asian Perspectives on Animal Ethics: Rethinking the Nonhuman*, ed. Neil Dalal and Chloë Taylor (London: Routledge, 2014), 129–147. McRae compares Dōgen's view with the doctrine of *double effect*, which considers negative side effects as permissible under certain conditions. The current chapter emphasizes that for Dōgen killing is never justified or legitimatized as "expedient means" (*upāya*). It is our karmic burden or fate that sins cannot be avoided at all times, but even if we understand why one had to commit a sin, seeing it from a "higher" or "enlightened" perspective does not change or cancel out the act. To evoke such a moral instinct, one only needs to imagine a human child held under Nansen's arm instead of the cat.

49. Douglas Mikkelson finds Dōgen's account of Nansen's killing the cat "ambivalent." He suggests that "do no evil" is *prescriptive* for unenlightened people but *descriptive* for the enlightened. In my opinion this talks around the question, because the real issue is whether "do no evil" is *prescriptive* for the enlightened too, as it should be. One place Mikkelson's reading goes astray is that he infers from the "discontinuous [temporal] moments" of cause and effect, which does apply to Dōgen's thought, the view that "from the standpoint of enlightenment, cause and effect can be seen as discontinuous." The latter contradicts Dōgen's teaching of the "simultaneity of cause and effect [*inga dōji* 因果同時]" and much of what has been said in this chapter. What Dōgen means is that in each discrete or discontinuous moment, causal connections are manifest in entirety such that they appear to the experiencer as "simultaneous." That Dōgen perceived causality as plain as daylight (*inga rekizen* 因果歴然) in this way and remained consistent in this regard is elaborated in Tsunoda, *Dogen-zenji no Shisōteki Kenkyū*, chapter 5. Compare Douglas K. Mikkelson, "Who Is Arguing about the Cat? Moral Action and Enlightenment According to Dōgen," in *Philosophy East and West* 47, no. 3 (1997): 383–397, especially 393f.

50. *Dōgen-zenji Zenshū*, 2:81. With a stretch of imagination, one can in fact argue that this is just a traditional "Buddhist" view of *washing*. One of the contrasts early Buddhism drew between Hinduism and itself was to point out that physically bathing in a river—in the Ganges, for example—does not wash off sins. Recall the following witty passage from *Therīgātā*: "Is it that frogs and turtles will all go to heaven, and so will water monitors and crocodiles, and anything that lives in water, as will killers of sheep and killers of pigs ... everyone who habitually does evil [just because they live or bathe

in water]?" Quoted from *Therigatha: Poems of the First Buddhist Women*, trans. Charles Hallisey (Cambridge, MA: Harvard University Press, 2015), 125.

51. *Dōgen-zenji Zenshū*, 1:245. Dōgen further states that "time is origination" and "origination is the fulfilment of a moment" (*Dōgen-zenji Zenshū*, 1:120). Note that this can also be taken as just "Buddhist" rather than making it Dōgen's original philosophic thought. SAIGUSA Mitsuyoshi, a leading Japanese Buddhologist who critically compares East Asian developments of Mahayana Buddhism with early Buddhist *Āgama* texts, points out: "From its earliest period, Buddhism has never regarded time as substance, but has nonetheless considered time, though not substance, as the basis of every actual thing or fact. The famous phrase 'Being *is* time' of Dōgen, the founder of the Sōtō school, which appears in the "Being-Time" (*uji* 有時) fascicle of *Shōbōgenzō*, refers us directly to the idea already present in the inception of Buddhist teaching." See NAKAMURA Hajime and SAIGUSA Mitsuyoshi, *Bauddha* (*Buddhist*) (Tokyo: Shōgakkan, 1987), 128.

52. *Dōgen-zenji Zenshū*, 1:240.

53. *Dōgen-zenji Zenshū*, 7:100. In relation to "Buddhism" in general, it is also worth bearing in mind here that Dōgen did not regard his teaching as that of the "Zen sect" (*Zen shū* 禅宗). His rejection of the label "Zen sect" is voiced with great clarity: "In India of the West and China of the East, there has never been the name 'Zen sect' from ancient times down to the present, though some people [today] rashly call themselves by this name, who are uninvited enemies of Buddhist ancestors and demons that destroy the Buddhist Way" (*Dōgen-zenji Zenshū*, 1:472); "You should know clearly that using 'Zen sect' to name it [i.e., Buddhist teaching] is an enormous mistake" (1:476). The same point is repeated by Dōgen a year and a half before his death (*Dōgen-zenji Zenshū*, 4:72–75).

54. *Dōgen-zenji Zenshū*, 7:66.

55. *Dōgen-zenji Zenshū*, 2:83.

56. *Dōgen-zenji Zenshū*, 2:89. As the forgoing discussion shows, it is the *act* that matters for Dōgen, not the material that makes up feces or urine. In this regard Dōgen distances himself from traditional religions that abhor what the body produces, such as feces, urine, blood, phlegm, and so forth, a tendency more noticeable in both early Buddhism and Hinduism. An illuminating perspective on the Indian tradition is given by George A. James, "Environment and Environmental Philosophy in India," in Callicott and McRae, *Environmental Philosophy in Asian Traditions of Thought*, 3–23, especially 6–15.

57. *Dōgen-zenji Zenshū*, 2:84.

58. *Dōgen-zenji Zenshū*, 2:83.

59. *Dōgen-zenji Zenshū*, 2:81.

60. *Dōgen-zenji Zenshū*, 2:90.

61. Note that Buddhism encourages compassion for all sentient beings, but it does not value all life forms simply as "equal"—for example, being born a human is superior to being born a fox. Likewise, recommendable patterns of conduct for humans are not just "natural." Regarding Dōgen's strict instructions of *washing*, IWATA Keiji explains: "[Following Dōgen's instructions,] one sets the body-mind into orderly shape, inside and outside, and engages in ascetic training. This is not mere formalism, for just as birds are birds, and fish are fish, humans must have forms for themselves as humans." IWATA Keiji, *Dōgen no Mita Uchū* (*The Universe Captured in Dōgen's Vision*) (Tokyo: Seidosha, 1989), 256–257.

62. *Dōgen-zenji Zenshū*, 2:90.

63. *Dōgen-zenji Zenshū*, 2:91.

64. *Dōgen-zenji Zenshū*, 2:86.

65. *Dōgen-zenji Zenshū*, 2:86. Although such toilet instructions may seem somewhat priggish, they continue to form part of everyday Buddhist training. Deane Curtin takes notice of the postings often found around toilets in Zen monasteries that remind us of the food cycle—that food becomes the self, and then not-self. Cf. Curtin, "Dōgen, Deep Ecology, and the Ecological Self," 274.

66. It is easy to overlook the philosophical significance of what may appear like mere monastery rules in Dōgen's texts. The interesting continuity between monastery rules and Dōgen's broader Buddhist philosophy is analyzed in KUREBAYASHI Kōdō, "Dōgen-zenji ni okeru Kanjin Fujō" ("The Idea of the Impurity of the Body in Dōgen Zenji"), in *Indogaku Bukkyōgaku Kenkyū* (*Journal of Indian and Buddhist Studies*) 15, no. 1 (1966–1967): 15–21.

67. *Dōgen-zenji Zenshū*, 7:56.

68. *Dōgen-zenji Zenshū*, 2:81.

69. In Dōgen's *shūshō ichinyo*, practice and attainment are felt as simultaneous by the experiencer, which can be regarded as another expression given to the idea of the "simultaneity of cause and effect [*inga dōji*]" mentioned in note 49. David Shaner offers a useful comment on the intuitive connection between time, changing attitude, and our relationship to nature. He writes, "Time, as conceived by Dōgen, is thus interpreted as a function of our own changing attitudes," while observing that some degrading attitudes can become "world-denying because they devalue an otherwise intimate relation with nature." Shaner is correct to stress that for Dōgen *time* coarises with our *attitudes*, which in turn influence our relationship with nature, though his attribution of *original enlightenment* (*hongaku*) to Dōgen may require some reconsideration (see note 25). Cf. David E. Shaner, "The Japanese Experience of Nature," in *Nature in Asian Traditions of Thought: Essays in Environmental Philosophy*, ed. by J. Baird Callicott and Roger T. Ames (Albany: SUNY Press, 1989), 163–182, especially 168–172.

70. Dōgen suggests that even washing our clothes is not just soaking laundry in water. It is to coparticipate in the vast and complex self-purifying process of nature that includes the sun, wind, and earth: "There are ways in which you wash clothes by using fire, wind, soil, water, and air. There are ways in which you cleanse earth, water, fire, wind, and air, by using earth, water, fire, wind, and air" (*Dōgen-zenji Zenshū*, 2:131). Most simply said, we dry and wear our clothes in the open environment as we roam on the surface of the planet.

71. Kenneth Kraft observes that should we follow Dōgen's teaching, "We would probably not produce any nuclear waste in the first place," while also pointing out that "tens of thousands of tons of atomic waste generated by nuclear reactors and weapon plants is a problem on a different scale." I mention this in passing because Buddhists today do face challenges that were not foreseeable in Dōgen's time. Cf. Kenneth Kraft, "Nuclear Ecology and Engaged Buddhism," in *Buddhism and Ecology: The Interconnection of Dharma and Deeds*, ed. Marilyn E. Tucker and Duncan R. Williams (Cambridge, MA: Harvard University Press, 1997), 281f.

72. In comparing Dōgen's philosophy with contemporary environmental ethics, TAKAHASHI Takao notes that the foundation of "nature's right" in Western literature can be sought more in terms of *habits*, from Dōgen's viewpoint. Cf. TAKAHASHI

Takao, "*Shōbōgenzō* Sansuikyō ni tsuite: Kankyō Rinrigaku e no ichishiten" ("On the Mountains and Waters Sutra in *Shōbōgenzō*: A Perspective on Environmental Ethics"), *Kumamoto Daigaku Bungakubu Ronsō* (*Kumamoto Journal of Culture and Humanities*) 38 (1993): 1–18.

73. *Dōgen-zenji Zenshū*, 7:77. Note that this remark belongs to Dōgen's relatively early years when barely a fascicle of *Shōbōgenzō* was written.

74. *Dōgen-zenji Zenshū*, 2:408–409, and 621 for a slightly variant text. I touched on the related notions of *karma over three time periods* (*sanjigō* 三時業) and *believing deep in cause and effect* (*shinjin inga* 深信因果) in note 33.

CHAPTER 15 | Planetary Philosophy and Social
Consensus Building

KUWAKO TOSHIO

THE JAPANESE ISLANDS are located at the northeast rim of the Pacific
Ocean. This location has brought the Japanese people not only rich benefits of nature but also various natural disasters. The islands are, so to speak,
a treasure house of natural disasters. In my interpretation, the tradition has
been formed through a long history in which the Japanese people have
struggled against the overwhelming power of nature and accumulated wisdom to cope with natural hazards such as earthquakes, tsunamis, volcanic
eruptions, typhoons, floods, droughts, and heavy snows.

In the twentieth century, human activity became another threat to the
living beings on this planet because human activity is one of the causes
of climate change, the destruction of biodiversity, and resource depletion.

I started my philosophical career by exploring the meaning of the recognition of and the actions of human beings toward nature. Comparing
the views of the relationship of human beings with nature in Western and
Eastern philosophy and, particularly, focusing my interest on traditional
Japanese thought, I devised two theoretical and practical notions—"placement of body" and "historical profile of space"—to grasp the relationship
between human beings and the natural environment. I also proposed an
understanding of landscape as "appearance to the self with bodily placement" and a method of recognition and creation of value structure in
space.[1]

I published *Environmental Philosophy: Making Use of Traditional
Japanese Thought* in 1999, which proposed the concept of "historical
profile of space" as an attempt to understand the relationship between
human beings and their environment. There, I examined the philosophies

of Saigyō, MUSŌ Soseki, and KUMAZAWA Bansan and applied them to the environmental issues that modern Japan is facing.[2] Since the publication of that book, I have been asked by the national government and local governments to work as a project coordinator, a project adviser, and a facilitator to resolve disputes concerning infrastructure such as river works, the building of dams and roads, and town revitalization. Almost all the projects have raised environmental-ethical issues. I am also engaged in important projects of nature regeneration and restoration, such as the reintroduction of the crested ibis on Sado Island and planning for the protection of the semitropical forests of Yambaru in Okinawa.

Through these activities, I have found that it is necessary to have both *practical theory* and *theoretical practice* to inform decision-making and social consensus building by means of the collaboration of administrative sectors, specialists, and citizens. The principles of my practices are as follows:

1. A triangular structure of value for ethical decision-making
2. A triangular structure for understanding human nature as beings that inhabit the planet Earth
3. A triangular structure for the recognition of space value to promote consensus building
4. A triangular structure for the relationship among stakeholders for social consensus building[3]

Practical ethics concerns the rules and regulations that guide human actions. If we want to act in an ethically appropriate way, we should functionalize the rules and regulations for decision-making. To that end, we must recognize the relationships among three elements: the ideas incorporated in the rules and regulations, social systems of these rules and regulations that embody the ideas, and each person's decision-making based on individual morality. We must develop an action-guiding theory based on this recognition.

Ethical action is the realization of our wishes expressed as ideal thoughts. When a wish becomes the driving force for individual decision-making, ethics becomes the foundation of that choice. Ideas must inform human actions in actual situations. Furthermore, we must answer the questions of how we choose an action and what rules and regulations are used to make that choice. If an ideal thought contains a notion of environment, we need a new model for human action directed toward the environment, which I call "planetary philosophy and planetary ethics." I posit the triangular structures of human actions through planetary ethics and decision-making because I think that when environmental philosophy and ethics are presented only as abstract philosophy, they cannot become the driving force of a real action.

The benefits derived from and the threats posed by nature for human beings form the foundation for thinking about the global environmental crisis. The scope of planetary ethics is a comprehensive understanding of both the benefits derived from and the threats posed by nature. If significant rain falls but does not harm human life, we do not call it a threat. We do not think that rain benefits human beings if the rain does not become drinking water or if we do not eat vegetables, fruits, meat, and fish that exist because of water irrigating the fields or filling in the rivers and lakes.

The increase in the temperature of the atmosphere by carbon dioxide emissions causes large-scale weather phenomena such as heavy rain or heavy snowfall because of the increase in atmospheric moisture. To be sure, the cause of earthquakes and tsunamis from the movement of crustal plates is the result of dynamics inside the earth, but the accident at the nuclear power plant in Fukushima Prefecture, which was destroyed by the tsunami resulting from the Great East Japan Earthquake, caused extensive radioactive contamination. The Japanese government built seawalls using a large quantity of concrete in order to mitigate damage from tsunamis, but this project resulted in the emission of a significant amount of carbon dioxide. As this example illustrates, there is complicated, reciprocal causation between human beings and the activities of this planet. We must have the ability to appropriately enjoy the benefits of nature while appropriately responding to threats from nature.

A key to building planetary ethics is to understand the geographical and geological conditions of the earth. This is especially important in the Japanese islands because of their spatial characteristics conditioned by the distribution and motion of tectonic plates and proximity to the northeastern Pacific Ocean. These conditions produce a great variety of natural benefits and destructive effects for the islands. Four tectonic plates formed the Japanese Islands: the Pacific plate, the Indo-Australian plate, the small Filipino plate, and the Eurasian plate.

Their motions cause earthquakes, tsunamis, and volcanic activity. On the other hand, the seasonal heavy rains, snows, and typhoons that the Japanese islands endure are weather phenomena caused by heat from the sun and atmospheric flow. Global warming is related to these atmospheric phenomena in complicated ways. The inner movements of the earth, though unaffected by humans, impact humans greatly. On the other hand, human beings contribute to these weather phenomena, principally by altering the chemistry of the atmosphere. The human choices affecting the atmosphere are a serious problem for environmental ethics. I call this philosophy "planetary philosophy" and the ethics of our actions on this planet "planetary ethics."[4]

But how can we construct a planetary ethic? As J. Baird Callicott suggests in *Earth's Insights*, the old adage, "Think globally and act locally," should be turned on its head.[5] We need to think locally, that is, derive environmental ethics from local conceptual resources and apply them to the new and unprecedented planetary or global challenges we face in the twenty-first century. Callicott also indicates that some "Rosetta Stone" is needed to harmonize and coordinate these locally turned and culturally embedded environmental ethics, but that task is beyond the scope of this chapter. Here, I would like to show the environmental-ethics implications we can draw from Japanese mythology, which is embedded in the historical profile of the local spaces where I have been engaged in consensus building.

15.1. Historical Profile of Space and Japanese Mythology

The Miyazaki prefectural government started a project of environmental restoration in 2012 that included the Jindai River. I am engaged in this project as an adviser. The primary goal is to regenerate a spring feeding it, but it is very difficult work because the riverbed was made of a thin board of melted tufa, which was brought down after the eruption of Mount Aso, a famous volcano with a huge caldera. The people enjoyed the benefits of this spring from ancient times, but the river was repaired by the Miyazaki prefectural government in the 1960s without the consensus of the local habitants. The river channel was changed for flood prevention. The riverbed was dug out and diked with concrete. The flood prevention function was achieved, but the ecosystem deteriorated, the fireflies and the fish disappeared, and the spring dried up.

The historical profile of the Jindai River, which flows through the town of Takachiho in Kyushu district, suggests one way to express planetary philosophy. The name "Jindai" means "the era of ancient gods." Near the river there is a spring called Amano-manai (Genuine Spring of Heaven). The description of the Takachiho myth says that when Ninigi, a grandson of Amaterasu (the sun goddess) descended from the heaven, he planted a seed of water on the ground where no water was found. In the

Takamagahara myth, Amaterasu, the grandmother of Ninigi, hid herself in a cave called Amanoiwato to escape from the bad behavior of her brother, Susanoo. It is said that all of the evil things that happened on the earth were because of the absence of the sun goddess. As a result of this grave situation, eight million gods gathered in the open space of the riverside, Amanoyasukawara, to find a solution through discussion.

In this myth, we can find a prototype of conflict and the Japanese way of building consensus. It is said in *Nihonshoki* that this is a story of conflict over land inheritance and water management, and the process of solving the problem. Amaterasu is said to have inherited good rice paddies (long, narrow rice paddies, surrounded by fences, and not adversely affected by risks of flood or drought), whereas Susanoo inherited bad rice paddies (wherein wood stumps were left, located near the river, and at risk of flood or drought). This resulted in a conflict between the sister and brother. This is a basic story of conflict over limited space and resources, as well as risk allocation through countless disasters.[6] Ancient gods got together to discuss this problem, which was solved by the outstanding performance of Omoikane (the god of wisdom), Amanouzume (the goddess of wisdom and entertainment) and Tajikarao (the god of power). This process consisted of a discussion involving everyone, the adoption of a well-considered proposal, and a relaxed atmosphere, all of which facilitated a solution.

Japanese mythology suggests that a lack of sunlight, such as a solar eclipse or the winter solstice, produces natural disasters. This myth is probably correlated with the lack of sunlight brought about by volcanic eruptions. A large quantity of volcanic ash from an eruption can appear in the atmosphere, cover the earth, shield the light of the sun, and cause a drop in temperature. A volcanic eruption on earth can yield other significant effects as well. Takachiho Town is located outside the outer rim of the volcanic caldera of Mount Aso, and it was built on the pyroclastic flow of the ancient eruption. In southern Kyushu, the Jōmon people were highly cultured 7,200 years ago, but they were devastated by the eruption of Kikai Caldera. In the remains of Uenohara, it was discovered that people living their ordinary lives were buried under thick volcanic ash called *shirasu*. We can imagine that some people survived the disaster and the myth of the sun goddess began.

15.2. Social Infrastructure Development in the Hii River

I learned the most in the Hiikawa basin, which flows through the Izumo district of Shimane. This is the area characterized by the Izumo myth, in which Susanoo was ousted from Takamagahara, the Heavenly Terrace, and arrived at Torikami Peak, the source of the Hiikawa River. There Susanoo met Kushinada, the goddess of the rice harvest. She was going to be sacrificed to Yamatano-orochi, the giant, eight-headed serpent, but Susanoo won the fight against the serpent, married Kushinada, and founded a new country. The enemy that Susanoo fought was the river Hiikawa, which looks like a serpent, so the fight symbolizes the control of natural disaster. The sword that Susanoo picked up from the tail of the serpent is known as "a sword that makes clouds in the sky." It is a ritual tool for controlling rainfall to minimize the threats of flood and drought.

The land development in the Hii River Basin has a long history in Japan, and it became part of a myth that has been passed down in the community. The project of repair in the Hii River Basin is one of the largest social-infrastructure development projects in Japan and has many regional characteristics. I have been engaged in the formulation of Basic Planning for the Revitalization of Towns along the Ohashi River, which is a trilateral joint project of MLIT (Ministry of Land, Infrastructure, Transportation and tourism), Shimane Prefecture, and Matsue City. This project has been positioned as a part of the so-called three-piece set, projects covering the whole area along the Hii River: (1) two dams (Obara and Shizumi) making up the Hii River flood control system, (2) a huge diversion of the Hii River, and (3) a project for the improvement of the Ohashi River (a tributary of the Hii River), which runs through the famous provincial city of Matsue. Although the Ohashi River is a tributary of the Hii River, the project for the improvement of the Ohashi River was extremely important both for the country and for the region because that river is the most important part of the whole Hii River system and we needed to consider the entire Hii River system to complete this project.

Originally, the project for the improvement of the Ohashi River had been placed within a flood control project. However, we knew from the beginning that this improvement project would have a substantial impact on the Matsue City area because it included a widening of the Ohashi River and an excavation of the riverbed, the construction of banks, the replacement of two bridges, and town development in bridge guard areas (such as the relocation of houses in the areas affected by the widening work, replacement of roads, related redevelopment of the urban areas, etc.). It is thus considered a project involving extremely complex values. People differed in opinion, as each person prioritized different values, which generated conflict as we tried to move forward with the project.[7]

Flood control works usually commence in the downstream area and proceed upstream. However, the flood control project in the Hii River was interrupted due to the land reclamation issue in Nakaumi in the downstream area, which suspended the project for thirty-seven years. In the meantime, two dams in the upper-stream area as well as the diversion of the Hii River were constructed, and the improvement of the Ohashi River was left as the only remaining issue.

In 2005, I received a request from the Izumo River Office of MLIT to cooperate in this large-scale national project. While the improvement of the Ohashi River essentially aims for improved flood control, we decided to call the project "Revitalization of Towns along the Ohashi River," as it involved various issues beyond mere flood control, such as the preservation of the environment, the improvement of landscape, and the enhancement of communities. I worked as a member of the Review Committee for Revitalization of Towns along the Ohashi River, in which citizens participated. I served as a facilitator in the meetings, drafted policies that were later adopted by the review committee, and acted as a liaison with citizens of the community.

15.3. Basic Principles for the Revitalization of Towns along the Ohashi River

The best way to understand how the project for the improvement of the Ohashi River involves various values may be referring to the "Basic Principles" adopted by the Review Committee for the Revitalization of Towns along the Ohashi River in December 2006. "Basic Principles" includes a text titled "Basic Concept for Town Development."

Matsue City, the Aquapolis of Izumo, will be developed based on the belief that the town, people, and water are inextricably linked. Izumo means "clouds spring" and refers to the cloud formations shaped by the area's unique climate. The town development will cover the whole area along the Hii River, which has shaped the Izumo culture, including the myth of Izumo and the Tatara ironmaking method. We will give sufficient consideration to all elements of the landscape that contribute to the origin of Matsue, such as Mount Daisen and Lake Shinji. Building upon the nature and climate where ancient gods are believed to live as well as the history and the culture from the Matsue Domain era, we aim to achieve town development where residents and visitors can appreciate and share the beauty of the changing seasons. We will preserve, in a manner appropriate for the community, the environment (including rivers, channels, farmlands, and wetlands), the landscape (including various waterfronts, traditional streetscapes, and historic sites), and the culture and livelihood of people there.[8]

The text of "Basic Concept" sets out the idea of the project Revitalization of Towns along the Ohashi River and attracts the attention of those who have concern for the improvement of the Ohashi River. The "Basic Concept" is given the role of specifying the goal that should be shared by those interested in the improvement project. It also includes the message that the project aims to harmonize various elements included in the "Basic Concept," even opposing elements between which compromise must be sought. Clarifying the idea of the project is the first step for its promotion. If local residents and those involved in the project do not agree on this idea, doubt and mistrust will arise as the project progresses. In contrast, if we specify a clear goal, we can always come back to this basic goal and review the situation when the discussion gets snarled. It is thus important to set a clear basic idea as the first step toward the promotion of the project.

Furthermore, the "Basic Concept" is not something that the project leader imposed in a top-down fashion. We have designed the process so that citizens can participate in the project from the concept formulation phase. This is the most important point in the Ohashi River project.

In order to draw up the "Basic Principles," we have assembled the committee to discuss and revise summaries in a totally open meeting with citizens. Of course, not all participants agreed with the project operator. In public projects, there is always a possibility that project operators will use tactics to discourage dissent. In the Ohashi River project, however, we have never used such tactics and have been committed to a fully open, democratic process. As a result, we have received some opinions critical of the project. The main reason for such opposition was mistrust among citizens as a result of the process employed in previous projects. Therefore, we needed to devote energy to relieve mistrust among citizens.

It takes a lot of work to consolidate citizens' trust. In contrast, an indiscreet remark by a person in charge of the project is enough to lose the trust of citizens. Therefore, communication management is important in a project. One of the important elements in communication management is sharing a project goal.

A social infrastructure development in a community changes its traditional spatial structure. Redesigning river spaces, including the construction or improvement of dams or diversions, drastically changes the life of residents living along the river. Road construction and land readjustment also have substantial impact on people's lives as such projects change spatial layouts. However, project operators do not always accurately perceive the possible impact that their project might cause. If they perceive only that their flood control project will make the community safer, they will be criticized by citizens and wonder why people do not understand that their work will benefit local residents. Such cases often occur when project operators do not understand what local residents really need. For example, even if the project improves safety, residents may doubt its value, feeling that it is beneficial only for those in the downstream area and will destroy the environment or landscape, or even their culture. Open and honest dialogue among all stakeholders helps to dispel such doubts. While the national, prefectural, and municipal governments are the main actors in the Ohashi River project, citizens are also actors, as we are promoting projects with citizen involvement.

15.4. Various Meanings of "Diversity"

Revitalization of Towns along the Ohashi River is an unprecedented program that aims to harmonize diverse values to address flood control, landscape and environment preservation, and the revitalization of towns. The phrase "diversity of values" may be somewhat abstract, and I need to discuss each of its elements in more detail.

When thinking about values, I focus on three factors. As all three are mutually related, I indicate them in a "triangle of values." The triangle of values consists of idea, system, and decision-making. The idea in the Ohashi River project includes "active town development" and "environmental consideration" as well as the ideal of "Aquapolis." Such an idea should be realized based on systems, such as laws or policies. However, not all systems have been developed in a way that is the most convenient to embody the ideals. In other words, some systems may become constraints for the realization of the idea. As in the case of the basic planning for Revitalization of Towns along the Ohashi River, when relevant actors in a project make decisions by way of discussion, along with philosophies and systems, options that relevant actors have for decision-making will be an issue. If philosophies are diverse, systems will also be diverse, and the diversity of options for those participating in the decision-making as well as the diversity of choices will be issues.

Troubles in the decision-making related to a social infrastructure development are often considered an issue of diversity of opinions among interested parties and, in that sense, as an issue of diversity of actual value judgments. However, such value judgments depend on what philosophies an actor brings to the table, and on institutional constraints or knowledge of these constraints he or she has.

Diversities of philosophies and systems related to certain values—as well as diversities of individual consciousness—have regional features. In problems related to dam construction or road improvement, there will be regional differences in terms of how local people perceive their town, what is dear to them, and how they wish to create a future vision. Project operators need to figure out how their project's idea is perceived by interested parties, what kinds of institutional support they need to realize their vision, and what intentions the interested parties have in participating in decision-making.

Changing the spatial structure of a community itself is a historical and cultural project. Some may think that creating a road will not change the culture. However, that is not correct. Creating a road does change people's lives and behavioral patterns. Changes in a space structure change the history and culture of the community concerned. Those involved in road improvement projects should be fully aware of this fact. Many simply believe that life in the community will be convenient with a road improvement. However, road construction can divide a community, lead to an increase in crime (due to easier access from outside), or hurt local business (as local customers can now travel to big cities to shop).

When people oppose a project, we should remember that such objections are made because of a diversity of philosophies. For example, one person might prioritize the preservation of the natural environment over convenience or the economy. Likewise, some institutional constraints can cause opposition when people make unacceptable claims. In some cases, changing institutional constraints can solve these problems.

In terms of history and culture, we also need to pay attention to the temporal elements of a regional space. In the project in Matsue, not only local history from ancient times, but also changes of the seasons and changes within a day are considered important elements. What is important here is that "changes of the times" is also an element that makes up diversity. As the project goes on, society and people will change: there will be generational changes in philosophies and systems of community development that make up people's triangle of values. The Ohashi River project had been suspended for thirty-seven years. During that period of suspension, the country of Japan and the region of Izumo have changed dramatically. The natural environment has also changed drastically. However, in the Japanese administrative system, there is a personnel reshuffle every two or three years and everyone is transferred to a new workplace. Therefore, it will be extremely difficult to understand the temporal trajectory of a project. We need to consider the fact that gaps in time consciousness between project operators and residents-citizens might cause a conflict of opinions.

15.5. Understanding Structures of Landscape

An experience concerning a landscape is personal or subjective. Unlike general or universal knowledge or technologies explained in the textbooks on civil-engineering techniques, the perception of each person and his or her interpretation of a space based on such perception can be different. These differing experiences and impressions make it difficult to universalize interpretations of regional space. Conflict between interpretations of a landscape causes conflict of opinions concerning social infrastructure development. Therefore, it is sometimes possible to understand the structure of conflict in a certain area by understanding its space structure, without even listening to interested parties. Especially in riverside areas, the interests of the upstream area and the downstream area as well as those of the right bank and the left bank often conflict. We can predict possible conflicts that will come up during a river improvement project simply by understanding the condition of the river and the surrounding areas.

For instance, the flood control project has been promoted in the Hii River to protect Matsue, a city in the downstream area. Many people were forced to relocate their homes for the construction of dams in the upperstream area and diversion of the Hii River. Long-established communities suffered substantial impact to protect Matsue City in the downstream area from flood disasters. We can easily imagine that people upstream think they are being sacrificed for the sake of people downstream. Similarly, flood disasters in Matsue are not caused by muddy streams bursting from their banks, but rather by the elevation of the water level of Lake Shinji. Therefore, houses will not be washed away by dike breaks but will suffer inundation at floor level, or, at worst, inundation above floor level. In such circumstances, if we visit the site, we can imagine that residents would request a development of levees, especially in the low area along the Ohashi River. In the downstream area of the Ohashi River, there is a stretch of rice paddies designated as an urbanization control area, and a rich ecosystem is preserved in the area along the Ohashi River. Therefore, we can also imagine that local environmentalists or ecosystem researchers would be concerned that the project would damage natural riches.

As discussed above, we can analyze diverse opinions and the reasons for such opinions within a landscape. If we get an overview of such diverse opinions as a whole, we understand the rivalries among such opinions and can make a conflict assessment. However, such schematic assessments should be fully backed up by concrete discussions and investigations. In order to have further insights into possible opposing opinions and their grounds, it is necessary to understand the history and the culture of the community concerned. In the process of engagement in the project, walking around the Izumo region with its rich, ancient culture, I kept thinking about how the climate, history, and culture of this region have influenced the inhabitants' way of thinking. By doing so, I can predict possible opinions when I serve as a facilitator in a concrete discussion. If I can predict possible opinions, I will not be surprised by any opinions. I will be prepared to address them and can steer the discussion toward agreement, not conflict.

We can observe not only dams, but also the condition of mountains, rivers, and communities in Izumo. The diversion of the Hii River is located where it spills out onto the Izumo Plain. If we observe the condition of the Hii River around that area, we find many white sandbars on the riverside. The headstream area of the Hii River is an old granite terrain where decayed rocks crumble into quartz and feldspar to make white sandbars. If you look at the Hii River as a huge serpent, each of these sandbars looks like a scale.

Ancient people portrayed the Hii River as a snake and understood floods as the violence of the serpent. Struggles to wipe out the violence of the serpent meant efforts for flood control, and it was a god called Susanoo who undertook that role. Susanoo wiped out the eight-headed serpent, married the goddess Kushinada, and created the country of Izumo. Susanoo is a god who has a power over natural disasters, and Kushinada is a goddess who blesses productive rice paddies using the water from the Hii River. The myth of Izumo is a story harmonizing opposite attitudes about nature: controlling the threats of the water while enjoying its blessings.

Based on such ideas, I have been engaged in the Ohashi River project. The "Basic Concept" is a summary of opinions of various people who participated in the discussions, but its direction largely coincided with what I have visualized based on the landscape of Izumo. People in the region have deep affection for and pride in the landscape of Izumo. The working group strived to express such pride and affection in the "Basic Concept." My main goal in project design and discussion is to honor and respect the culture of the community concerned, including the mythology I have just mentioned. As long as a project team or facilitator has this kind of respectful sprit, local people will trust them. In the modern age, local communities have experienced drastic changes, and many people are indifferent to or unaware of important values accumulated in their community. If those formally involved in the project do not attend to these values, people may think that it is not necessary to discuss them within a familiar landscape, or they may doubt traditional values. By expressing understanding of such values, a facilitator will be trusted by citizens as someone who respects their opinions.

Building relationships of trust is the most important, albeit the most difficult, work in a consensus building. Actual construction works are easily appreciated because they are visible. In contrast, the creation of a process for consensus building will only be documented and cannot be observed in a spatial structure. Although the work of consensus building is not fully recognized in Japan, it is indispensable in order to promote a smooth and peaceful completion of a project.

15.6. Toward a Creative Consensus Building

The goal of town development and river improvement is to change spatial structures to improve the quality of a community. However, even though project operators believe their project is productive, members of the community my fear that it will be destructive to the community. If project operators believe that important values should be preserved and passed down and that the project should be developed creatively to resolve conflicts, they will win the sympathy of local people and will be able to build a relationship of mutual trust.

Let us discuss the creation of new values in relation to the triangle of values I mentioned earlier. The triangle is a relationship consisting of three factors, which are the abstract idea, the institutionalized system, and individual decision-making. In the Ohashi River project, these factors are related to the project's goals, including the safety of flood control, preservation of the environment, maintenance of the landscape, and revitalization of urban areas. These values can conflict with each other. If we dredge the Ohashi riverbed deeply in order to improve the safety of flood control, it will lead to larger volumes of saltwater incursion at high tide into the estuarial region, which will affect the farming of freshwater clams. If we give up the excavation and construct high levees, they will destroy the waterfront landscape. Controlling floods, maintaining ecosystem processes and functions, preserving landscapes, and revitalizing towns are all important values, but in an actual project, they will conflict. Such conflicts are related to the personal priorities of each individual, based on his or her particular values and situation in the spaces affected. Those who place ultimate priority on safety from floods, those who give primary consideration to the environment, and, for example, tourist agents who care about the beauty of the landscape will have different opinions. Those who wish to promote the project and those who have a cautious attitude toward it will make different remarks in a discussion, and they may face a conflict of opinions. In consensus building, we aim to create a new idea while recognizing these different opinions. The "Basic Concepts" that we articulated integrate, as noted, four values: flood control, ecosystem health, beauty of the landscape, and revitalization of towns. These "Basic Concepts" have played an important role in articulating a value system that minimizes conflict.

Whether existing systems (rivers, roads, town development systems, etc.) suit a new idea may not be apparent from the beginning. If we are to create a new value, we may need to develop a new social system to realize such a value. Considering this point, in the "Basic Concepts" we said, "With regard to the landscape, we will continue to consider it, taking into account the systems related to town development." This means that we will take into account consensus building not only for the actual project of social system development, but also for the development of systems related to the creation of new values.

We pursued the Ohashi River project in a way that promotes open and democratic discussions. Likewise, the process of citizens' participation was fully discussed by the project team. We designed the discussions so that all interested parties could attend and explain their own opinions. The space where decision-making takes place is as important as the philosophies being discussed. As decision-making is done through consensus, a communication space must be designed to promote consensus building. Unlike Western people, the Japanese do not debate with one another straightforwardly. Therefore, we need a little ingenuity to make communications smooth. I have acquired techniques to communicate indirectly, using various tools. Opposing opinions often morph into attacks on the person expressing contrary opinions. If opposing opinions take the form of attacks on the personality of another, the atmosphere for a discussion will be poisoned. Techniques for indirect communications should keep participants from falling into direct conflict with others and, by focusing on the issue itself, discourage personal attacks on those who have an opposing opinion. A person expressing his or her viewpoint should be considered a person suggesting a different possibility for problem-solving. It is important to reach a way forward that is convincing for as many people as possible. In this sense, a consensus building should be a creative one.

The actors promoting a project should have definite ideas about each one of the values of idea, system, and decision-making. As I explained earlier, this basic structure encompasses a diversity of values in itself, but at the same time, idea, system, and decision-making are limited by diverse elements. Existing systems are supported by old philosophies. However, in the course of historical changes, there are systems that need to be changed. Likewise, individuals also need to change themselves to achieve their aims.

I believe that a consensus building is a wonderful opportunity for a personal transformation. Even among those who oppose a project, as a new idea emerges, there will be people who wish to change their own ideas to support it. Within a group of persons with the same opinion, it is hard to change opinions, and in some cases, those who change their opinions are treated as traitors. We need a reason—or a "good cause" in old-fashioned terms—to change opinions. We thus need to enable people to explain that they have changed their opinions to support an important aim, which can be a good cause. A process of consensus building enables opposing people to explain the reasons they have changed their opinions and reached an agreement. It is important that people are able to say that they have changed their opinions not for personal interests but for society. Of course, it is important that it is not a hard compromise, which sacrifices their personal interests.

The flexibility of project operators for opinion changes will be also important. As I mentioned earlier, the "Basic Concepts" of the Ohashi River project include a reference to system development. A social infrastructure development project will be welcomed by the community and can move forward only when a new idea, systems supporting the new idea, and decision-makers move forward in harmony.

15.7. Conclusion

The planetary philosophy of environmental ethics makes it possible to promote sustainability and a flourishing life for human beings. We must maintain a global viewpoint concerning our actions in which we address the workings of nature on the planet and ascertain the benefits and threats that human activity might pose. But the scale of most human activities—even those with global effects—is local. Therefore, we must establish a philosophy and techniques of social consensus building that have the power to overcome disputes over the benefits bestowed by and the threats posed by nature.

It is possible to construct an appropriate process of consensus building through the philosophy and practice of project management using the triangular scheme of ethical decision-making explained above. This process is grounded in a profound respect for the Japanese mythological tradition embraced by many of the stakeholders affected by environmental projects. Planetary philosophy stresses the importance of human adaptation to natural disasters and suggests the importance of the integration of mitigation and adaptation in environmental management. People's understanding of adaptation promotes their recognition of the importance of mitigation.[9]

Notes

1. KUWAKO Toshio, *Philosophy of Environment in Landscape* (Tokyo: Tokyo University Press, 2008); KUWAKO Toshio, *Philosophy of Life and Landscape* (Tokyo: Iwanami Shoten, 2013).

2. KUWAKO Toshio, *Kankyō no tetsugaku: Nihon no shisō o gendai ni ikasu (Environmental Philosophy: Making Use of Traditional Japanese Thought)* (Tokyo: Kodansha, 1999).

3. KUWAKO Toshio, *Project Management of Consensus Building* (Tokyo: Corona, 2016); Lawrence Susskind, Sarah McKearnan, and Jennifer Thomas-Larmer, eds. *Consensus Building Handbook: A Comprehensive Guide to Reaching Agreement* (Thousand Oaks, CA: Sage, 1999).

4. Charles H. Langmuir and Wally Broecker, *How to Build a Habitable Planet* (Princeton, NJ: Princeton University Press, 2013).

5. J. Baird Callicott, *Earth's Insights: A Multicultural Survey of Ecological Ethics from the Mediterranean Basin to Australian Outback* (Berkeley: University of California Press, 1994)

6. KURANO Keiji, *Kojiki* (Tokyo: Iwanami Shoten, 1911); and SAKAMOTO Taro, *Nihonshoki* (Tokyo: Iwanami Shoten, 2003).

7. Construction Office, Chugoku District Construction Bureau, Ministry of Construction, ed., *Hiikawashi*, 1995.

8. For more information about this region, please see http://www.pref.shimane.lg.jp/hiikawakandogawa/index.data/kihonkeikakugenan.pdf.

9. The first half of this chapter was read at the 2015 Uehiro-Carnegie-Oxford Conference "Global Warming: Environmental Ethics and Its Practice," which took place October 28–29, 2015. By the courtesy of the foundation, I incorporate the manuscript in this chapter.

A Plea for Environmental Philosophy as an Extension of Natural Philosophy

J. BAIRD CALLICOTT

A.1. The Topos of *Mu* and the Predicative Self

My first up-close-and-personal encounter with Japanese environmental philosophy came in the boreal summer of 1989 during a weeklong event held in and around Kyoto titled "Elmwood Symposium on New Paradigm Thinking and Traditional Japanese Culture." Elmwood is the name of the neighborhood in Berkeley, California, where Fritjof Capra lived. He founded the Elmwood Institute in 1984, which was transformed into the Center for Ecoliteracy in 1995 and relocated to downtown Berkeley. Intellectually, Capra may be situated in the living tradition of natural philosophy that began in Ionia on the eastern fringes of the Greek ambit in the early sixth century BCE. More about Capra and the symposium he helped organize shortly; first, a word about natural philosophy.

The first Western philosophy was natural philosophy and started off with crude speculation about the stuff of which the world is composed (Thales: water; Anaximenes: air), the forces moving that stuff around (Anaxagoras: mind; Empedocles: love and strife), the laws governing change and transformation (Heraclitus: the logos), and the contours of the cosmos (Anaximander: a drum-shaped central earth surrounded by wheels of fire enclosed in vented tubes of fire-hardened air). From such primitive beginnings, ancient Greek natural philosophy rapidly evolved by a process that might be characterized as a diachronic dialectic of ideas: the speculation of one thinker, followed by its rational criticism by a subsequent thinker together with that thinker's more subtle speculation. In a matter of only three centuries or so, this ancient Greek diachronic dialectic of ideas produced the atomic theory of matter and the concept of infinite space in which infinitely many world-orders are scattered (Leucippus and Democritus), calculated a good approximation of the actual circumference of the earth and the degree at which the earth's axis tilts (Eratosthenes), and even produced the idea that the earth is one among the planets orbiting a central sun (Aristarchus).

The still ongoing diachronic dialectic of ideas about the nature of nature—today known as science—was interrupted in Christendom for centuries by various scourges, mainly by dogmatic religious zealotry and barbarous mayhem. For a long time it passed into the hands of Islamic custodians, who further developed it, especially mathematically, before dogmatic religious zealotry in the caliphate again managed to snuff out rational inquiry into the nature of nature. But whenever and wherever the *anattā* of ancient Greek natural philosophy was reincarnated, its new embodiers built on the foundations laid down by the ancient Greek natural philosophers and the structures resting on those foundations erected by the medieval Muslim natural philosophers. Copernicus pointed out that he was not the first to develop a heliocentric astronomy; Gassendi acknowledged his debt to Lucretius and Epicurus, who, in turn, adopted the atomism of Leucippus and Democritus; Darwin cited Empedocles as the (admittedly primitive) originator of his basic concept of natural selection. Descartes united Euclid's geometry with Omar Khayyám's algebra to create analytic geometry.

Capra is a quantum physicist by training, who, with many other physicists, such as Werner Heisenberg and Irwin Schrödinger, realized that the second scientific revolution, which occurred at the turn of the twentieth century, had profound metaphysical implications—as did the first. Like Schrödinger, his fellow Austrian, Capra found similarities between the metaphysical implications of quantum physics and South and East Asian philosophy. He set out his comparative philosophy in *The Tao of Physics: An Exploration of the Parallels between Modern Physics and Eastern Mysticism*, published in 1975. Capra tended to conflate Asian traditions of thought, virtually making Brahman, Buddhadhātu, and the Dao simply different names for the same universal being. Further, the physics espoused by Capra—known as "the bootstrap model of strong-force interactions"—fell out of fashion in physics just as *The Tao of Physics* arrived in bookstores. The quantum-physics community largely abandoned the bootstrap model in favor of quantum chromodynamics and quarks—now known as the standard model—because of the simultaneous and coincidental creation a new particle, called ψ at the Stanford Linear Accelerator and J at MIT's Brookhaven National Laboratory. So dramatic was that turn of the physics worm that it became known as the "November Revolution," because November 1974 was the month during which the Stanford and MIT physicists had stumbled on the same thing. Nonetheless, *The Tao of Physics*—which included Capra's acknowledgment that his personal mystical experiences were catalyzed by psychedelics—became a New Age sensation. (Even more dramatic and better known to the general public, the standard model was confirmed by the well-publicized creation of the Higgs boson in the Large Hadron Collider near Geneva, Switzerland, in 2012.)

I had read *The Tao of Physics* when it was first published, of course. That was a decade before I had any genuine scholarly acquaintance with Asian traditions of thought, nor was I a close student of the blow-by-blow developments in the arcane field of quantum physics. And so I was as enthusiastic about the book as any other middle-aged hippie. With his charismatic demeanor and personality, Capra became something of a celebrity and thus attracted the attention of NOMURA Shingo, a Japanese philanthropist, who invited Capra to assemble a group of American environmentalists—by then Capra had begun to explore the metaphysical implications of ecology—to meet and exchange ideas with our Japanese counterparts. Capra's entourage was diverse, consisting of environmental activists, journalists, and public intellectuals. I was the only academically credentialed philosopher among us.

I vividly remember the first meeting with our Japanese counterparts, which was led by MATSUOKA Seigo, an ontologist. We Americans were all stunned and left speechless by his postmodern discourse. This suave, supremely self-confident, young Japanese scholar spoke glibly of the "topos of *mu*" and the "predicative self" (the latter phrase echoing NISHIDA Kitarō's "logic of the predicate," as I finally learn from Augustin Berque's chapter herein, and the former was coined by NAKAMURA Yūjirō, who deconstructed Nishida's philosophy). We Americans thought that we had come to exchange ideas about environmental ethics and ecophilosophy, not to exchange ideas about the self in an urbane and pomo argot, a topic to which our intimidator repeatedly demanded we return. All the other Americans looked to me to save us from the utter embarrassment of being out-discoursed by a Japanese sophisticate—and not in his own language, but in ours. I managed to stammer something out that barely passed as engaging our Japanese counterparts, but I also felt a bit betrayed. Isn't a discussion of the self not just anthropocentric but egocentric? What, I silently seethed, does that have to do with environmental ethics and ecophilosophy, for Christ's sake?

The answer to that question is *everything*—as I now realize about a quarter century later. I now think that the nature of the self—or better how to conceive and experience the self—is the central philosophical question of environmental ethics and indeed of ecophilosophy. While the term *topos* is used in a technical sense by Aristotle—the meaning of which remains a matter of scholarly dispute—the natural sense of the phrase "topos of *mu*" is the place of no-thing, of emptiness, of Buddhist *Śūnyatā*. In regard to the self, it is the Buddhist *anattā*, no-self, but in many ways the "topos of *mu*" is a better characterization of the Buddhist understanding of the self than the term "no-self," because the self is not nothing. There is a topos, but when we unravel it we are left with *mu*—no-thing; that is, nothing. As in Berque's contribution to this collection, there was a good bit of discussion at the Elmwood Symposium about the peculiarities of the Japanese language. The upshot of the notion of the predicative self is as much about what is absent, the subject, as what is present, the predicate, in the term "predicative self." As Berque points out, English and other European languages are, as it were, subject centered; Japanese, our interlocutor indicated, and Berque here confirms, is predicate centered.

At the risk of gross oversimplification, the prevailing Western self is still very much the legacy of Descartes—here too confirmed by Berque. Here's another embarrassing flash from the past, again vividly remembered. My first philosophy course at what is now Rhodes College—then it was named Southwestern at Memphis—was taught by a faculty team led by Charles Bigger and consisted of a series of lectures surveying Western philosophy. During Dr. Bigger's lecture on Descartes, this is what I wrote in my notebook: "Be a Cartesian Dualist!" Why did Cartesian dualism resonate with me so naturally and passionately? Because I already was one. And so was everyone else I ever met, up to that point in my life. Descartes articulated mind-body dualism in a particularly clear, radical, and vivid way. But mind-body dualism had been a cornerstone of Western philosophy from its origins in the sixth century BCE, beginning with Pythagoras, echoed by Empedocles a century later, and staunchly and persistently reinforced by Plato a century after that. Some of the ancient Greek philosophers had other ideas about the *psyche*—some more beautiful and others more subtle than the Pythagorean-Platonic-Cartesian idea. As to more beautiful, Anaximenes thought that air was the ambient universal soul stuff, of which we partake with every breath. As to more subtle, Aristotle regarded the *psyche* as only an aspect of ontologically robust organisms—the actualization of a potential function of the corporeal organism. He captures the idea best in his remark that if the eye were a free-living organism, sight would be its soul. We might express the Aristotelian idea of the psyche in contemporary terms thusly: an emergent epiphenomenon of the fully functioning central nervous system.

For better or worse, Pythagorean-Platonic soul-body dualism was modified and institutionalized in Christianity and then resecularized by Descartes. As a result, the Western self is a sort of a dimensionless psychic atom or "monad," to adopt the terminology of Leibniz, residing in the body. (I discuss Steve Odin's interpretation of monads in chapter 7 further on in this afterword.) The atomic self looks out on an alien world through the portals of the body's sensory organs. It is as externally related to other selves as it is to the body in which it resides and to the "external world"—a phrase that is all too common in twentieth-century Anglo-American analytic philosophy (and still all too common in the undead corpse of that school of philosophy lurching along now in the twenty-first century).

Ecophilosophy demands a reconception and a corresponding re-experiencing of the self in relational terms. Why? Because we are all thoroughly embedded in a complex skein of socioecological relationships. And these relationships are internal, not external. The mechanistic worldview of Gassendi, Descartes, and Newton is often epitomized, for illustrative purposes, by pool balls on a pool table. The identity of each ball is independent of its relationships to the other balls. The one-ball remains the one-ball, in other words, in all its changing spatial relationships and collisions with all the other balls. Its relationships are all external. In the evolutionary-ecological worldview that is emerging in contemporary environmental philosophy, organisms are internally related. In the evolutionary aspect of that worldview, deer, for example, have become deer in a dialectical relationship with the plants that they eat, the predators and parasites that eat them, and with the characteristics—such as temperature maxima and minima, seasonal variation, annual rainfall—of their habitat. In its ecological aspect, deer and all other aerobic animals are internally related to plants via the oxygen, nitrogen, and carbon cycles, and their population dynamics are internally related to those of their predators, their parasites; to weather anomalies; and to the hundreds of other variables that mutually and reciprocally affect them.

With the Human Microbiome Project we are beginning to realize that multicelled organisms, certainly our human selves included, are not individual organisms after all but highly integrated and tightly orchestrated ecosystems. Our personal somatic cells are outnumbered ten to one by our microbial symbionts (commensals, mutualists, and parasites) belonging to thousands of species. Digestion would be impossible without the help of some gut-living microbes; and others in various bodily niches coconstitute our immune systems. The first paradigm in ecology portrayed ecosystems as superorganisms—"super" referring to their large size in comparison with macro-organisms. We are now learning that macro-organisms are actually superecosystems—"super" in this case referring not to size but to the degree to which they are relationally integrated and symbiotic.

To discover its individual identity, the Western self engages in introspection. Part II of Descartes's *Discours de la Méthode* provides the classic example: "Le commencement de l'hiver, m'arrêta en un quartier où, ne trouvant aucune conversation qui me divertit ... je demeurois tout le jour enfermé seul dans un poêle, où j'avois tout le loisir de m'entretenir de mes pensées." Descartes overwinters in an unspecified place (the location of which is still a mystery) and, uninterested in social interaction, he remains alone all day and directs his attention to his own thoughts. The predicative or ecological self discovers its individual identity as the unique nexus of a complex set of socioenvironmental relationships. I, for example, am the son of an artist, who politically characterized himself as a communist in the 1930s and, in his later years, metaphysically as a theosophist. I was born into a racially segregated society in an American city of the Deep South. Its ley lines; towering hardwoods; summer heat and humidity; muddy waters; delta blues, hard gospel, and rock-and-roll music; turnip greens, blackeyed peas, and bar-b-que—all that and much, much more local color, culture, cuisine, and landscape shaped my very being as a child, adolescent, and young man. (As a kid I loved to read Civil War novels, written for teenagers, always hoping that, at the end, the South would have won the war—and always being disappointed.) I was on one side or the other of a classroom lectern every September from age six to seventy-four in the Memphis public school system, Rhodes College, Syracuse University (where I did my postgraduate studies) and the several universities that employed me. I was a foot soldier in the southern civil rights movement, marching in demonstrations led by Martin Luther King Jr. on behalf of the Memphis sanitation workers' strike. And I was there when he was assassinated, a literally life-altering event for me. I lived as a southern expatriate for twenty-five years in the Wisconsin sand counties, which also helped shape the identities of John Muir and Aldo Leopold, whose earth-born insights helped shape me. I am reluctant to name my several domestic partners over the years, but I am who I am in no small part because of my associations with them and their families. Pull the threads of all these interwoven relationships—environmental and social—and when they are all unraveled there is no me there. The there that remains there is the topos of *mu*.

And one more thing contra Descartes: There is no such thing as one's own thoughts. As Descartes himself remarked (in the context of relegating animals to the res extensa as soulless automata), language and thought are inextricably united—no language, he argued, no thought. And as Wittgenstein drolly pointed out, there can be no such thing as a private language. Language lives in a community; it's a thoroughly social phenomenon. Thus, mutatis mutandis, thoughts do not exist in minds, but in the common cognitive ether that we take in with every breath. (Maybe Anaximenes was on to something.) Accordingly, I regard my work as a philosopher not to be inventing and publishing proprietary ideas, but as finding the right language to articulate the embryonic ideas gestating in the communal zeitgeist.

And why is the predicative or ecological self of such supreme importance to think and to experience? Because: as the relationships—in which each of us is embedded and which constitute our very being—have become global in reach and evermore tangled and complex, the whole that they constitute has also become ever more delicate and fragile. We must collectively lavish the utmost care on the biosocial whole. The atomic self is just about the most dangerous idea to think and to experience because it blinds us to the integrity of the biosphere and the global human civilization embedded in it—on both of which we are utterly and abjectly dependent, not only for our individual identities, but for our very lives. There's no Other over there and myself here. There's just mutual codependence and dynamic mutual definition.

The exposition and promulgation and the axiological and normative implications of conceiving and experiencing oneself predicatively or ecologically is certainly one great gift of Japanese environmental philosophy to the rest of the world. In addition to Berque's exposition in the first chapter of this collection, its axiological and normative implications for both business ethics and environmental ethics are explored by James McRae in the third chapter on "mutualistic relationships" and "symbiotic flourishing." The whole second part of this book is devoted to "the Japanese understanding of the person as a being fundamentally grounded in a social and environmental context," as the editors put it in their introduction—that is, in other words, to the predicative or ecological self. In chapter 4, Graham Parkes explores the deeper intellectual history of the concept in ancient Chinese Daoism as well as in classical Japanese Buddhism. And in chapter 5, INUTSUKA Yū indicates how a permutation of it is manifest in the twentieth-century philosophy of WATSUJI Tetsurō. As I am emphasizing here in this afterword, and as Steve Bein emphasizes in chapter 6, the socioenvironmental crisis, now epitomized by global climate change, poses an existentialist as well as an existential threat—"existential" in the currently popular sense of a threat to our very existence (at least as we know it and now enjoy it) and "existentialist" in the philosophical sense of a threat to our identities individually and collectively.

In chapter 7, Steve Odin gives a Japanese-philosophy spin to Leibniz's concept of a monad. Leibniz himself was addressing the main metaphysical problem bequeathed to his immediate successors by Descartes: how mind and body can possibly interact. The body is extended and unthinking, essentially a machine among other machines, both natural and artificial, in a mechanical universe. The mind is thinking and unextended. There can thus be no mechanical causal relationship between the two. Spinoza would solve the problem by positing the existence of one Substance with infinitely many attributes, of which we are aware of only two: thought and extension. There is, Spinoza believed, no actual interaction between them, but, because they are two attributes of one Substance, the two are synced up. In other words, as change occurs in one attribute a corresponding change occurs in the other(s). This is Spinoza's doctrine of "psychophysical parallelism." Thus when one accidentally hits one's thumb with a hammer and feels pain, the injury to the body does not cause the experience in the psyche; rather the latter is the psychic analog of the former. And the same explanation in reverse accounts for what seems like a wish in the psyche causing one's physical arm to swing the errant hammer. Leibniz's solution to the problem of mind-body interaction was more mathematical, as one might expect from the coinventor of the differential calculus. Again, Descartes had characterized the res extensa and the res cogitans in contrasting terms—the former is extended and unthinking; the latter thinking and unextended. Ah, but a geometrical point is unextended (dimensionless), and so Leibniz made it into a thinking thing, a monad. Indeed, without some definite attribute a point would be nothing at all. It is not extended, and the only Cartesian alternative left for it to be is to be thinking. And for Leibniz, (in)famously, there are no windows in a monad! That is, a monad's consciousness is externally related to the consciousnesses of all the other monads. Via Whitehead's process modification of Leibniz's monadology, Indra's Net, and still other philosophical massaging, Odin manages to internally relate Leibniz's monads—thus making them very un-Leibnizian.

This underlying theme running through many of the chapters of this book in various permutations, which I am calling the predicative or ecological self, resurfaces in the penultimate chapter. ISHIDA Masato reflects on the possibility of an environmental ethic consistent with Dōgen's nondualism; and he does so in the extreme context of radioactive pollutants in the aftermath of the Fukushima Daiichi nuclear power plant meltdown.

A.2. What's Missing: Natural Philosophy

There is another undercurrent running through many of the chapters of this book, which is symptomatic of a darker side of Japanese environmental philosophy. And there is an undercurrent that is not running through them—a robust natural philosophy—the absence of which may be responsible for that darker side of Japanese environmental philosophy. And in the remainder of this afterword, I want to bring the former to the surface and make a topos for the latter. And I want to compare the dark side of Japanese environmental philosophy with an even darker side of American environmental philosophy.

Midori Kagawa-Fox quotes the journalist and democracy advocate NAKAE Chōmin, who wrote, "From the past to the present [late nineteenth century], there has been no philosophy in Japan." Kagawa-Fox goes on to note that philosophy got going in Japan at about the same time that "professional philosophy" got going in the West—roughly at the turn of the twentieth century. And it might be added that the more extreme professional philosophers in the West also think that from the past until the emergence of professional philosophy there has been not only no philosophy in Japan (or anywhere else in Asia), there had been no philosophy in the West—until they came along. The study of Plato, Aristotle, Descartes, and Kant is not a part of the curriculum in some American philosophy departments. The study of these literally amateur philosophers is regarded as the remit of historians of ideas. At best these historical "philosophers" can be credited with identifying some challenging philosophical "puzzles," which those professional philosophers who are particularly "clever" can definitively solve. In any case, as Kagawa-Fox notes, Nakae's dictum became famous, so much so that philosophy in Japan at first consisted (and to some extent still does) of the academic study of Western philosophy, especially that of Kant, Mill, Hegel, and Heidegger.

Kagawa-Fox helpfully provides a brief history of (modern) Japanese philosophy, but she assumes that her readers only need know when the Edo/Tokugawa period began and ended, to be followed by the Meiji period. The interesting story of the advent of philosophy in Japan is understandable only against the background of the political history of Japan during the last four centuries of the second millennium. So I begin this second part of the afterword by sketching in some basic information.

The period from 1603 to 1868 is variously called Tokugawa or Edo. That's because during that interval Japan was ruled from the city of Edo (which was renamed Tokyo, meaning "Eastern Capital," in 1868), by the feudal military regime of the Tokugawa family clan. *Shōgun* ("general") was the title of the head Tokugawa honcho. Thus this form of government is known as a shogunate. The *daimyō* were the barons and earls; and the *samurai* were the knights of the shogun's round table (to explain one interesting story by allusion to another). Until the last decades of the Tokugawa shogunate, Japan was closed to foreign trade (except with China and the Netherlands). With limited foreign influence, Japan thus evolved culturally in isolation from the cosmopolitanism evolving to one degree or another in the rest of the world. Edo was a period of relative peace, social stability, and, as noted in the introduction, environmental integrity, stability, and beauty.

American gunboat diplomacy in the person of Commodore Matthew Perry, who sailed four warships into Edo harbor in 1853, forced Japan to engage more promiscuously in commercial and cultural intercourse with the West. Perry's arrival demonstrated in a particularly dramatic way the vulnerability of Japan to foreign powers equipped with modern weapons technologies. But external pressure was not the only thing that doomed the Tokugawa shogunate. There were internal tensions as well—those typically arising as a rigidly hierarchical social structure reaches the cracking point of ossification. During the Tokugawa shogunate, the nominal capital remained Kyoto and the emperor remained on his throne, but the shogun ruled from Edo castle. In 1867, a revolutionary opposition gathered forces and defeated the army of Shogun TOKUGAWA Yoshinobu in 1868, who resigned his generalship later that year. The imperial palace was moved to Tokyo (formerly Edo), but the country was ruled not by the titular head of state, but by his ministers and their oligarchical cronies. Emperor Mutsuhito took the name Meiji (meaning "Enlightened Policy") and endorsed the *Gokajō no Goseimon*—the Charter Oath or, more literally, the Five-Article Oath—which in effect created a constitutional monarchy not at all unlike that of Great Britain. The new government in Tokyo set Japan on a course of rapid modernization complete with a putatively classless society, market economy, industrialization, militarization, cosmopolitanization, and a mass migration from the countryside to the cities. Among the things imported from the West was philosophy.

Only upon the narrowest definition of "philosophy" was there no philosophy in Japan prior to the importation of Western philosophy (ignoring the even more absurdly narrow restriction of the reference of the term to professional Anglo-American analytic philosophy). One might as well say that there was no religion in Japan prior to the arrival of aggressive Christian missionaries. After all, there is no God Almighty in Buddhism; and Shinto might be dismissed by some pedantic language police as a corpus of superstition about nature sprites. Moreover, Buddhism is as much a philosophical tradition as it is a religious tradition. As noted at the beginning of this afterword, a signal characteristic of Western philosophy is a diachronic dialectic of ideas. And one certainly finds that in the history of Japanese Buddhist thought; that is, as we may confidently say, in classical Japanese Buddhist philosophy. The diachronic dialectic of ideas in classical Japanese Buddhist philosophy, however, was not in the modality of natural philosophy as in the West, but did have to do with nature in another way. Is the Buddhadhātu present in nonhuman sentient beings, but not in plants; or do all living beings participate in Buddha-nature? And are animals and even plants fellow travelers with Buddhist monks on the path to enlightenment? Questions such as these were taken up, progressively, by Saichō (767–822), Kūkai (774–835), Ryōgen (912–985), and Chūjin (1065–1138), most notably.

A distinctly *Japanese* modern philosophy emerged with the formation of the Kyoto school, led by NISHIDA Kitarō, who was born in the first decade of the Meiji Restoration. Nishida, in particular, and the Kyoto school, in general, created a hybrid philosophy (with hybrid vigor) by expressing the subtle concepts of classical Japanese Buddhist philosophy in Western philosophical form. As Nishida absorbed and transformed the ideas of Hegel, Schopenhauer, Royce, and Bergson, so the next generation of philosophers in the Kyoto school, some handpicked by Nishida, absorbed and transformed the ideas of their own European contemporaries. One member of that second generation of Kyoto school philosophers is WATSUJI Tetsurō. (Although he left the faculty of Kyoto Imperial University and ended up in a position at Tokyo Imperial University, intellectually he remains a member of the Kyoto school, as Kagawa-Fox points out.)

In her "brief history of Japanese philosophy" Kagawa-Fox considers Watsuji as ranking equal to Nishida in the pantheon of modern Japanese philosophers. She suggests that, in contrast to Nishida, Watsuji found Confucianism a more useful conceptual resource than Buddhism for Japanese ethics. Watsuji is discussed in many of the chapters in this book. And my paean here to the relational, predicative, or ecological self is as thoroughly Watsujian as it is Nishidaesque. However, just as the emergence of modern Japanese philosophy can be understood only against the background of the Tokugawa-Meiji transition, so only against the background of the political history of Japan during his active career can we fully appreciate the development of Watsuji's environmental philosophy. Kagawa-Fox hints at a more broadly politico-historical contextualization of Watsuji's philosophy by noting that he provided a philosophical foundation for Japan's imperial form of constitutional monarchy and makes reference to his writings in "prewar Japan," noting that in comparison with Nishida's fusion of Buddhist philosophy with that of the West, Watsuji also fused Japanese "cultural values" with it. In 1927–1928, Watsuji traveled to Germany to study with Martin Heidegger; and Heidegger's influence on Watsuji is greater than that of all his other Western contemporaries.

Among American "continental philosophers," Heidegger's work is most often read in a historical and political vacuum. Victor Farias has extensively documented Heidegger's association with the Nazi Party; and Heidegger's recently published *Black Notebooks* convict the author by his own words of deeply ingrained and unapologetic anti-Semitism. Michael E. Zimmerman and Charles Bambach have provided much more measured and nuanced politico-historical contextualizations of Heidegger's philosophy. They have extensively documented the resonance that much of it has with German National Socialist ideology, especially with *Blut-und-Boden* ideas, romantic nationalism, and linguistic and racial superiority. One does not need to look too deeply into Watsuji's writings to find similar themes. Steve Bein makes the observation—but only in a footnote—that "Watsuji was closely associated with the expansionist imperial government during World War II" and that some scholars have (outrageously in my opinion) compared his politics to Osama bin Laden's. It would be as unfair as it would be uncharitable to say that both Heidegger and Watsuji were propagandists for the fascist regimes in their respective countries before and during World War II. Rather, in Watsuji's own terms of mutualism and co-identity formation, we might rather say that there was a mutual influence running between their respective philosophies and the politico-historical contexts of their respective times and places.

My appeal, in this regard, is not primarily polemical, so much as it is hermeneutical. To repeat: A full understanding and indeed appreciation of the philosophies of both Heidegger and Watsuji—as well, the appeal of Heidegger's philosophy for Watsuji—requires contextualization in the political histories of their times and places. And I would say the same about the philosophy of Plato, which I admire above all others (and which is sensitively discussed by YAMAUCHI Tomosaburō in chapter 9). Plato was sympathetic with the antidemocratic party in Athens, and several of his close relatives were among the reactionary (and bloodthirsty) Thirty Tyrants, who briefly ruled Athens after it lost the Peloponnesian War and before what we might here call the Demos Restoration. Among the first things the Athenian democrats did upon being restored to power was to put Socrates on trial and convict and execute him. And that certainly served to intensify Plato's antidemocratic political sympathies. Thus only against the political history of Athens is it possible to fully understand and appreciate Plato's philosophy, most especially that found in his master-piece, the *Republic*, wherein democracy is second only to tyranny as the worst form of government. (Personally, I'm in agreement with Winston Churchill who famously quipped that democracy is indeed the worst form of government—except for all the others.)

To be sure, Watsuji is critical of Heidegger, especially of the lat-ter's overemphasis on temporality and underemphasis on spatiality, as INUTSUKA Yu points out in chapter 5, and on Heidegger's overempha-sis on individuality and underemphasis on sociality. Which raises a most interesting question: Why in a dense and turbid tome, *Sein und Zeit*, which is all about being and time, do we find nothing about the revolutionary integration of space and time in the general theory of relativity, which was published in 1915? There might be a historical-political answer to that question. Indeed, there are some interesting parallels. The Nazi Party formed in 1920 and the storm troopers (aka Brownshirts) emerged a year later. The SS (aka Blackshirts) formed in 1925 as party leader Adolph Hitler's personal bodyguard. The first annual party conference was held at Nuremberg in 1927, the same year that *Sein und Zeit* was published. The party condemned the *Jüdische Physik* of Albert Einstein and insisted on the superiority of *Deutsche Physik* or *Arische Physik*. But for what-ever reason, although written in the twentieth century, Heidegger's neglect of the revelations about space and time in twentieth-century natural phi-losophy makes his philosophy of being and time merely a historical curi-osity, no less than had he been nattering on about the ontological status of phlogiston or the luminiferous ether. And I suppose one could pose the same question to Watsuji scholars. Why was Heidegger's neglect of ideas about space and time in Western natural philosophy not a point on which Watsuji dwelt in his critique of Heidegger? There might also be a political-historical answer to that question too—but not necessarily the same political-historical answer to the question concerning Heidegger.

Watsuji is best known in the West for his book *Fūdo*, translated into English by Geoffrey Bownas under the title *Climate and Culture* (and translated by Augustin Berque into French under the tile *Le Milieu Humain*). It is one thing to emphasize, as I do here, the way the socioenvironmental specifics of a place constitute the self and provide an alternative way of conceiving of one's unique identity, but quite another to characterize the way they constitute a people's identity collectively. I should note that the connection between climate and national character has a long history going back to Herodotus, who, in the *Inquiries*, attributed the peculiarities of the Egyptians largely to the torrid climate and environment of Egypt and the virtues of the Greeks in part to the ideal climates of Ionia and the Greek mainland.

Despite the racial and ethnic diversity of the United States, American thinkers have fallen prey to a similar nationalistic temptation. It was not exactly the North American climate—which is itself quite diverse—but the mythical North American wilderness that is supposed to have shaped a unique and purportedly superior American character. This idea was popularly expressed in his monumental *Winning the West* by the bellicose Theodore Roosevelt and also in nakedly racist terms. In brief, the encounter of the Nordic race with the North American wilderness engendered the vaunted American national character—or so said TR. This idea was more politely and academically expressed by historian Frederick Jackson Turner; and afterward named "the frontier thesis." And the frontier thesis was deployed as a rationale for wilderness preservation by Aldo Leopold in the 1920s.

Leopold too, I should note, was a contemporary of Heidegger and also visited Germany a few years after Watsuji did. Leopold probably never heard of Heidegger and there is no evidence that he sympathized with Hitler, who had come to power two years prior to Leopold's 1935 visit, or with Hitler's Nazi Party. Leopold was a natural philosopher, exploring the ontological, axiological, and normative implications of evolutionary biology and ecology. Because it has taken the form of metascience and because science itself is now international, natural environmental philosophy tempers nationalistic impulses rather than aggravates such impulses.

Watsuji's philosophy figures prominently in the first chapter of this volume, by Augustin Berque, but the only historical context is intellectual and linguistic, not political. Chapter 5 by Inutsuka is concerned with a close comparison of Watsuji and Heidegger and includes a sub-section titled "Discussing 'Sensation' in Watsuji's 'Consideration of National Character'"—which, one would think, would provide on open-ing to reflect on more than "sensation" in that work. But the larger con-text of national character, with its racial and political overtones, is not discussed. The following chapter by Steve Bein closely compares Watsuji with Algirdas Julien Greimas, but again, no larger historical context is provided. TOYODA Mitsuyo clearly summarizes Watsuji's reflections on climate and national character, but with no hint of a critical appraisal thereof in the body of her text. In a footnote, she acknowledges criticism of Watsuji's "characterization of ethnicity based on climate" (without refer-ence to any critics), but only as a "stereotype of culture." In an earlier essay not included in this book, Steve Odin, as Toyoda goes on to point out in the same footnote, suggested some affinity between "Watsuji's ethical phi-losophy" and "environmental ethics as outlined by Leopold." If Leopold has a Japanese counterpart it would not be Watsuji but IMANISHI Kinji.

From the perspective of the larger sociocultural contextualization that I am urging here, compare the way Watsuji puts *fūdo* (however translated, but most usually as "climate") in service of nationalistic and racial politics, and the more generous and empathetic universalism of Imanishi, another figure whom Berque introduces and interprets. Imanishi was a younger contemporary of Watsuji and worked across the campus from the Kyoto school philosophers in Kyoto University's Primate Research Institute. According to Berque, a cardinal principle of Imanishi's "interpretation of nature"—that is, his natural philosophy—is "to consider that any liv-ing being, including the human, is a member of a global society, which Imanishi called *seibutsu zentai shakai* . . . , 'the whole society of the liv-ing,' on which grounds a scientist is entitled to feel something in common with the animal he or she observes, and penetrate, so to speak hermeneuti-cally, into this animal's proper world." Compare Heidegger's niggardly declamation in a 1929 lecture that animals are "world-poor" (and worse in the *Black Notebooks* that Jews are "worldless," having no *Boden* in which they are rooted). Part of the difference between Watsuji's nationalism and Imanishi's universalism is due, I contend, to the fact that Imanishi, like Leopold, was a natural philosopher, while Watsuji was influenced by the antinaturalism of Heidegger, an intellectual descendant of Husserl, who railed against naturalism (aka science).

I myself have undertaken an extensive critical examination of the wil-derness idea in American environmental philosophy in the context of American political history. Perhaps most bluntly, I have argued that the wilderness idea served to erase from the American mind the presence of robust populations of indigenous peoples in the continent on which the neo-European United States was founded and over which it expanded. In effect, the wilderness idea was a tool of the greatest and still the most unrepentant episode of ethnic cleansing and genocide in human history. It was during the 1920s that Leopold deployed the frontier thesis in his pleas for wilderness preservation. By the 1940s the frontier thesis no longer appears in Leopold's advocacy of wilderness. Instead, one finds a scientific rationale. Wilderness might serve as a control or "base-datum of normality" against which we might measure successes and failures in land use for agriculture, forestry, and the like. In his last thoughts on wilderness in *A Sand County Almanac*, Leopold de-Americanizes the concept and renders it "the raw material out of which man [in general] has hammered the artifact called civilization." And he goes on to eulogize "the rich diversity of the world's cultures ... corresponding [to the] diversity in the wilds that gave them birth." Admittedly, nonetheless, Leopold never challenged the concept of wilderness itself nor comprehended, let alone acknowledged, its historical-political erasure function in American historiography.

Why am I raking up all this muck? First, as the US presidential election of 2016 dramatically demonstrated, nationalism and racism are rampant even in a country composed almost entirely of immigrants and their descendants from the four corners of the earth, to say nothing of its manifestation in a number of other countries around the world. Let us hope that such tendencies are not aided and abetted by environmental philosophy, however innocently and inadvertently. If Imanishi and Leopold are at all indicative, an environmental philosophy conceived as an extension of or a subarea of natural philosophy—a metascientific environmental philosophy—resists nationalistic and racist temptations. By contrast, as we see, the antinatural phenomenological strain of environmental philosophy—at least as represented by Heidegger and Watsuji—can aggravate such impulses. Second, the twentieth-first-century environmental crisis, epitomized by global climate change, is, well, global in spatial scale. It thus requires a global philosophical consensus, which is best inspired and informed by international science. Third, and more generally, I raise these issues because environmental philosophers, Western and Asian, American and Japanese, must heed the dictum of Plato's character, Socrates, in the *Republic* and "follow the argument whithersoever it may lead." A good environmental philosophy is necessarily a just and honest environmental philosophy. We must embrace the good and reject the bad in our precursors, but to do so, we must first examine their thinking in the clear light of day.

INDEX

mu, 170, 297–302. *See also* nothingness
Muir, John, 167, 229, 292
mujō, 138
mujō seppō, 177
MUSŌ Soseki, 151, 272
myths (-ology), 8–9, 42, 170, 179, 185,
    195–215, 217–224, 231–238,
    274–277, 282–283, 286, 300

Nāgārjuna, 66
NAKAE Chōmin, 196, 198, 202, 212, 295
Nansen, 252–254, 265n39, 266n46
natural philosophy, 287–302
Nausicaä of the Valley of the Wind,
    138–139, 210
Nazi party, 298–300
Nietzsche, Friedrich, 23, 159–160, 199
Nihonjinron, 81
ningen, 93, 109–116
ningen sonzai, 6–7, 20, 105
Ninigi (-no-Mikoto), 217, 219, 274–275
NINOMIYA Sontoku, xiv, 197
NISHI Amane, 197–198, 202, 212
NISHIDA Kitarō, 14, 128–129, 159, 196,
    198–200, 212, 289, 297–298
no-self, 3, 37, 66, 92, 103n30, 290. See
    also *anātman*
Noh theater, 17, 137–138, 152
nonanthropocentrism, 88, 143n52,
    230–231
nonzero-sumness, 56–57
nothingness, 8, 128–129, 137, 169–174.
    See also *mu*
nuclear power, 2, 9, 80, 83, 113, 116, 138,
    201–202, 227, 243–269, 273, 295

Ohashi River, 10, 276–285
OKADA Mamiko, 218
OKAKURA Tenshin, 199
Okinawa, 272
Olympics, xi, 51
OMINE Akira, 29, 36–37
ontology, 13–14, 21, 24, 89, 131, 133,
    141–142n4, 232, 248, 259–260,
    262n8, 264–265n31, 289–290,
    299–300

original enlightenment. See *hongaku*
other-power, 36–37, 39, 41, 43

Perrow, Charles, 113
perspective-taking, 7, 123, 130–141
Plato, 8, 112, 159–175, 290–291, 295,
    299, 302
Polanyi, Michael, 222
poverty, ix, xiv, 51, 53, 161, 167, 171
pragmatism, 88, 128, 130
pratītya-samutpāda, 66
primatology, 5, 23–28
property rights, 180–183
Pure Land, 5, 29–46, 257
purifying, 10, 232, 247, 256–257,
    260–261, 268n70
purity, 207–208, 261

radiation, 2, 9, 79, 82, 202, 227–228,
    243–245, 247, 259, 261n2, 273
reciprocity, x, 25, 49–50, 56, 84, 133, 139,
    211, 273, 291
Reich, Warren T., 234
relata, 55
religion, 2, 8–10, 25–26, 31–34, 38–39,
    46n30, 67, 116–117, 136–137, 162,
    164, 166, 170, 183, 186, 195–215,
    218–219, 221, 233, 243, 254,
    267n56, 288, 297
respect, x, xi, xiv, 6, 8, 23, 30, 47, 51, 59,
    70–72, 79, 84, 111, 145–148, 150,
    173, 180–181, 183–184, 188, 200,
    205, 209–211, 231, 233, 237–240,
    283, 286
rhythm, 6, 87–104, 114
rice, xii–xiii, 43, 72, 185, 208, 211,
    219–221, 237, 275–276, 281–282
right, 30, 37, 4, 54, 57, 65, 78, 81,
    131–132, 134, 160–161, 164, 168,
    171, 180, 181, 183, 192, 207, 221,
    237, 244–245, 252, 255, 281, 293
rigimuge, 136
rinri, 92–93, 96, 111, 115, 200, 203–204
risk, 50, 101, 113, 179, 185, 186,
    275, 290
Ritte, Walter Jr., 43